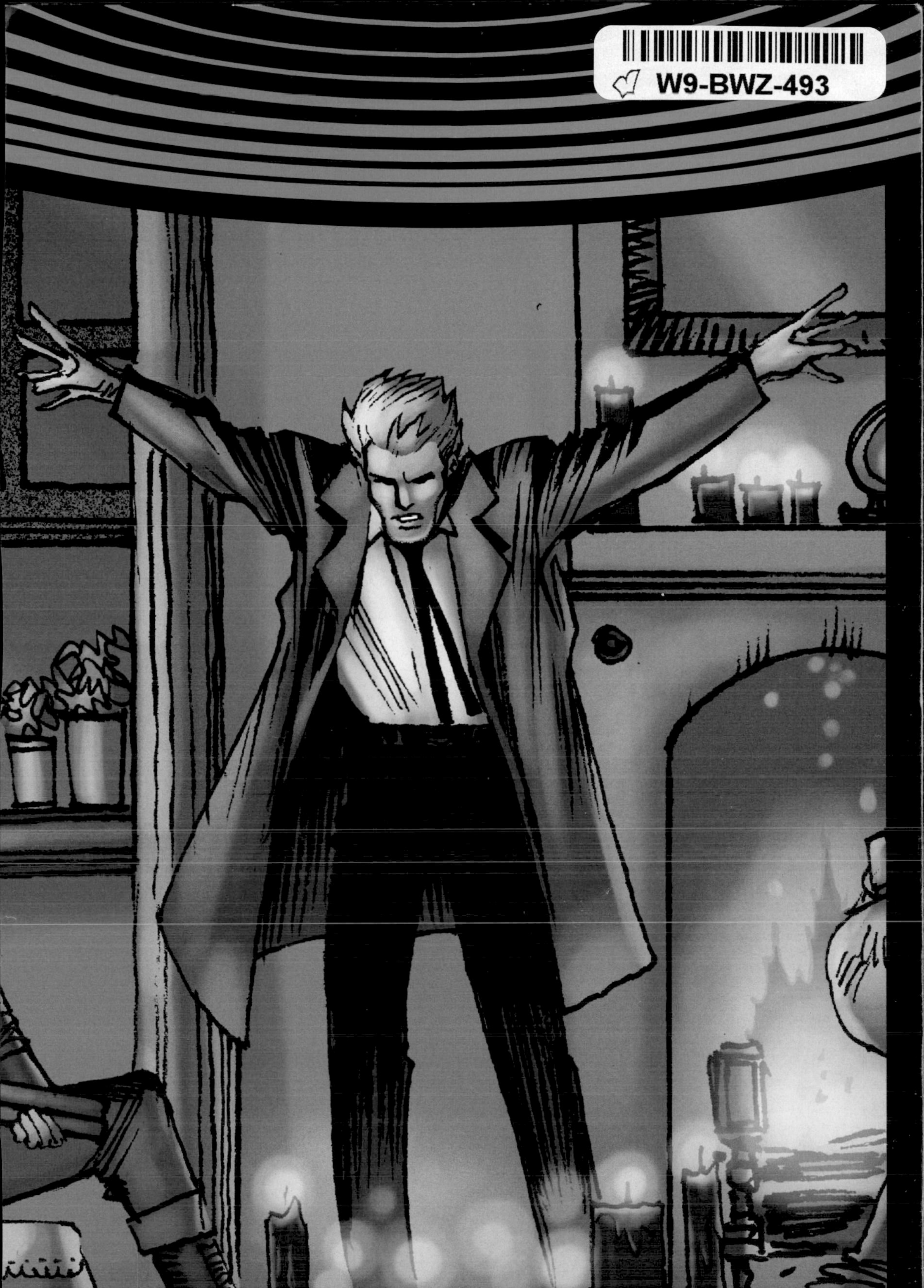

THE HELLBLAZER

VOL. 1 THE POISON TRUTH

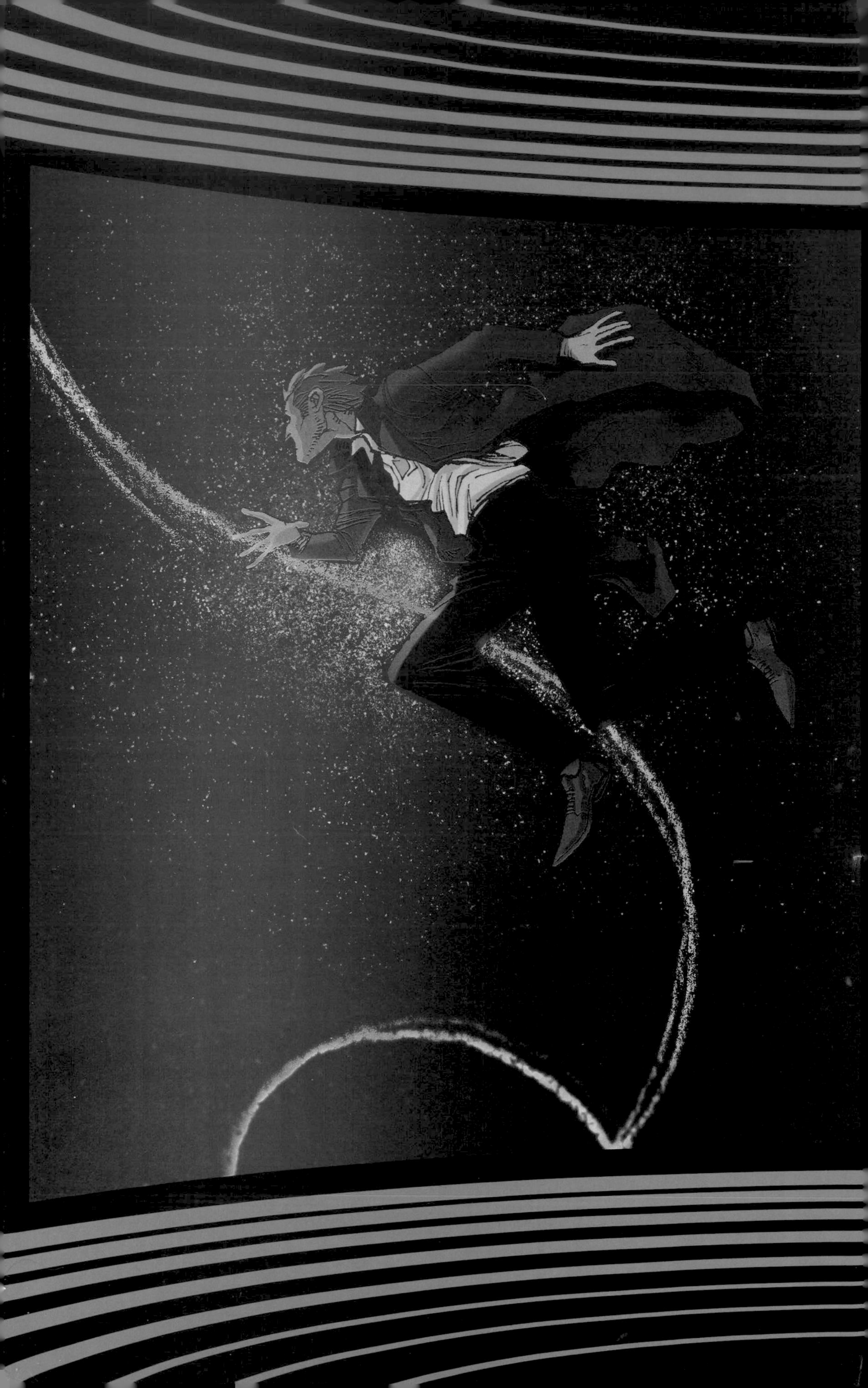

THE HELLBLAZER

VOL. 1 THE POISON TRUTH

SIMON OLIVER
writer

MORITAT * **PIA GUERRA**
JOSÉ MARZÁN JR.
artists

ANDRE SZYMANOWICZ * **MORITAT**
CARRIE STRACHAN * **TONY AVIÑA**
colorists

SAL CIPRIANO
letterer

MORITAT
collection cover art

MORITAT
JOHN CASSADAY with **PAUL MOUNTS**
original series covers

JOHN CONSTANTINE created by ALAN MOORE, STEVE BISSETTE,
JOHN TOTLEBEN and JAMIE DELANO & JOHN RIDGWAY

KRISTY QUINN Editor - Original Series • **JESSICA CHEN** Associate Editor - Original Series
JEB WOODARD Group Editor - Collected Editions • **SCOTT NYBAKKEN** Editor - Collected Edition
STEVE COOK Design Director - Books

BOB HARRAS Senior VP - Editor-in-Chief, DC Comics

DIANE NELSON President • **DAN DiDIO** Publisher • **JIM LEE** Publisher • **GEOFF JOHNS** President & Chief Creative Officer
AMIT DESAI Executive VP - Business & Marketing Strategy, Direct to Consumer & Global Franchise Management
SAM ADES Senior VP - Direct to Consumer • **BOBBIE CHASE** VP - Talent Development • **MARK CHIARELLO** Senior VP - Art, Design & Collected Editions
JOHN CUNNINGHAM Senior VP - Sales & Trade Marketing • **ANNE DePIES** Senior VP - Business Strategy, Finance & Administration
DON FALLETTI VP - Manufacturing Operations • **LAWRENCE GANEM** VP - Editorial Administration & Talent Relations
ALISON GILL Senior VP - Manufacturing & Operations • **HANK KANALZ** Senior VP - Editorial Strategy & Administration
JAY KOGAN VP - Legal Affairs • **THOMAS LOFTUS** VP - Business Affairs • **JACK MAHAN** VP - Business Affairs
NICK J. NAPOLITANO VP - Manufacturing Administration • **EDDIE SCANNELL** VP - Consumer Marketing
COURTNEY SIMMONS Senior VP - Publicity & Communications • **JIM (SKI) SOKOLOWSKI** VP - Comic Book Specialty Sales & Trade Marketing
NANCY SPEARS VP - Mass, Book, Digital Sales & Trade Marketing

THE HELLBLAZER VOL. 1: THE POISON TRUTH

DC Comics, 2900 West Alameda Ave.w Burbank, CA 91505
Printed by LSC Communications, Salem, VA, USA. 2/24/17.
First Printing. ISBN: 978-1-4012-6886-2

Library of Congress Cataloging-in-Publication Data is available.

PEFC Certified
Printed on paper from sustainably managed forests, controlled sources
PEFC/29-31-337
www.pefc.org

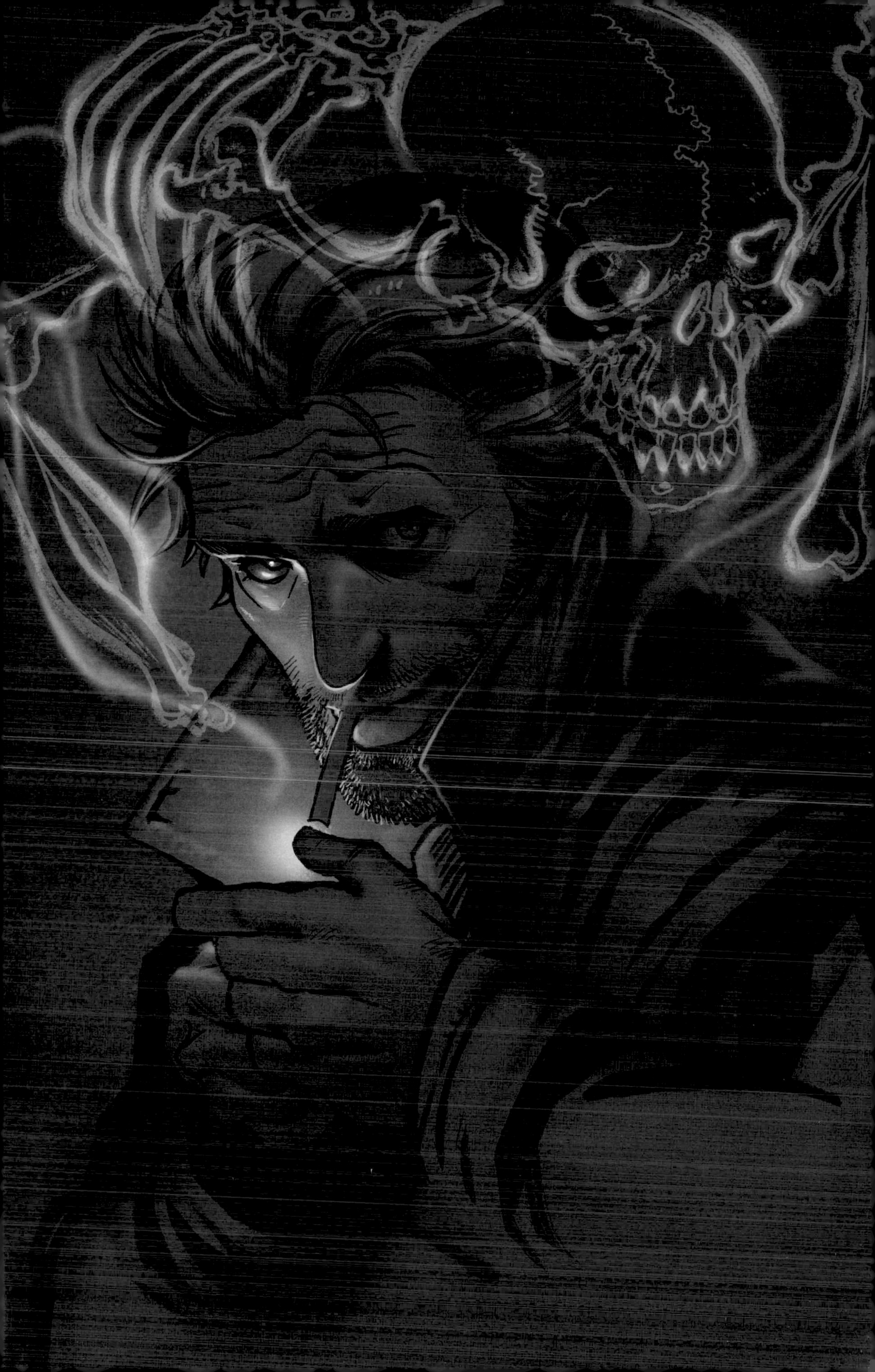

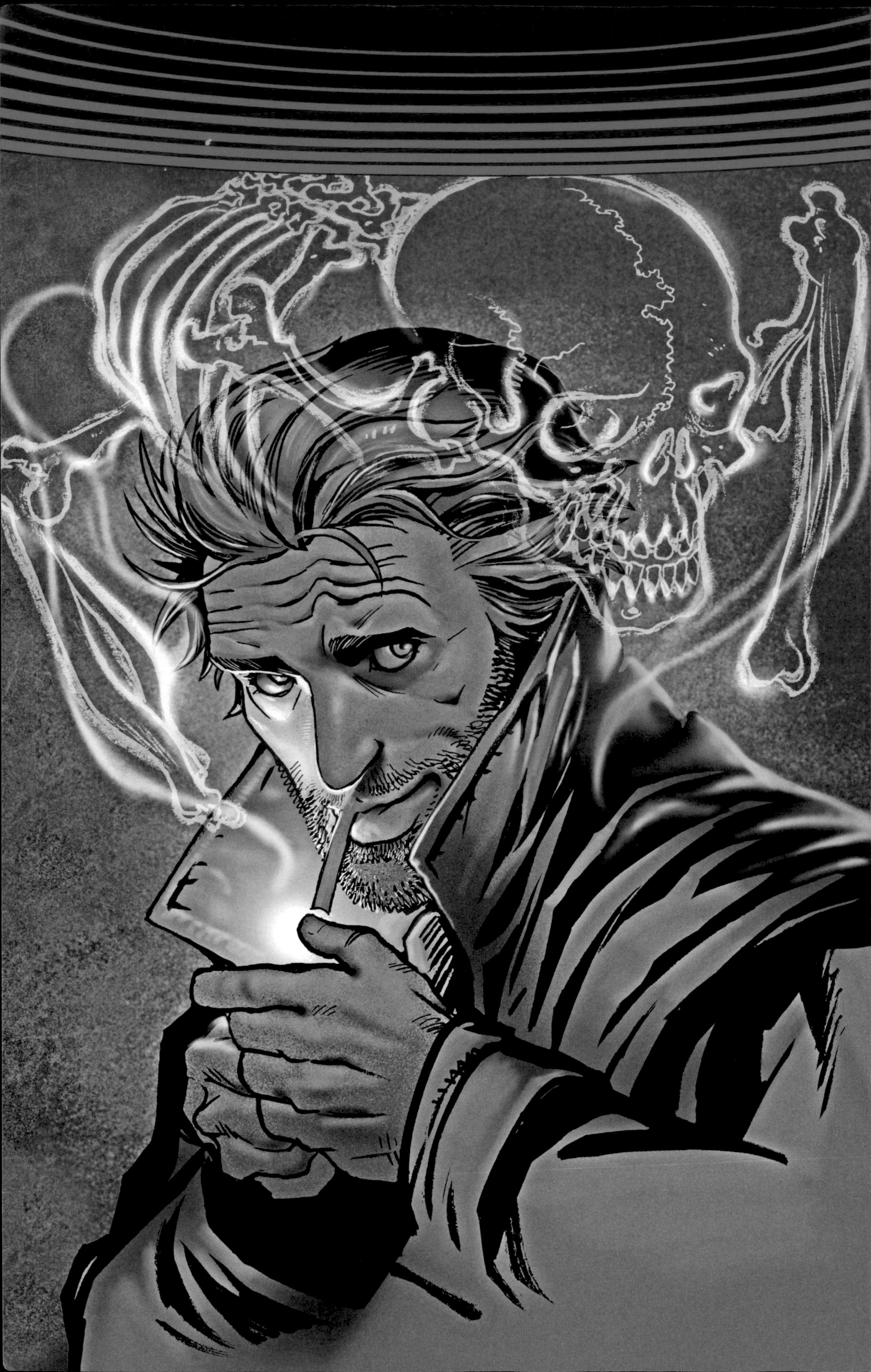

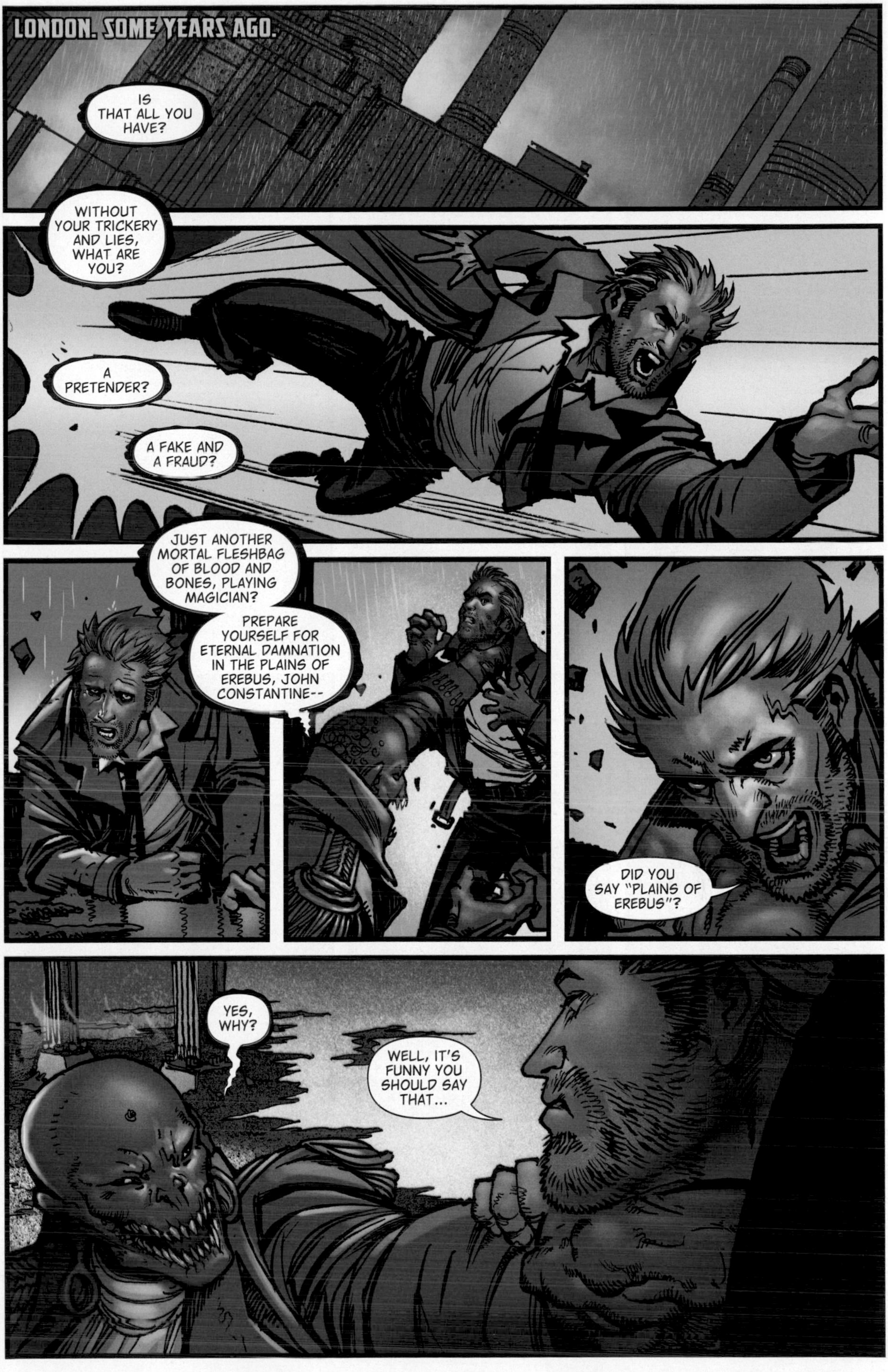
LONDON. SOME YEARS AGO.
IS THAT ALL YOU HAVE?
WITHOUT YOUR TRICKERY AND LIES, WHAT ARE YOU?
A PRETENDER?
A FAKE AND A FRAUD?
JUST ANOTHER MORTAL FLESHBAG OF BLOOD AND BONES, PLAYING MAGICIAN?
PREPARE YOURSELF FOR ETERNAL DAMNATION IN THE PLAINS OF EREBUS, JOHN CONSTANTINE--
DID YOU SAY "PLAINS OF EREBUS"?
YES, WHY?
WELL, IT'S FUNNY YOU SHOULD SAY THAT...

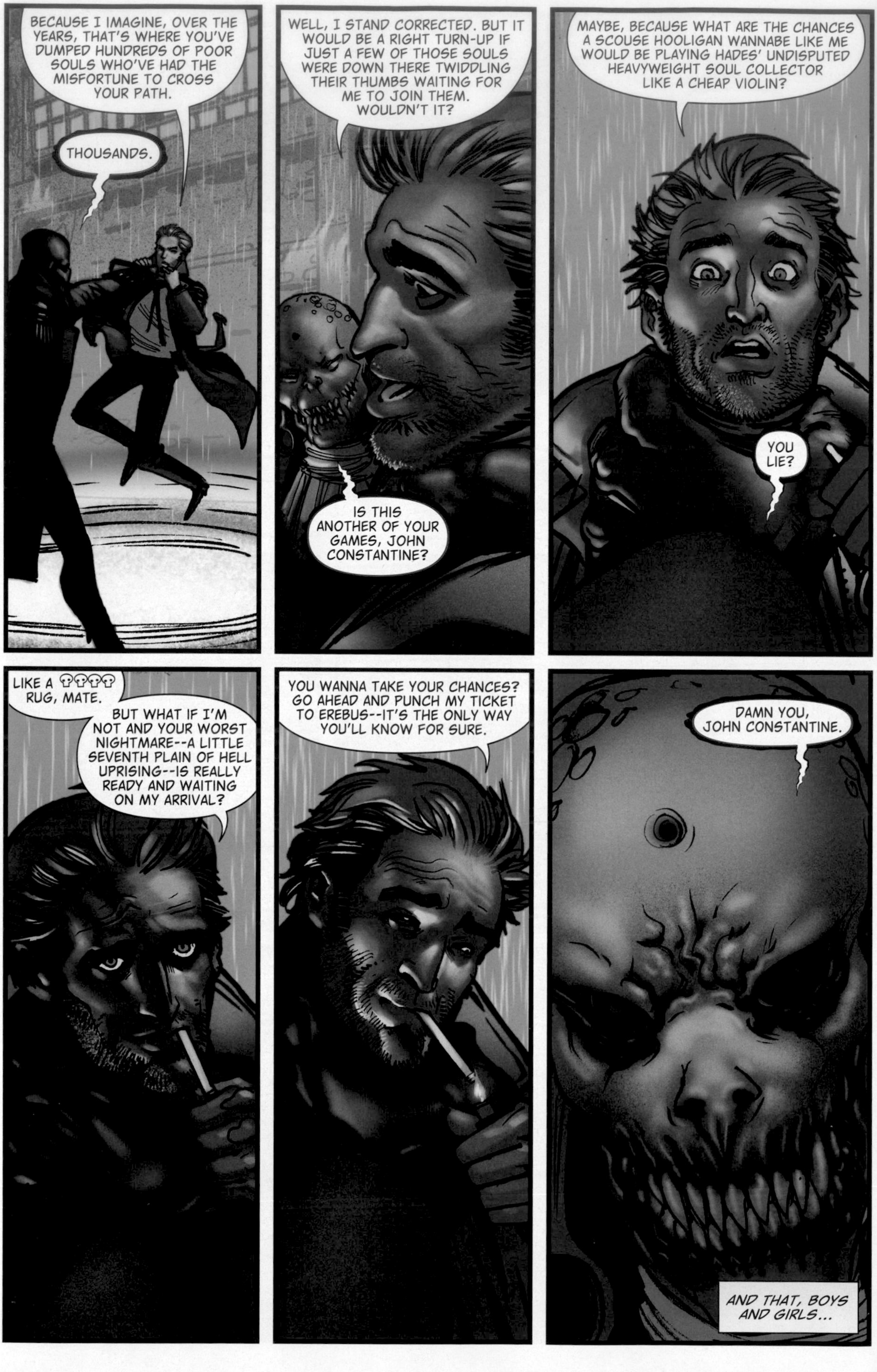
BECAUSE I IMAGINE, OVER THE YEARS, THAT'S WHERE YOU'VE DUMPED HUNDREDS OF POOR SOULS WHO'VE HAD THE MISFORTUNE TO CROSS YOUR PATH.
THOUSANDS.
WELL, I STAND CORRECTED. BUT IT WOULD BE A RIGHT TURN-UP IF JUST A FEW OF THOSE SOULS WERE DOWN THERE TWIDDLING THEIR THUMBS WAITING FOR ME TO JOIN THEM. WOULDN'T IT?
IS THIS ANOTHER OF YOUR GAMES, JOHN CONSTANTINE?
MAYBE, BECAUSE WHAT ARE THE CHANCES A SCOUSE HOOLIGAN WANNABE LIKE ME WOULD BE PLAYING HADES' UNDISPUTED HEAVYWEIGHT SOUL COLLECTOR LIKE A CHEAP VIOLIN?
YOU LIE?
LIKE A RUG, MATE.
BUT WHAT IF I'M NOT AND YOUR WORST NIGHTMARE--A LITTLE SEVENTH PLAIN OF HELL UPRISING--IS REALLY READY AND WAITING ON MY ARRIVAL?
YOU WANNA TAKE YOUR CHANCES? GO AHEAD AND PUNCH MY TICKET TO EREBUS--IT'S THE ONLY WAY YOU'LL KNOW FOR SURE.
DAMN YOU, JOHN CONSTANTINE.
AND THAT, BOYS AND GIRLS...

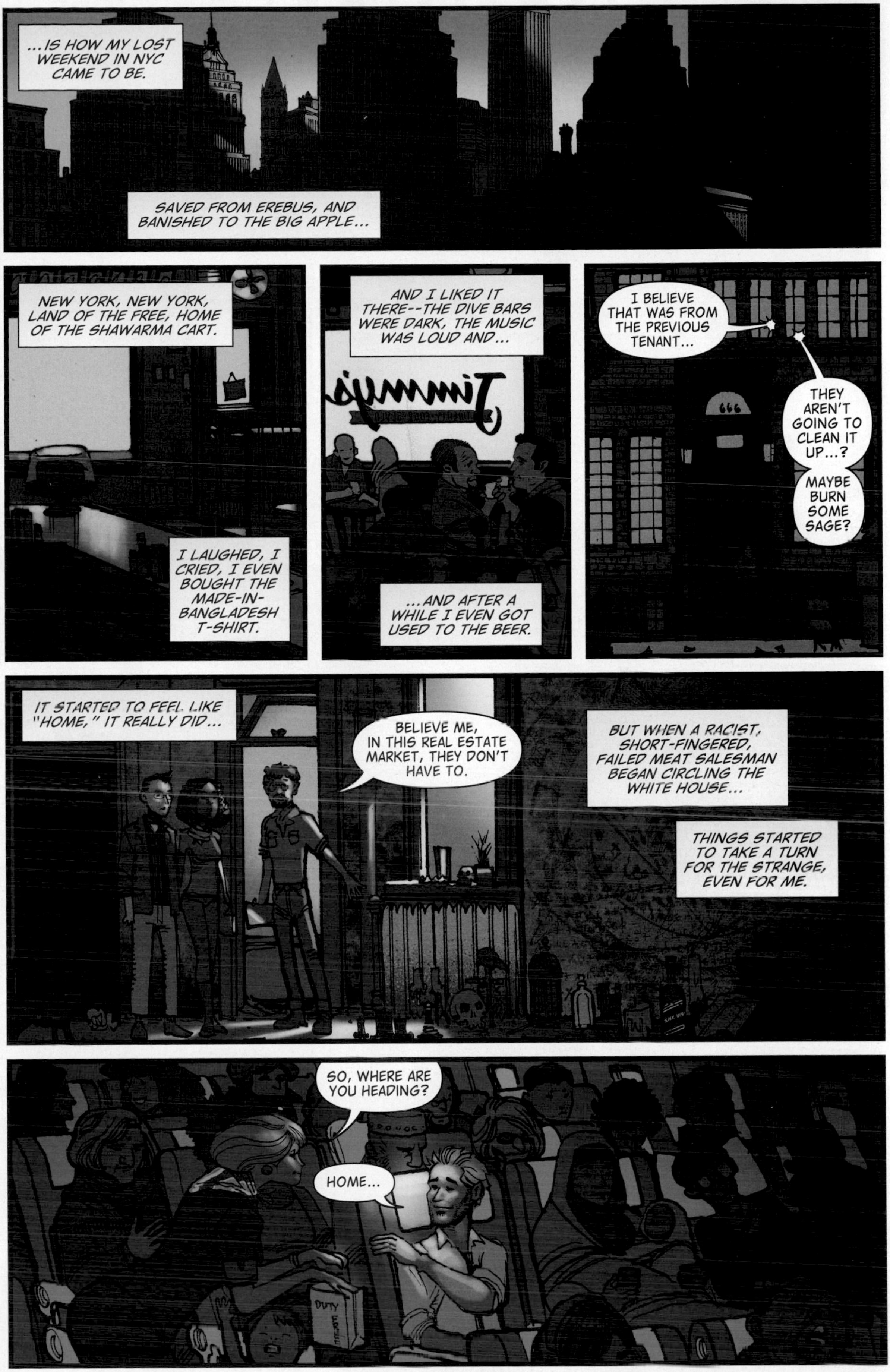
...IS HOW MY LOST WEEKEND IN NYC CAME TO BE.
SAVED FROM EREBUS, AND BANISHED TO THE BIG APPLE...
NEW YORK, NEW YORK, LAND OF THE FREE, HOME OF THE SHAWARMA CART.
I LAUGHED, I CRIED, I EVEN BOUGHT THE MADE-IN-BANGLADESH T-SHIRT.
AND I LIKED IT THERE--THE DIVE BARS WERE DARK, THE MUSIC WAS LOUD AND...
...AND AFTER A WHILE I EVEN GOT USED TO THE BEER.
I BELIEVE THAT WAS FROM THE PREVIOUS TENANT...
THEY AREN'T GOING TO CLEAN IT UP...?
MAYBE BURN SOME SAGE?
666
IT STARTED TO FEEL LIKE "HOME," IT REALLY DID...
BELIEVE ME, IN THIS REAL ESTATE MARKET, THEY DON'T HAVE TO.
BUT WHEN A RACIST, SHORT-FINGERED, FAILED MEAT SALESMAN BEGAN CIRCLING THE WHITE HOUSE...
THINGS STARTED TO TAKE A TURN FOR THE STRANGE, EVEN FOR ME.
SO, WHERE ARE YOU HEADING?
HOME...
DUTY FREE

REBIRTH

Writer: Simon Oliver Artist: Moritat
Colorists: Andre Szymanowicz and Moritat Letterer: Sal Cipriano
Cover Artist: Moritat Variant Cover Artist: Duncan Fegredo
Associate Editor: Jessica Chen Editor: Kristy Quinn

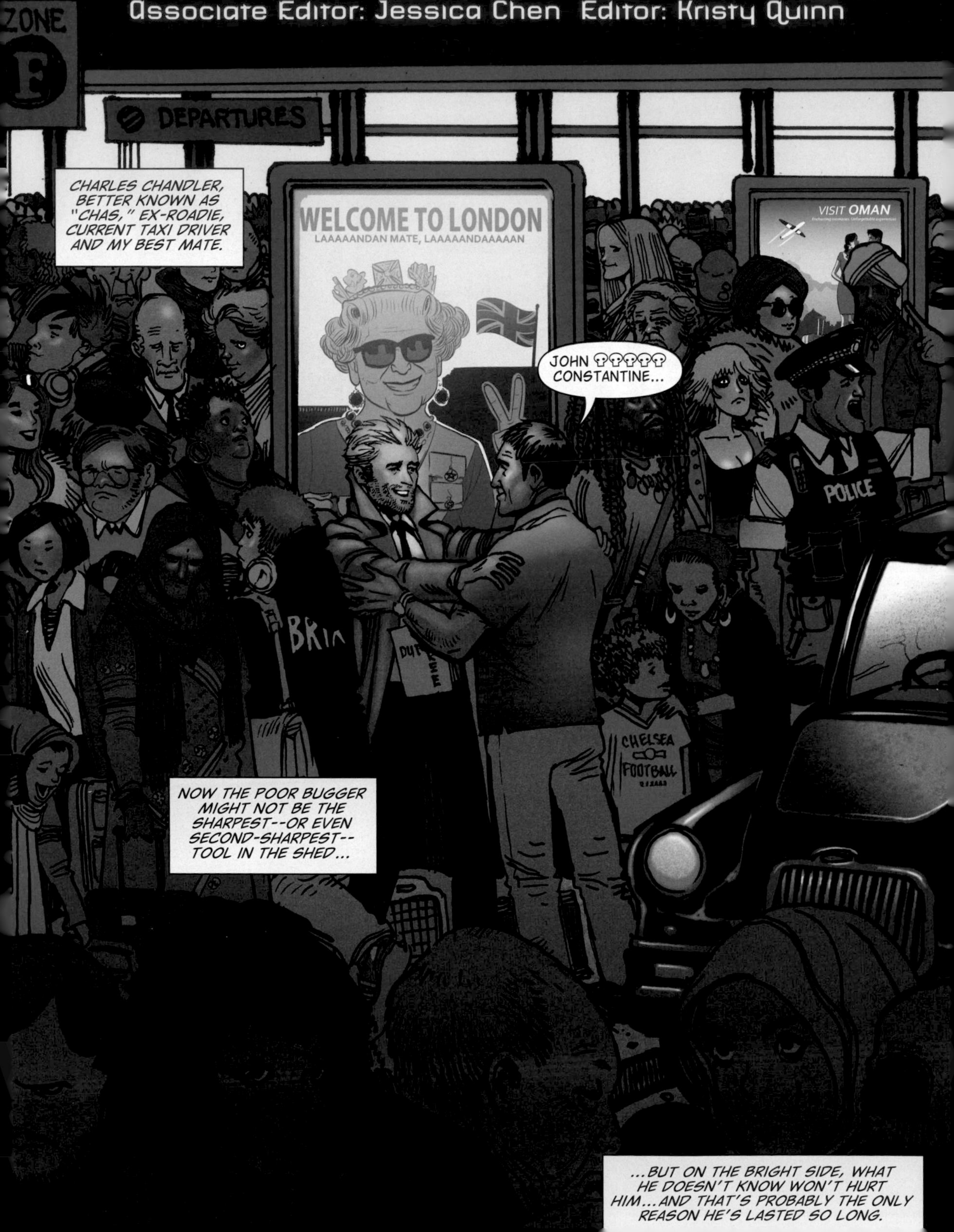
ZONE F
DEPARTURES
CHARLES CHANDLER, BETTER KNOWN AS "CHAS," EX-ROADIE, CURRENT TAXI DRIVER AND MY BEST MATE.
WELCOME TO LONDON
LAAAAANDAN MATE, LAAAAANDAAAAAN
VISIT OMAN
JOHN
CONSTANTINE...
POLICE
CHELSEA FOOTBALL
NOW THE POOR BUGGER MIGHT NOT BE THE SHARPEST--OR EVEN SECOND-SHARPEST--TOOL IN THE SHED...
...BUT ON THE BRIGHT SIDE, WHAT HE DOESN'T KNOW WON'T HURT HIM...AND THAT'S PROBABLY THE ONLY REASON HE'S LASTED SO LONG.

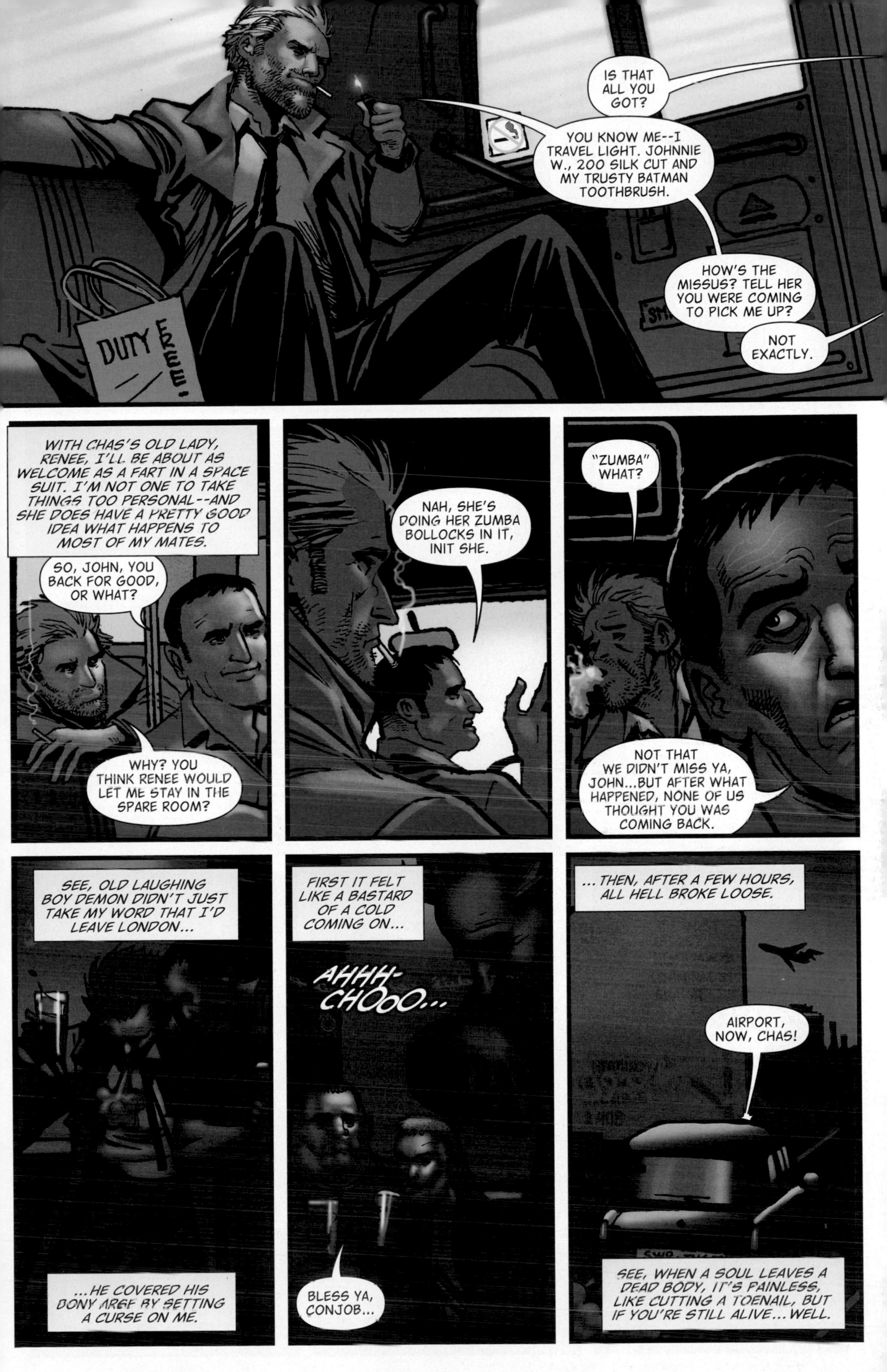
IS THAT ALL YOU GOT?
YOU KNOW ME--I TRAVEL LIGHT. JOHNNIE W., 200 SILK CUT AND MY TRUSTY BATMAN TOOTHBRUSH.
HOW'S THE MISSUS? TELL HER YOU WERE COMING TO PICK ME UP?
NOT EXACTLY.
DUTY FREE!
WITH CHAS'S OLD LADY, RENEE, I'LL BE ABOUT AS WELCOME AS A FART IN A SPACE SUIT. I'M NOT ONE TO TAKE THINGS TOO PERSONAL--AND SHE DOES HAVE A PRETTY GOOD IDEA WHAT HAPPENS TO MOST OF MY MATES.
SO, JOHN, YOU BACK FOR GOOD, OR WHAT?
WHY? YOU THINK RENEE WOULD LET ME STAY IN THE SPARE ROOM?
NAH, SHE'S DOING HER ZUMBA BOLLOCKS IN IT, INIT SHE.
"ZUMBA" WHAT?
NOT THAT WE DIDN'T MISS YA, JOHN...BUT AFTER WHAT HAPPENED, NONE OF US THOUGHT YOU WAS COMING BACK.
SEE, OLD LAUGHING BOY DEMON DIDN'T JUST TAKE MY WORD THAT I'D LEAVE LONDON...
...HE COVERED HIS BONY ARSE BY SETTING A CURSE ON ME.
FIRST IT FELT LIKE A BASTARD OF A COLD COMING ON...
AHHH-CHOOO...
BLESS YA, CONJOB...
...THEN, AFTER A FEW HOURS, ALL HELL BROKE LOOSE.
AIRPORT, NOW, CHAS!
SEE, WHEN A SOUL LEAVES A DEAD BODY, IT'S PAINLESS, LIKE CUTTING A TOENAIL, BUT IF YOU'RE STILL ALIVE...WELL.

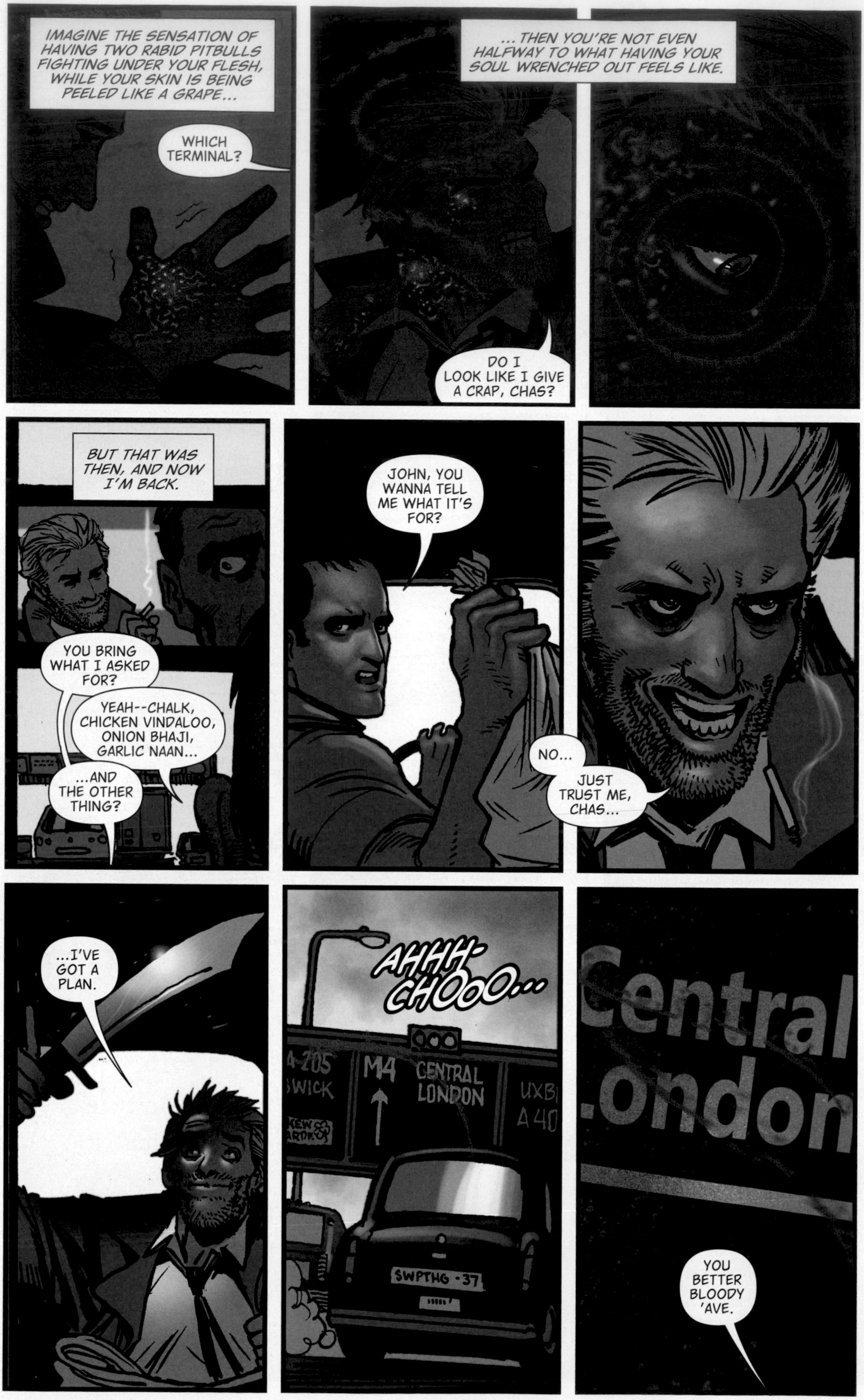
IMAGINE THE SENSATION OF HAVING TWO RABID PITBULLS FIGHTING UNDER YOUR FLESH, WHILE YOUR SKIN IS BEING PEELED LIKE A GRAPE...
WHICH TERMINAL?
...THEN YOU'RE NOT EVEN HALFWAY TO WHAT HAVING YOUR SOUL WRENCHED OUT FEELS LIKE.
DO I LOOK LIKE I GIVE A CRAP, CHAS?
BUT THAT WAS THEN, AND NOW I'M BACK.
YOU BRING WHAT I ASKED FOR?
YEAH--CHALK, CHICKEN VINDALOO, ONION BHAJI, GARLIC NAAN...
...AND THE OTHER THING?
JOHN, YOU WANNA TELL ME WHAT IT'S FOR?
NO...
JUST TRUST ME, CHAS...
...I'VE GOT A PLAN.
AHHH-CHOOOO...
M4
CENTRAL LONDON
SWPTHG -37
Central London
YOU BETTER BLOODY 'AVE.

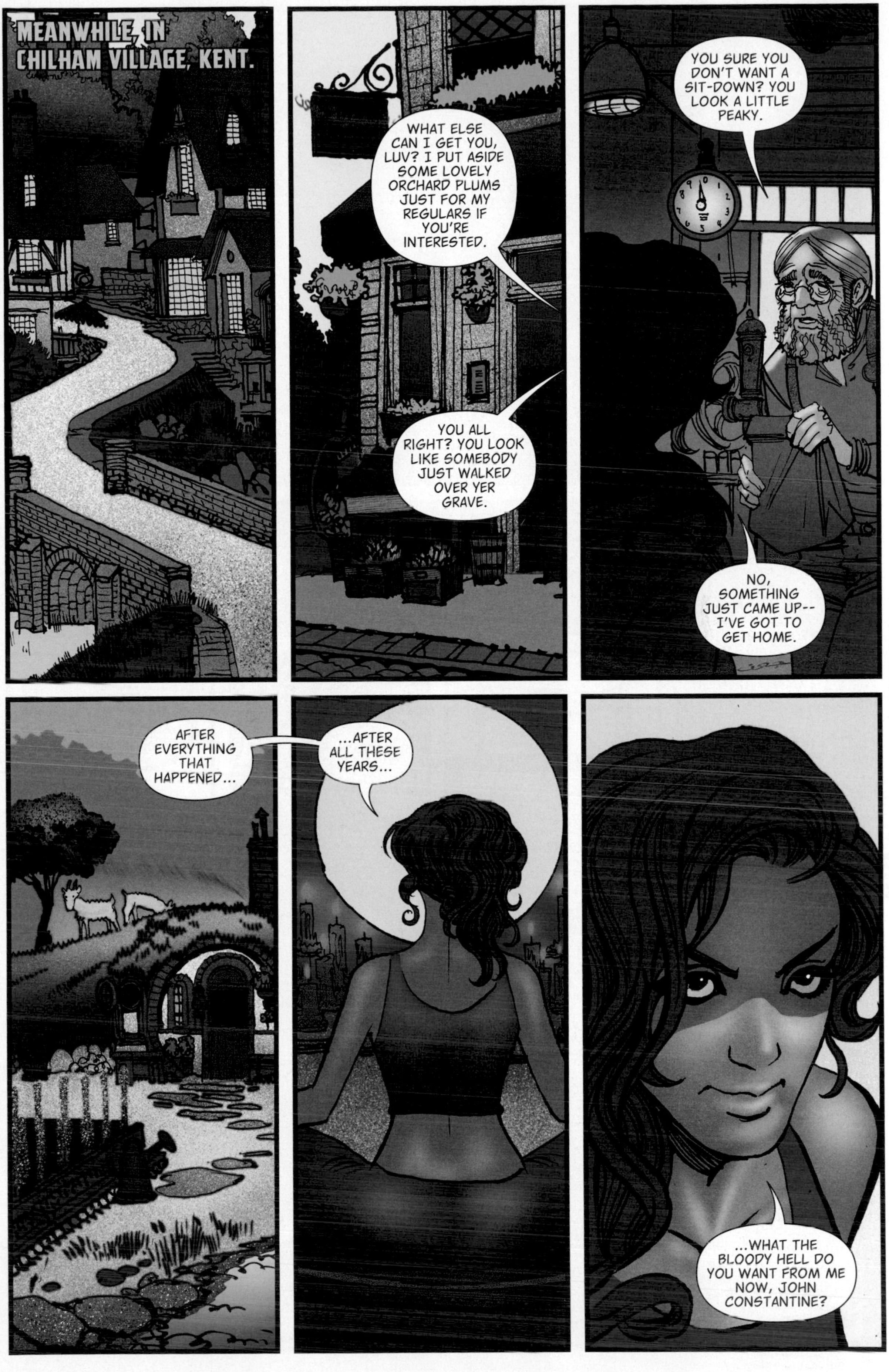
MEANWHILE, IN CHILHAM VILLAGE, KENT.
WHAT ELSE CAN I GET YOU, LUV? I PUT ASIDE SOME LOVELY ORCHARD PLUMS JUST FOR MY REGULARS IF YOU'RE INTERESTED.
YOU ALL RIGHT? YOU LOOK LIKE SOMEBODY JUST WALKED OVER YER GRAVE.
YOU SURE YOU DON'T WANT A SIT-DOWN? YOU LOOK A LITTLE PEAKY.
NO, SOMETHING JUST CAME UP-- I'VE GOT TO GET HOME.
AFTER EVERYTHING THAT HAPPENED...
...AFTER ALL THESE YEARS...
...WHAT THE BLOODY HELL DO YOU WANT FROM ME NOW, JOHN CONSTANTINE?

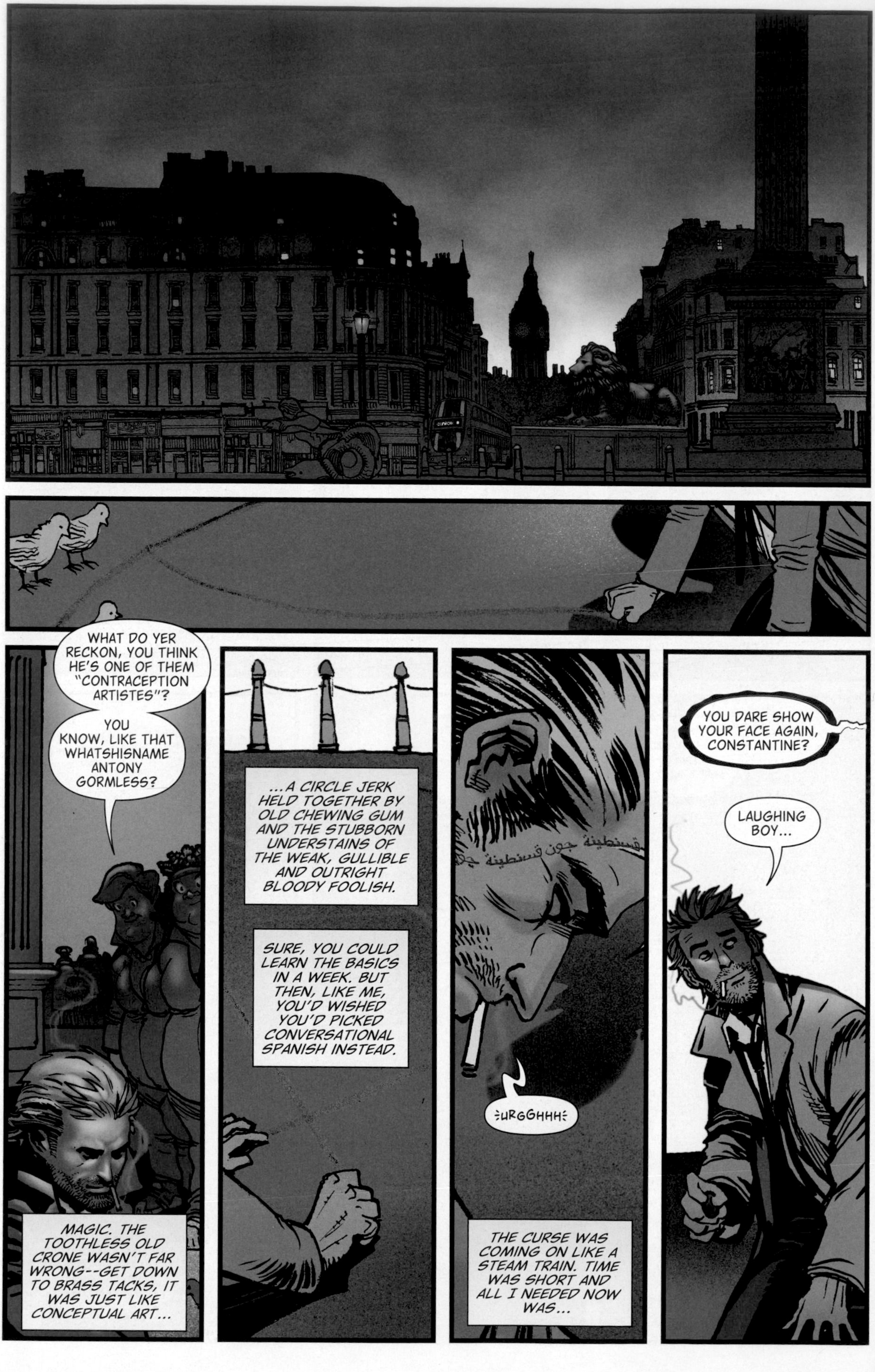

WHAT DO YER RECKON, YOU THINK HE'S ONE OF THEM "CONTRACEPTION ARTISTES"?
YOU KNOW, LIKE THAT WHATSHISNAME ANTONY GORMLESS?
MAGIC. THE TOOTHLESS OLD CRONE WASN'T FAR WRONG--GET DOWN TO BRASS TACKS, IT WAS JUST LIKE CONCEPTUAL ART...
...A CIRCLE JERK HELD TOGETHER BY OLD CHEWING GUM AND THE STUBBORN UNDERSTAINS OF THE WEAK, GULLIBLE AND OUTRIGHT BLOODY FOOLISH.
SURE, YOU COULD LEARN THE BASICS IN A WEEK. BUT THEN, LIKE ME, YOU'D WISHED YOU'D PICKED CONVERSATIONAL SPANISH INSTEAD.
URGGHHH
THE CURSE WAS COMING ON LIKE A STEAM TRAIN. TIME WAS SHORT AND ALL I NEEDED NOW WAS...
YOU DARE SHOW YOUR FACE AGAIN, CONSTANTINE?
LAUGHING BOY...

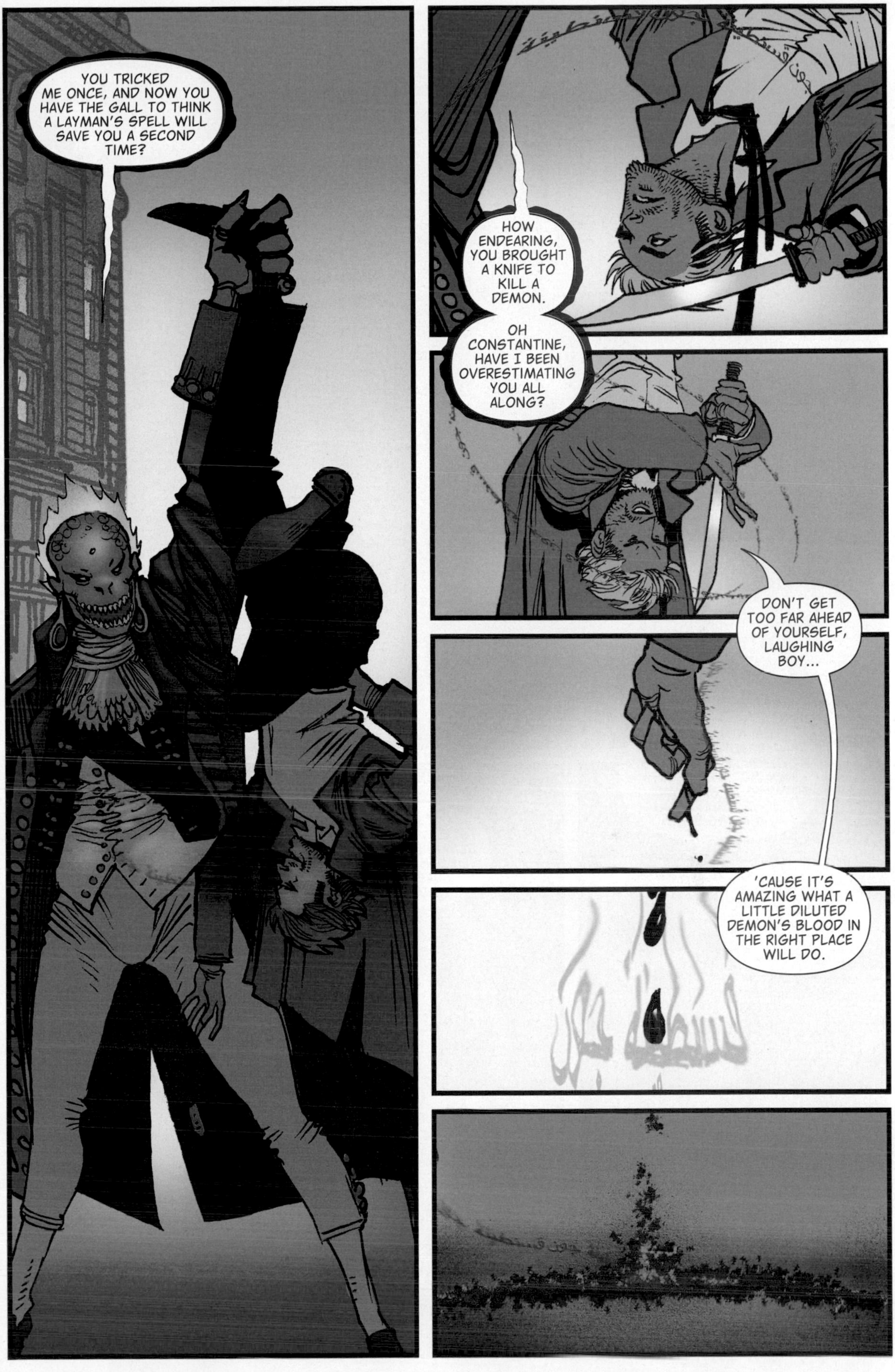
YOU TRICKED ME ONCE, AND NOW YOU HAVE THE GALL TO THINK A LAYMAN'S SPELL WILL SAVE YOU A SECOND TIME?
HOW ENDEARING, YOU BROUGHT A KNIFE TO KILL A DEMON.
OH CONSTANTINE, HAVE I BEEN OVERESTIMATING YOU ALL ALONG?
DON'T GET TOO FAR AHEAD OF YOURSELF, LAUGHING BOY...
'CAUSE IT'S AMAZING WHAT A LITTLE DILUTED DEMON'S BLOOD IN THE RIGHT PLACE WILL DO.

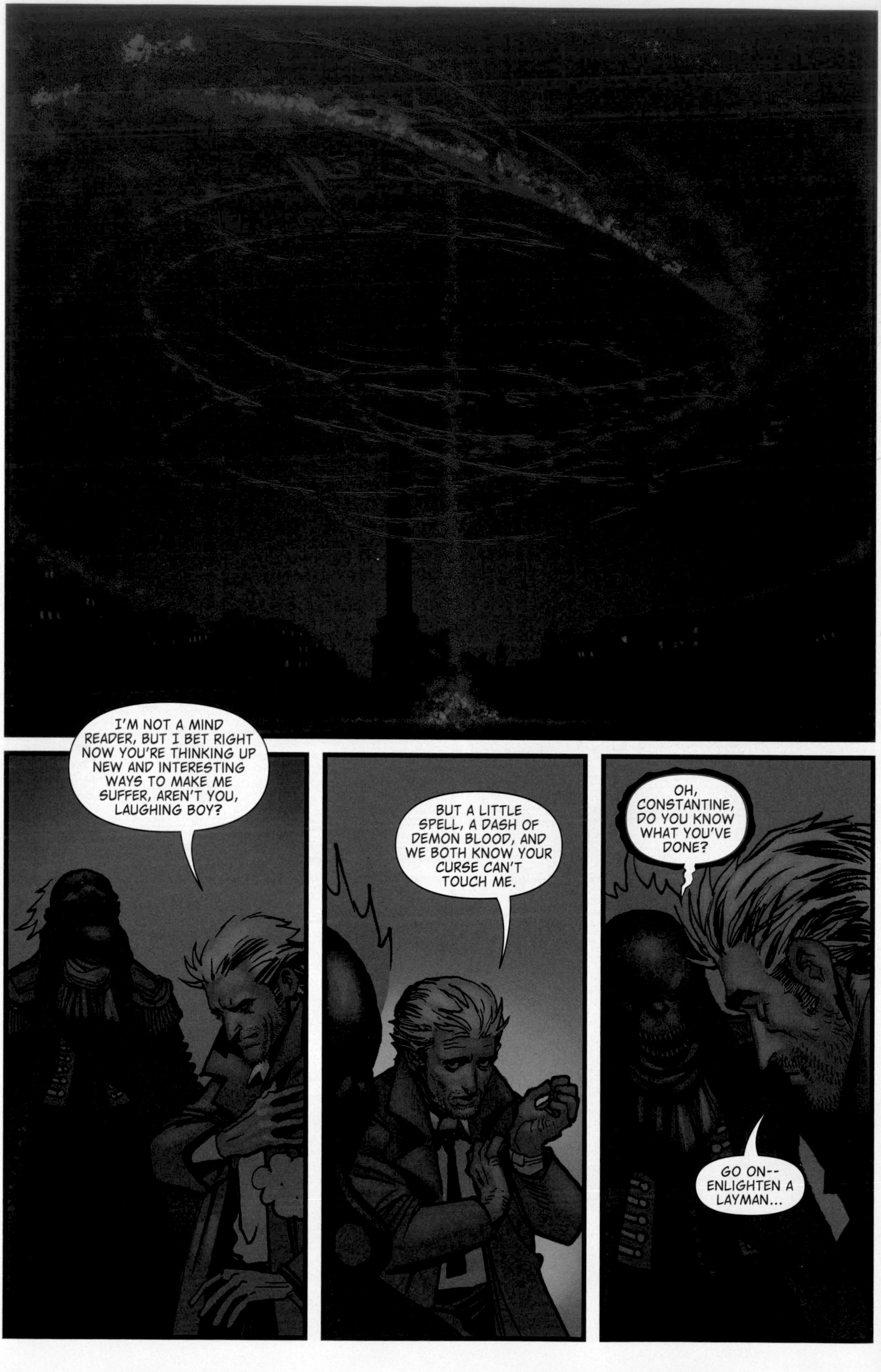
I'M NOT A MIND READER, BUT I BET RIGHT NOW YOU'RE THINKING UP NEW AND INTERESTING WAYS TO MAKE ME SUFFER, AREN'T YOU, LAUGHING BOY?
BUT A LITTLE SPELL, A DASH OF DEMON BLOOD, AND WE BOTH KNOW YOUR CURSE CAN'T TOUCH ME.
OH, CONSTANTINE, DO YOU KNOW WHAT YOU'VE DONE?
GO ON--ENLIGHTEN A LAYMAN...

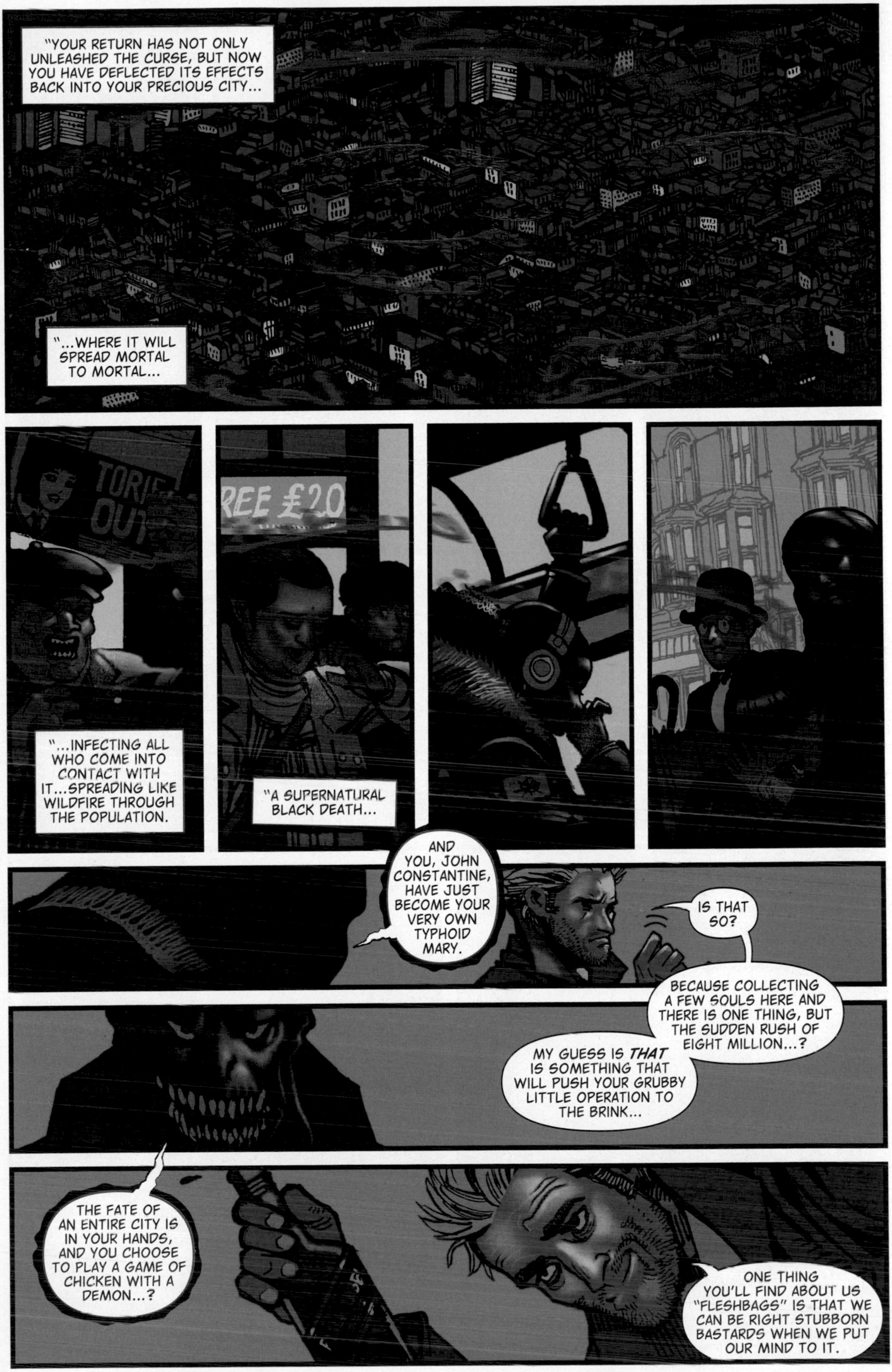
"YOUR RETURN HAS NOT ONLY UNLEASHED THE CURSE, BUT NOW YOU HAVE DEFLECTED ITS EFFECTS BACK INTO YOUR PRECIOUS CITY...
"...WHERE IT WILL SPREAD MORTAL TO MORTAL...
TORIES OUT
"...INFECTING ALL WHO COME INTO CONTACT WITH IT...SPREADING LIKE WILDFIRE THROUGH THE POPULATION.
"A SUPERNATURAL BLACK DEATH...
AND YOU, JOHN CONSTANTINE, HAVE JUST BECOME YOUR VERY OWN TYPHOID MARY.
IS THAT SO?
BECAUSE COLLECTING A FEW SOULS HERE AND THERE IS ONE THING, BUT THE SUDDEN RUSH OF EIGHT MILLION...?
MY GUESS IS *THAT* IS SOMETHING THAT WILL PUSH YOUR GRUBBY LITTLE OPERATION TO THE BRINK...
THE FATE OF AN ENTIRE CITY IS IN YOUR HANDS, AND YOU CHOOSE TO PLAY A GAME OF CHICKEN WITH A DEMON...?
ONE THING YOU'LL FIND ABOUT US "FLESHBAGS" IS THAT WE CAN BE RIGHT STUBBORN BASTARDS WHEN WE PUT OUR MIND TO IT.

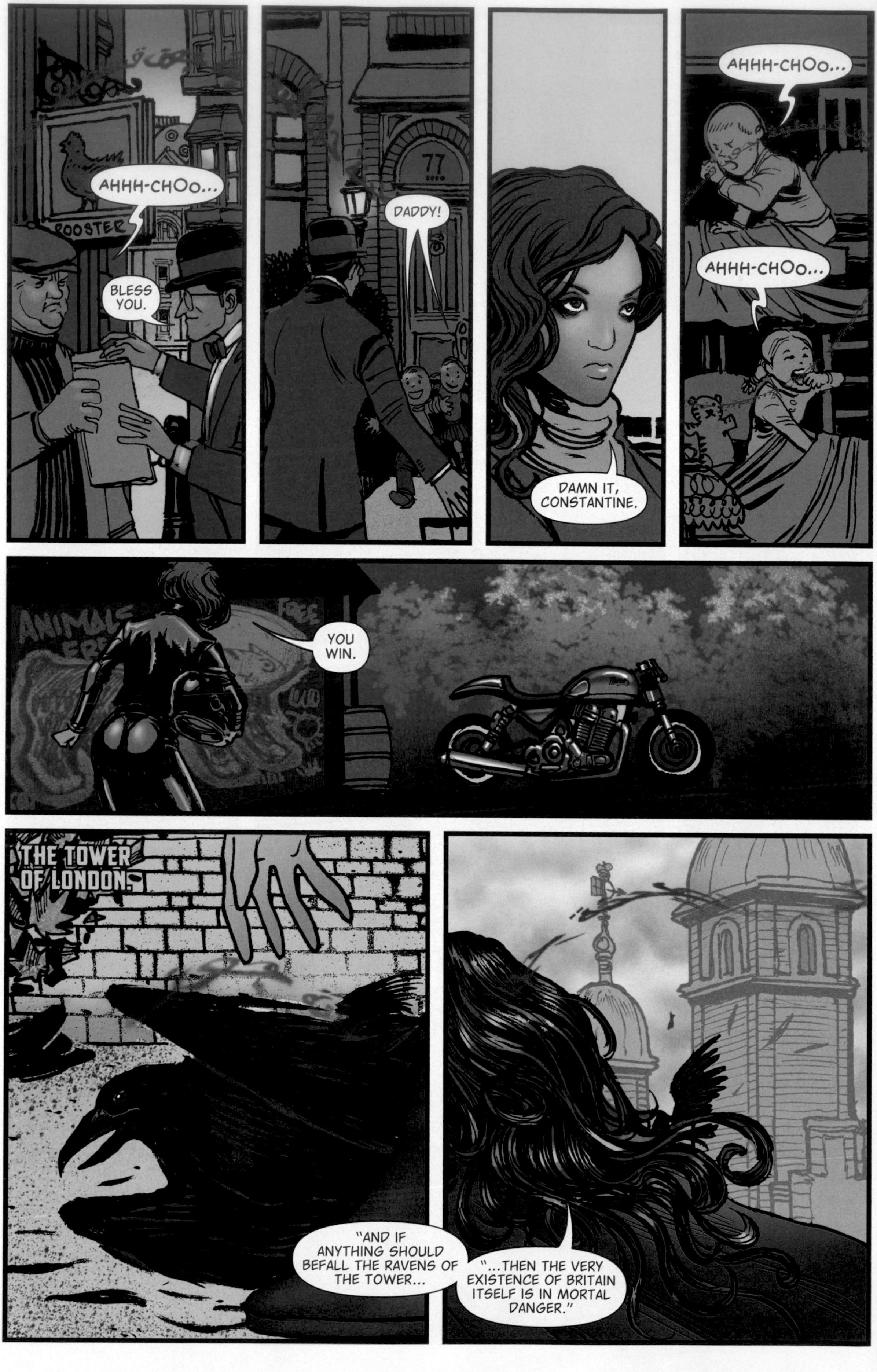
AHHH-CHOo...
BLESS YOU.
ROOSTER
77
DADDY!
DAMN IT, CONSTANTINE.
AHHH-CHOo...
AHHH-CHOo...
YOU WIN.
THE TOWER OF LONDON.
"AND IF ANYTHING SHOULD BEFALL THE RAVENS OF THE TOWER...
"...THEN THE VERY EXISTENCE OF BRITAIN ITSELF IS IN MORTAL DANGER."

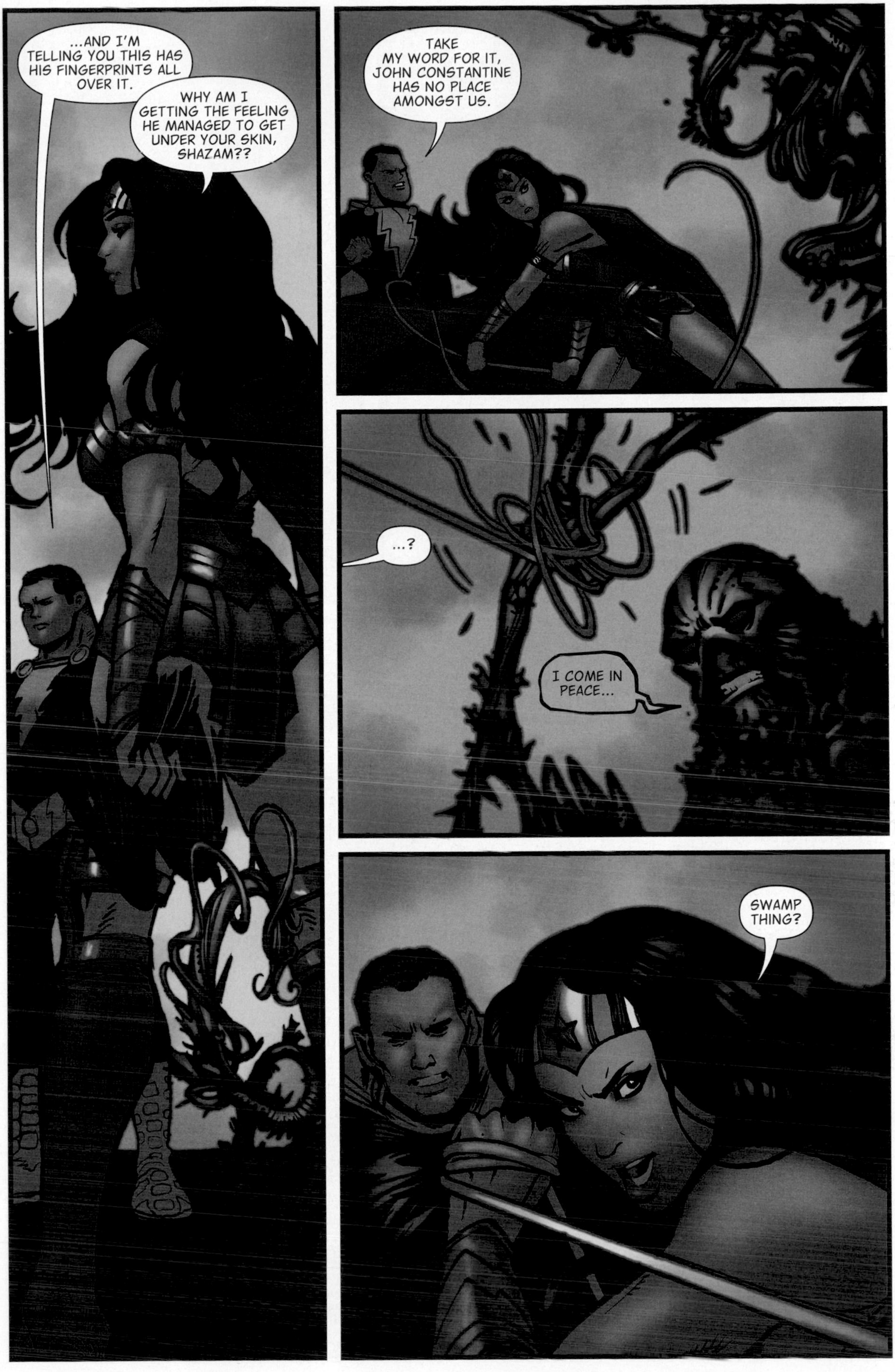
...AND I'M TELLING YOU THIS HAS HIS FINGERPRINTS ALL OVER IT.
WHY AM I GETTING THE FEELING HE MANAGED TO GET UNDER YOUR SKIN, SHAZAM??
TAKE MY WORD FOR IT, JOHN CONSTANTINE HAS NO PLACE AMONGST US.
...?
I COME IN PEACE...
SWAMP THING?

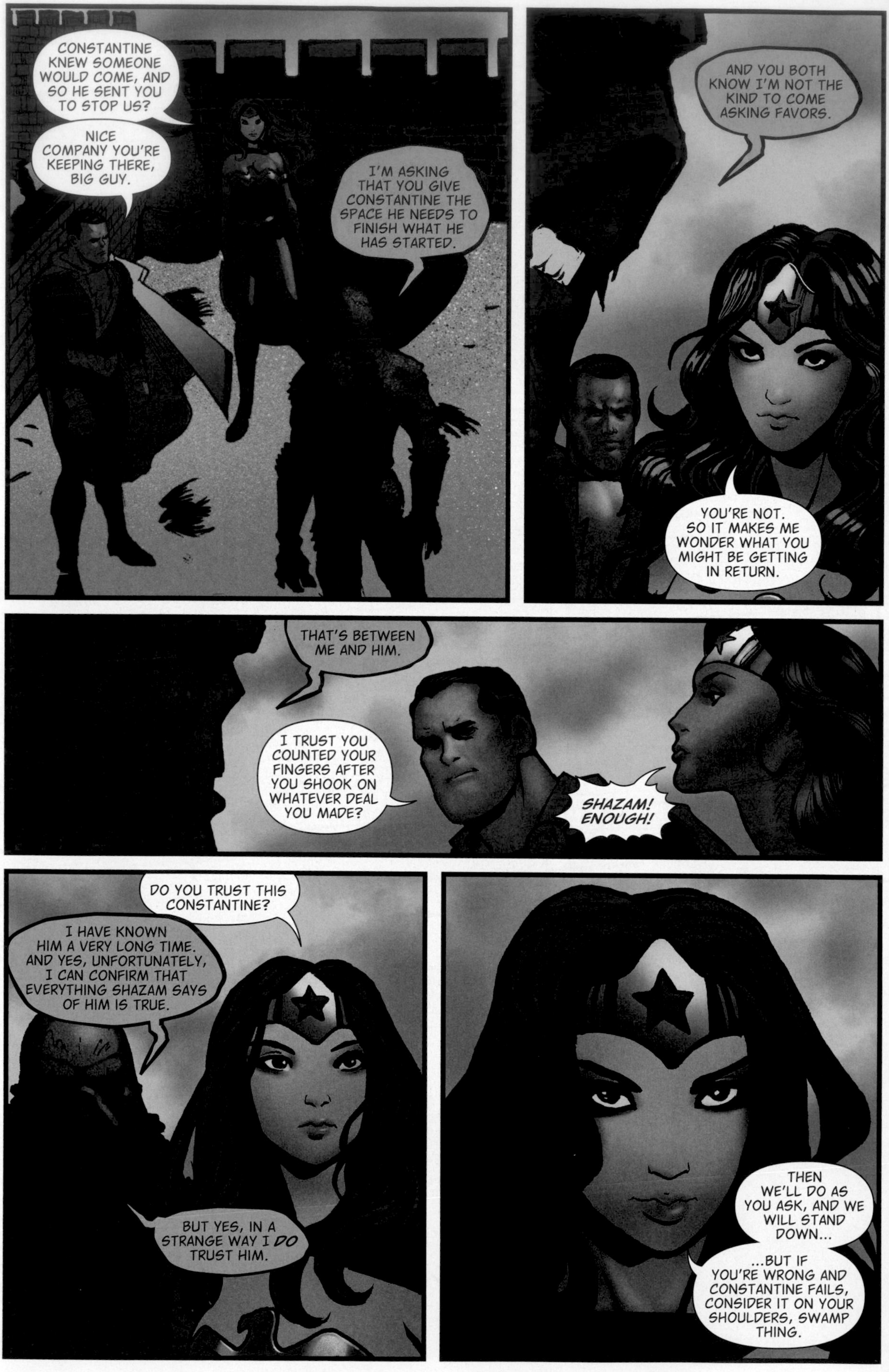
CONSTANTINE KNEW SOMEONE WOULD COME, AND SO HE SENT YOU TO STOP US?
NICE COMPANY YOU'RE KEEPING THERE, BIG GUY.
I'M ASKING THAT YOU GIVE CONSTANTINE THE SPACE HE NEEDS TO FINISH WHAT HE HAS STARTED.
AND YOU BOTH KNOW I'M NOT THE KIND TO COME ASKING FAVORS.
YOU'RE NOT. SO IT MAKES ME WONDER WHAT YOU MIGHT BE GETTING IN RETURN.
THAT'S BETWEEN ME AND HIM.
I TRUST YOU COUNTED YOUR FINGERS AFTER YOU SHOOK ON WHATEVER DEAL YOU MADE?
SHAZAM! ENOUGH!
DO YOU TRUST THIS CONSTANTINE?
I HAVE KNOWN HIM A VERY LONG TIME. AND YES, UNFORTUNATELY, I CAN CONFIRM THAT EVERYTHING SHAZAM SAYS OF HIM IS TRUE.
BUT YES, IN A STRANGE WAY I DO TRUST HIM.
THEN WE'LL DO AS YOU ASK, AND WE WILL STAND DOWN...
...BUT IF YOU'RE WRONG AND CONSTANTINE FAILS, CONSIDER IT ON YOUR SHOULDERS, SWAMP THING.

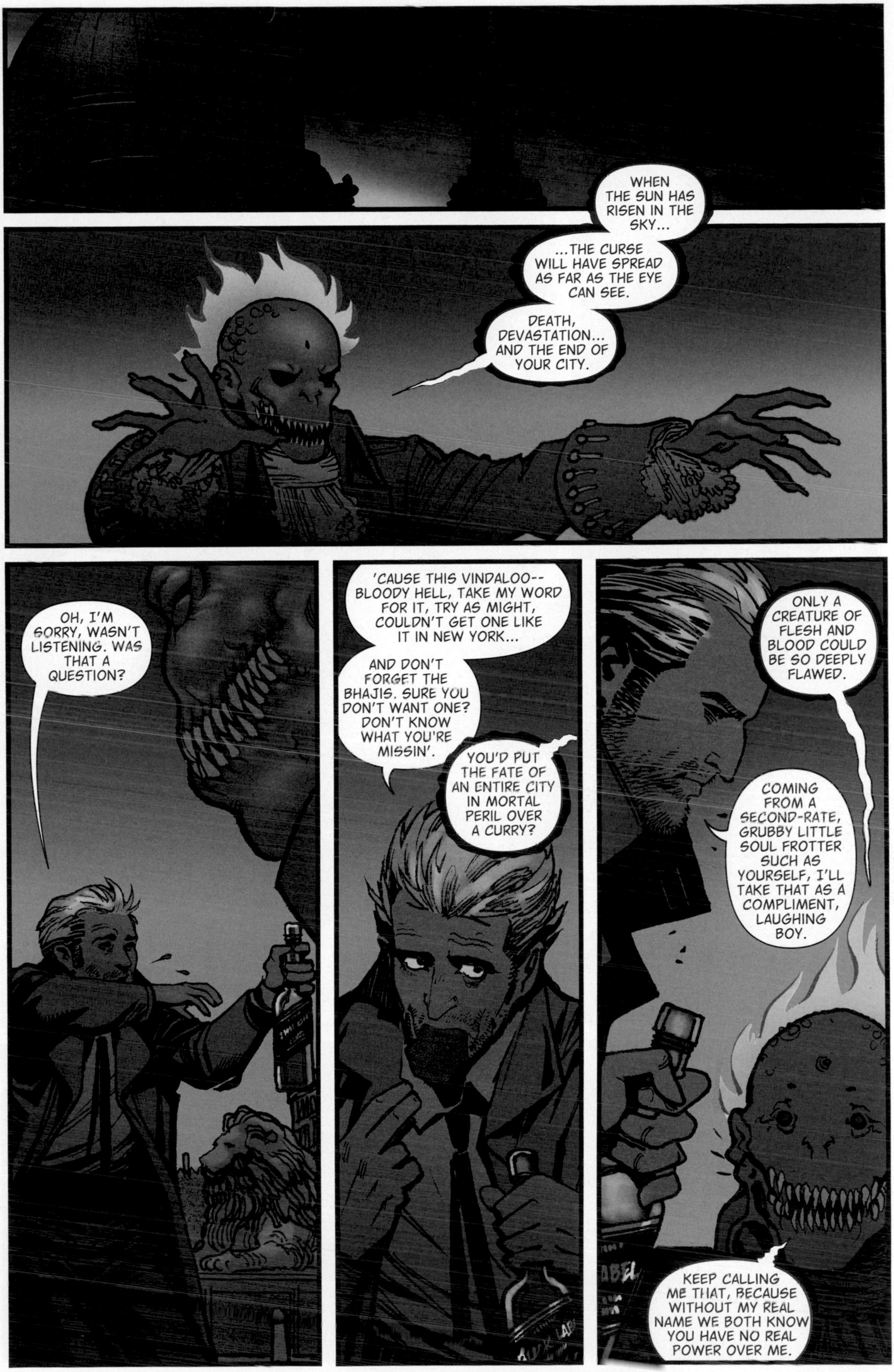
WHEN THE SUN HAS RISEN IN THE SKY...
...THE CURSE WILL HAVE SPREAD AS FAR AS THE EYE CAN SEE.
DEATH, DEVASTATION... AND THE END OF YOUR CITY.
OH, I'M SORRY, WASN'T LISTENING. WAS THAT A QUESTION?
'CAUSE THIS VINDALOO-- BLOODY HELL, TAKE MY WORD FOR IT, TRY AS MIGHT, COULDN'T GET ONE LIKE IT IN NEW YORK...
AND DON'T FORGET THE BHAJIS. SURE YOU DON'T WANT ONE? DON'T KNOW WHAT YOU'RE MISSIN'.
YOU'D PUT THE FATE OF AN ENTIRE CITY IN MORTAL PERIL OVER A CURRY?
ONLY A CREATURE OF FLESH AND BLOOD COULD BE SO DEEPLY FLAWED.
COMING FROM A SECOND-RATE, GRUBBY LITTLE SOUL FROTTER SUCH AS YOURSELF, I'LL TAKE THAT AS A COMPLIMENT, LAUGHING BOY.
KEEP CALLING ME THAT, BECAUSE WITHOUT MY REAL NAME WE BOTH KNOW YOU HAVE NO REAL POWER OVER ME.

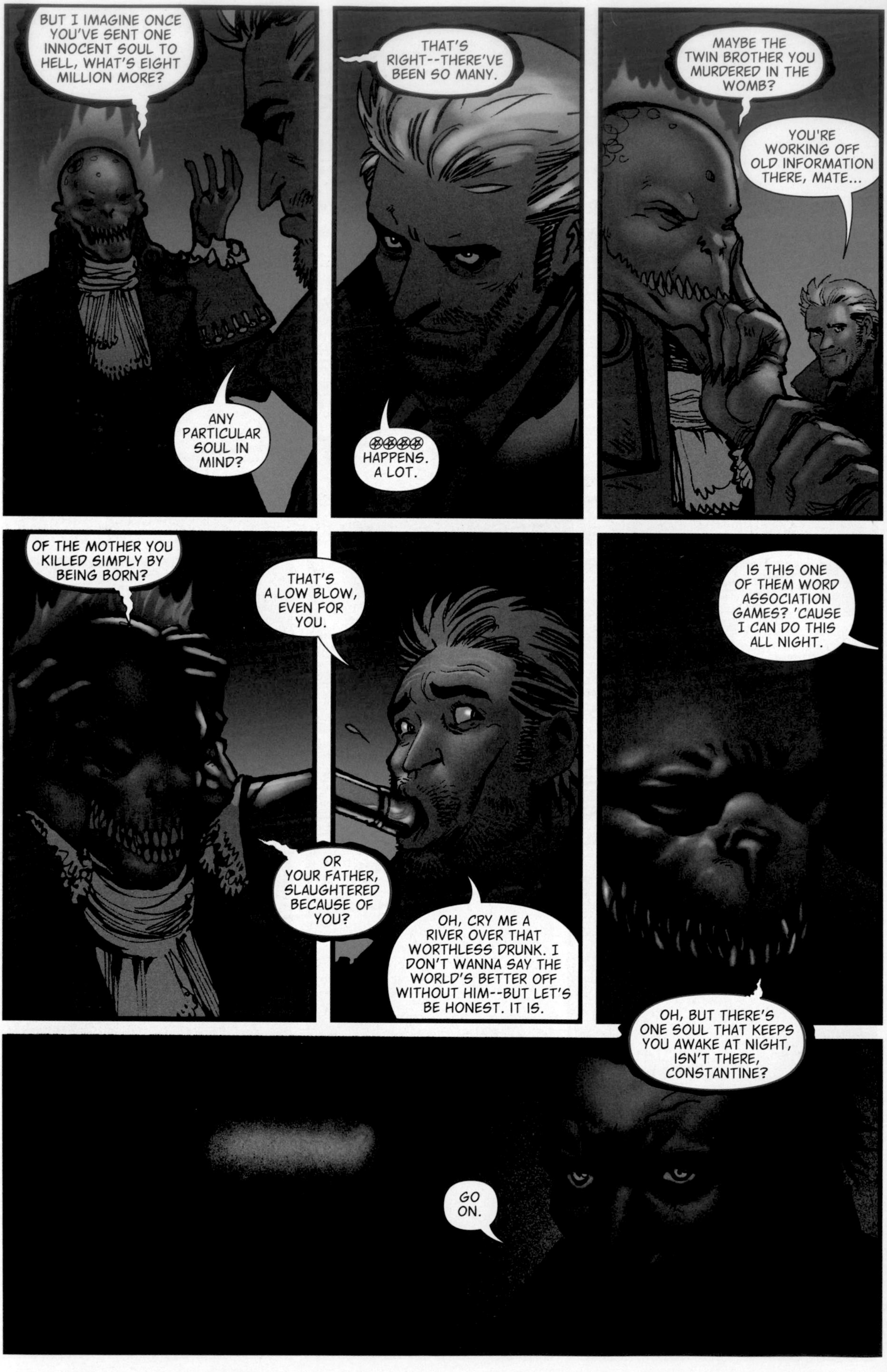
BUT I IMAGINE ONCE YOU'VE SENT ONE INNOCENT SOUL TO HELL, WHAT'S EIGHT MILLION MORE?
ANY PARTICULAR SOUL IN MIND?
THAT'S RIGHT--THERE'VE BEEN SO MANY.
HAPPENS. A LOT.
MAYBE THE TWIN BROTHER YOU MURDERED IN THE WOMB?
YOU'RE WORKING OFF OLD INFORMATION THERE, MATE...
OF THE MOTHER YOU KILLED SIMPLY BY BEING BORN?
THAT'S A LOW BLOW, EVEN FOR YOU.
OR YOUR FATHER, SLAUGHTERED BECAUSE OF YOU?
OH, CRY ME A RIVER OVER THAT WORTHLESS DRUNK. I DON'T WANNA SAY THE WORLD'S BETTER OFF WITHOUT HIM--BUT LET'S BE HONEST. IT IS.
IS THIS ONE OF THEM WORD ASSOCIATION GAMES? 'CAUSE I CAN DO THIS ALL NIGHT.
OH, BUT THERE'S ONE SOUL THAT KEEPS YOU AWAKE AT NIGHT, ISN'T THERE, CONSTANTINE?
GO ON.

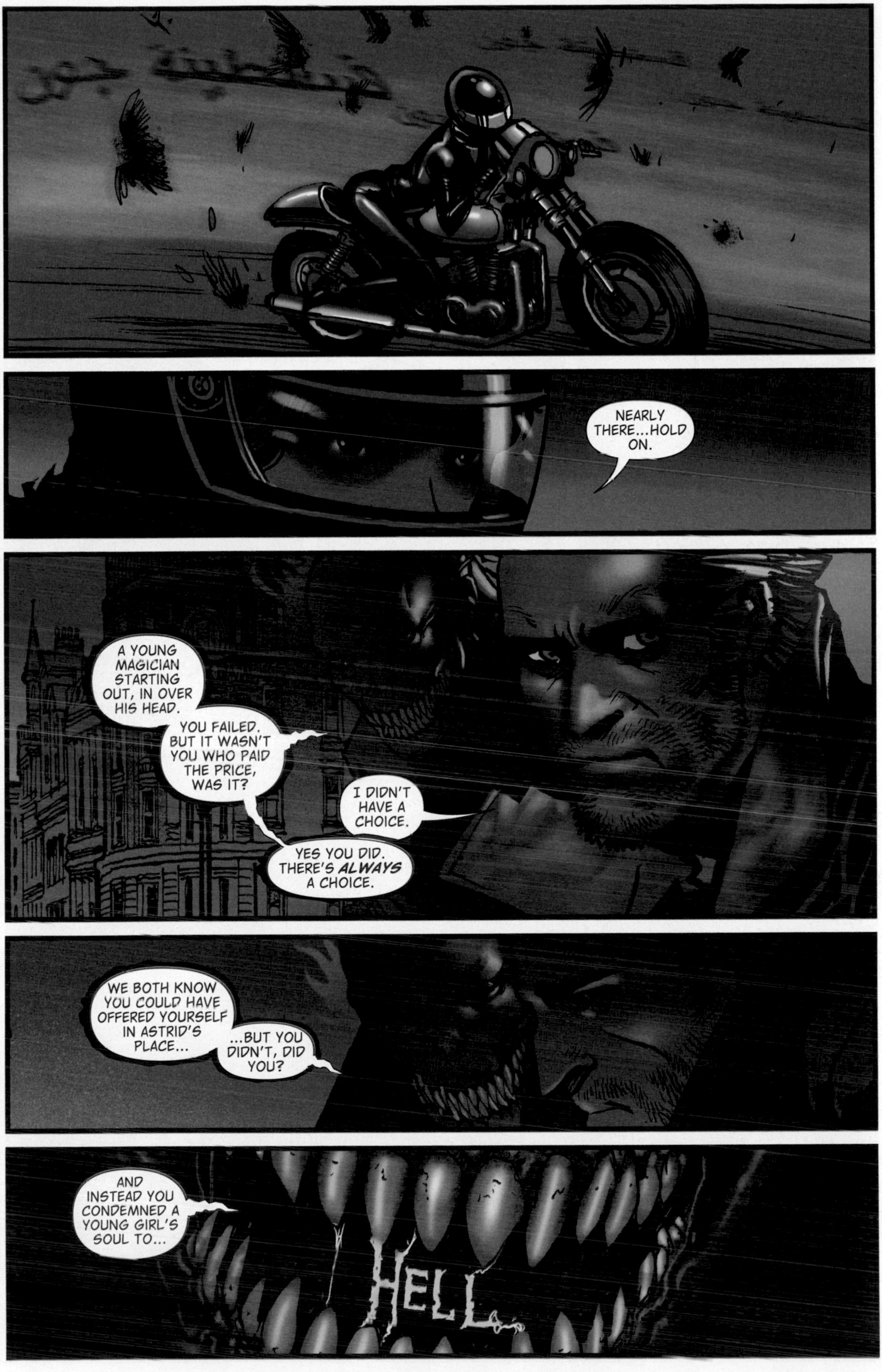
NEARLY THERE...HOLD ON.
A YOUNG MAGICIAN STARTING OUT, IN OVER HIS HEAD.
YOU FAILED. BUT IT WASN'T YOU WHO PAID THE PRICE, WAS IT?
I DIDN'T HAVE A CHOICE.
YES YOU DID. THERE'S *ALWAYS* A CHOICE.
WE BOTH KNOW YOU COULD HAVE OFFERED YOURSELF IN ASTRID'S PLACE...
...BUT YOU DIDN'T, DID YOU?
AND INSTEAD YOU CONDEMNED A YOUNG GIRL'S SOUL TO...
HELL

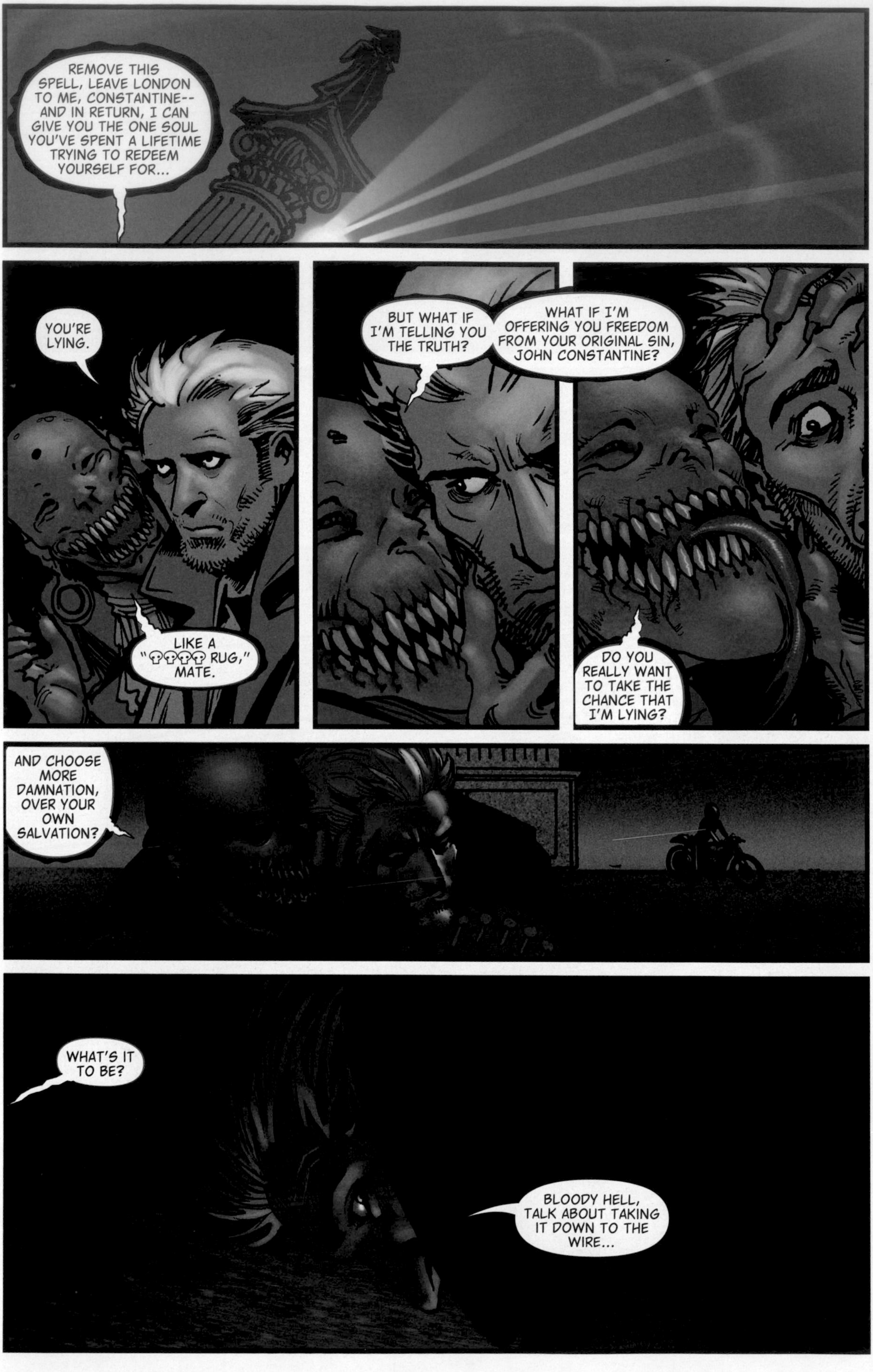
REMOVE THIS SPELL, LEAVE LONDON TO ME, CONSTANTINE-- AND IN RETURN, I CAN GIVE YOU THE ONE SOUL YOU'VE SPENT A LIFETIME TRYING TO REDEEM YOURSELF FOR...
YOU'RE LYING.
LIKE A "♰♰♰♰ RUG," MATE.
BUT WHAT IF I'M TELLING YOU THE TRUTH?
WHAT IF I'M OFFERING YOU FREEDOM FROM YOUR ORIGINAL SIN, JOHN CONSTANTINE?
DO YOU REALLY WANT TO TAKE THE CHANCE THAT I'M LYING?
AND CHOOSE MORE DAMNATION, OVER YOUR OWN SALVATION?
WHAT'S IT TO BE?
BLOODY HELL, TALK ABOUT TAKING IT DOWN TO THE WIRE...

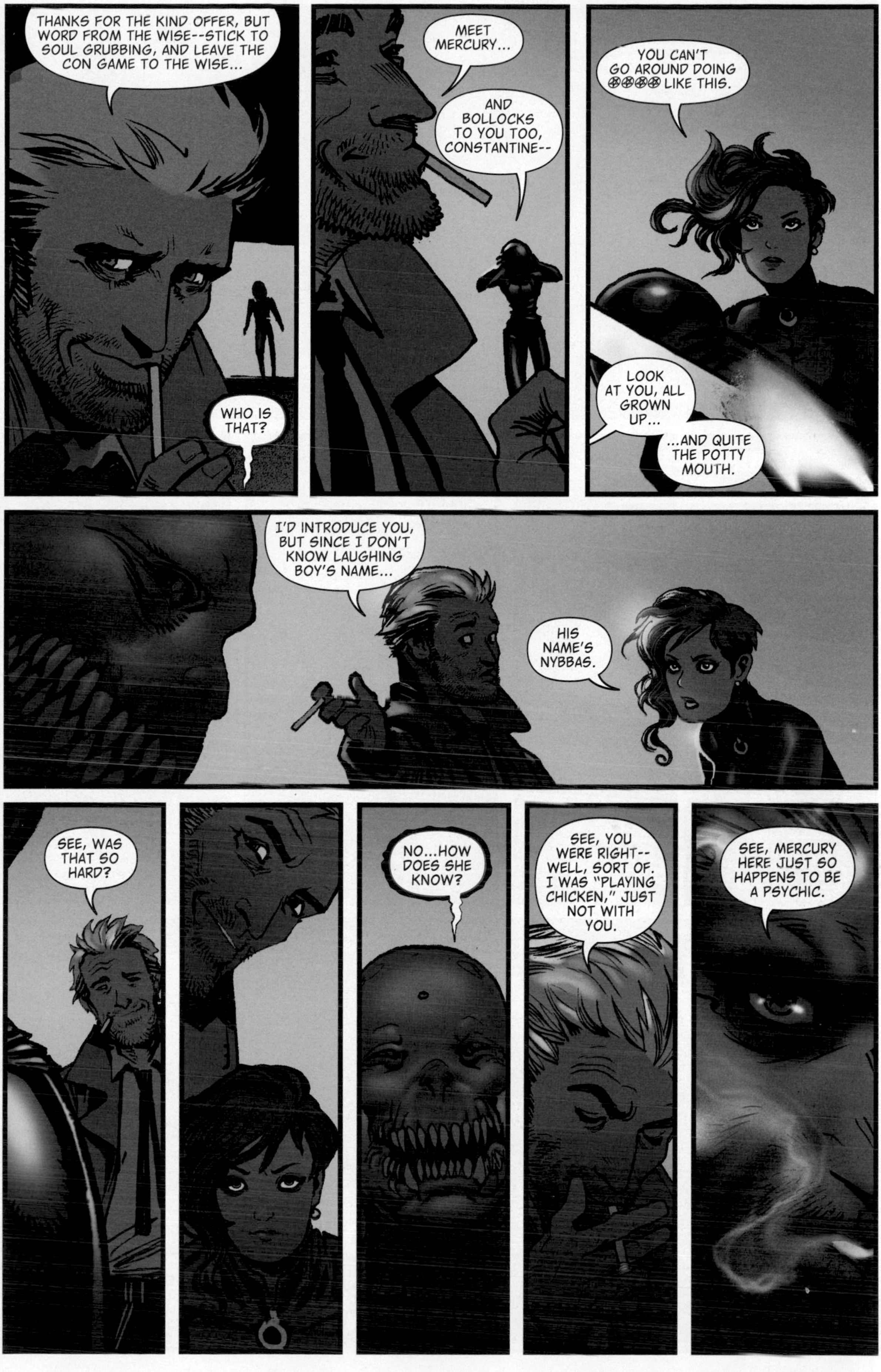
THANKS FOR THE KIND OFFER, BUT WORD FROM THE WISE--STICK TO SOUL GRUBBING, AND LEAVE THE CON GAME TO THE WISE...
WHO IS THAT?
MEET MERCURY...
AND BOLLOCKS TO YOU TOO, CONSTANTINE--
YOU CAN'T GO AROUND DOING ⊗⊗⊗⊗ LIKE THIS.
LOOK AT YOU, ALL GROWN UP...
...AND QUITE THE POTTY MOUTH.
I'D INTRODUCE YOU, BUT SINCE I DON'T KNOW LAUGHING BOY'S NAME...
HIS NAME'S NYBBAS.
SEE, WAS THAT SO HARD?
NO...HOW DOES SHE KNOW?
SEE, YOU WERE RIGHT-- WELL, SORT OF. I WAS "PLAYING CHICKEN," JUST NOT WITH YOU.
SEE, MERCURY HERE JUST SO HAPPENS TO BE A PSYCHIC.

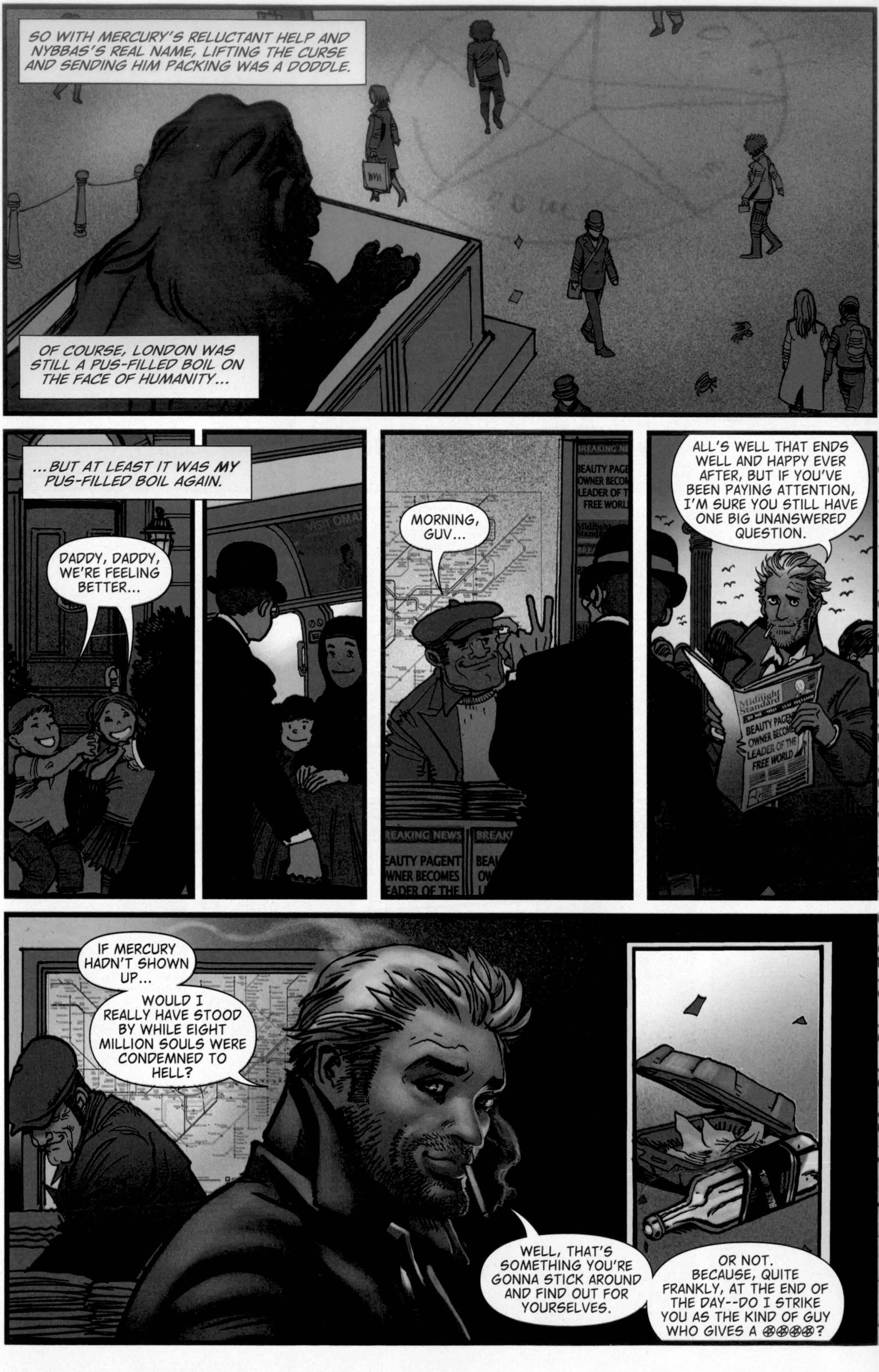
SO WITH MERCURY'S RELUCTANT HELP AND NYBBAS'S REAL NAME, LIFTING THE CURSE AND SENDING HIM PACKING WAS A DODDLE.
OF COURSE, LONDON WAS STILL A PUS-FILLED BOIL ON THE FACE OF HUMANITY...
...BUT AT LEAST IT WAS MY PUS-FILLED BOIL AGAIN.
DADDY, DADDY, WE'RE FEELING BETTER...
BREAKING NEWS
BEAUTY PAGENT OWNER BECOMES LEADER OF THE FREE WORLD
MORNING, GUV...
ALL'S WELL THAT ENDS WELL AND HAPPY EVER AFTER, BUT IF YOU'VE BEEN PAYING ATTENTION, I'M SURE YOU STILL HAVE ONE BIG UNANSWERED QUESTION.
Midnight Standard
BEAUTY PAGENT OWNER BECOMES LEADER OF THE FREE WORLD
IF MERCURY HADN'T SHOWN UP...
WOULD I REALLY HAVE STOOD BY WHILE EIGHT MILLION SOULS WERE CONDEMNED TO HELL?
WELL, THAT'S SOMETHING YOU'RE GONNA STICK AROUND AND FIND OUT FOR YOURSELVES.
OR NOT. BECAUSE, QUITE FRANKLY, AT THE END OF THE DAY--DO I STRIKE YOU AS THE KIND OF GUY WHO GIVES A ⊗⊗⊗⊗?

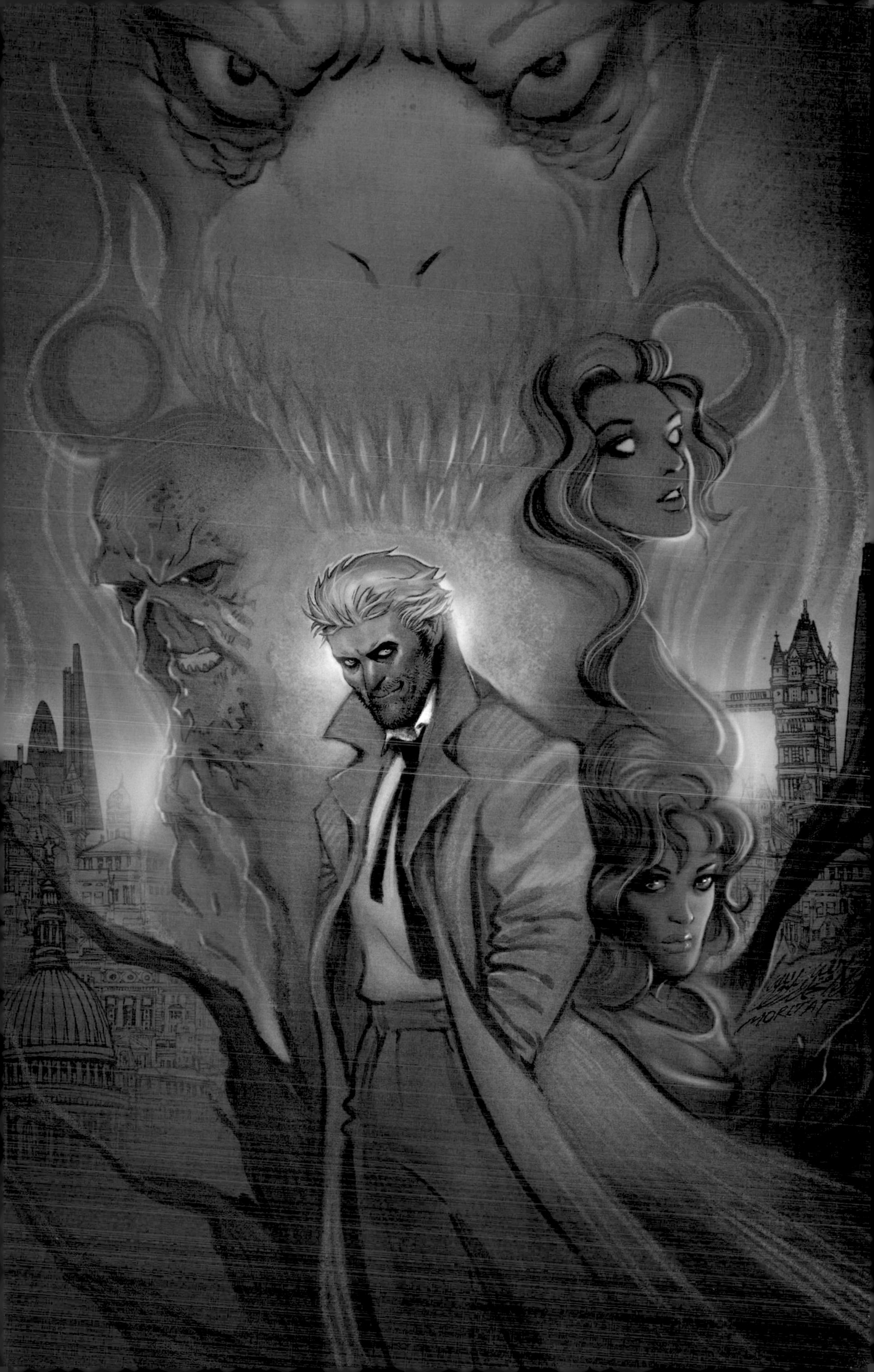

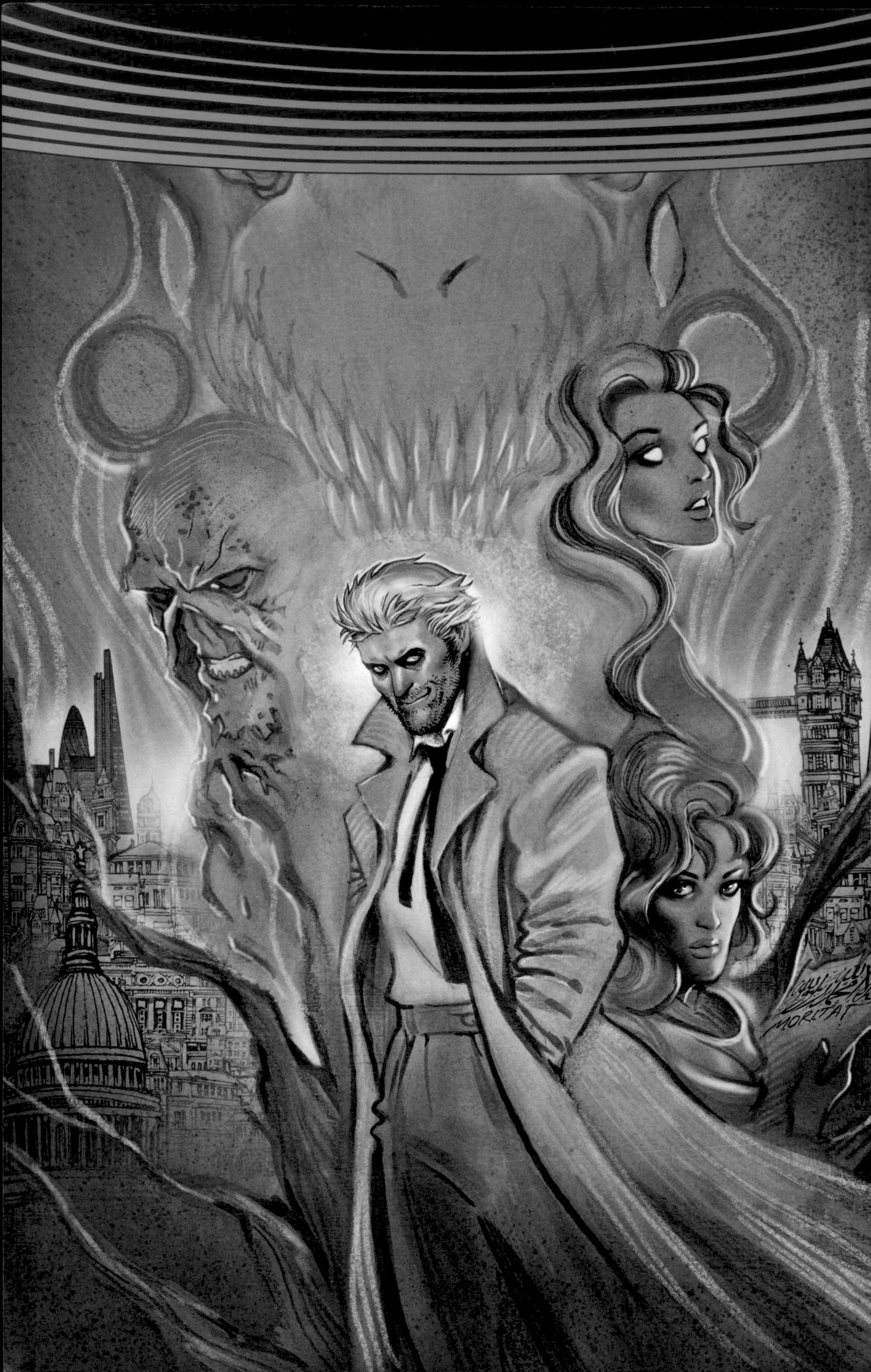
MORITAT

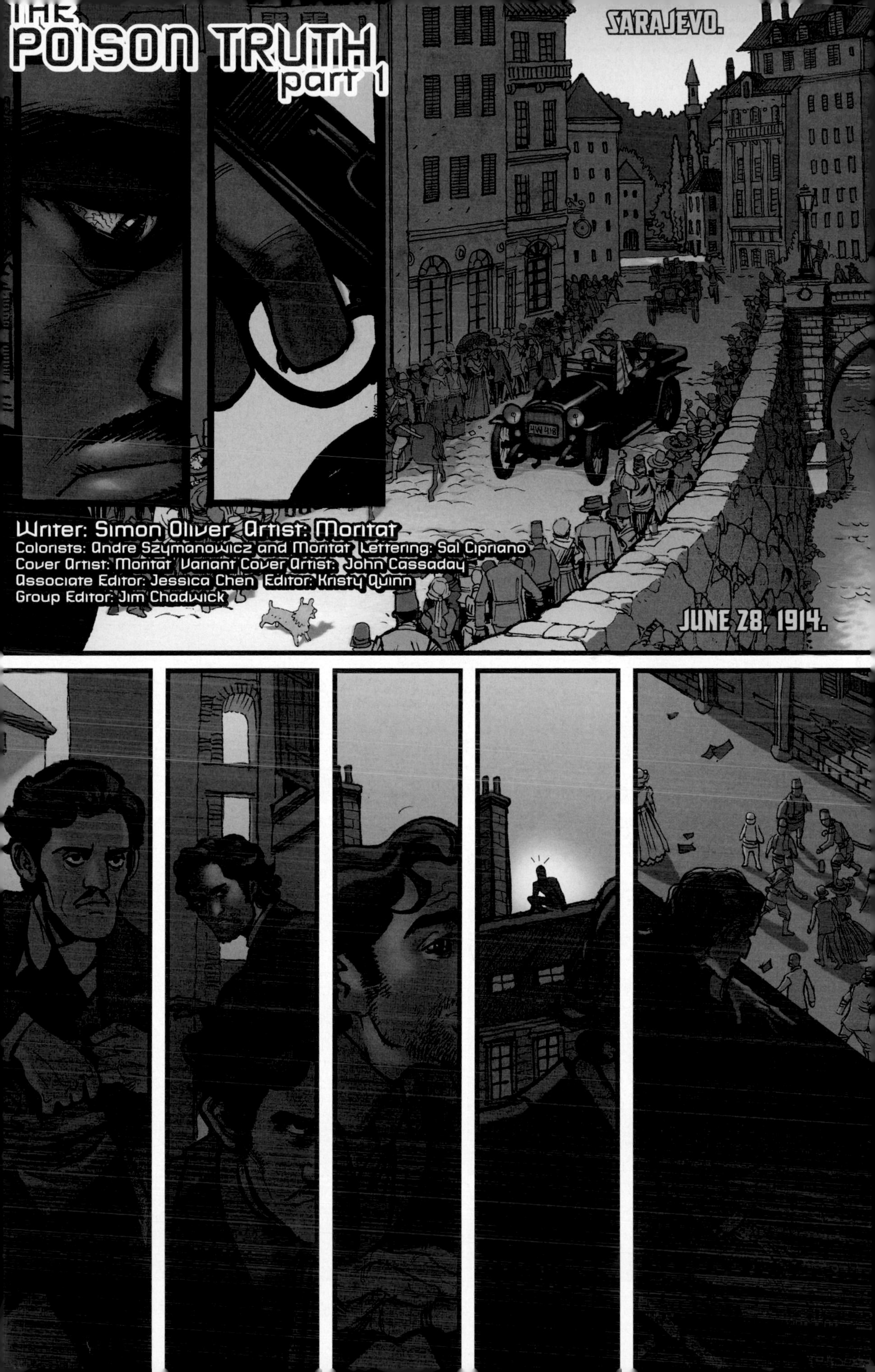

THE POISON TRUTH part 1
SARAJEVO.
4W 418
Writer: Simon Oliver Artist: Moritat
Colorists: Andre Szymanowicz and Moritat Lettering: Sal Cipriano
Cover Artist: Moritat Variant Cover Artist: John Cassaday
Associate Editor: Jessica Chen Editor: Kristy Quinn
Group Editor: Jim Chadwick
JUNE 28, 1914.

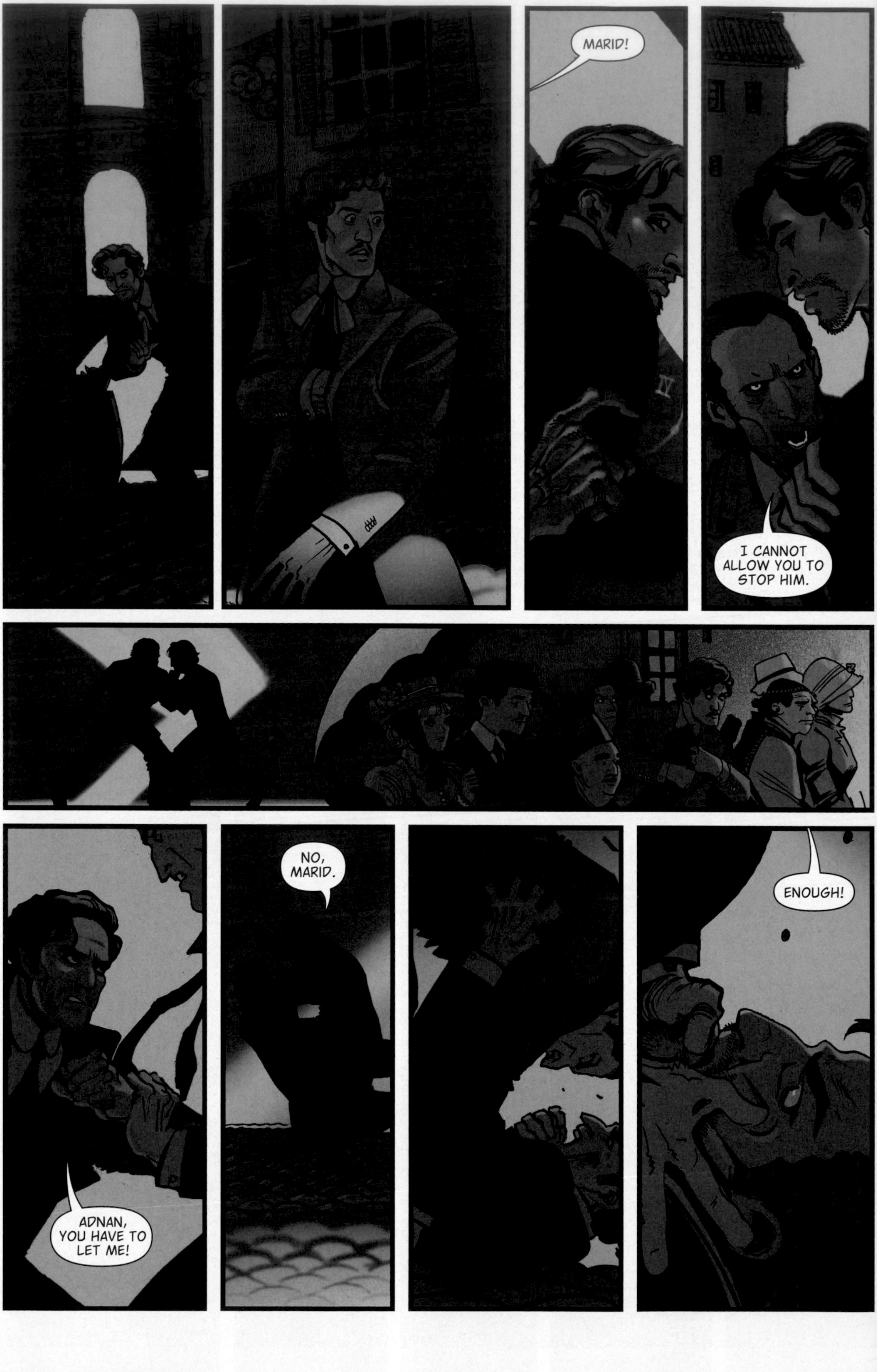
MARID!
I CANNOT ALLOW YOU TO STOP HIM.
ADNAN, YOU HAVE TO LET ME!
NO, MARID.
ENOUGH!

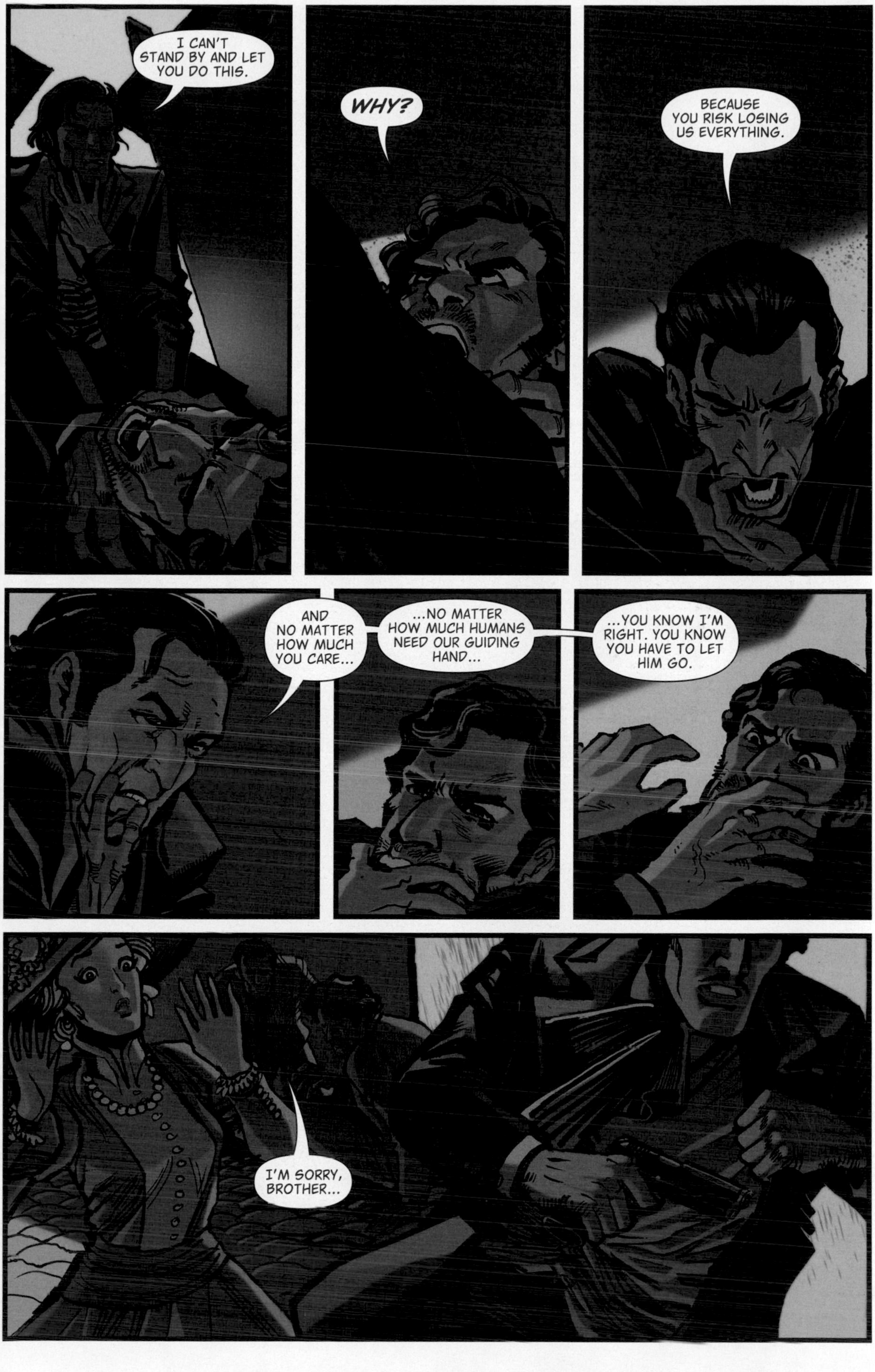
I CAN'T STAND BY AND LET YOU DO THIS.
WHY?
BECAUSE YOU RISK LOSING US EVERYTHING.
AND NO MATTER HOW MUCH YOU CARE...
...NO MATTER HOW MUCH HUMANS NEED OUR GUIDING HAND...
...YOU KNOW I'M RIGHT. YOU KNOW YOU HAVE TO LET HIM GO.
I'M SORRY, BROTHER...

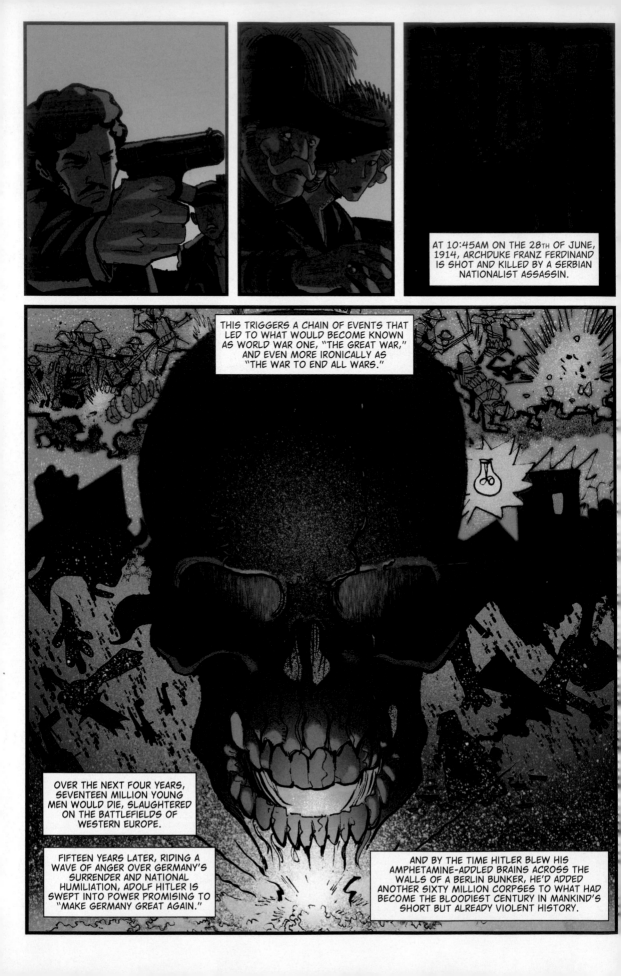

AT 10:45AM ON THE 28TH OF JUNE, 1914, ARCHDUKE FRANZ FERDINAND IS SHOT AND KILLED BY A SERBIAN NATIONALIST ASSASSIN.

THIS TRIGGERS A CHAIN OF EVENTS THAT LED TO WHAT WOULD BECOME KNOWN AS WORLD WAR ONE, "THE GREAT WAR," AND EVEN MORE IRONICALLY AS "THE WAR TO END ALL WARS."

OVER THE NEXT FOUR YEARS, SEVENTEEN MILLION YOUNG MEN WOULD DIE, SLAUGHTERED ON THE BATTLEFIELDS OF WESTERN EUROPE.

FIFTEEN YEARS LATER, RIDING A WAVE OF ANGER OVER GERMANY'S SURRENDER AND NATIONAL HUMILIATION, ADOLF HITLER IS SWEPT INTO POWER PROMISING TO "MAKE GERMANY GREAT AGAIN."

AND BY THE TIME HITLER BLEW HIS AMPHETAMINE-ADDLED BRAINS ACROSS THE WALLS OF A BERLIN BUNKER, HE'D ADDED ANOTHER SIXTY MILLION CORPSES TO WHAT HAD BECOME THE BLOODIEST CENTURY IN MANKIND'S SHORT BUT ALREADY VIOLENT HISTORY.

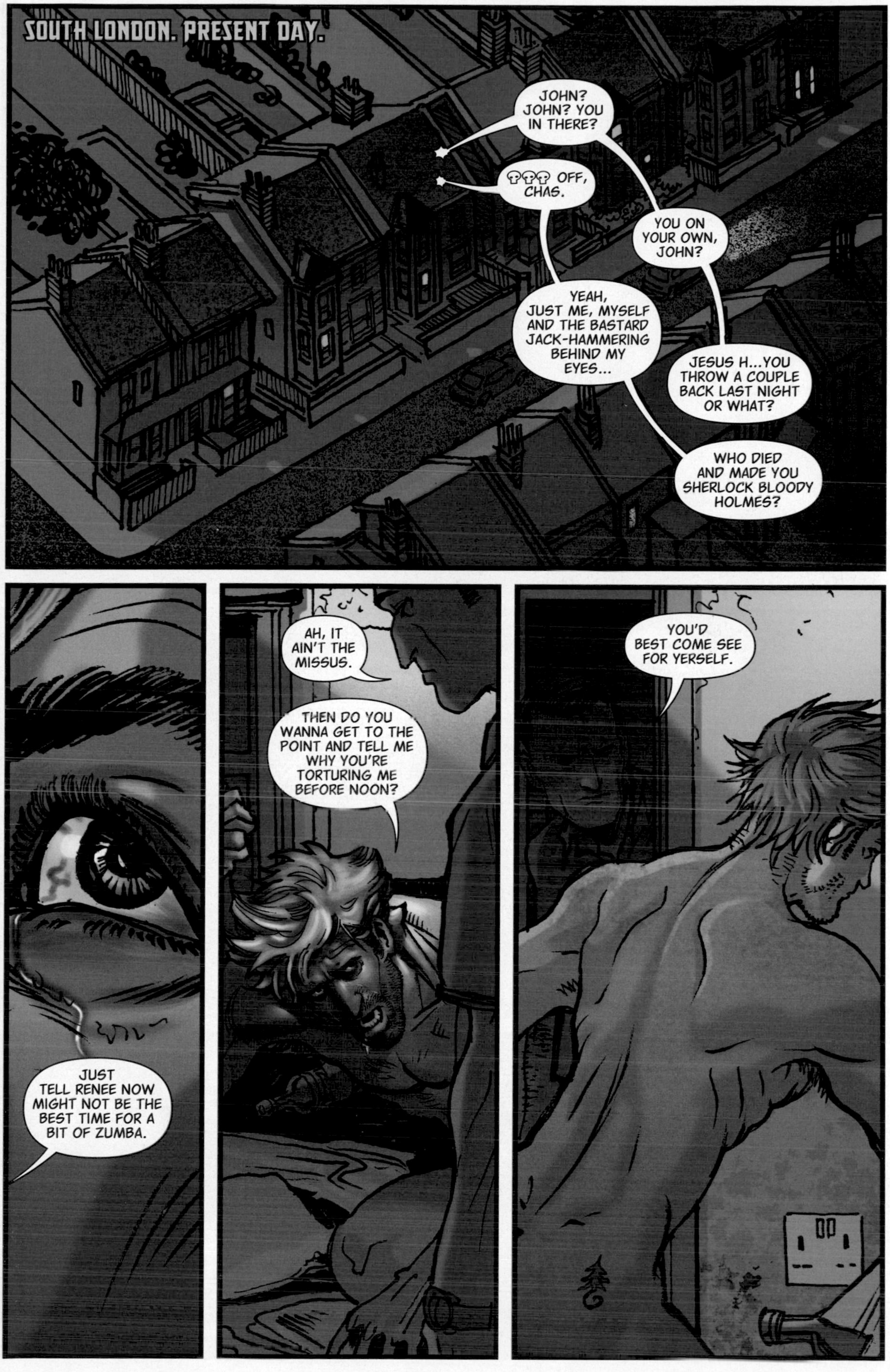
SOUTH LONDON. PRESENT DAY.
JOHN? JOHN? YOU IN THERE?
OFF, CHAS.
YOU ON YOUR OWN, JOHN?
YEAH, JUST ME, MYSELF AND THE BASTARD JACK-HAMMERING BEHIND MY EYES...
JESUS H...YOU THROW A COUPLE BACK LAST NIGHT OR WHAT?
WHO DIED AND MADE YOU SHERLOCK BLOODY HOLMES?
JUST TELL RENEE NOW MIGHT NOT BE THE BEST TIME FOR A BIT OF ZUMBA.
AH, IT AIN'T THE MISSUS.
THEN DO YOU WANNA GET TO THE POINT AND TELL ME WHY YOU'RE TORTURING ME BEFORE NOON?
YOU'D BEST COME SEE FOR YERSELF.

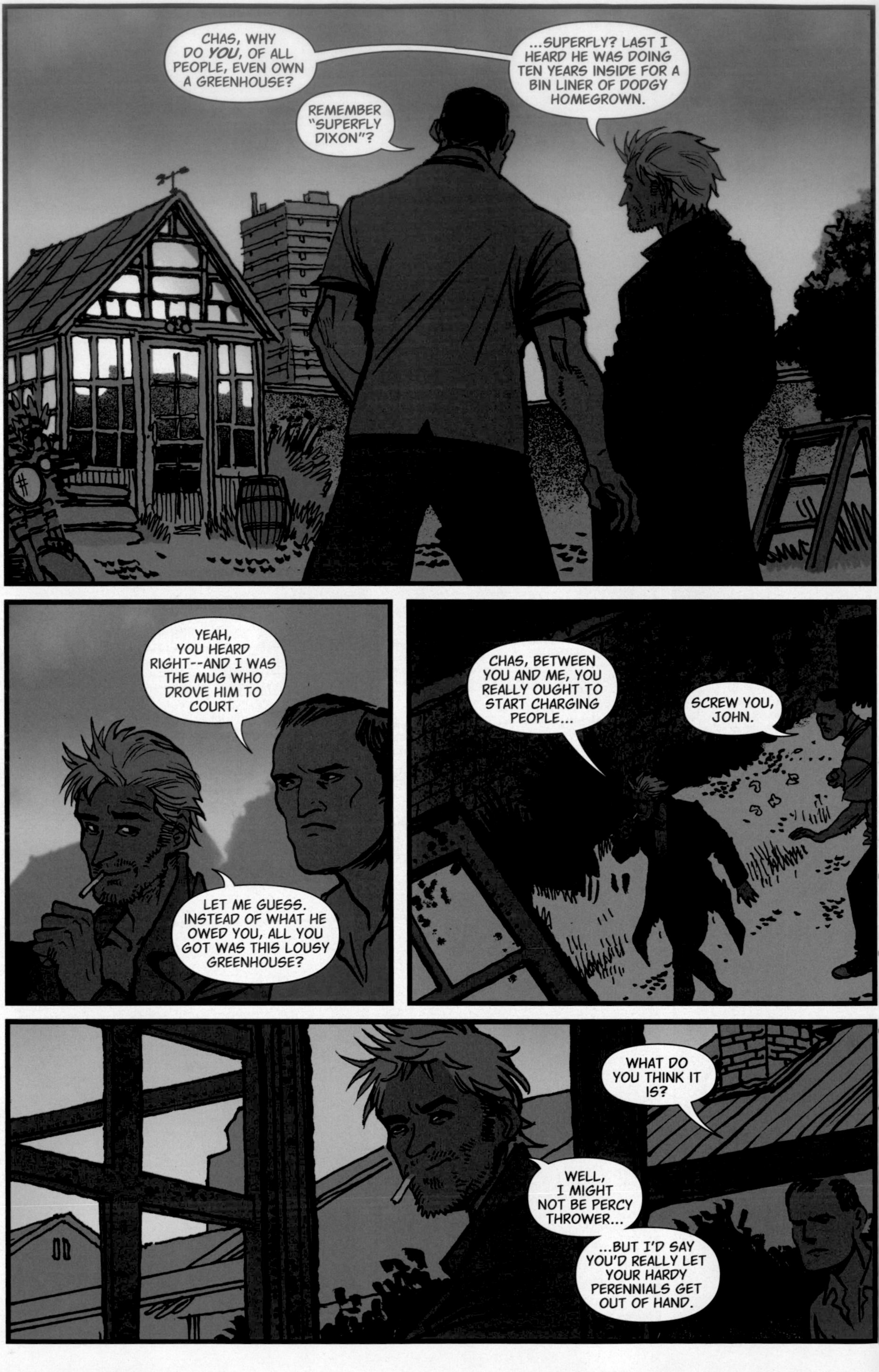
CHAS, WHY DO *YOU*, OF ALL PEOPLE, EVEN OWN A GREENHOUSE?
REMEMBER "SUPERFLY DIXON"?
...SUPERFLY? LAST I HEARD HE WAS DOING TEN YEARS INSIDE FOR A BIN LINER OF DODGY HOMEGROWN.
YEAH, YOU HEARD RIGHT--AND I WAS THE MUG WHO DROVE HIM TO COURT.
LET ME GUESS. INSTEAD OF WHAT HE OWED YOU, ALL YOU GOT WAS THIS LOUSY GREENHOUSE?
CHAS, BETWEEN YOU AND ME, YOU REALLY OUGHT TO START CHARGING PEOPLE...
SCREW YOU, JOHN.
WHAT DO YOU THINK IT IS?
WELL, I MIGHT NOT BE PERCY THROWER...
...BUT I'D SAY YOU'D REALLY LET YOUR HARDY PERENNIALS GET OUT OF HAND.

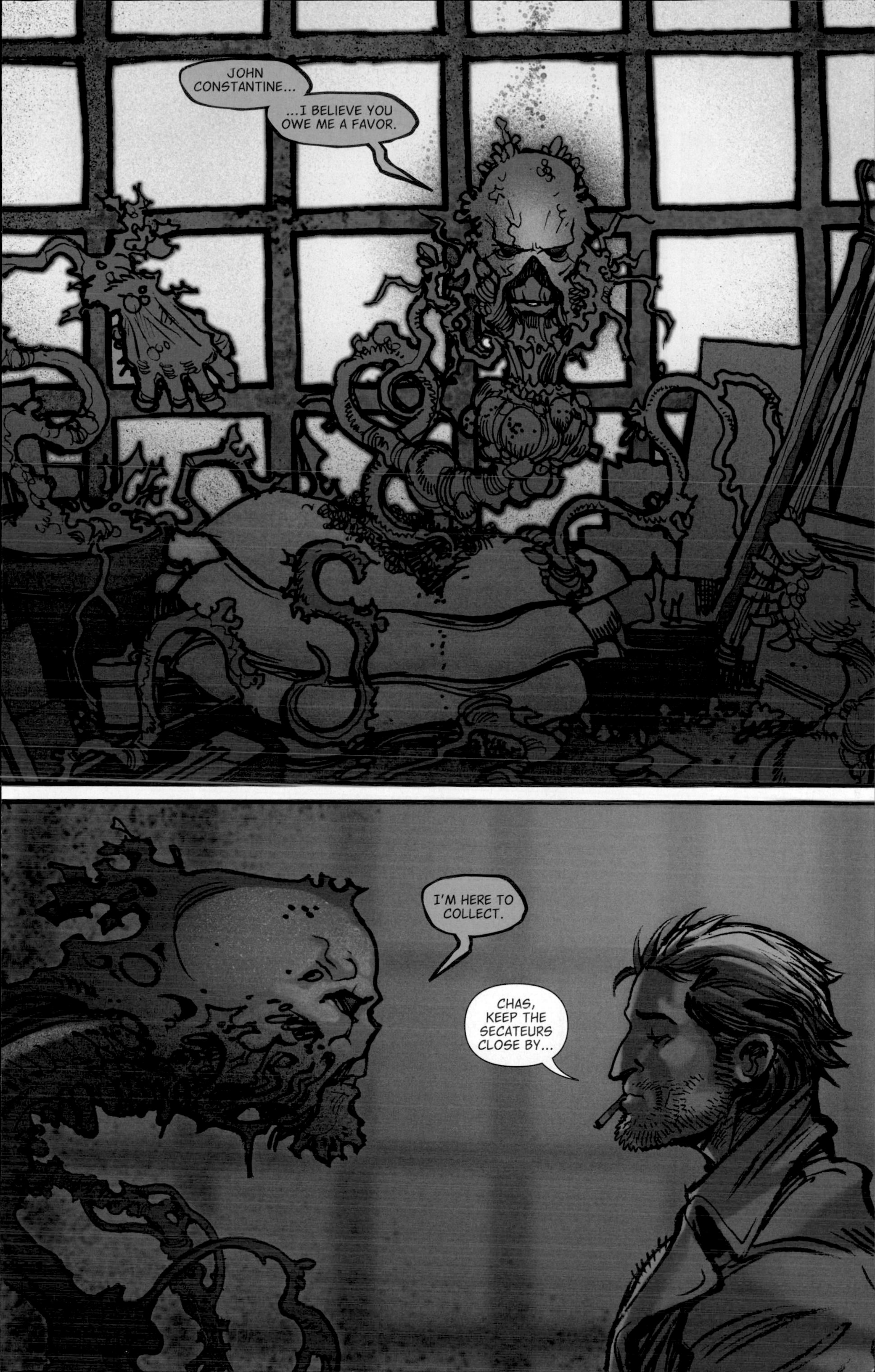
JOHN CONSTANTINE...
...I BELIEVE YOU OWE ME A FAVOR.
I'M HERE TO COLLECT.
CHAS, KEEP THE SECATEURS CLOSE BY...

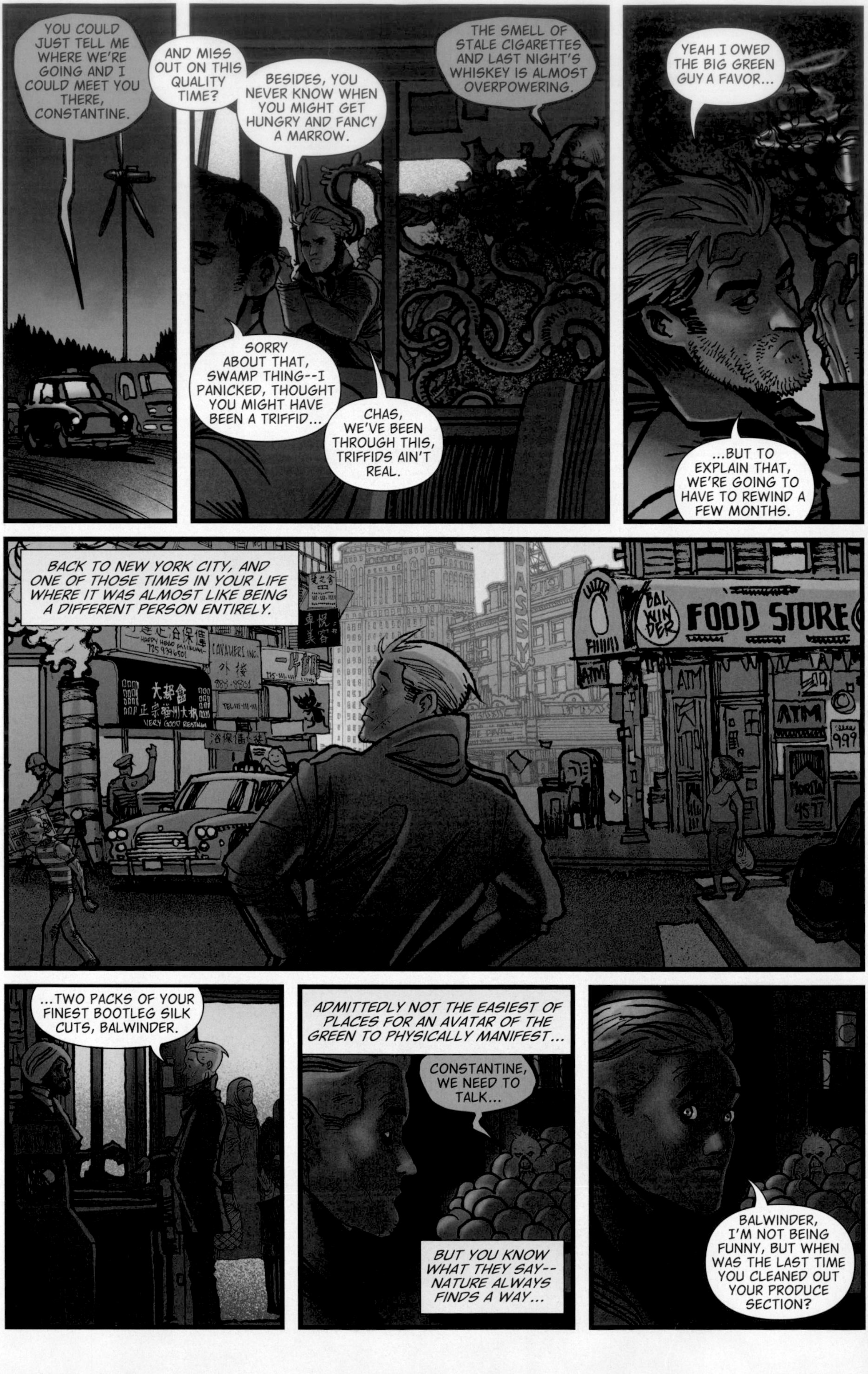
YOU COULD JUST TELL ME WHERE WE'RE GOING AND I COULD MEET YOU THERE, CONSTANTINE.
AND MISS OUT ON THIS QUALITY TIME?
BESIDES, YOU NEVER KNOW WHEN YOU MIGHT GET HUNGRY AND FANCY A MARROW.
SORRY ABOUT THAT, SWAMP THING--I PANICKED, THOUGHT YOU MIGHT HAVE BEEN A TRIFFID...
CHAS, WE'VE BEEN THROUGH THIS, TRIFFIDS AIN'T REAL.
THE SMELL OF STALE CIGARETTES AND LAST NIGHT'S WHISKEY IS ALMOST OVERPOWERING.
YEAH I OWED THE BIG GREEN GUY A FAVOR...
...BUT TO EXPLAIN THAT, WE'RE GOING TO HAVE TO REWIND A FEW MONTHS.
BACK TO NEW YORK CITY, AND ONE OF THOSE TIMES IN YOUR LIFE WHERE IT WAS ALMOST LIKE BEING A DIFFERENT PERSON ENTIRELY.
FOOD STORE
ATM
VERY GOOD RESTAURANT
...TWO PACKS OF YOUR FINEST BOOTLEG SILK CUTS, BALWINDER.
ADMITTEDLY NOT THE EASIEST OF PLACES FOR AN AVATAR OF THE GREEN TO PHYSICALLY MANIFEST...
CONSTANTINE, WE NEED TO TALK...
BUT YOU KNOW WHAT THEY SAY-- NATURE ALWAYS FINDS A WAY...
BALWINDER, I'M NOT BEING FUNNY, BUT WHEN WAS THE LAST TIME YOU CLEANED OUT YOUR PRODUCE SECTION?

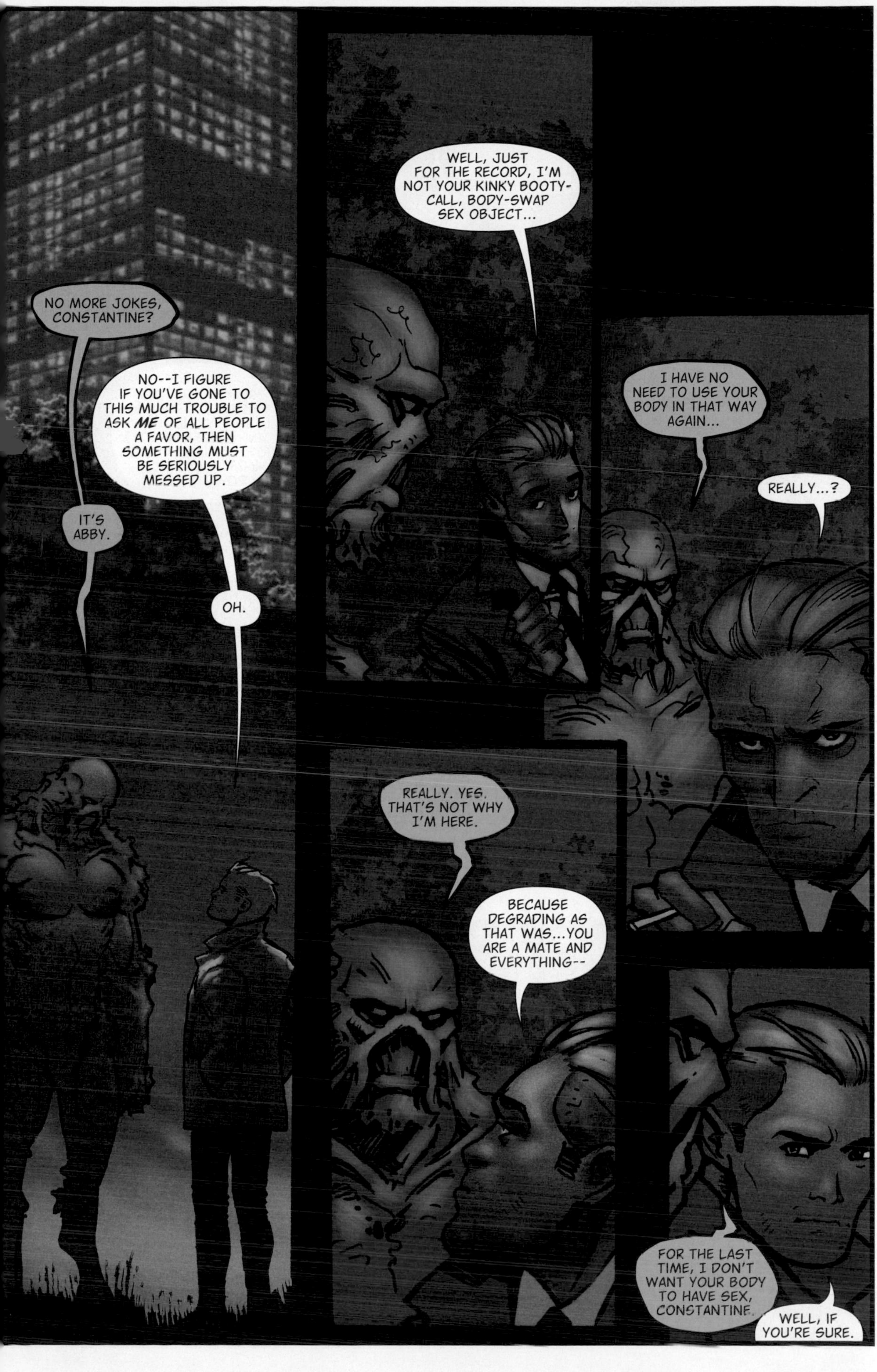
NO MORE JOKES, CONSTANTINE?
NO--I FIGURE IF YOU'VE GONE TO THIS MUCH TROUBLE TO ASK *ME* OF ALL PEOPLE A FAVOR, THEN SOMETHING MUST BE SERIOUSLY MESSED UP.
IT'S ABBY.
OH.
WELL, JUST FOR THE RECORD, I'M NOT YOUR KINKY BOOTY-CALL, BODY-SWAP SEX OBJECT...
I HAVE NO NEED TO USE YOUR BODY IN THAT WAY AGAIN...
REALLY...?
REALLY. YES. THAT'S NOT WHY I'M HERE.
BECAUSE DEGRADING AS THAT WAS...YOU ARE A MATE AND EVERYTHING--
FOR THE LAST TIME, I DON'T WANT YOUR BODY TO HAVE SEX, CONSTANTINE.
WELL, IF YOU'RE SURE.

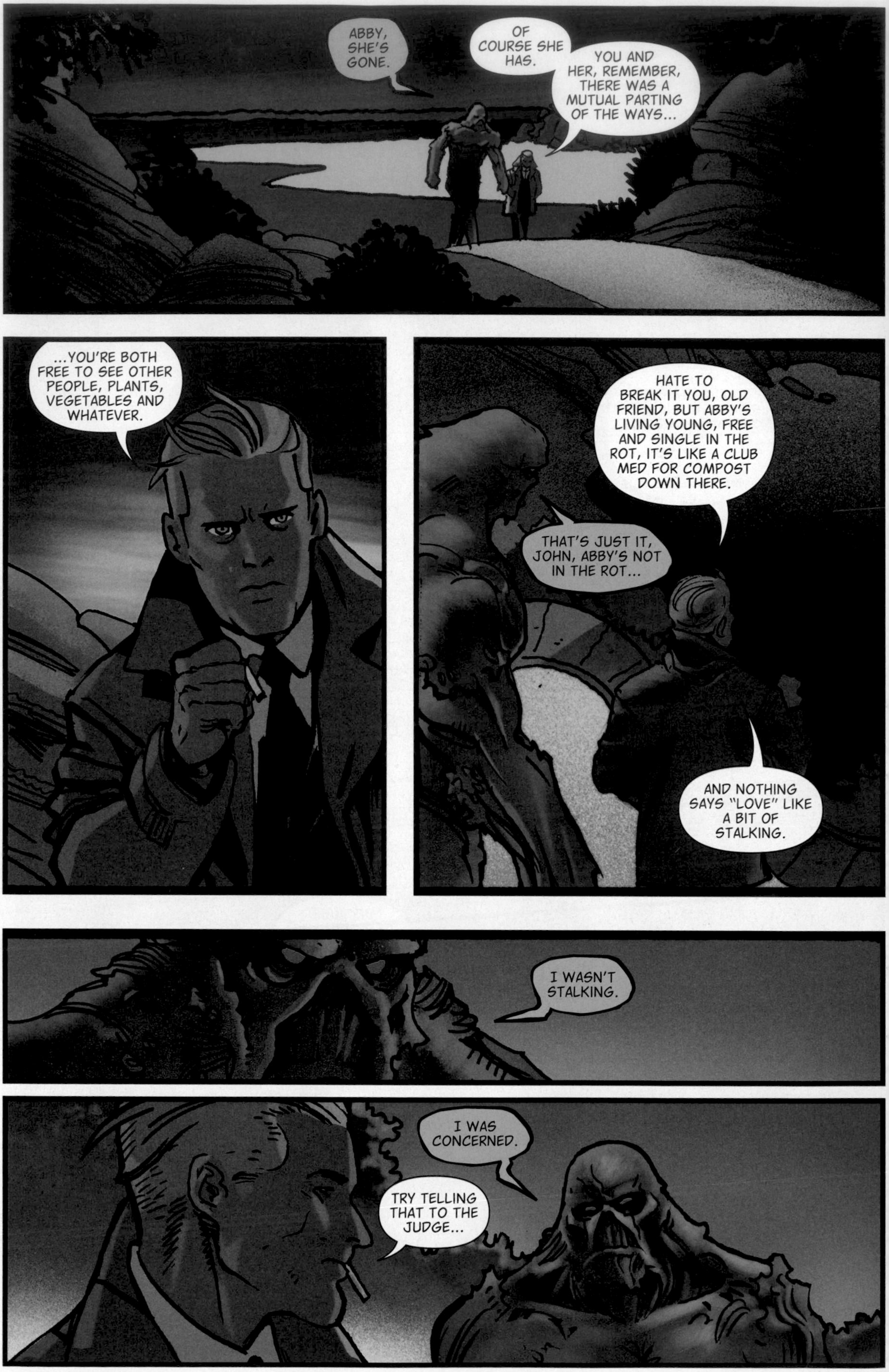
ABBY, SHE'S GONE.
OF COURSE SHE HAS.
YOU AND HER, REMEMBER, THERE WAS A MUTUAL PARTING OF THE WAYS...
...YOU'RE BOTH FREE TO SEE OTHER PEOPLE, PLANTS, VEGETABLES AND WHATEVER.
HATE TO BREAK IT YOU, OLD FRIEND, BUT ABBY'S LIVING YOUNG, FREE AND SINGLE IN THE ROT, IT'S LIKE A CLUB MED FOR COMPOST DOWN THERE.
THAT'S JUST IT, JOHN, ABBY'S NOT IN THE ROT...
AND NOTHING SAYS "LOVE" LIKE A BIT OF STALKING.
I WASN'T STALKING.
I WAS CONCERNED.
TRY TELLING THAT TO THE JUDGE...

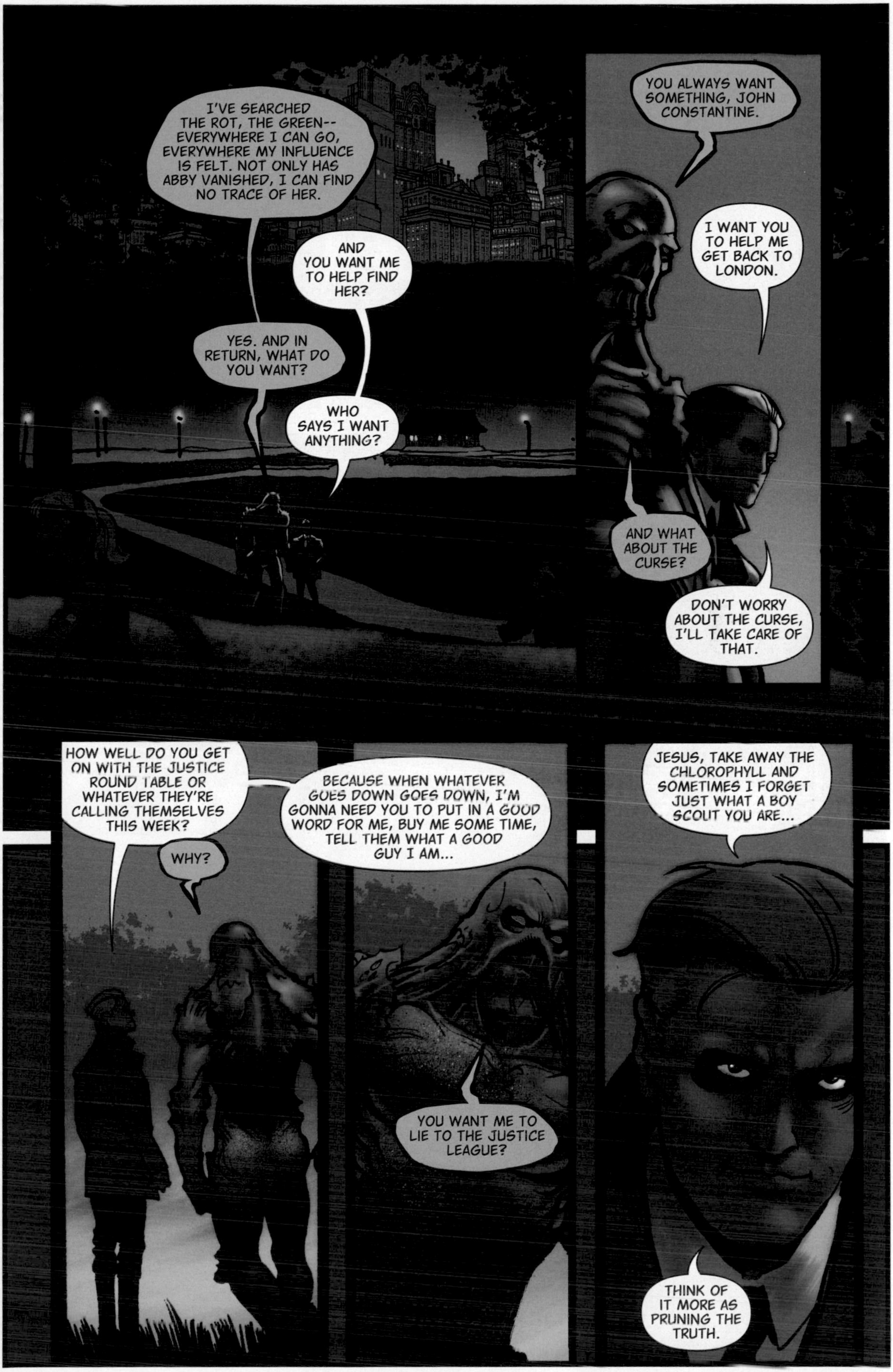
I'VE SEARCHED THE ROT, THE GREEN-- EVERYWHERE I CAN GO, EVERYWHERE MY INFLUENCE IS FELT. NOT ONLY HAS ABBY VANISHED, I CAN FIND NO TRACE OF HER.
AND YOU WANT ME TO HELP FIND HER?
YES. AND IN RETURN, WHAT DO YOU WANT?
WHO SAYS I WANT ANYTHING?
YOU ALWAYS WANT SOMETHING, JOHN CONSTANTINE.
I WANT YOU TO HELP ME GET BACK TO LONDON.
AND WHAT ABOUT THE CURSE?
DON'T WORRY ABOUT THE CURSE, I'LL TAKE CARE OF THAT.
HOW WELL DO YOU GET ON WITH THE JUSTICE ROUND TABLE OR WHATEVER THEY'RE CALLING THEMSELVES THIS WEEK?
WHY?
BECAUSE WHEN WHATEVER GOES DOWN GOES DOWN, I'M GONNA NEED YOU TO PUT IN A GOOD WORD FOR ME, BUY ME SOME TIME, TELL THEM WHAT A GOOD GUY I AM...
YOU WANT ME TO LIE TO THE JUSTICE LEAGUE?
JESUS, TAKE AWAY THE CHLOROPHYLL AND SOMETIMES I FORGET JUST WHAT A BOY SCOUT YOU ARE...
THINK OF IT MORE AS PRUNING THE TRUTH.

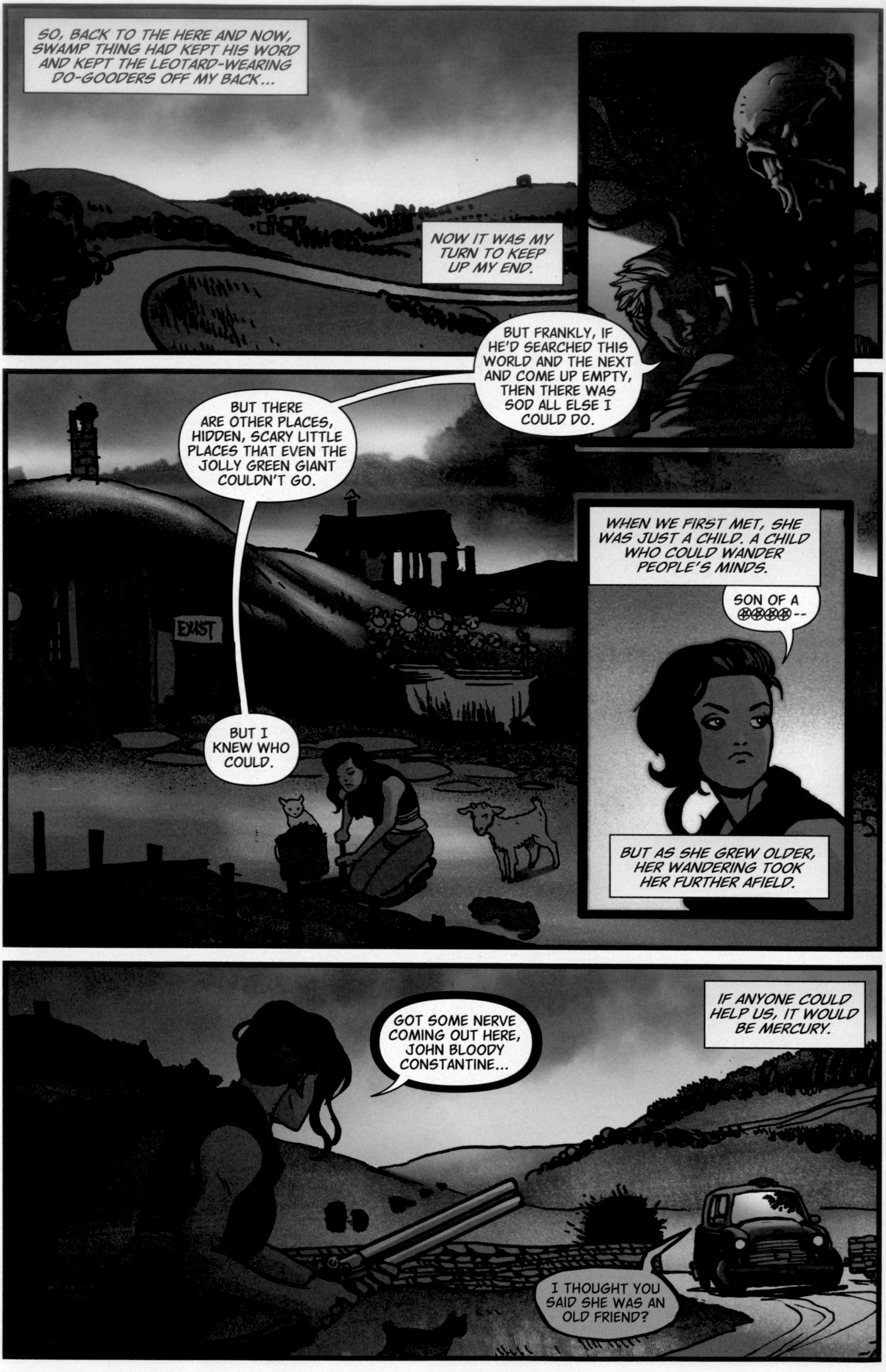
SO, BACK TO THE HERE AND NOW, SWAMP THING HAD KEPT HIS WORD AND KEPT THE LEOTARD-WEARING DO-GOODERS OFF MY BACK...
NOW IT WAS MY TURN TO KEEP UP MY END.
BUT FRANKLY, IF HE'D SEARCHED THIS WORLD AND THE NEXT AND COME UP EMPTY, THEN THERE WAS SOD ALL ELSE I COULD DO.
BUT THERE ARE OTHER PLACES, HIDDEN, SCARY LITTLE PLACES THAT EVEN THE JOLLY GREEN GIANT COULDN'T GO.
BUT I KNEW WHO COULD.
EXIST
WHEN WE FIRST MET, SHE WAS JUST A CHILD. A CHILD WHO COULD WANDER PEOPLE'S MINDS.
SON OF A ⊗⊗⊗⊗--
BUT AS SHE GREW OLDER, HER WANDERING TOOK HER FURTHER AFIELD.
GOT SOME NERVE COMING OUT HERE, JOHN BLOODY CONSTANTINE...
IF ANYONE COULD HELP US, IT WOULD BE MERCURY.
I THOUGHT YOU SAID SHE WAS AN OLD FRIEND?

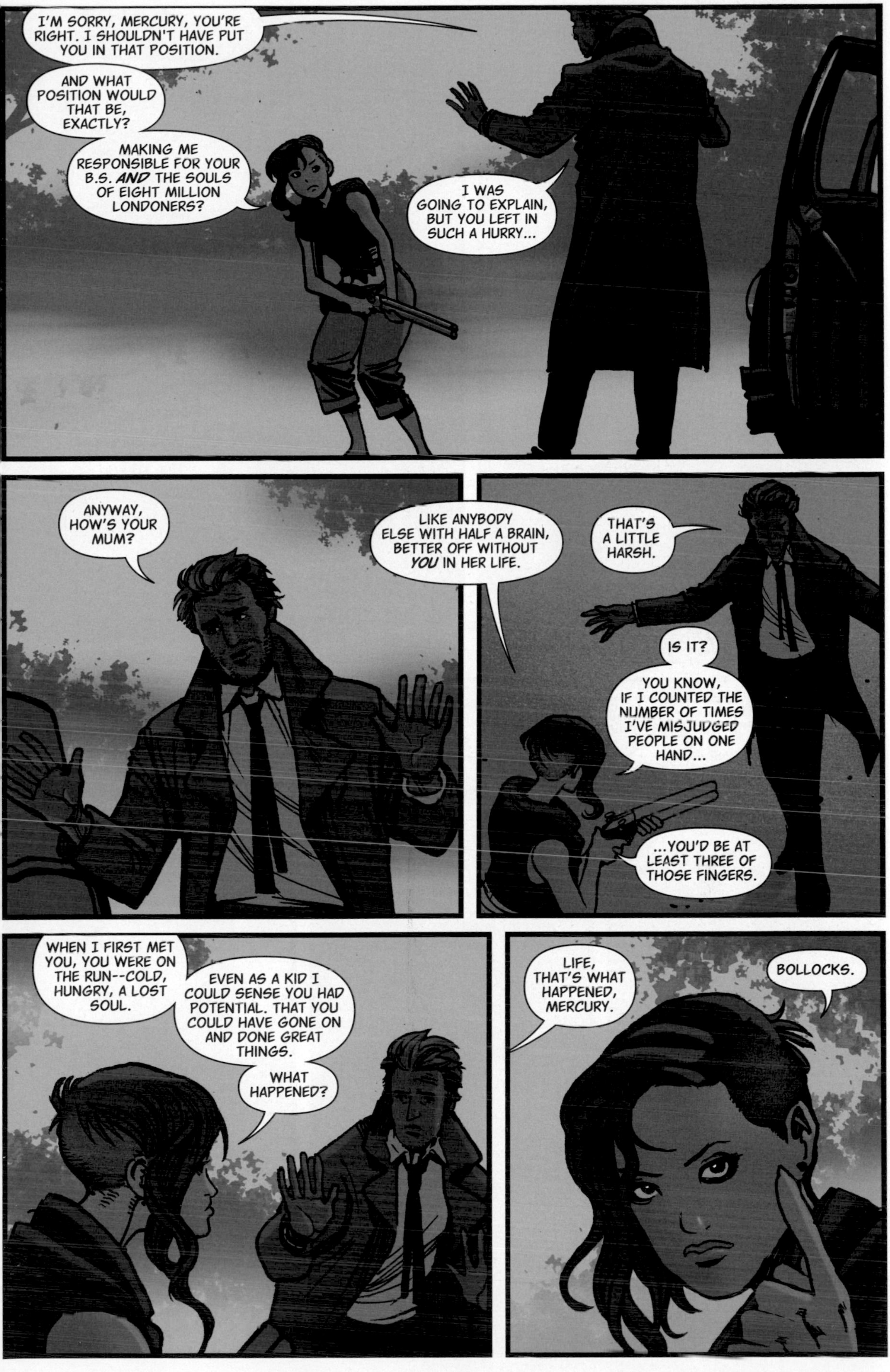
I'M SORRY, MERCURY, YOU'RE RIGHT. I SHOULDN'T HAVE PUT YOU IN THAT POSITION.
AND WHAT POSITION WOULD THAT BE, EXACTLY?
MAKING ME RESPONSIBLE FOR YOUR B.S. AND THE SOULS OF EIGHT MILLION LONDONERS?
I WAS GOING TO EXPLAIN, BUT YOU LEFT IN SUCH A HURRY...
ANYWAY, HOW'S YOUR MUM?
LIKE ANYBODY ELSE WITH HALF A BRAIN, BETTER OFF WITHOUT YOU IN HER LIFE.
THAT'S A LITTLE HARSH.
IS IT?
YOU KNOW, IF I COUNTED THE NUMBER OF TIMES I'VE MISJUDGED PEOPLE ON ONE HAND...
...YOU'D BE AT LEAST THREE OF THOSE FINGERS.
WHEN I FIRST MET YOU, YOU WERE ON THE RUN--COLD, HUNGRY, A LOST SOUL.
EVEN AS A KID I COULD SENSE YOU HAD POTENTIAL. THAT YOU COULD HAVE GONE ON AND DONE GREAT THINGS.
WHAT HAPPENED?
LIFE, THAT'S WHAT HAPPENED, MERCURY.
BOLLOCKS.

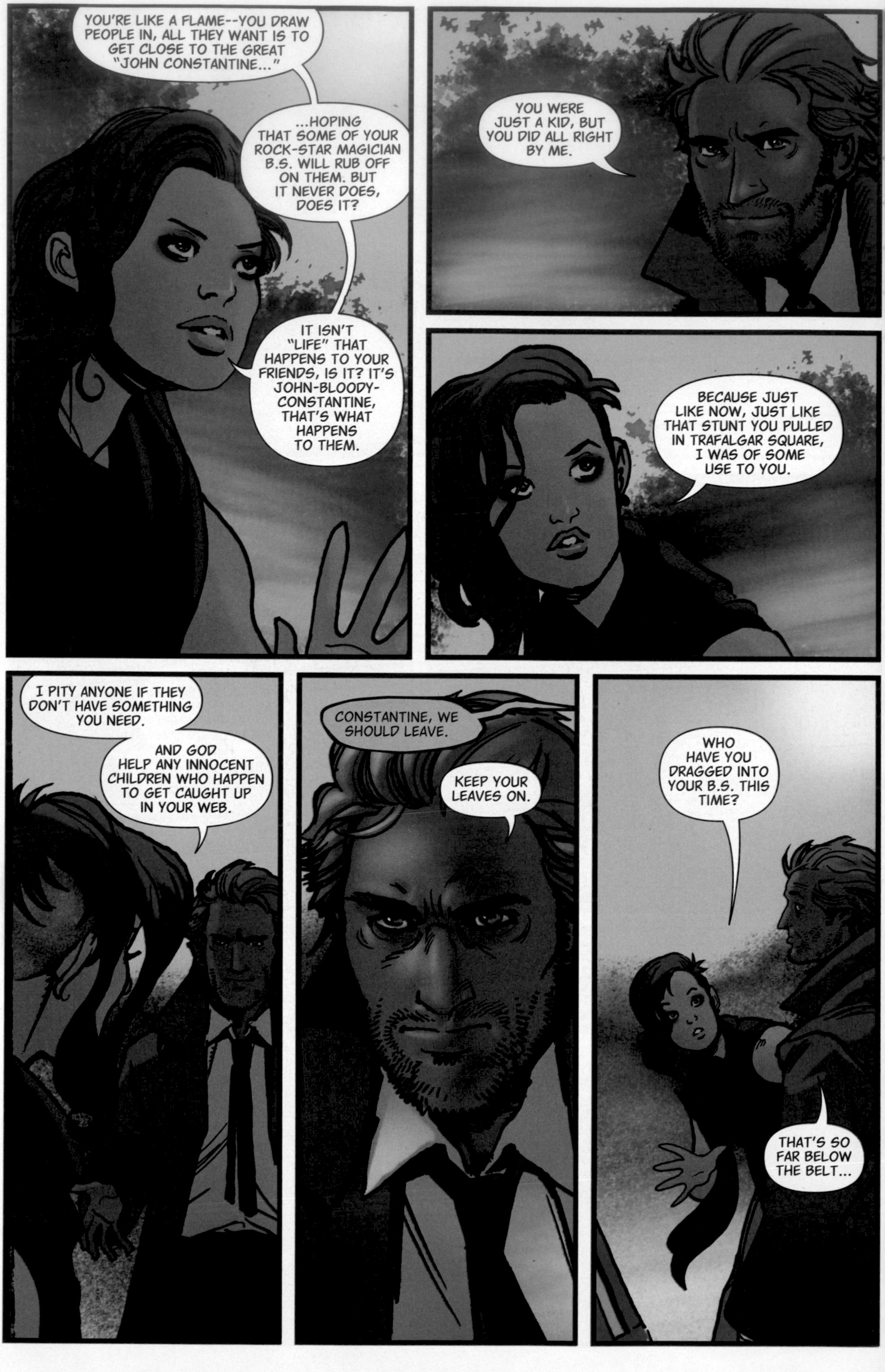
YOU'RE LIKE A FLAME--YOU DRAW PEOPLE IN, ALL THEY WANT IS TO GET CLOSE TO THE GREAT "JOHN CONSTANTINE..."
...HOPING THAT SOME OF YOUR ROCK-STAR MAGICIAN B.S. WILL RUB OFF ON THEM. BUT IT NEVER DOES, DOES IT?
IT ISN'T "LIFE" THAT HAPPENS TO YOUR FRIENDS, IS IT? IT'S JOHN-BLOODY-CONSTANTINE, THAT'S WHAT HAPPENS TO THEM.
YOU WERE JUST A KID, BUT YOU DID ALL RIGHT BY ME.
BECAUSE JUST LIKE NOW, JUST LIKE THAT STUNT YOU PULLED IN TRAFALGAR SQUARE, I WAS OF SOME USE TO YOU.
I PITY ANYONE IF THEY DON'T HAVE SOMETHING YOU NEED.
AND GOD HELP ANY INNOCENT CHILDREN WHO HAPPEN TO GET CAUGHT UP IN YOUR WEB.
CONSTANTINE, WE SHOULD LEAVE.
KEEP YOUR LEAVES ON.
WHO HAVE YOU DRAGGED INTO YOUR B.S. THIS TIME?
THAT'S SO FAR BELOW THE BELT...

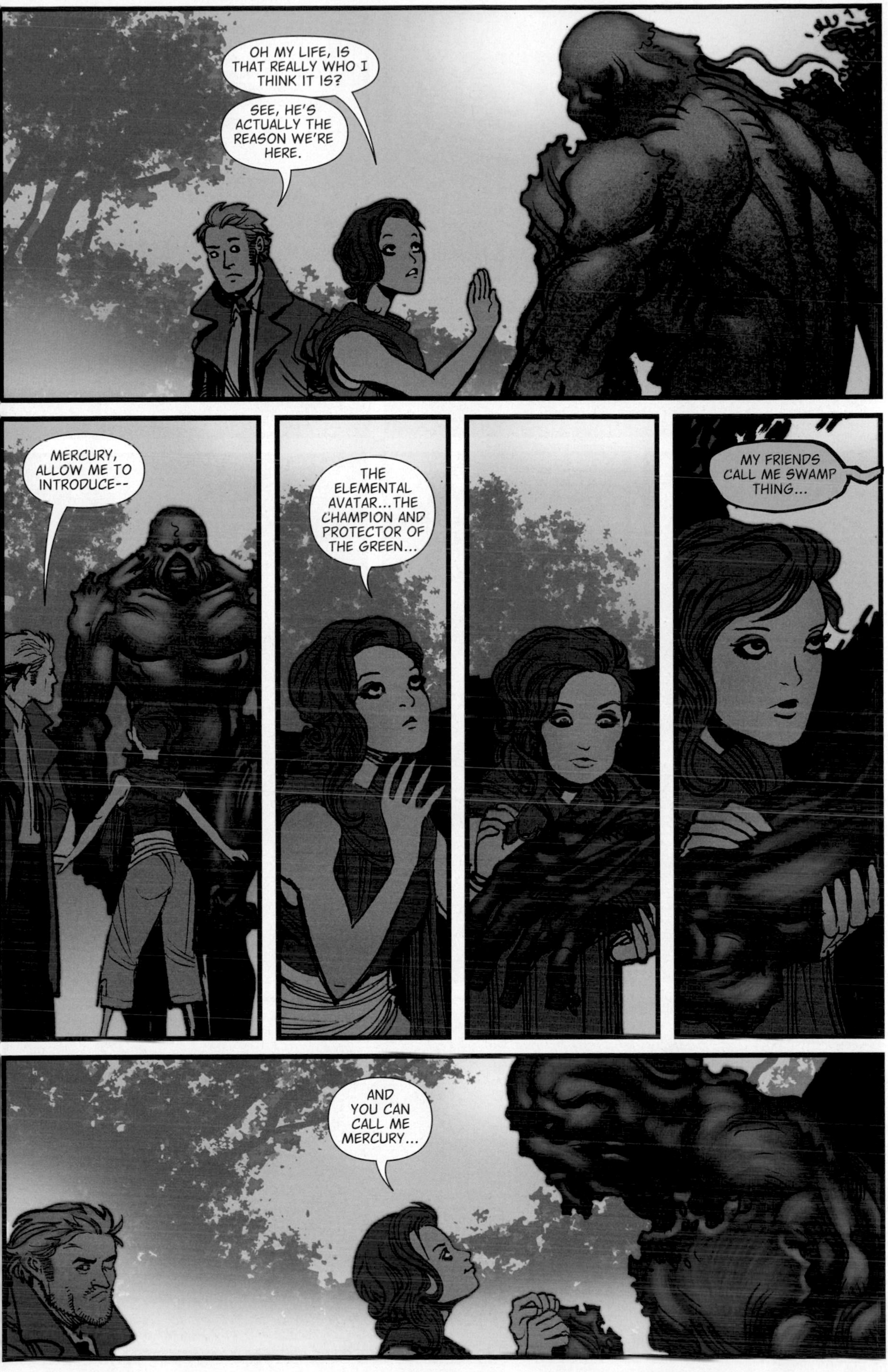
OH MY LIFE, IS THAT REALLY WHO I THINK IT IS?
SEE, HE'S ACTUALLY THE REASON WE'RE HERE.
MERCURY, ALLOW ME TO INTRODUCE--
THE ELEMENTAL AVATAR...THE CHAMPION AND PROTECTOR OF THE GREEN...
MY FRIENDS CALL ME SWAMP THING...
AND YOU CAN CALL ME MERCURY...

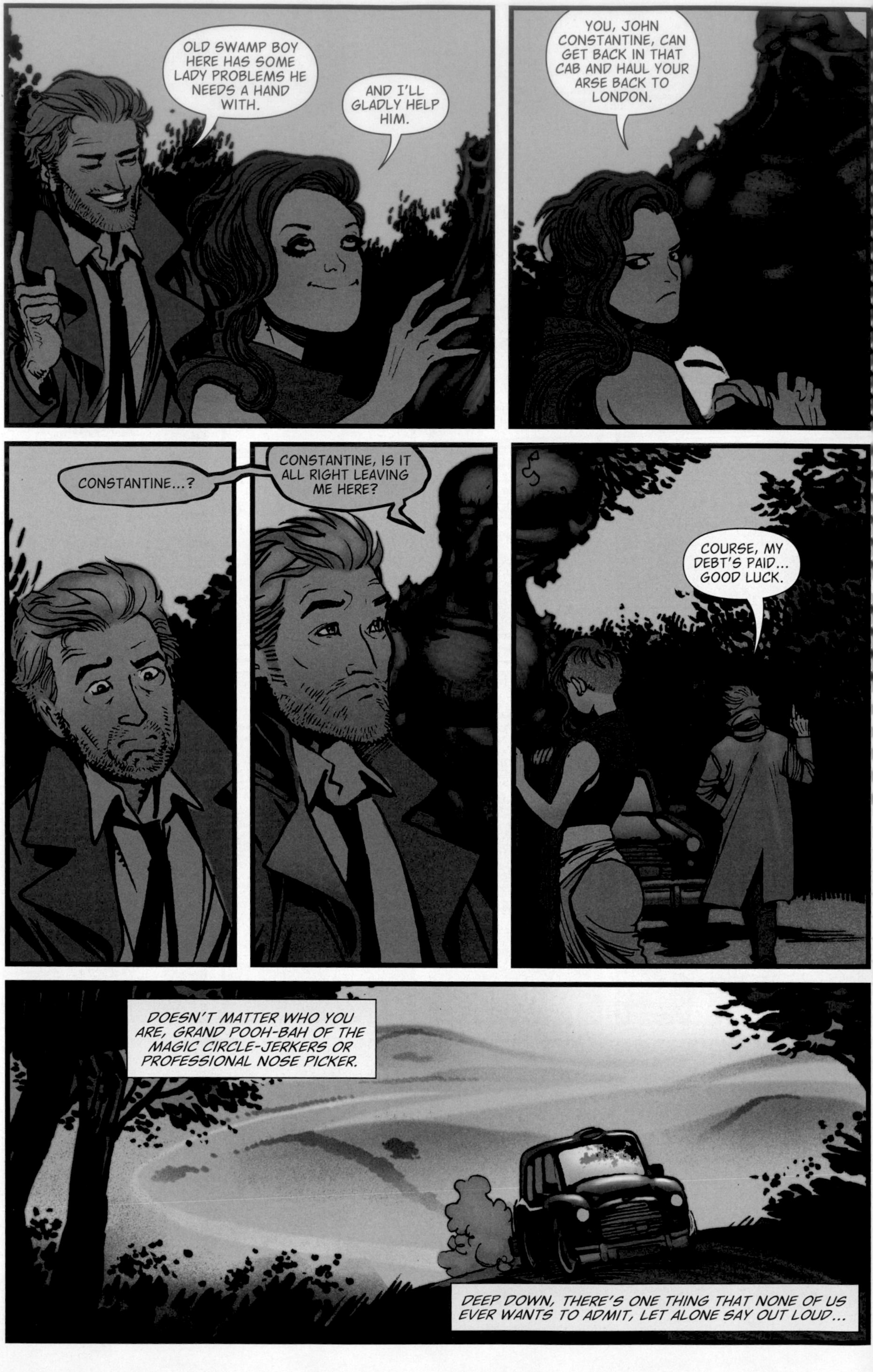
OLD SWAMP BOY HERE HAS SOME LADY PROBLEMS HE NEEDS A HAND WITH.
AND I'LL GLADLY HELP HIM.
YOU, JOHN CONSTANTINE, CAN GET BACK IN THAT CAB AND HAUL YOUR ARSE BACK TO LONDON.
CONSTANTINE...?
CONSTANTINE, IS IT ALL RIGHT LEAVING ME HERE?
COURSE, MY DEBT'S PAID... GOOD LUCK.
DOESN'T MATTER WHO YOU ARE, GRAND POOH-BAH OF THE MAGIC CIRCLE-JERKERS OR PROFESSIONAL NOSE PICKER.
DEEP DOWN, THERE'S ONE THING THAT NONE OF US EVER WANTS TO ADMIT, LET ALONE SAY OUT LOUD...

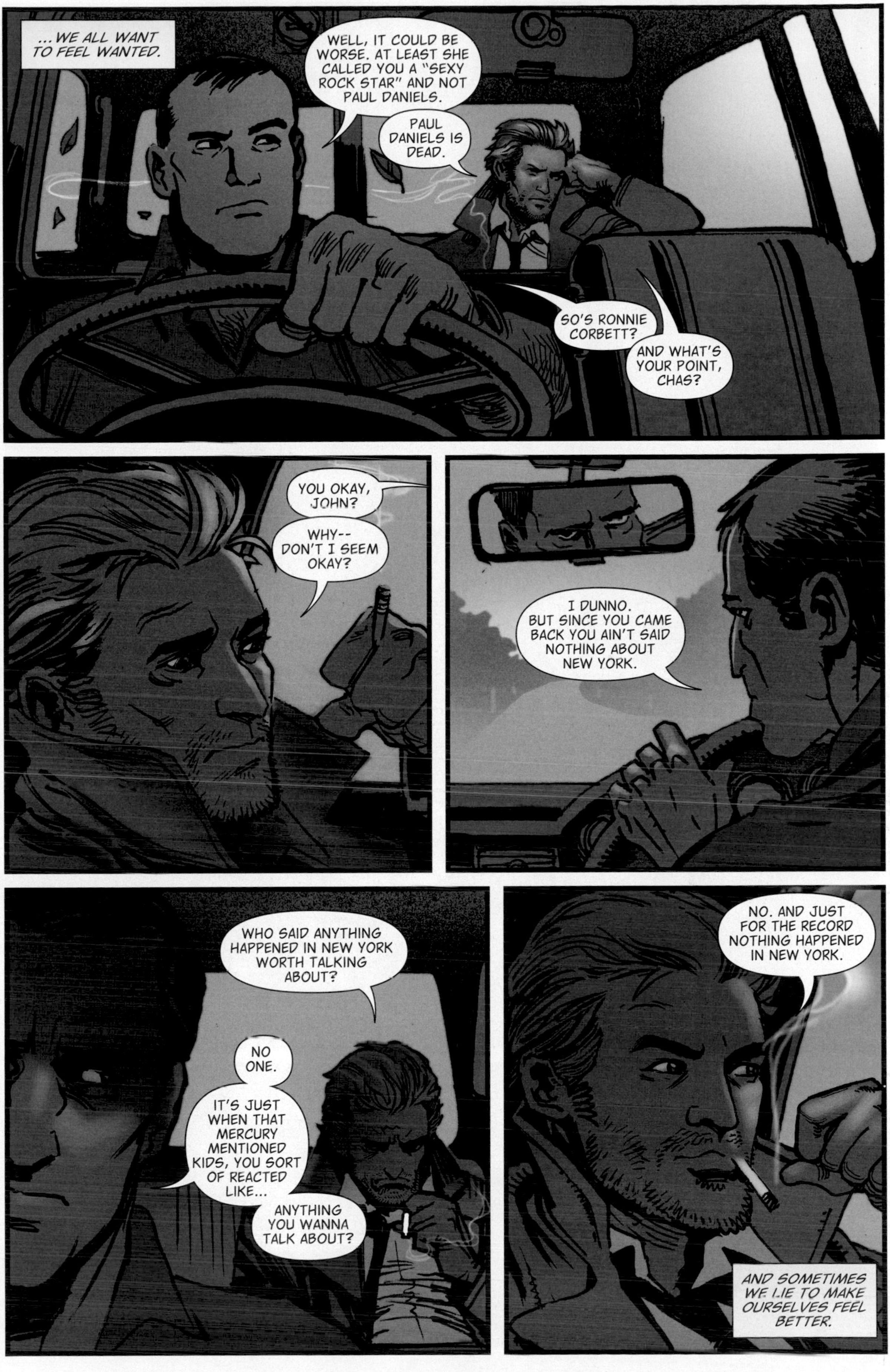
...WE ALL WANT TO FEEL WANTED.
WELL, IT COULD BE WORSE. AT LEAST SHE CALLED YOU A "SEXY ROCK STAR" AND NOT PAUL DANIELS.
PAUL DANIELS IS DEAD.
SO'S RONNIE CORBETT?
AND WHAT'S YOUR POINT, CHAS?
YOU OKAY, JOHN?
WHY-- DON'T I SEEM OKAY?
I DUNNO. BUT SINCE YOU CAME BACK YOU AIN'T SAID NOTHING ABOUT NEW YORK.
WHO SAID ANYTHING HAPPENED IN NEW YORK WORTH TALKING ABOUT?
NO ONE.
IT'S JUST WHEN THAT MERCURY MENTIONED KIDS, YOU SORT OF REACTED LIKE...
ANYTHING YOU WANNA TALK ABOUT?
NO. AND JUST FOR THE RECORD NOTHING HAPPENED IN NEW YORK.
AND SOMETIMES WE LIE TO MAKE OURSELVES FEEL BETTER.

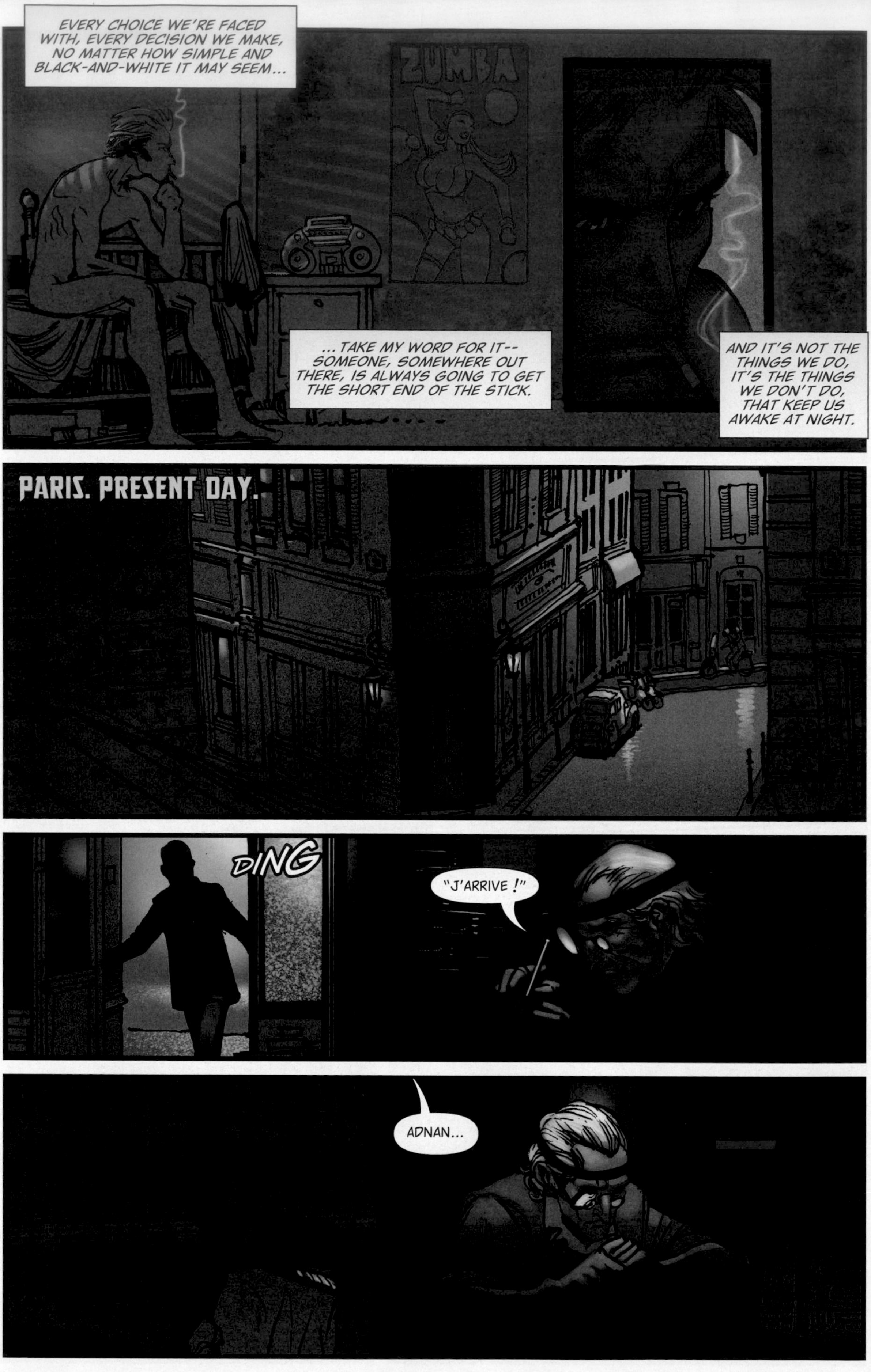
EVERY CHOICE WE'RE FACED WITH, EVERY DECISION WE MAKE, NO MATTER HOW SIMPLE AND BLACK-AND-WHITE IT MAY SEEM...
ZUMBA
...TAKE MY WORD FOR IT-- SOMEONE, SOMEWHERE OUT THERE, IS ALWAYS GOING TO GET THE SHORT END OF THE STICK.
AND IT'S NOT THE THINGS WE DO, IT'S THE THINGS WE DON'T DO, THAT KEEP US AWAKE AT NIGHT.
PARIS. PRESENT DAY.
DING
"J'ARRIVE !"
ADNAN...

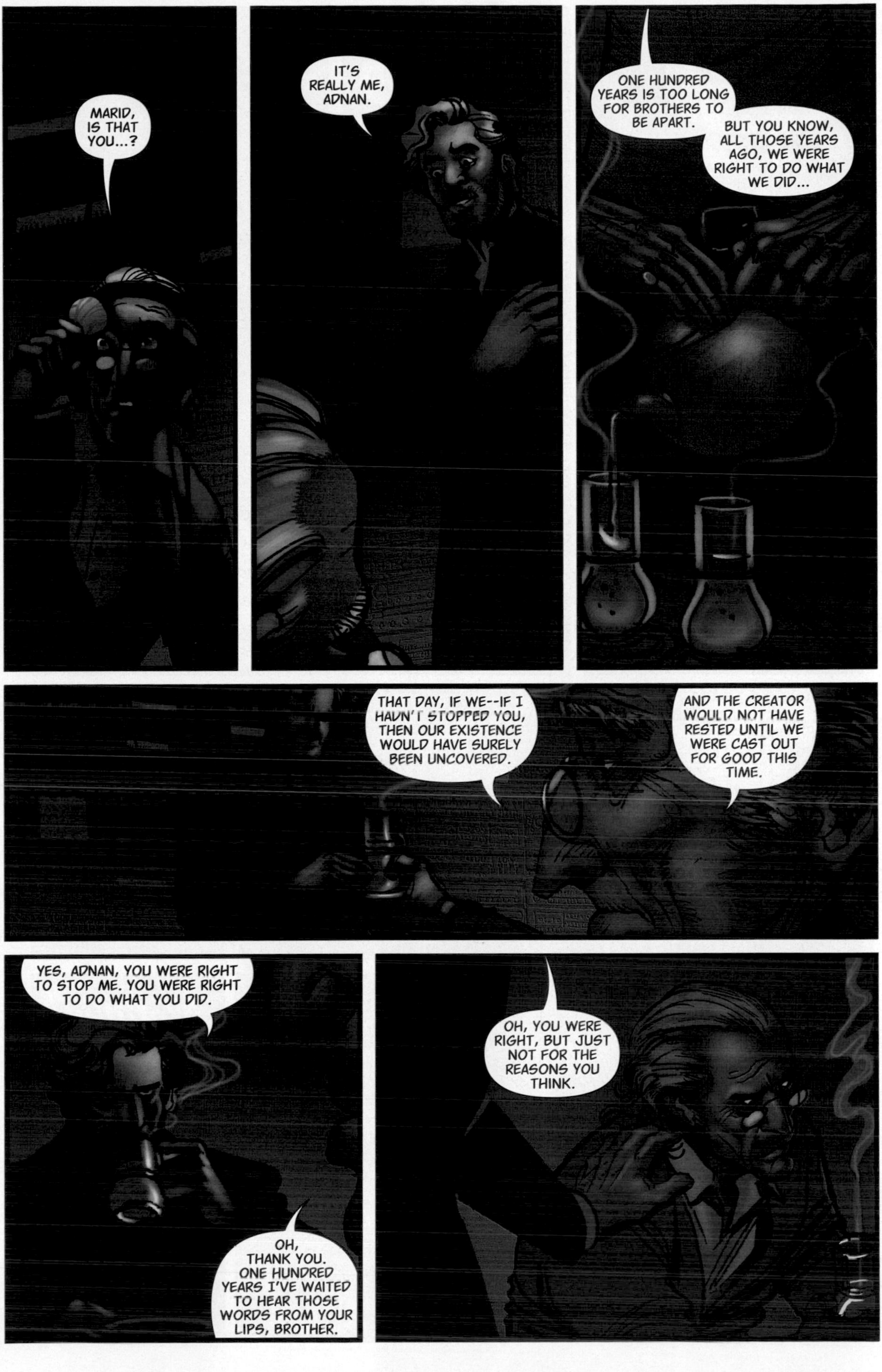
MARID, IS THAT YOU...?
IT'S REALLY ME, ADNAN.
ONE HUNDRED YEARS IS TOO LONG FOR BROTHERS TO BE APART.
BUT YOU KNOW, ALL THOSE YEARS AGO, WE WERE RIGHT TO DO WHAT WE DID...
THAT DAY, IF WE--IF I HADN'T STOPPED YOU, THEN OUR EXISTENCE WOULD HAVE SURELY BEEN UNCOVERED.
AND THE CREATOR WOULD NOT HAVE RESTED UNTIL WE WERE CAST OUT FOR GOOD THIS TIME.
YES, ADNAN, YOU WERE RIGHT TO STOP ME. YOU WERE RIGHT TO DO WHAT YOU DID.
OH, THANK YOU. ONE HUNDRED YEARS I'VE WAITED TO HEAR THOSE WORDS FROM YOUR LIPS, BROTHER.
OH, YOU WERE RIGHT, BUT JUST NOT FOR THE REASONS YOU THINK.

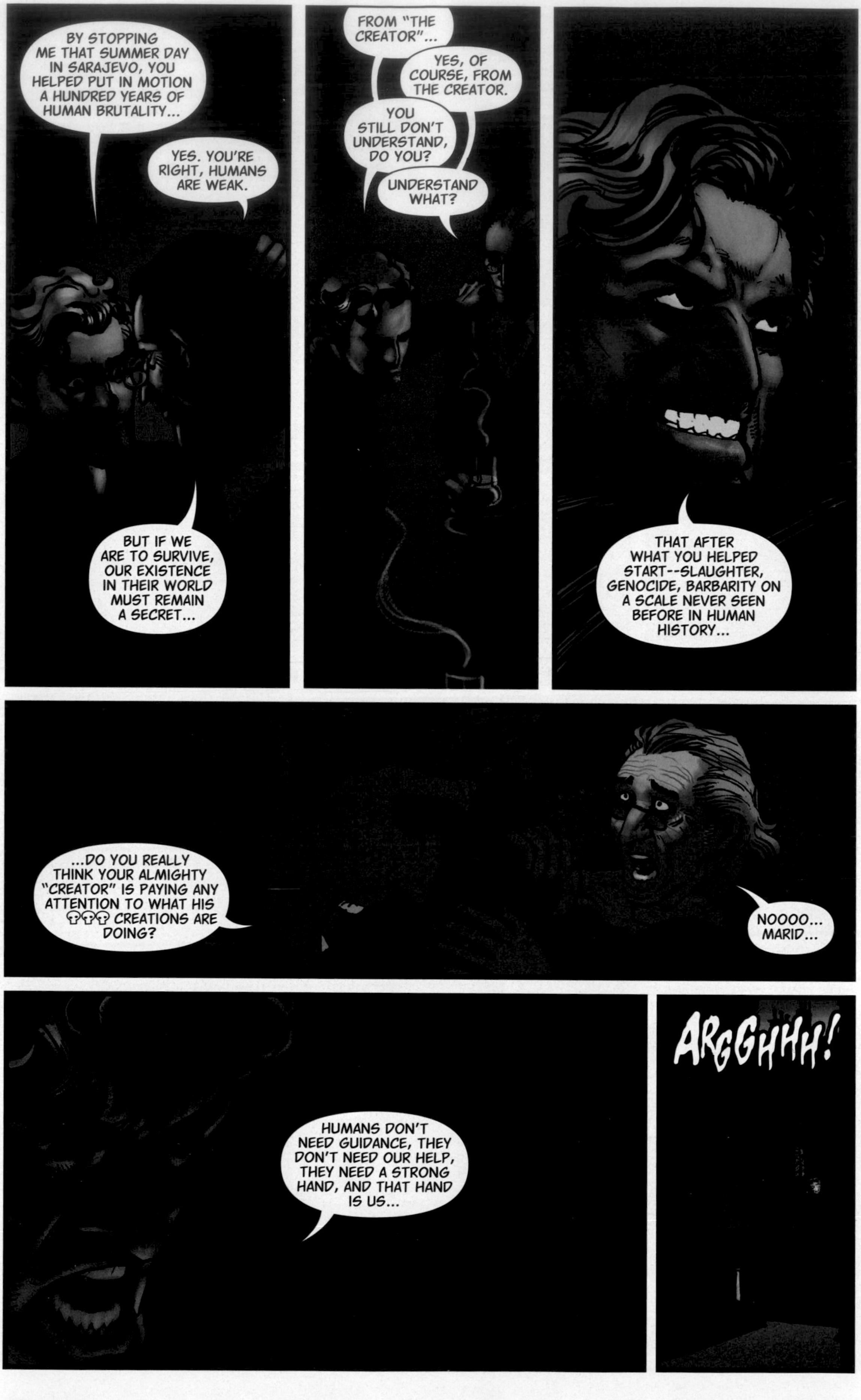
BY STOPPING ME THAT SUMMER DAY IN SARAJEVO, YOU HELPED PUT IN MOTION A HUNDRED YEARS OF HUMAN BRUTALITY...
YES. YOU'RE RIGHT, HUMANS ARE WEAK.
BUT IF WE ARE TO SURVIVE, OUR EXISTENCE IN THEIR WORLD MUST REMAIN A SECRET...
FROM "THE CREATOR"...
YES, OF COURSE, FROM THE CREATOR.
YOU STILL DON'T UNDERSTAND, DO YOU?
UNDERSTAND WHAT?
THAT AFTER WHAT YOU HELPED START--SLAUGHTER, GENOCIDE, BARBARITY ON A SCALE NEVER SEEN BEFORE IN HUMAN HISTORY...
...DO YOU REALLY THINK YOUR ALMIGHTY "CREATOR" IS PAYING ANY ATTENTION TO WHAT HIS CREATIONS ARE DOING?
NOOOO... MARID...
HUMANS DON'T NEED GUIDANCE, THEY DON'T NEED OUR HELP, THEY NEED A STRONG HAND, AND THAT HAND IS US...
ARGGHHH!

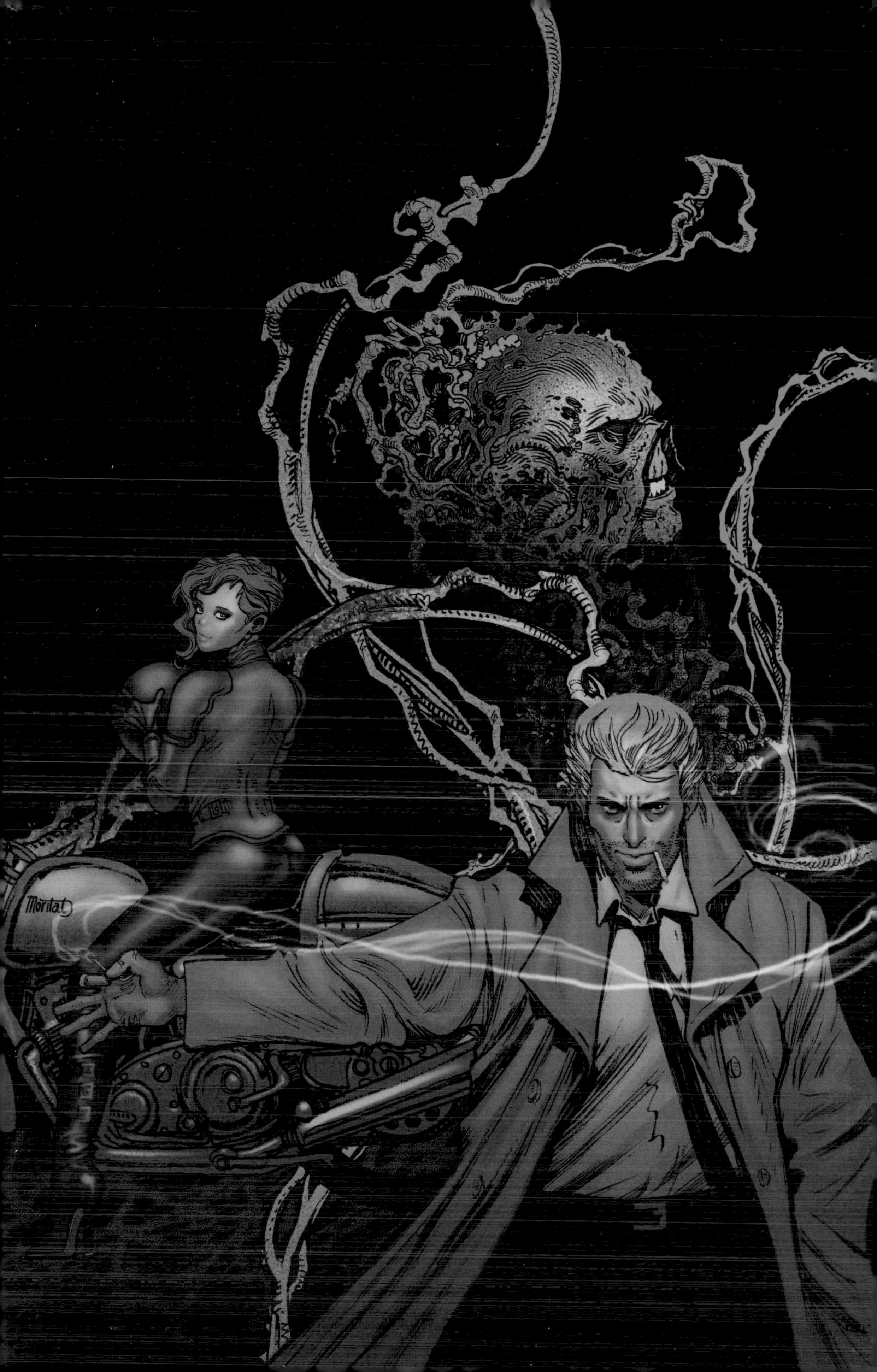
Moritat

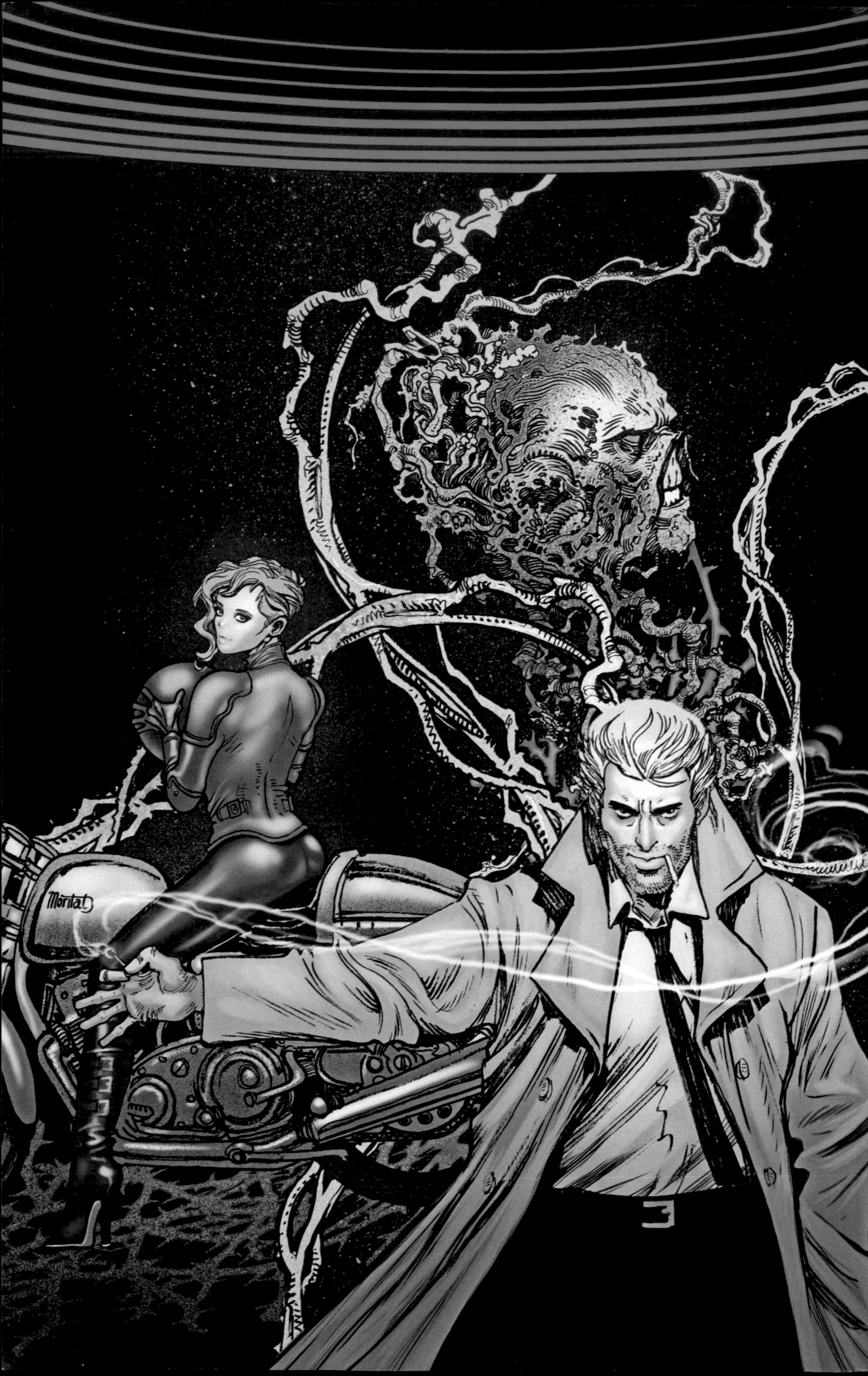
Moritat

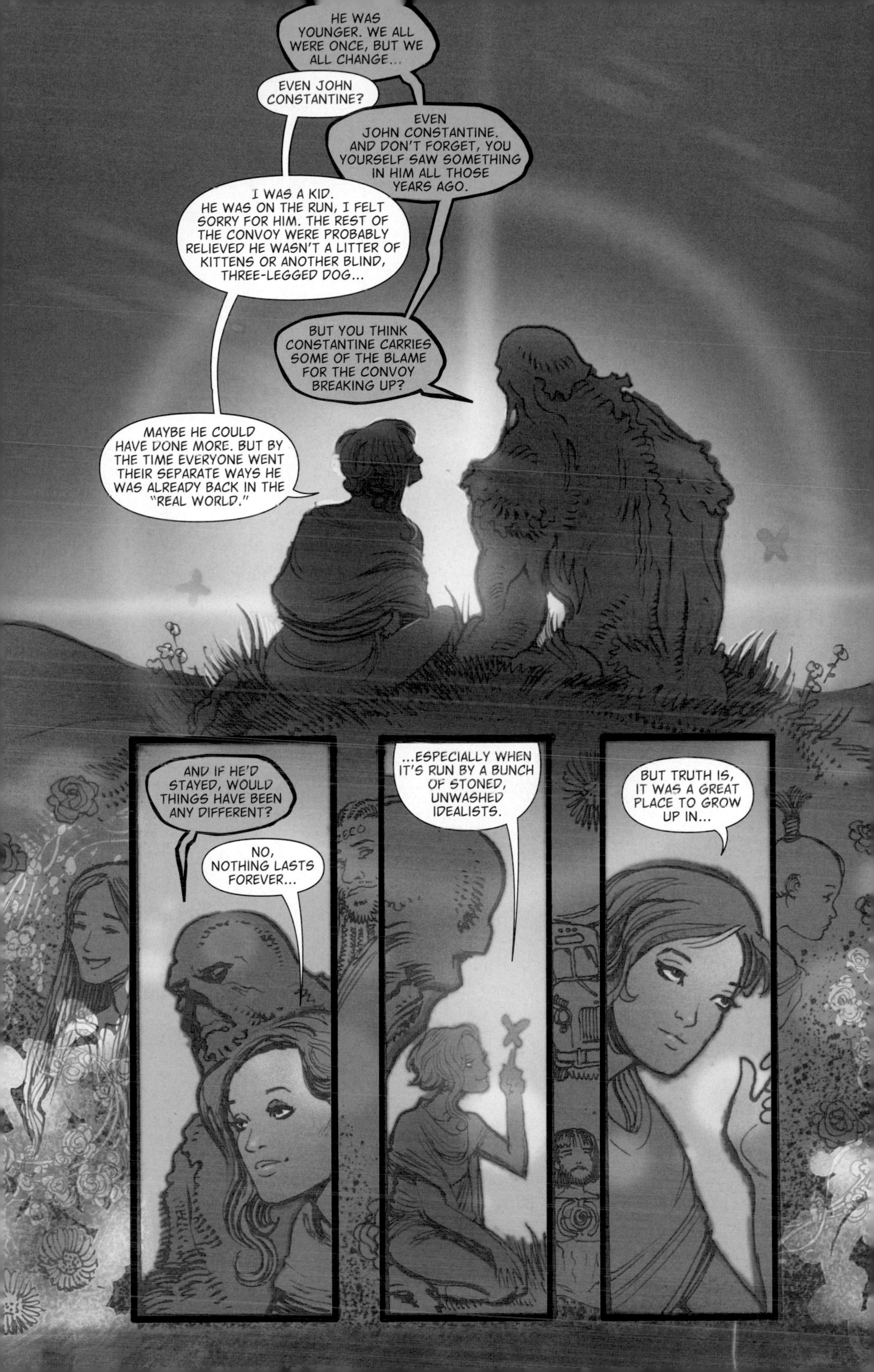
HE WAS YOUNGER. WE ALL WERE ONCE, BUT WE ALL CHANGE...
EVEN JOHN CONSTANTINE?
EVEN JOHN CONSTANTINE. AND DON'T FORGET, YOU YOURSELF SAW SOMETHING IN HIM ALL THOSE YEARS AGO.
I WAS A KID. HE WAS ON THE RUN, I FELT SORRY FOR HIM. THE REST OF THE CONVOY WERE PROBABLY RELIEVED HE WASN'T A LITTER OF KITTENS OR ANOTHER BLIND, THREE-LEGGED DOG...
BUT YOU THINK CONSTANTINE CARRIES SOME OF THE BLAME FOR THE CONVOY BREAKING UP?
MAYBE HE COULD HAVE DONE MORE. BUT BY THE TIME EVERYONE WENT THEIR SEPARATE WAYS HE WAS ALREADY BACK IN THE "REAL WORLD."
AND IF HE'D STAYED, WOULD THINGS HAVE BEEN ANY DIFFERENT?
NO, NOTHING LASTS FOREVER...
...ESPECIALLY WHEN IT'S RUN BY A BUNCH OF STONED, UNWASHED IDEALISTS.
BUT TRUTH IS, IT WAS A GREAT PLACE TO GROW UP IN...

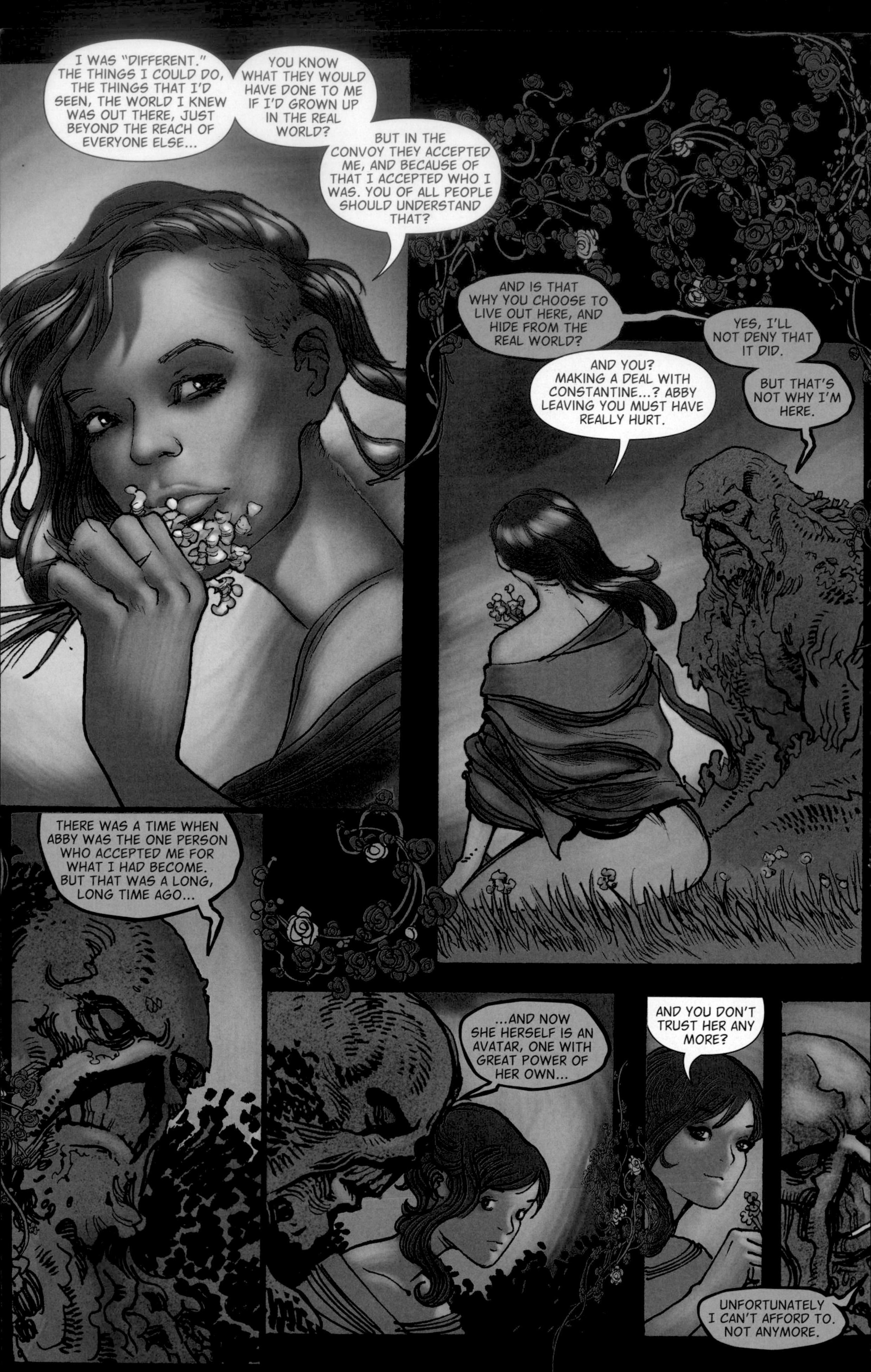

I WAS "DIFFERENT." THE THINGS I COULD DO, THE THINGS THAT I'D SEEN, THE WORLD I KNEW WAS OUT THERE, JUST BEYOND THE REACH OF EVERYONE ELSE...
YOU KNOW WHAT THEY WOULD HAVE DONE TO ME IF I'D GROWN UP IN THE REAL WORLD?
BUT IN THE CONVOY THEY ACCEPTED ME, AND BECAUSE OF THAT I ACCEPTED WHO I WAS. YOU OF ALL PEOPLE SHOULD UNDERSTAND THAT?
AND IS THAT WHY YOU CHOOSE TO LIVE OUT HERE, AND HIDE FROM THE REAL WORLD?
YES, I'LL NOT DENY THAT IT DID.
AND YOU? MAKING A DEAL WITH CONSTANTINE...? ABBY LEAVING YOU MUST HAVE REALLY HURT.
BUT THAT'S NOT WHY I'M HERE.
THERE WAS A TIME WHEN ABBY WAS THE ONE PERSON WHO ACCEPTED ME FOR WHAT I HAD BECOME. BUT THAT WAS A LONG, LONG TIME AGO...
...AND NOW SHE HERSELF IS AN AVATAR, ONE WITH GREAT POWER OF HER OWN...
AND YOU DON'T TRUST HER ANY MORE?
UNFORTUNATELY I CAN'T AFFORD TO. NOT ANYMORE.

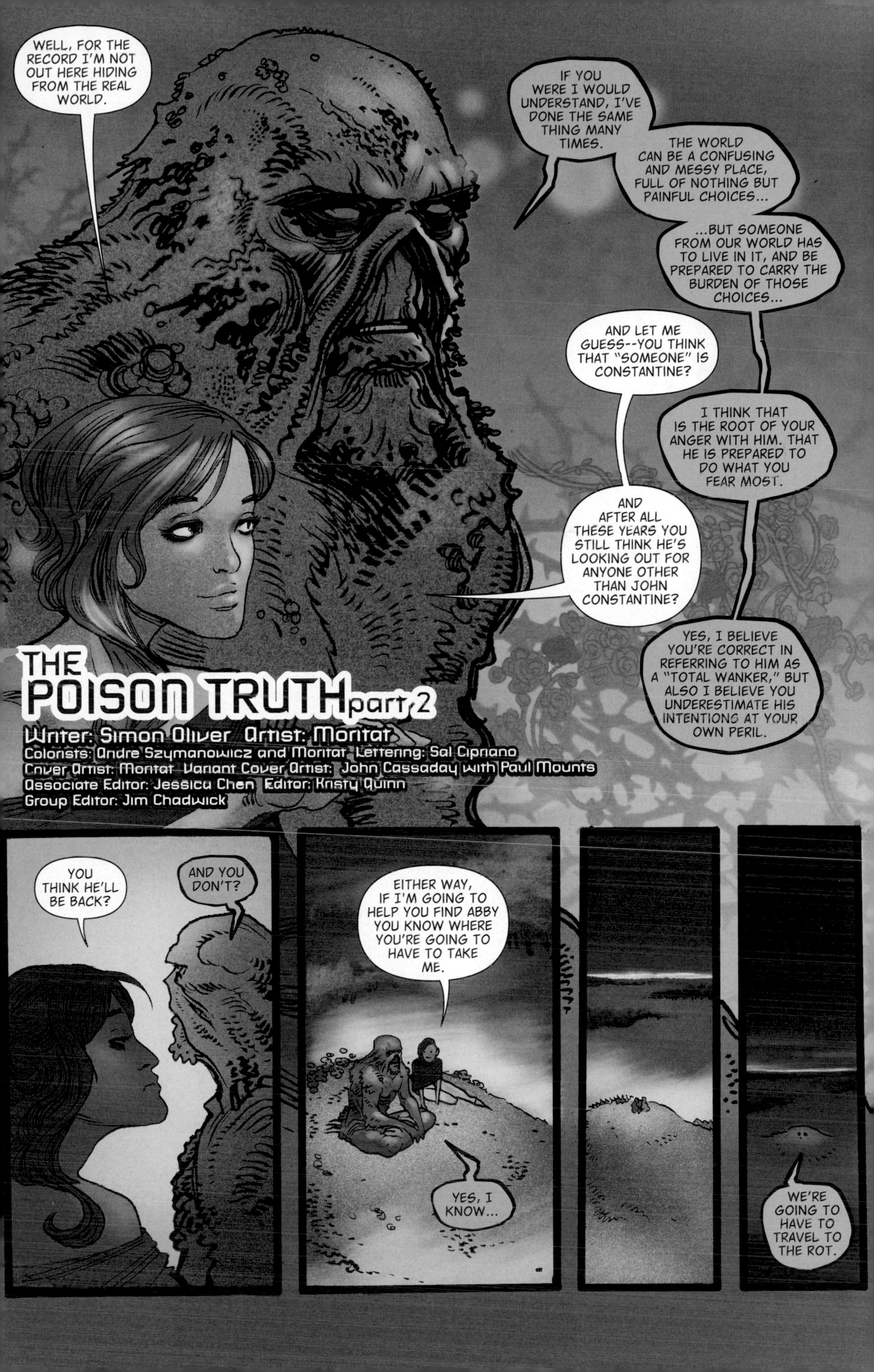
WELL, FOR THE RECORD I'M NOT OUT HERE HIDING FROM THE REAL WORLD.
IF YOU WERE I WOULD UNDERSTAND, I'VE DONE THE SAME THING MANY TIMES.
THE WORLD CAN BE A CONFUSING AND MESSY PLACE, FULL OF NOTHING BUT PAINFUL CHOICES...
...BUT SOMEONE FROM OUR WORLD HAS TO LIVE IN IT, AND BE PREPARED TO CARRY THE BURDEN OF THOSE CHOICES...
AND LET ME GUESS--YOU THINK THAT "SOMEONE" IS CONSTANTINE?
I THINK THAT IS THE ROOT OF YOUR ANGER WITH HIM. THAT HE IS PREPARED TO DO WHAT YOU FEAR MOST.
AND AFTER ALL THESE YEARS YOU STILL THINK HE'S LOOKING OUT FOR ANYONE OTHER THAN JOHN CONSTANTINE?
YES, I BELIEVE YOU'RE CORRECT IN REFERRING TO HIM AS A "TOTAL WANKER," BUT ALSO I BELIEVE YOU UNDERESTIMATE HIS INTENTIONS AT YOUR OWN PERIL.
THE POISON TRUTH part 2
Writer: Simon Oliver Artist: Moritat
Colorists: Andre Szymanowicz and Moritat Lettering: Sal Cipriano
Cover Artist: Moritat Variant Cover Artist: John Cassaday with Paul Mounts
Associate Editor: Jessica Chen Editor: Kristy Quinn
Group Editor: Jim Chadwick
YOU THINK HE'LL BE BACK?
AND YOU DON'T?
EITHER WAY, IF I'M GOING TO HELP YOU FIND ABBY YOU KNOW WHERE YOU'RE GOING TO HAVE TO TAKE ME.
YES, I KNOW...
WE'RE GOING TO HAVE TO TRAVEL TO THE ROT.

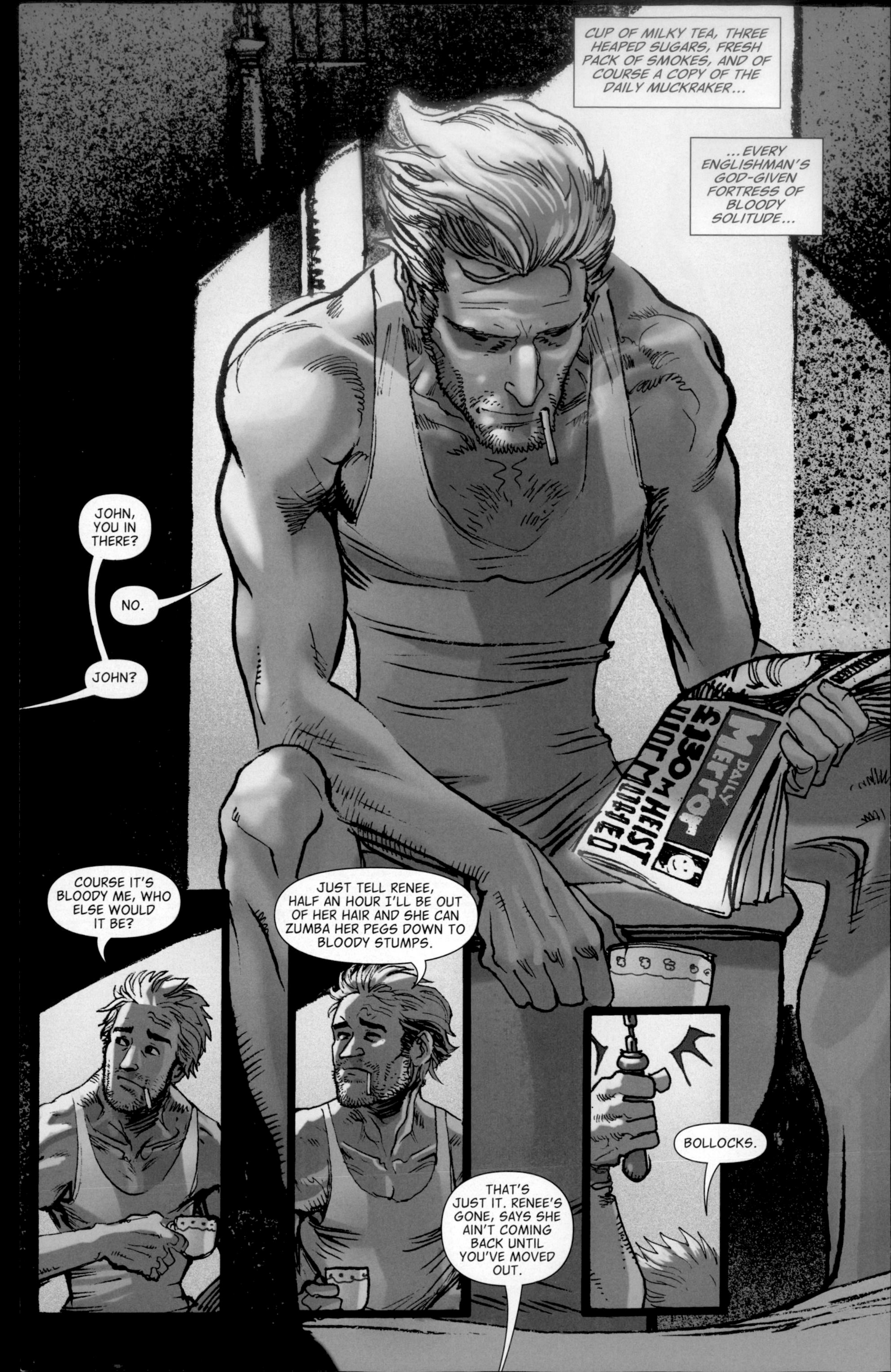
CUP OF MILKY TEA, THREE HEAPED SUGARS, FRESH PACK OF SMOKES, AND OF COURSE A COPY OF THE DAILY MUCKRAKER...
...EVERY ENGLISHMAN'S GOD-GIVEN FORTRESS OF BLOODY SOLITUDE...
JOHN, YOU IN THERE?
NO.
JOHN?
COURSE IT'S BLOODY ME, WHO ELSE WOULD IT BE?
JUST TELL RENEE, HALF AN HOUR I'LL BE OUT OF HER HAIR AND SHE CAN ZUMBA HER PEGS DOWN TO BLOODY STUMPS.
THAT'S JUST IT. RENEE'S GONE, SAYS SHE AIN'T COMING BACK UNTIL YOU'VE MOVED OUT.
BOLLOCKS.

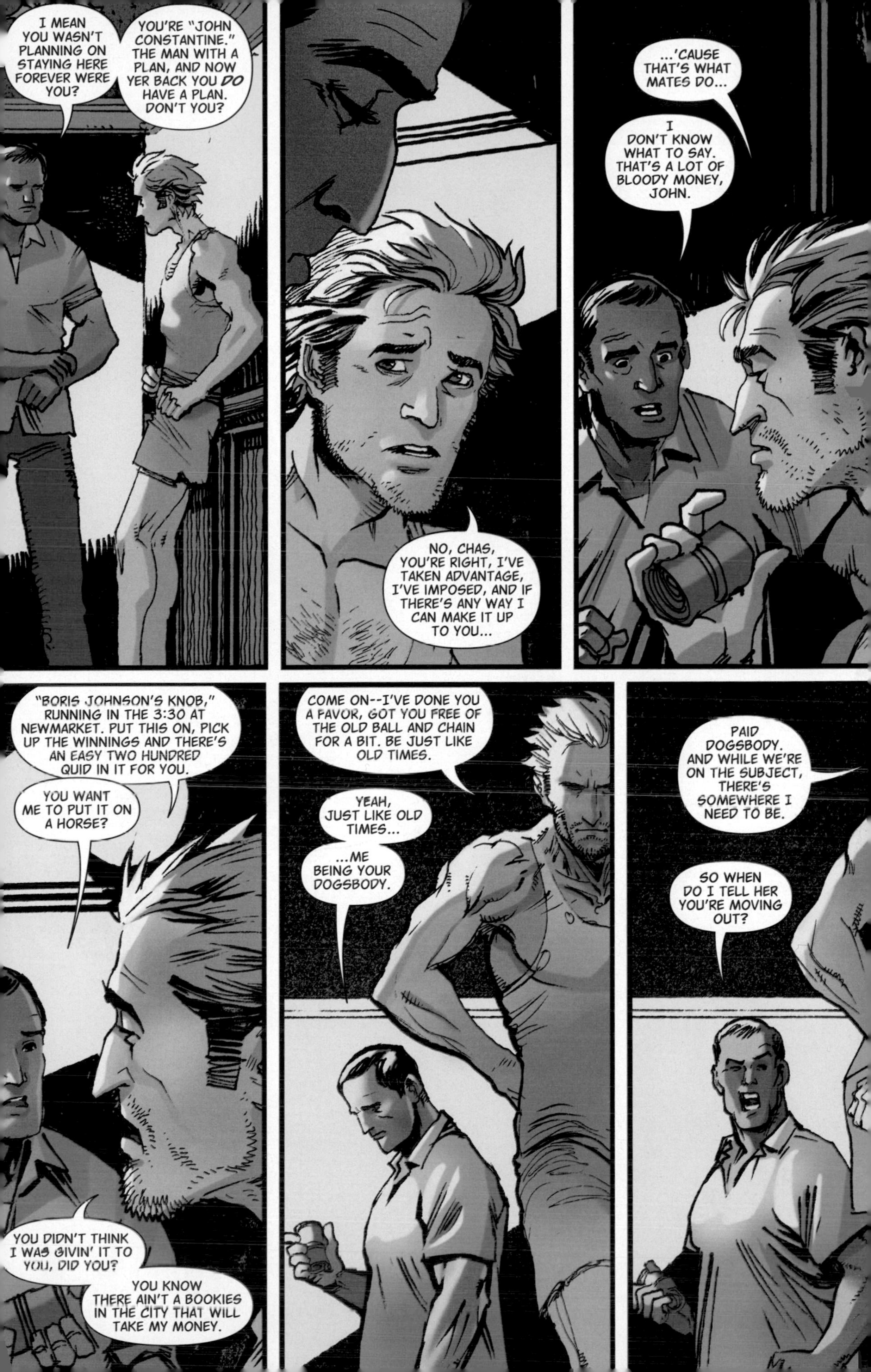
I MEAN YOU WASN'T PLANNING ON STAYING HERE FOREVER WERE YOU?
YOU'RE "JOHN CONSTANTINE." THE MAN WITH A PLAN, AND NOW YER BACK YOU DO HAVE A PLAN. DON'T YOU?
NO, CHAS, YOU'RE RIGHT, I'VE TAKEN ADVANTAGE, I'VE IMPOSED, AND IF THERE'S ANY WAY I CAN MAKE IT UP TO YOU...
...'CAUSE THAT'S WHAT MATES DO...
I DON'T KNOW WHAT TO SAY. THAT'S A LOT OF BLOODY MONEY, JOHN.
"BORIS JOHNSON'S KNOB," RUNNING IN THE 3:30 AT NEWMARKET. PUT THIS ON, PICK UP THE WINNINGS AND THERE'S AN EASY TWO HUNDRED QUID IN IT FOR YOU.
YOU WANT ME TO PUT IT ON A HORSE?
YOU DIDN'T THINK I WAS GIVIN' IT TO YOU, DID YOU?
YOU KNOW THERE AIN'T A BOOKIES IN THE CITY THAT WILL TAKE MY MONEY.
COME ON--I'VE DONE YOU A FAVOR, GOT YOU FREE OF THE OLD BALL AND CHAIN FOR A BIT. BE JUST LIKE OLD TIMES.
YEAH, JUST LIKE OLD TIMES...
...ME BEING YOUR DOGSBODY.
PAID DOGSBODY. AND WHILE WE'RE ON THE SUBJECT, THERE'S SOMEWHERE I NEED TO BE.
SO WHEN DO I TELL HER YOU'RE MOVING OUT?

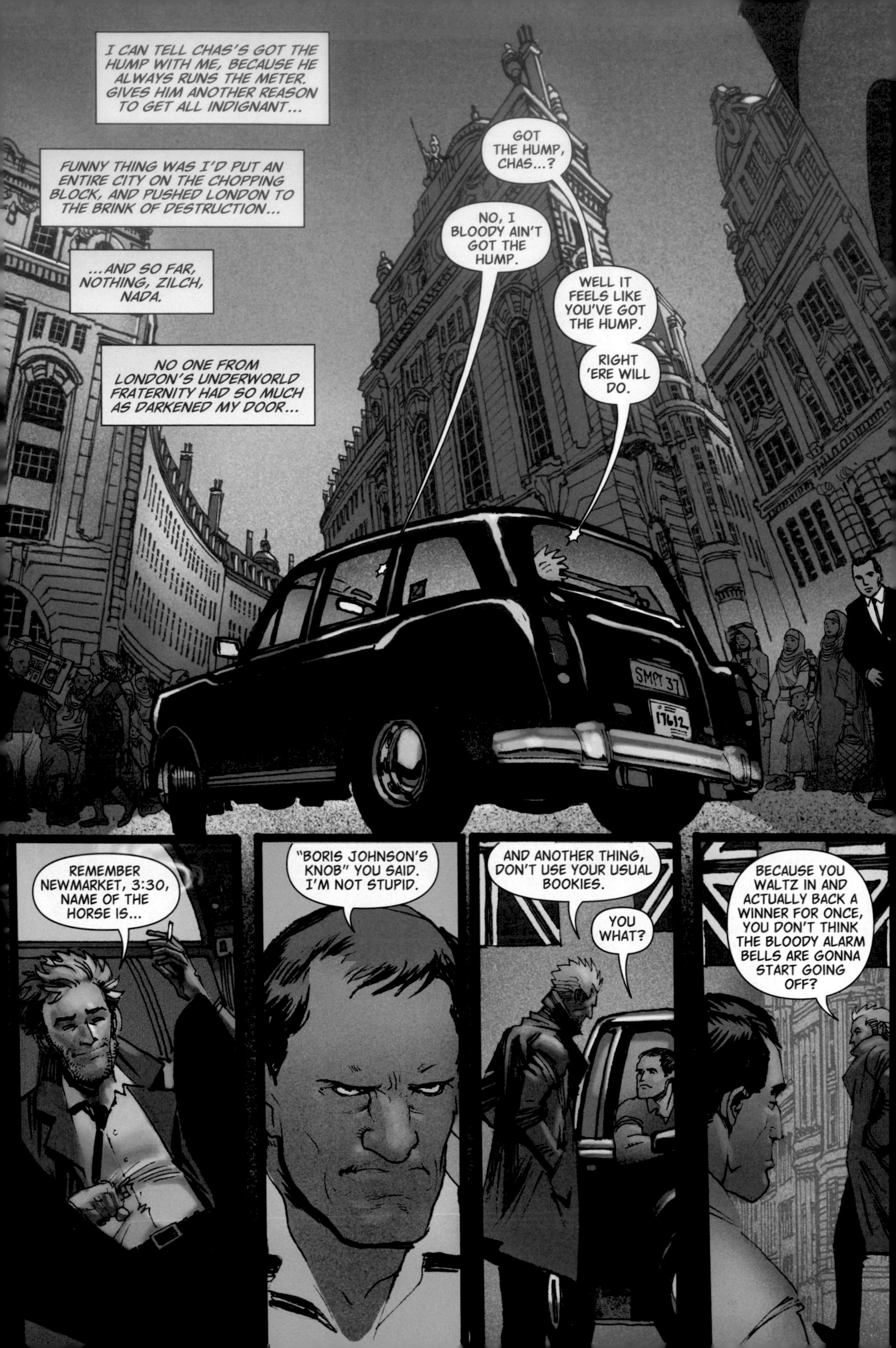
I CAN TELL CHAS'S GOT THE HUMP WITH ME, BECAUSE HE ALWAYS RUNS THE METER. GIVES HIM ANOTHER REASON TO GET ALL INDIGNANT...
FUNNY THING WAS I'D PUT AN ENTIRE CITY ON THE CHOPPING BLOCK, AND PUSHED LONDON TO THE BRINK OF DESTRUCTION...
...AND SO FAR, NOTHING, ZILCH, NADA.
NO ONE FROM LONDON'S UNDERWORLD FRATERNITY HAD SO MUCH AS DARKENED MY DOOR...
GOT THE HUMP, CHAS...?
NO, I BLOODY AIN'T GOT THE HUMP.
WELL IT FEELS LIKE YOU'VE GOT THE HUMP.
RIGHT 'ERE WILL DO.
SMPT 37
17612
REMEMBER NEWMARKET, 3:30, NAME OF THE HORSE IS...
"BORIS JOHNSON'S KNOB" YOU SAID. I'M NOT STUPID.
AND ANOTHER THING, DON'T USE YOUR USUAL BOOKIES.
YOU WHAT?
BECAUSE YOU WALTZ IN AND ACTUALLY BACK A WINNER FOR ONCE, YOU DON'T THINK THE BLOODY ALARM BELLS ARE GONNA START GOING OFF?

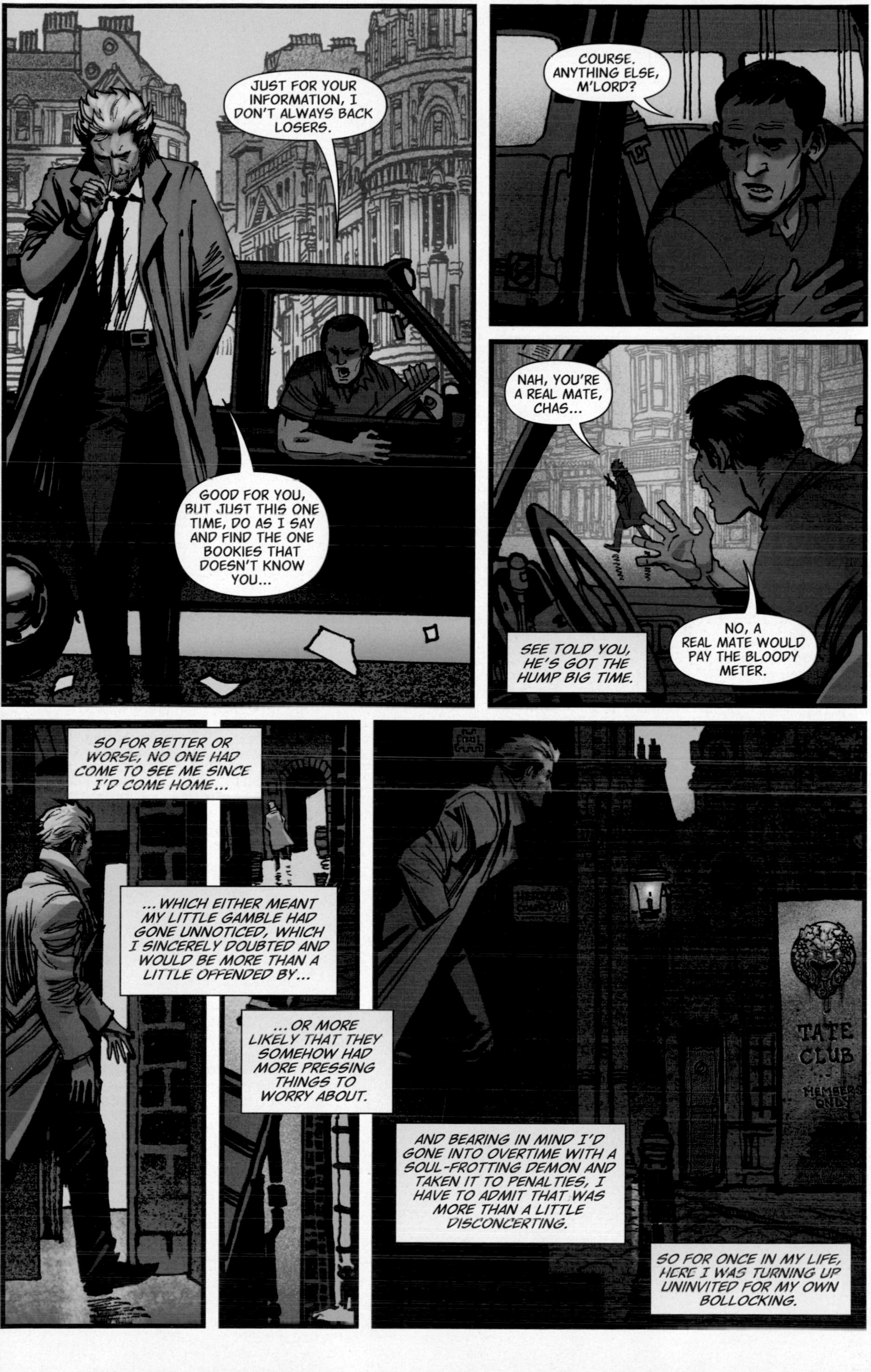
JUST FOR YOUR INFORMATION, I DON'T ALWAYS BACK LOSERS.
GOOD FOR YOU, BUT JUST THIS ONE TIME, DO AS I SAY AND FIND THE ONE BOOKIES THAT DOESN'T KNOW YOU...
COURSE. ANYTHING ELSE, M'LORD?
NAH, YOU'RE A REAL MATE, CHAS...
SEE TOLD YOU, HE'S GOT THE HUMP BIG TIME.
NO, A REAL MATE WOULD PAY THE BLOODY METER.
SO FOR BETTER OR WORSE, NO ONE HAD COME TO SEE ME SINCE I'D COME HOME...
...WHICH EITHER MEANT MY LITTLE GAMBLE HAD GONE UNNOTICED, WHICH I SINCERELY DOUBTED AND WOULD BE MORE THAN A LITTLE OFFENDED BY...
...OR MORE LIKELY THAT THEY SOMEHOW HAD MORE PRESSING THINGS TO WORRY ABOUT.
TATE CLUB
MEMBERS ONLY
AND BEARING IN MIND I'D GONE INTO OVERTIME WITH A SOUL-FROTTING DEMON AND TAKEN IT TO PENALTIES, I HAVE TO ADMIT THAT WAS MORE THAN A LITTLE DISCONCERTING.
SO FOR ONCE IN MY LIFE, HERE I WAS TURNING UP UNINVITED FOR MY OWN BOLLOCKING.

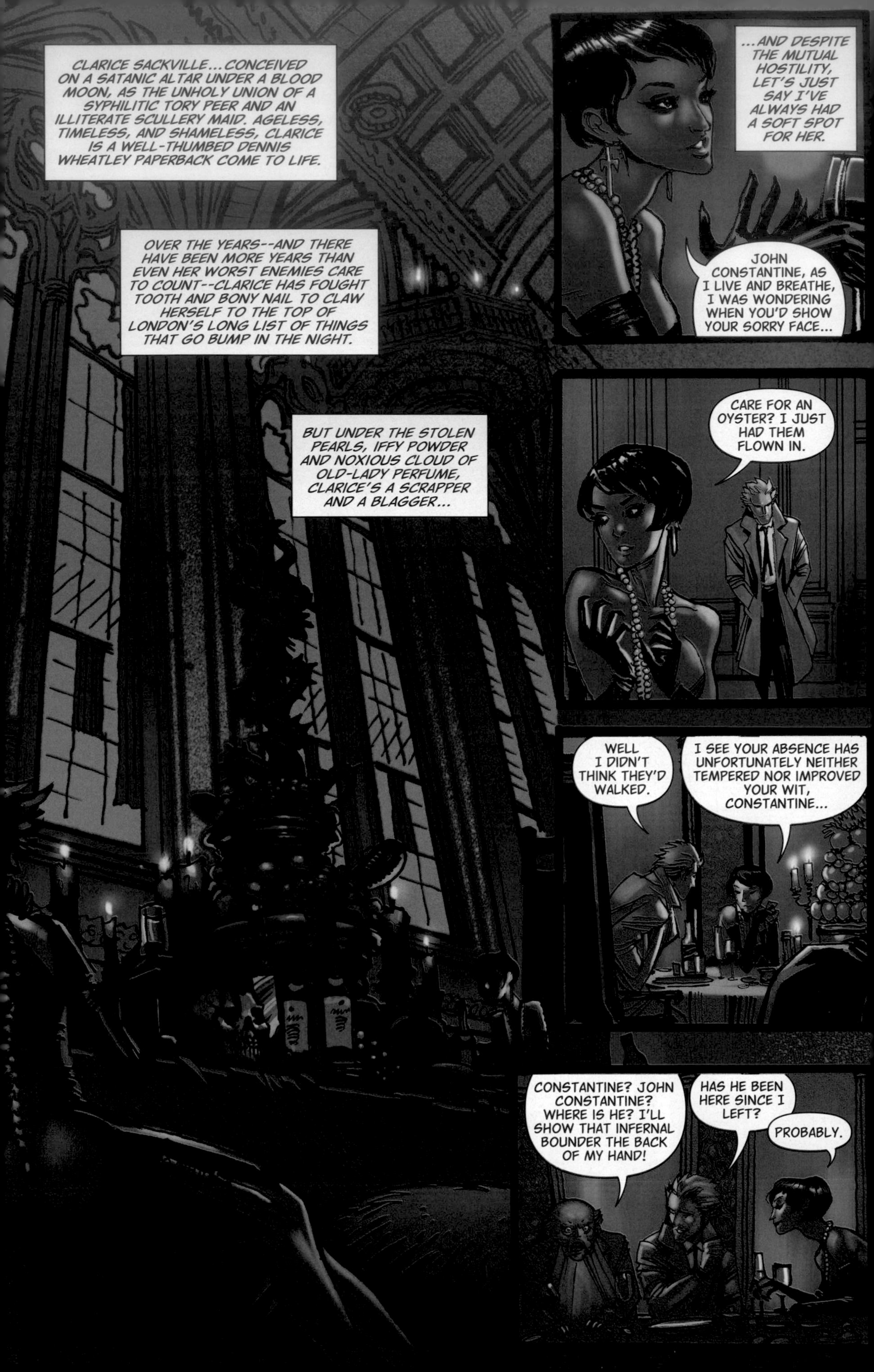
CLARICE SACKVILLE...CONCEIVED ON A SATANIC ALTAR UNDER A BLOOD MOON, AS THE UNHOLY UNION OF A SYPHILITIC TORY PEER AND AN ILLITERATE SCULLERY MAID. AGELESS, TIMELESS, AND SHAMELESS, CLARICE IS A WELL-THUMBED DENNIS WHEATLEY PAPERBACK COME TO LIFE.
OVER THE YEARS--AND THERE HAVE BEEN MORE YEARS THAN EVEN HER WORST ENEMIES CARE TO COUNT--CLARICE HAS FOUGHT TOOTH AND BONY NAIL TO CLAW HERSELF TO THE TOP OF LONDON'S LONG LIST OF THINGS THAT GO BUMP IN THE NIGHT.
BUT UNDER THE STOLEN PEARLS, IFFY POWDER AND NOXIOUS CLOUD OF OLD-LADY PERFUME, CLARICE'S A SCRAPPER AND A BLAGGER...
...AND DESPITE THE MUTUAL HOSTILITY, LET'S JUST SAY I'VE ALWAYS HAD A SOFT SPOT FOR HER.
JOHN CONSTANTINE, AS I LIVE AND BREATHE, I WAS WONDERING WHEN YOU'D SHOW YOUR SORRY FACE...
CARE FOR AN OYSTER? I JUST HAD THEM FLOWN IN.
WELL I DIDN'T THINK THEY'D WALKED.
I SEE YOUR ABSENCE HAS UNFORTUNATELY NEITHER TEMPERED NOR IMPROVED YOUR WIT, CONSTANTINE...
CONSTANTINE? JOHN CONSTANTINE? WHERE IS HE? I'LL SHOW THAT INFERNAL BOUNDER THE BACK OF MY HAND!
HAS HE BEEN HERE SINCE I LEFT?
PROBABLY.

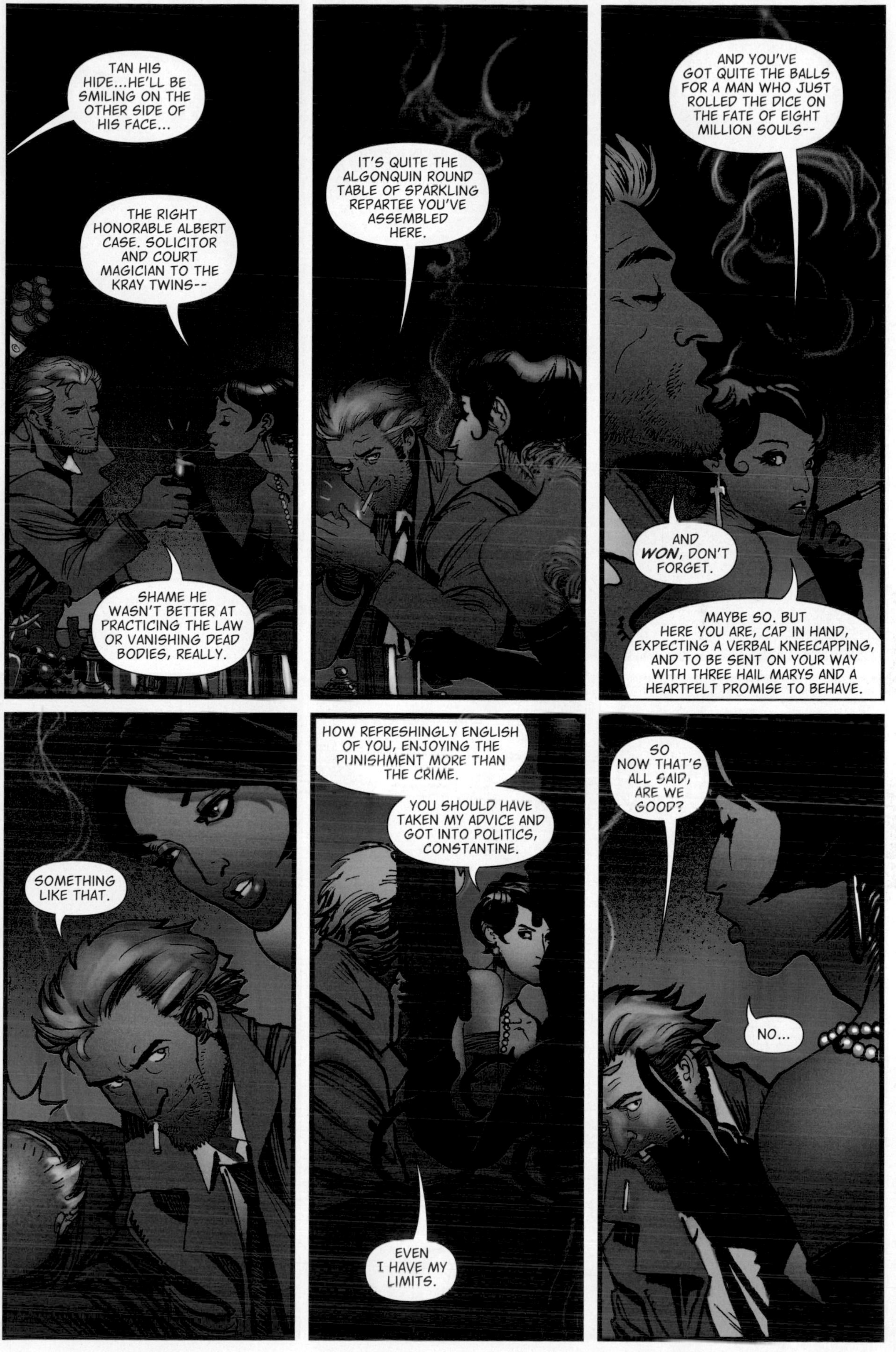
TAN HIS HIDE...HE'LL BE SMILING ON THE OTHER SIDE OF HIS FACE...
THE RIGHT HONORABLE ALBERT CASE. SOLICITOR AND COURT MAGICIAN TO THE KRAY TWINS--
SHAME HE WASN'T BETTER AT PRACTICING THE LAW OR VANISHING DEAD BODIES, REALLY.
IT'S QUITE THE ALGONQUIN ROUND TABLE OF SPARKLING REPARTEE YOU'VE ASSEMBLED HERE.
AND YOU'VE GOT QUITE THE BALLS FOR A MAN WHO JUST ROLLED THE DICE ON THE FATE OF EIGHT MILLION SOULS--
AND WON, DON'T FORGET.
MAYBE SO. BUT HERE YOU ARE, CAP IN HAND, EXPECTING A VERBAL KNEECAPPING, AND TO BE SENT ON YOUR WAY WITH THREE HAIL MARYS AND A HEARTFELT PROMISE TO BEHAVE.
SOMETHING LIKE THAT.
HOW REFRESHINGLY ENGLISH OF YOU, ENJOYING THE PUNISHMENT MORE THAN THE CRIME.
YOU SHOULD HAVE TAKEN MY ADVICE AND GOT INTO POLITICS, CONSTANTINE.
EVEN I HAVE MY LIMITS.
SO NOW THAT'S ALL SAID, ARE WE GOOD?
NO...

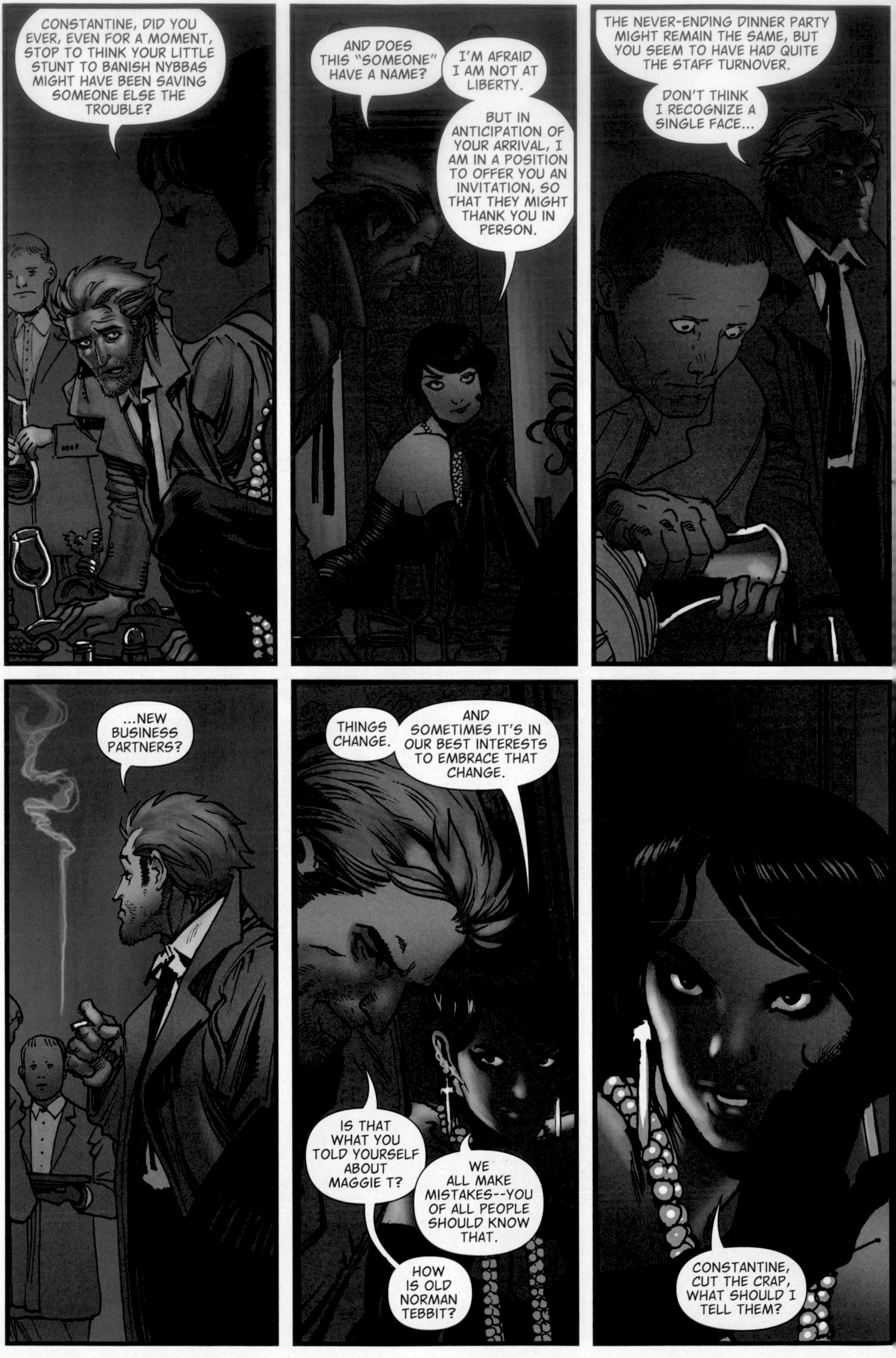
CONSTANTINE, DID YOU EVER, EVEN FOR A MOMENT, STOP TO THINK YOUR LITTLE STUNT TO BANISH NYBBAS MIGHT HAVE BEEN SAVING SOMEONE ELSE THE TROUBLE?
AND DOES THIS "SOMEONE" HAVE A NAME?
I'M AFRAID I AM NOT AT LIBERTY.
BUT IN ANTICIPATION OF YOUR ARRIVAL, I AM IN A POSITION TO OFFER YOU AN INVITATION, SO THAT THEY MIGHT THANK YOU IN PERSON.
THE NEVER-ENDING DINNER PARTY MIGHT REMAIN THE SAME, BUT YOU SEEM TO HAVE HAD QUITE THE STAFF TURNOVER.
DON'T THINK I RECOGNIZE A SINGLE FACE...
...NEW BUSINESS PARTNERS?
THINGS CHANGE.
AND SOMETIMES IT'S IN OUR BEST INTERESTS TO EMBRACE THAT CHANGE.
IS THAT WHAT YOU TOLD YOURSELF ABOUT MAGGIE T?
WE ALL MAKE MISTAKES--YOU OF ALL PEOPLE SHOULD KNOW THAT.
HOW IS OLD NORMAN TEBBIT?
CONSTANTINE, CUT THE CRAP, WHAT SHOULD I TELL THEM?

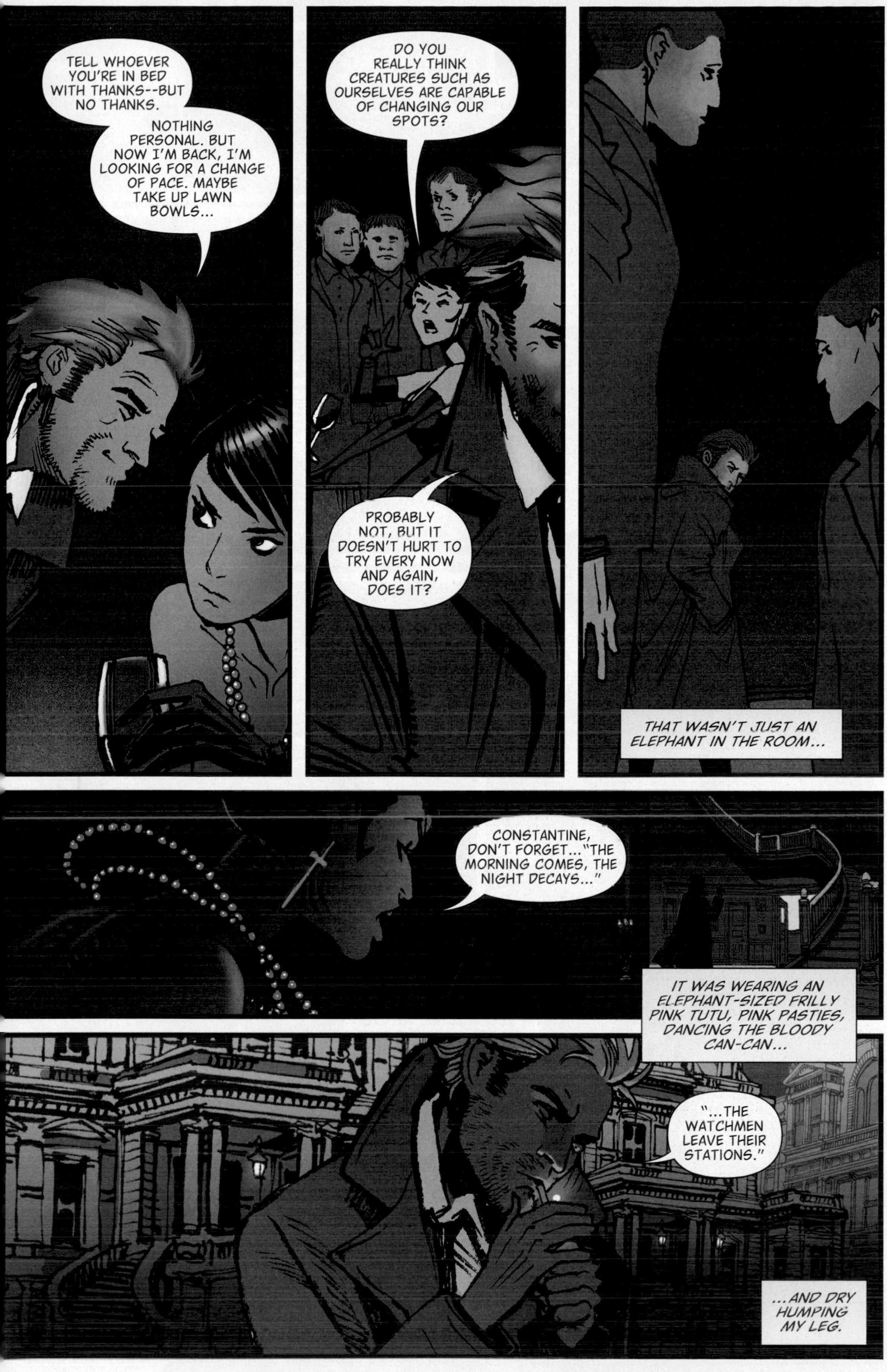
TELL WHOEVER YOU'RE IN BED WITH THANKS--BUT NO THANKS.
NOTHING PERSONAL. BUT NOW I'M BACK, I'M LOOKING FOR A CHANGE OF PACE. MAYBE TAKE UP LAWN BOWLS...
DO YOU REALLY THINK CREATURES SUCH AS OURSELVES ARE CAPABLE OF CHANGING OUR SPOTS?
PROBABLY NOT, BUT IT DOESN'T HURT TO TRY EVERY NOW AND AGAIN, DOES IT?
THAT WASN'T JUST AN ELEPHANT IN THE ROOM...
CONSTANTINE, DON'T FORGET..."THE MORNING COMES, THE NIGHT DECAYS..."
IT WAS WEARING AN ELEPHANT-SIZED FRILLY PINK TUTU, PINK PASTIES, DANCING THE BLOODY CAN-CAN...
"...THE WATCHMEN LEAVE THEIR STATIONS."
...AND DRY HUMPING MY LEG.

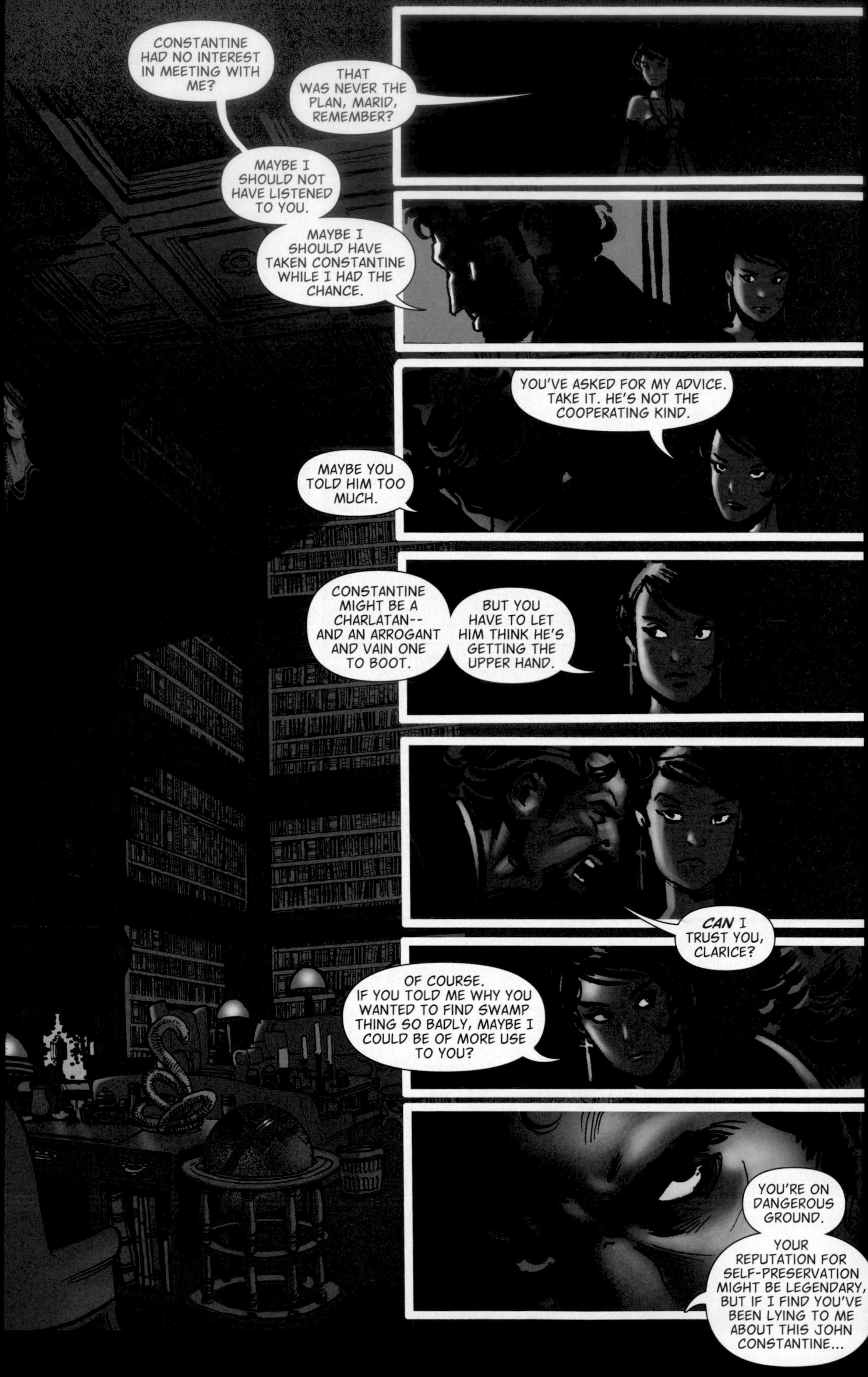
CONSTANTINE HAD NO INTEREST IN MEETING WITH ME?
THAT WAS NEVER THE PLAN, MARID, REMEMBER?
MAYBE I SHOULD NOT HAVE LISTENED TO YOU.
MAYBE I SHOULD HAVE TAKEN CONSTANTINE WHILE I HAD THE CHANCE.
YOU'VE ASKED FOR MY ADVICE. TAKE IT. HE'S NOT THE COOPERATING KIND.
MAYBE YOU TOLD HIM TOO MUCH.
CONSTANTINE MIGHT BE A CHARLATAN-- AND AN ARROGANT AND VAIN ONE TO BOOT.
BUT YOU HAVE TO LET HIM THINK HE'S GETTING THE UPPER HAND.
CAN I TRUST YOU, CLARICE?
OF COURSE. IF YOU TOLD ME WHY YOU WANTED TO FIND SWAMP THING SO BADLY, MAYBE I COULD BE OF MORE USE TO YOU?
YOU'RE ON DANGEROUS GROUND.
YOUR REPUTATION FOR SELF-PRESERVATION MIGHT BE LEGENDARY, BUT IF I FIND YOU'VE BEEN LYING TO ME ABOUT THIS JOHN CONSTANTINE...

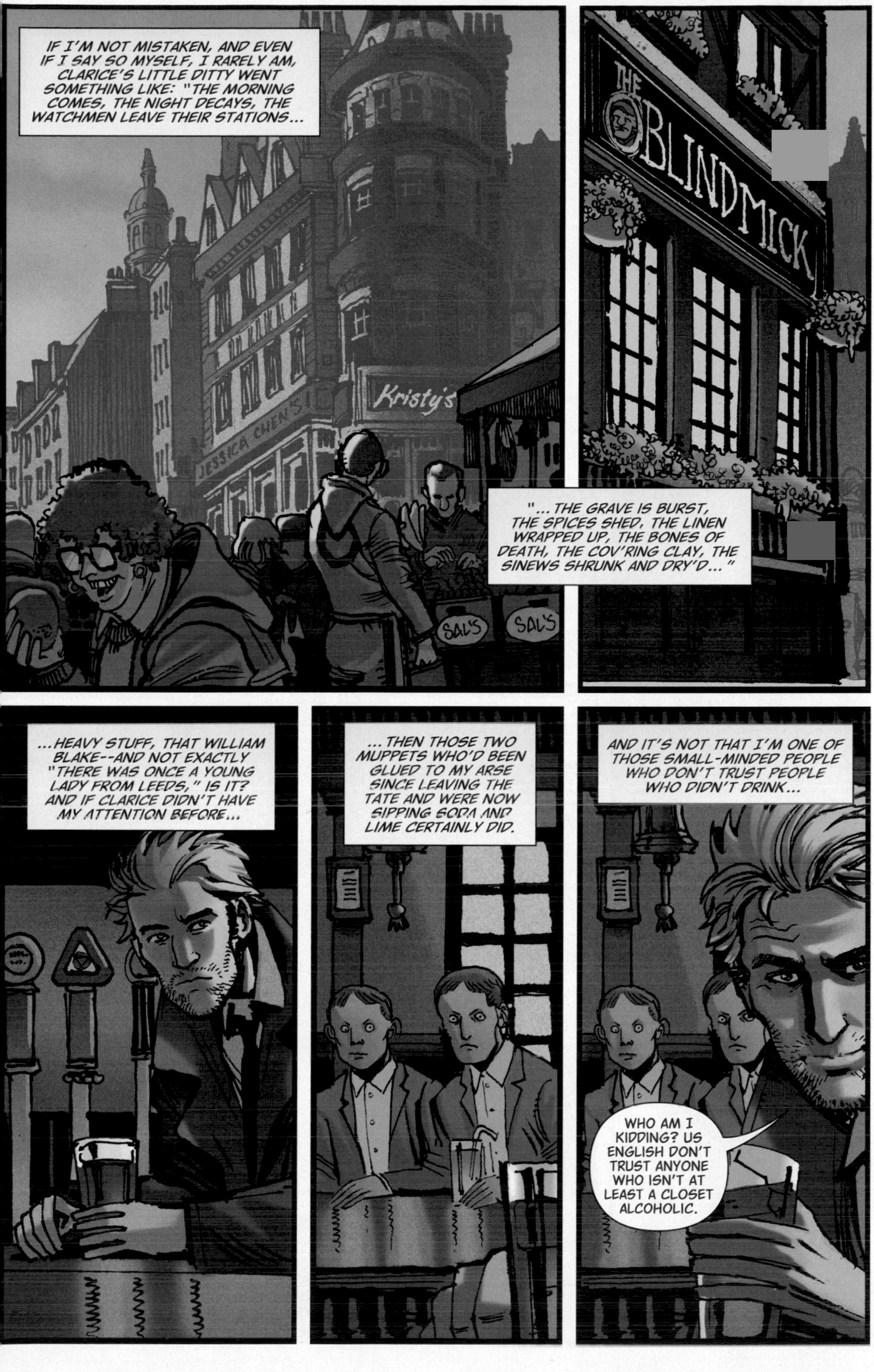
IF I'M NOT MISTAKEN, AND EVEN IF I SAY SO MYSELF, I RARELY AM, CLARICE'S LITTLE DITTY WENT SOMETHING LIKE: "THE MORNING COMES, THE NIGHT DECAYS, THE WATCHMEN LEAVE THEIR STATIONS...
JESSICA CHEN'S
Kristy's
SAL'S
SAL'S
THE BLINDMICK
"...THE GRAVE IS BURST, THE SPICES SHED, THE LINEN WRAPPED UP, THE BONES OF DEATH, THE COV'RING CLAY, THE SINEWS SHRUNK AND DRY'D..."
...HEAVY STUFF, THAT WILLIAM BLAKE--AND NOT EXACTLY "THERE WAS ONCE A YOUNG LADY FROM LEEDS," IS IT? AND IF CLARICE DIDN'T HAVE MY ATTENTION BEFORE...
...THEN THOSE TWO MUPPETS WHO'D BEEN GLUED TO MY ARSE SINCE LEAVING THE TATE AND WERE NOW SIPPING SODA AND LIME CERTAINLY DID.
AND IT'S NOT THAT I'M ONE OF THOSE SMALL-MINDED PEOPLE WHO DON'T TRUST PEOPLE WHO DIDN'T DRINK...
WHO AM I KIDDING? US ENGLISH DON'T TRUST ANYONE WHO ISN'T AT LEAST A CLOSET ALCOHOLIC.

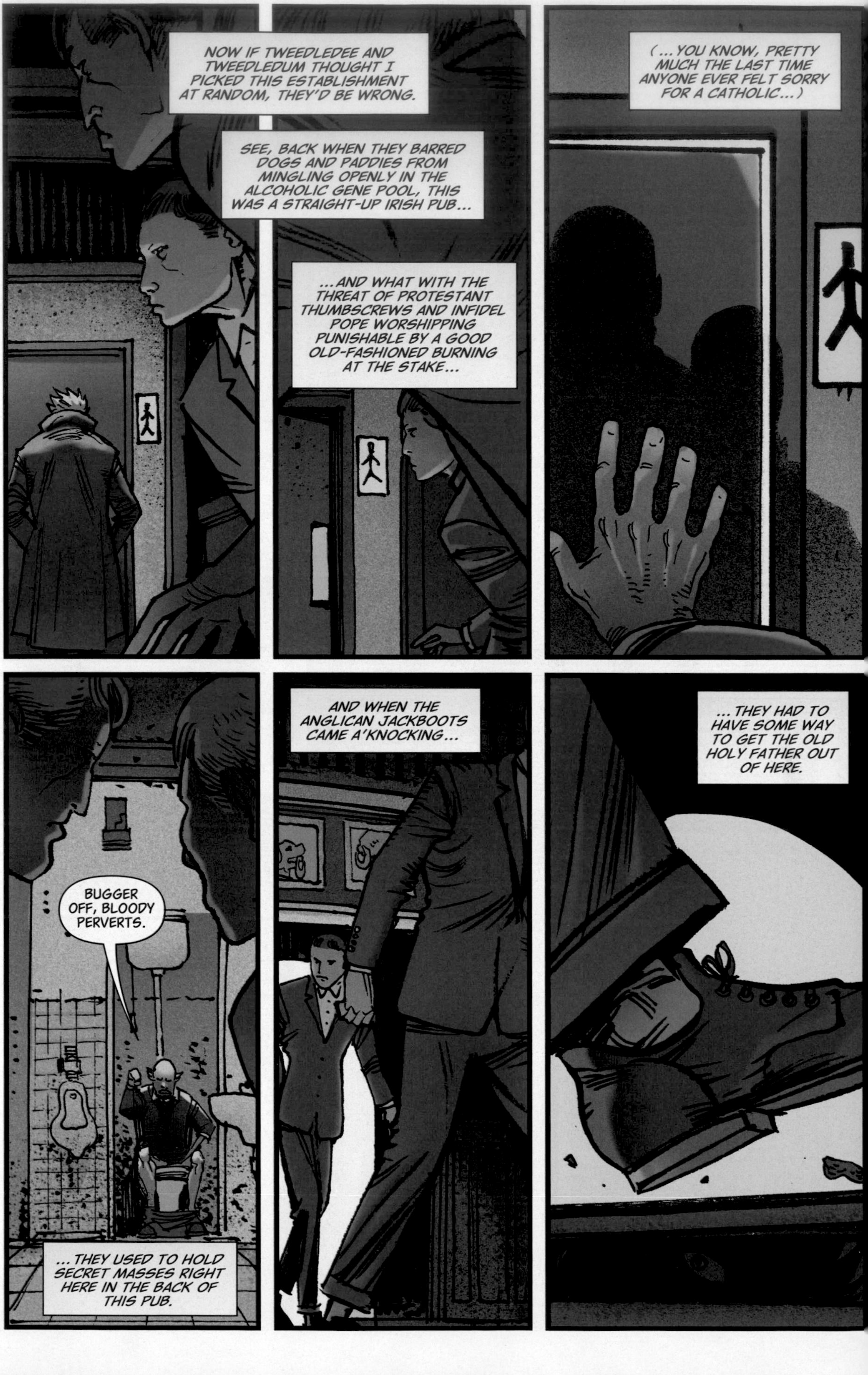
NOW IF TWEEDLEDEE AND TWEEDLEDUM THOUGHT I PICKED THIS ESTABLISHMENT AT RANDOM, THEY'D BE WRONG.
SEE, BACK WHEN THEY BARRED DOGS AND PADDIES FROM MINGLING OPENLY IN THE ALCOHOLIC GENE POOL, THIS WAS A STRAIGHT-UP IRISH PUB...
...AND WHAT WITH THE THREAT OF PROTESTANT THUMBSCREWS AND INFIDEL POPE WORSHIPPING PUNISHABLE BY A GOOD OLD-FASHIONED BURNING AT THE STAKE...
(...YOU KNOW, PRETTY MUCH THE LAST TIME ANYONE EVER FELT SORRY FOR A CATHOLIC...)
BUGGER OFF, BLOODY PERVERTS.
...THEY USED TO HOLD SECRET MASSES RIGHT HERE IN THE BACK OF THIS PUB.
AND WHEN THE ANGLICAN JACKBOOTS CAME A'KNOCKING...
...THEY HAD TO HAVE SOME WAY TO GET THE OLD HOLY FATHER OUT OF HERE.

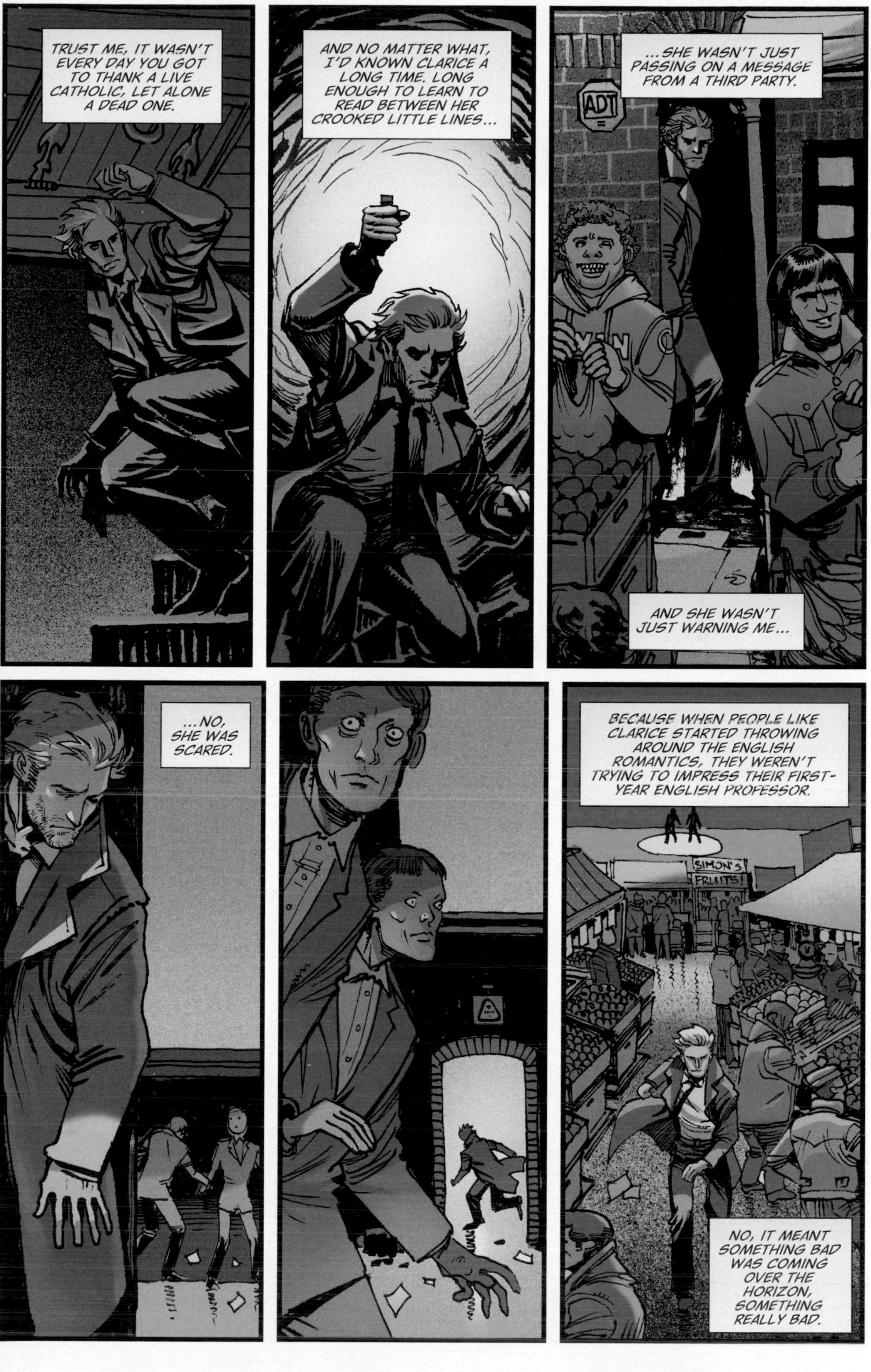
TRUST ME, IT WASN'T EVERY DAY YOU GOT TO THANK A LIVE CATHOLIC, LET ALONE A DEAD ONE.
AND NO MATTER WHAT, I'D KNOWN CLARICE A LONG TIME. LONG ENOUGH TO LEARN TO READ BETWEEN HER CROOKED LITTLE LINES...
...SHE WASN'T JUST PASSING ON A MESSAGE FROM A THIRD PARTY.
ADT
AND SHE WASN'T JUST WARNING ME...
...NO, SHE WAS SCARED.
BECAUSE WHEN PEOPLE LIKE CLARICE STARTED THROWING AROUND THE ENGLISH ROMANTICS, THEY WEREN'T TRYING TO IMPRESS THEIR FIRST-YEAR ENGLISH PROFESSOR.
SIMON'S FRUITS!
NO, IT MEANT SOMETHING BAD WAS COMING OVER THE HORIZON, SOMETHING REALLY BAD.

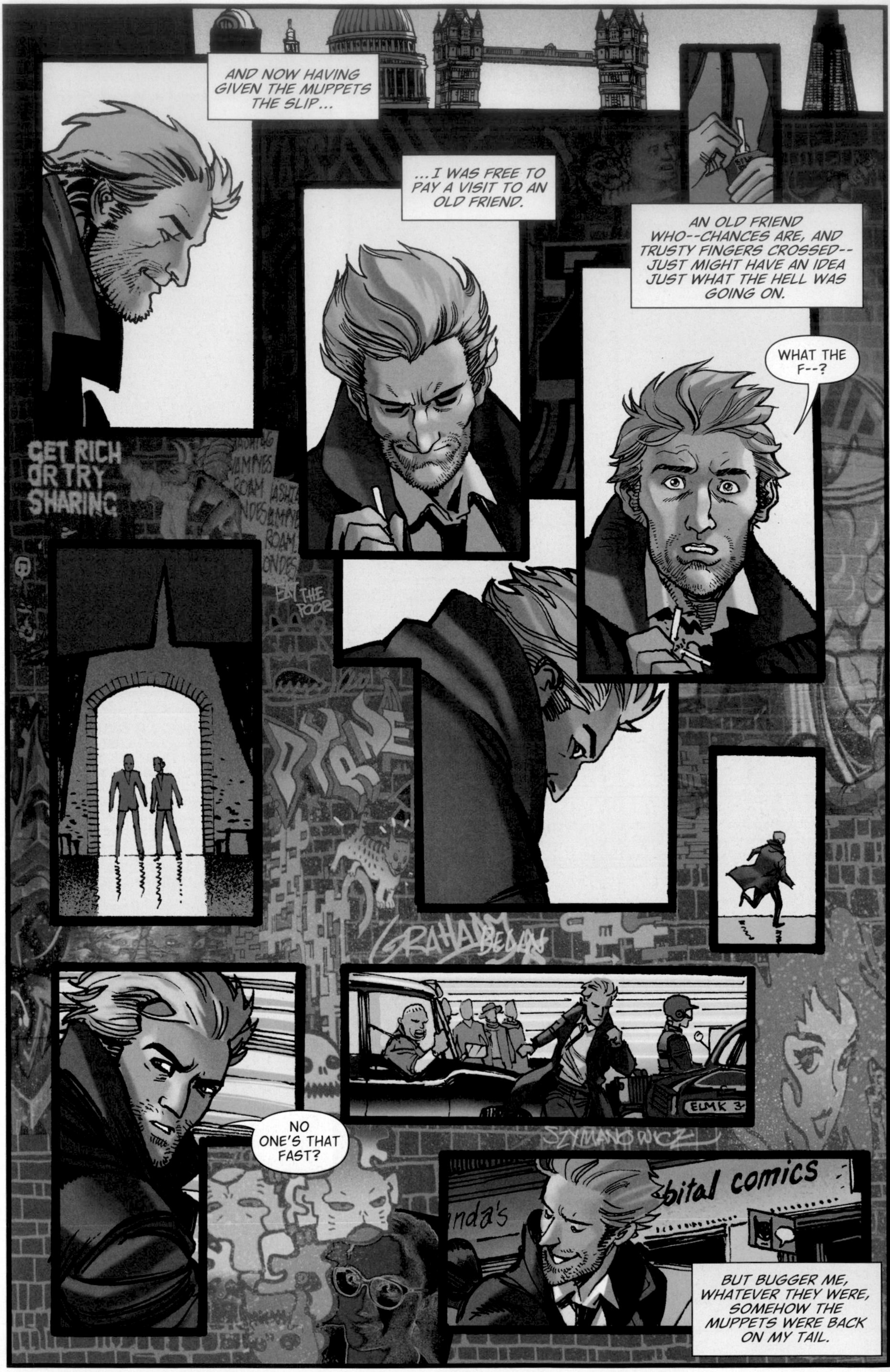
AND NOW HAVING GIVEN THE MUPPETS THE SLIP...
...I WAS FREE TO PAY A VISIT TO AN OLD FRIEND.
AN OLD FRIEND WHO--CHANCES ARE, AND TRUSTY FINGERS CROSSED--JUST MIGHT HAVE AN IDEA JUST WHAT THE HELL WAS GOING ON.
WHAT THE F--?
GET RICH OR TRY SHARING
NO ONE'S THAT FAST?
bital comics
BUT BUGGER ME, WHATEVER THEY WERE, SOMEHOW THE MUPPETS WERE BACK ON MY TAIL.

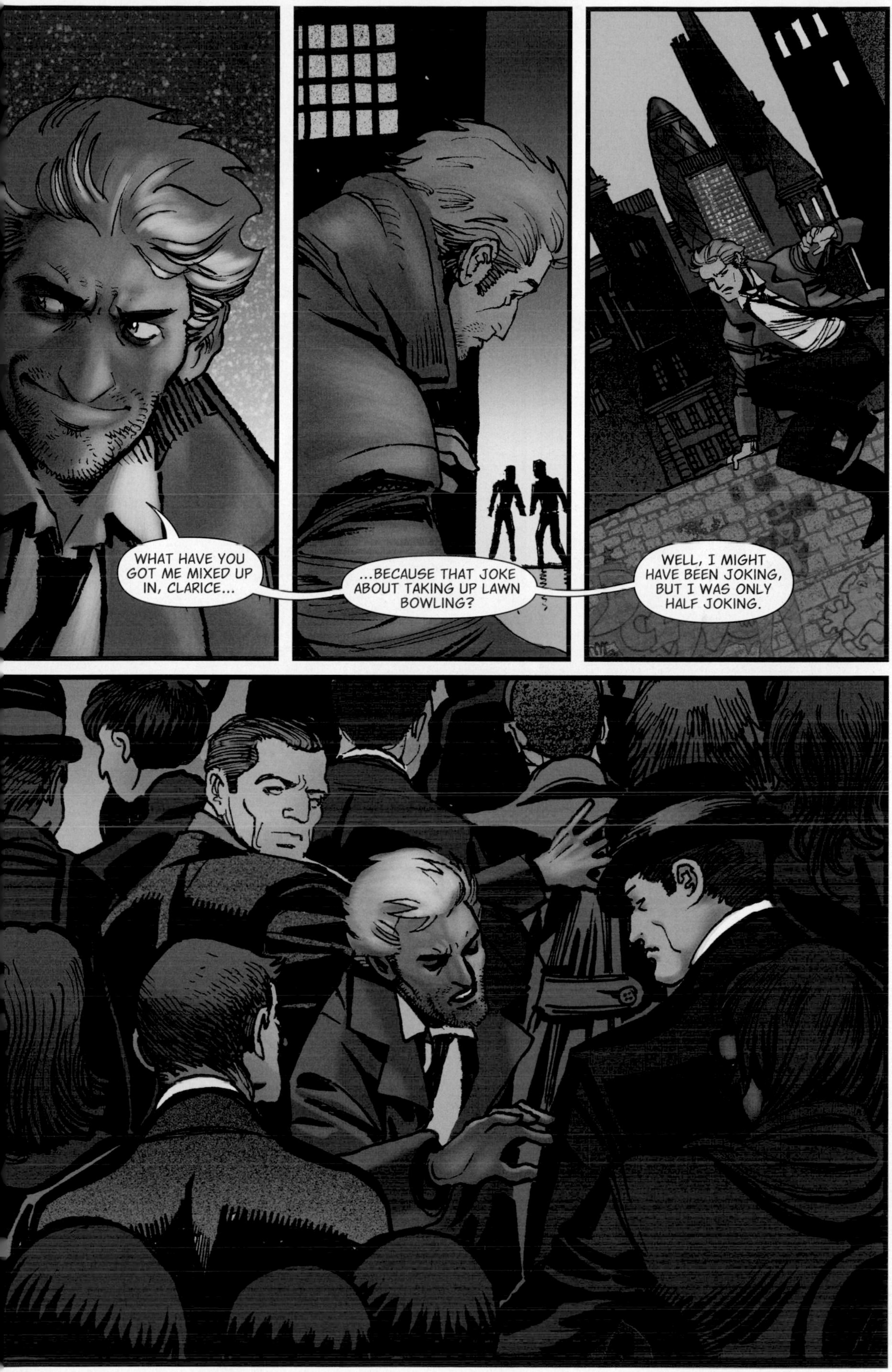
WHAT HAVE YOU GOT ME MIXED UP IN, CLARICE...
...BECAUSE THAT JOKE ABOUT TAKING UP LAWN BOWLING?
WELL, I MIGHT HAVE BEEN JOKING, BUT I WAS ONLY HALF JOKING.

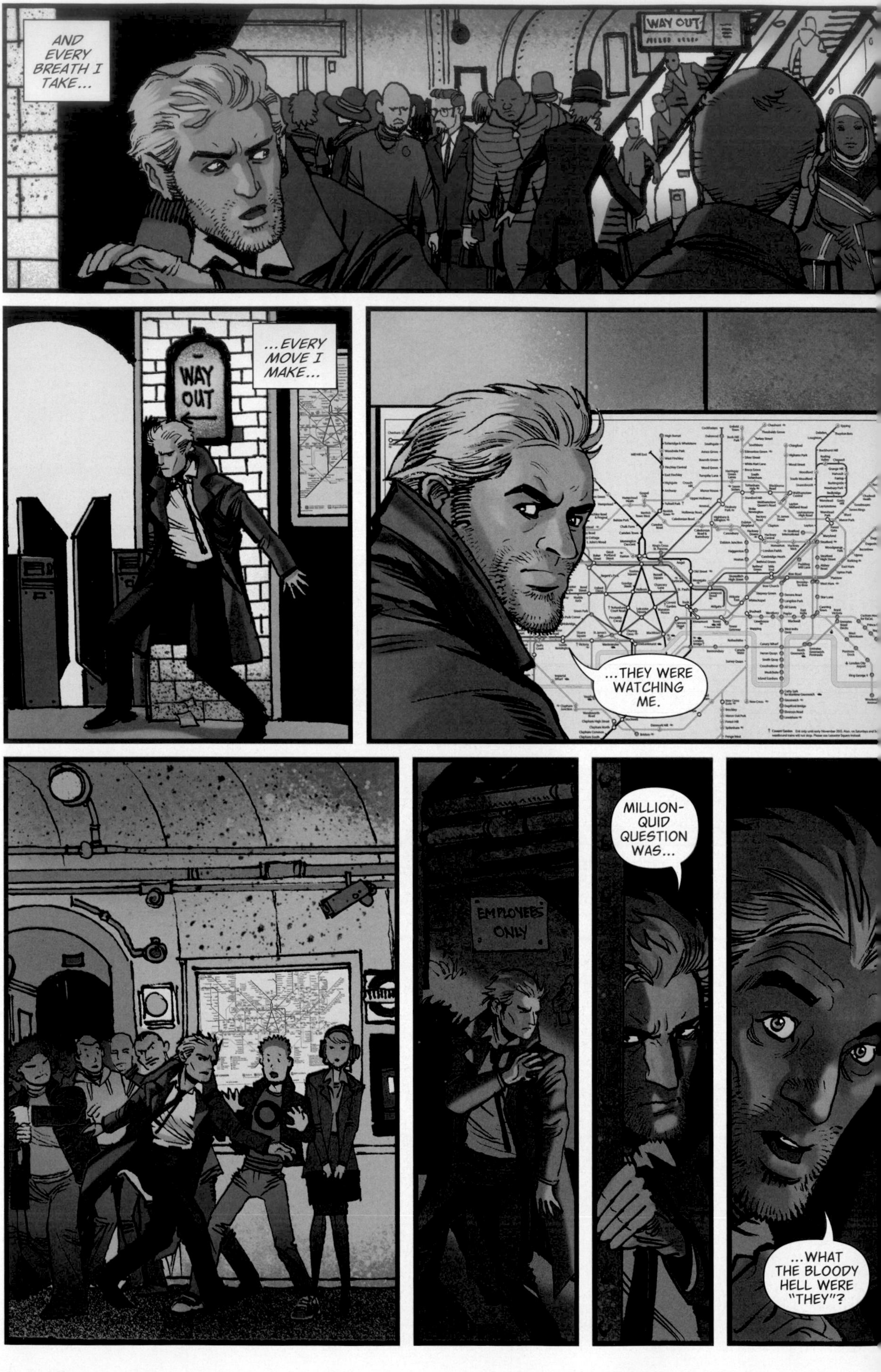
AND EVERY BREATH I TAKE...
WAY OUT
...EVERY MOVE I MAKE...
WAY OUT
...THEY WERE WATCHING ME.
EMPLOYEES ONLY
MILLION-QUID QUESTION WAS...
...WHAT THE BLOODY HELL WERE "THEY"?

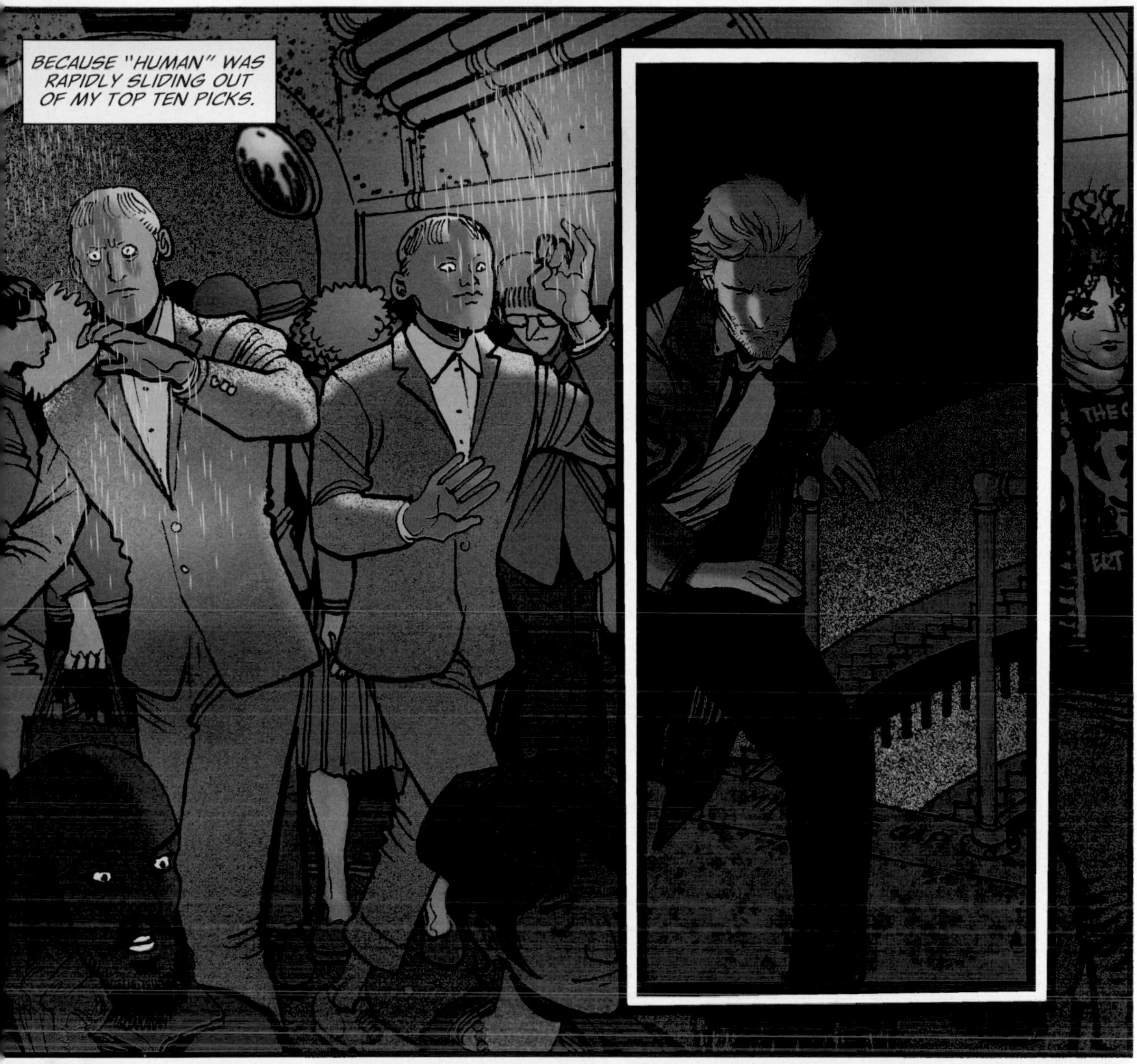
BECAUSE "HUMAN" WAS RAPIDLY SLIDING OUT OF MY TOP TEN PICKS.

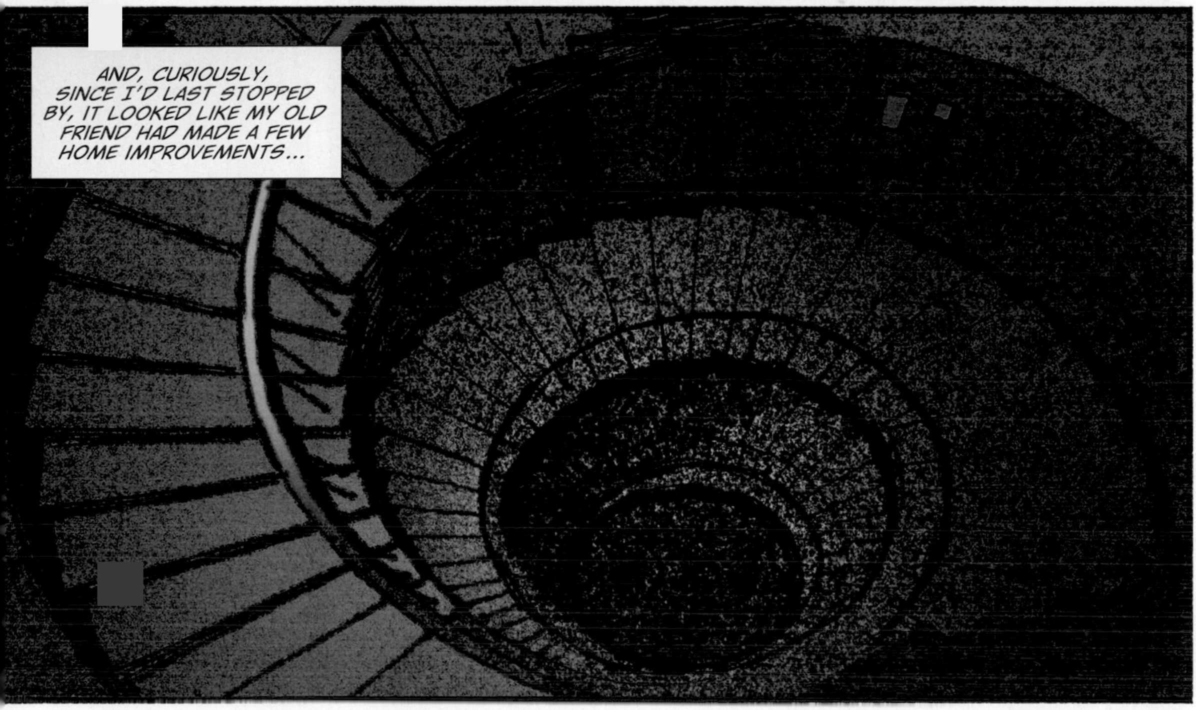
AND, CURIOUSLY, SINCE I'D LAST STOPPED BY, IT LOOKED LIKE MY OLD FRIEND HAD MADE A FEW HOME IMPROVEMENTS...

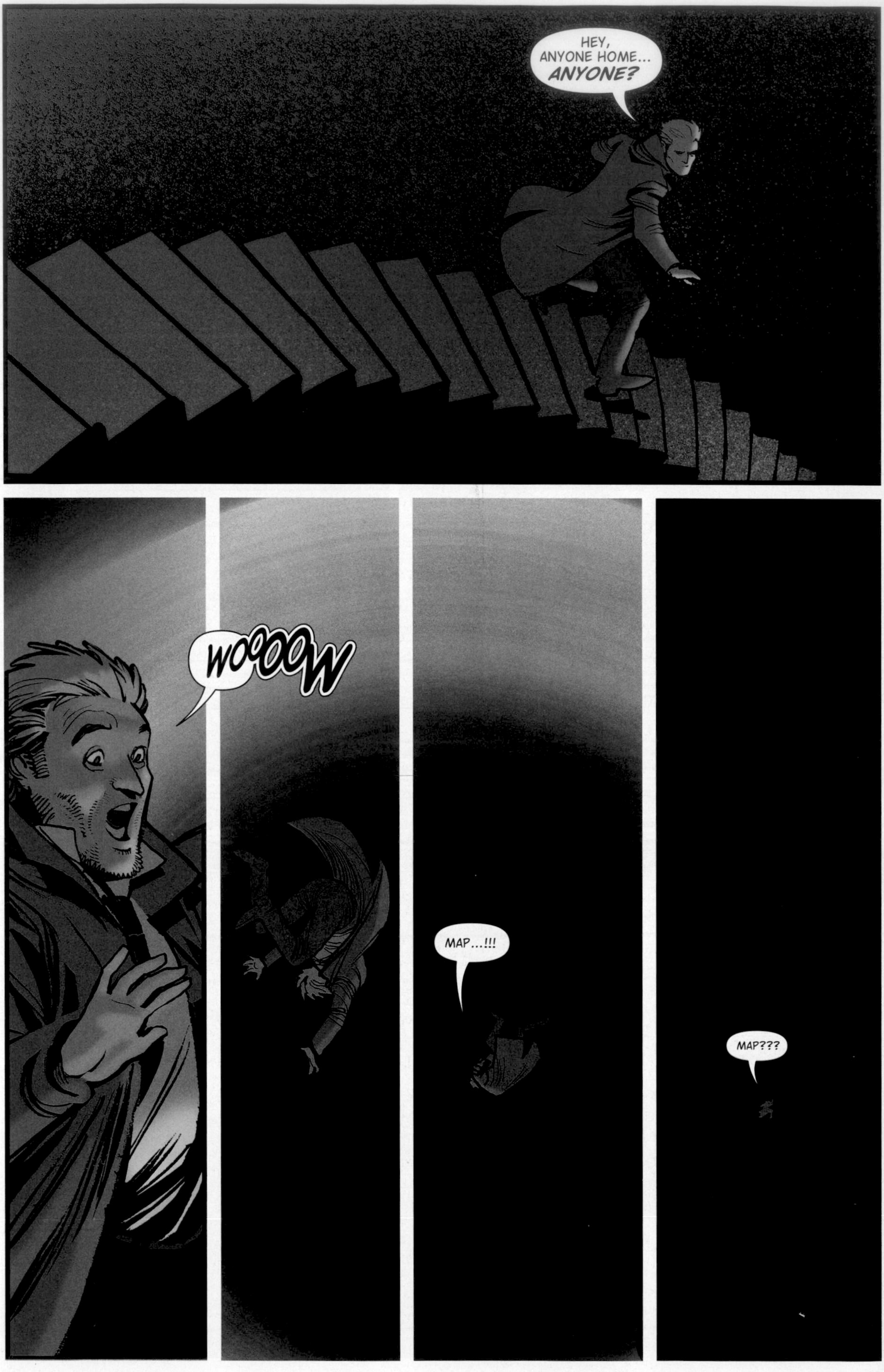
HEY, ANYONE HOME... ANYONE?
WOOOOW
MAP...!!!
MAP???

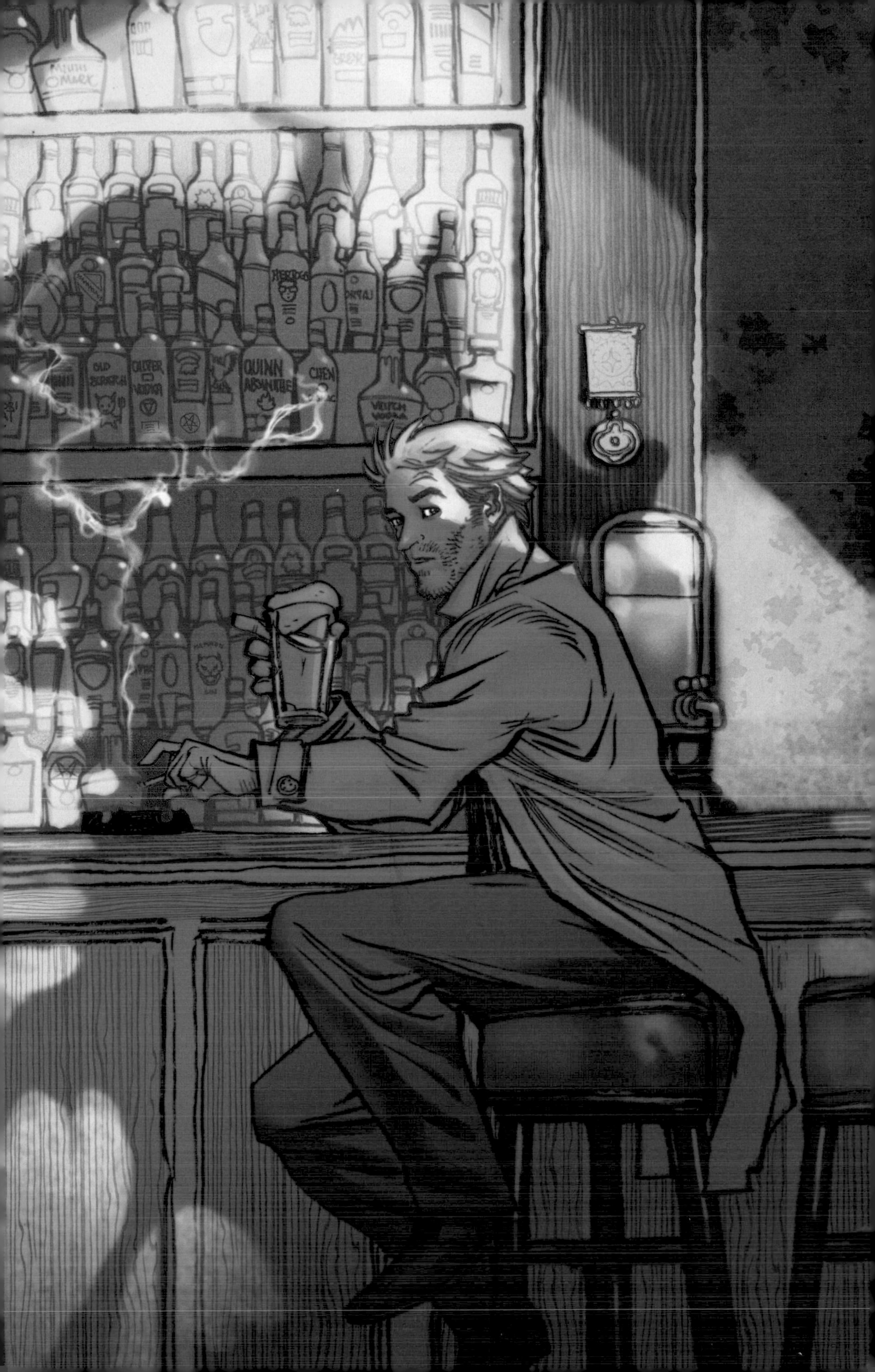
QUINN ABSINTHE
CHEN

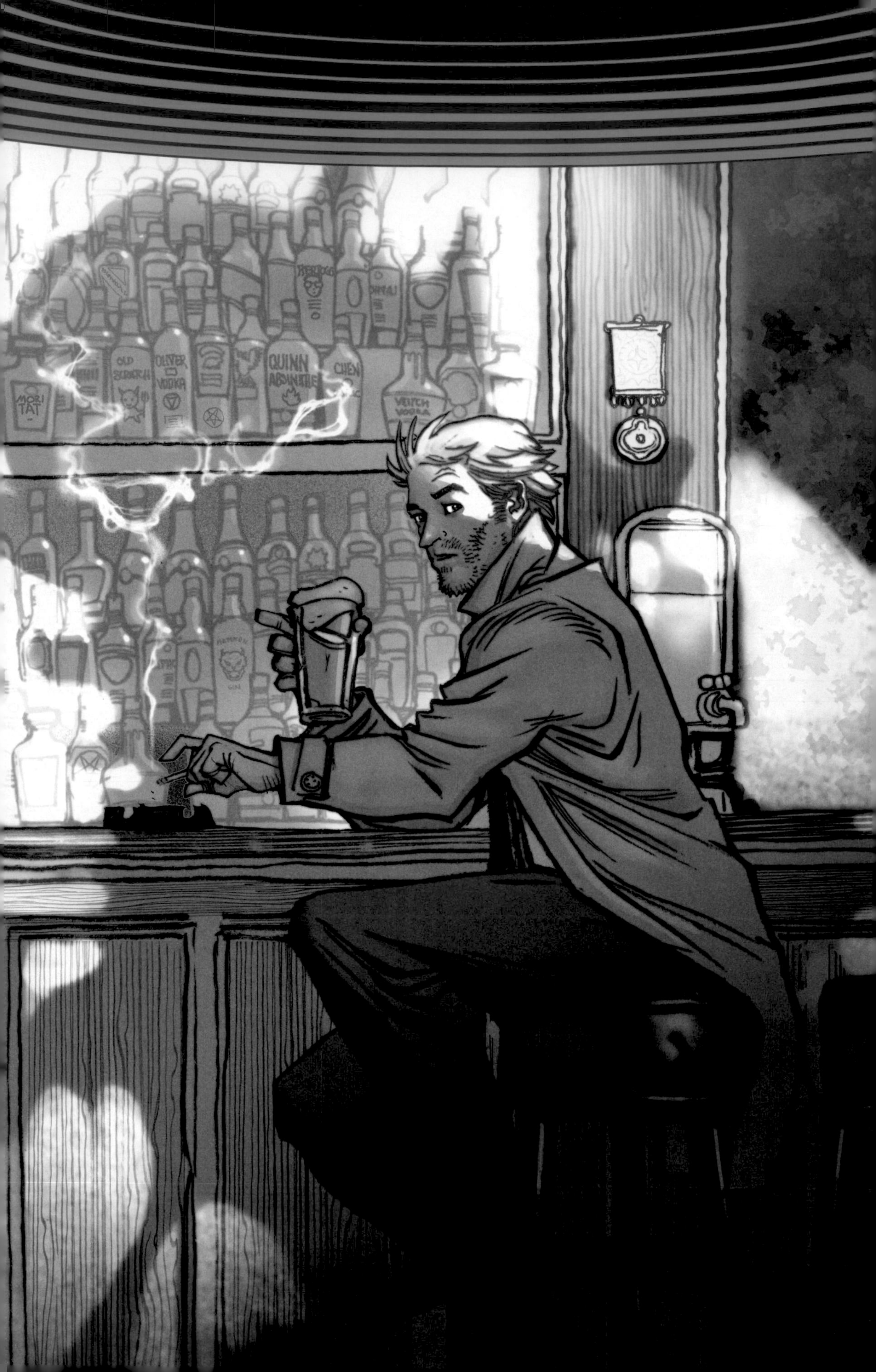
MORI TAT
OLD SCRATCH
OLIVER VODKA
QUINN ABSINTHE
CHEN
VEITCH VODKA

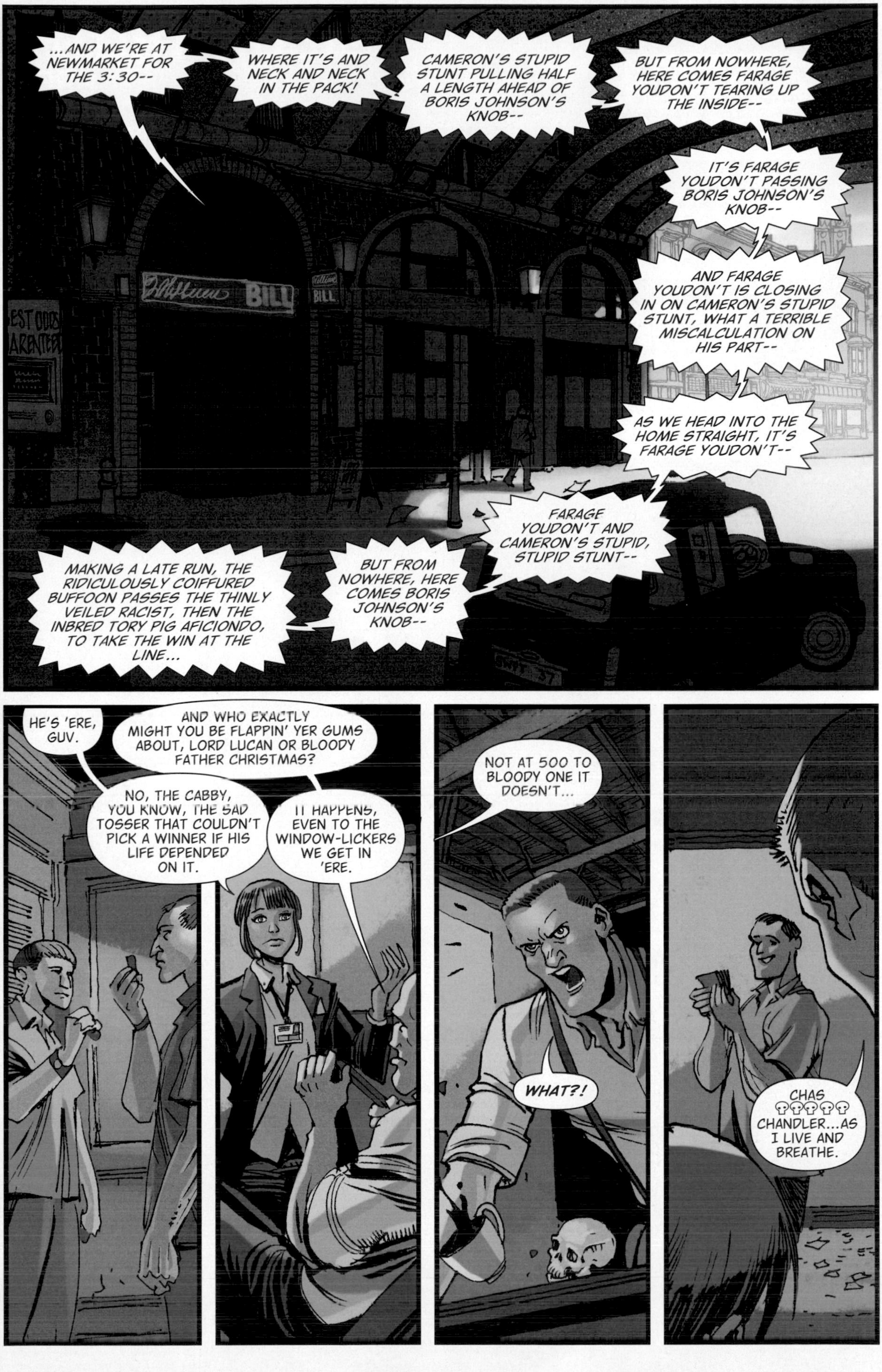
...AND WE'RE AT NEWMARKET FOR THE 3:30--
WHERE IT'S AND NECK AND NECK IN THE PACK!
CAMERON'S STUPID STUNT PULLING HALF A LENGTH AHEAD OF BORIS JOHNSON'S KNOB--
BUT FROM NOWHERE, HERE COMES FARAGE YOUDON'T TEARING UP THE INSIDE--
IT'S FARAGE YOUDON'T PASSING BORIS JOHNSON'S KNOB--
AND FARAGE YOUDON'T IS CLOSING IN ON CAMERON'S STUPID STUNT, WHAT A TERRIBLE MISCALCULATION ON HIS PART--
AS WE HEAD INTO THE HOME STRAIGHT, IT'S FARAGE YOUDON'T--
FARAGE YOUDON'T AND CAMERON'S STUPID, STUPID STUNT--
BUT FROM NOWHERE, HERE COMES BORIS JOHNSON'S KNOB--
MAKING A LATE RUN, THE RIDICULOUSLY COIFFURED BUFFOON PASSES THE THINLY VEILED RACIST, THEN THE INBRED TORY PIG AFICIONDO, TO TAKE THE WIN AT THE LINE...
HE'S 'ERE, GUV.
AND WHO EXACTLY MIGHT YOU BE FLAPPIN' YER GUMS ABOUT, LORD LUCAN OR BLOODY FATHER CHRISTMAS?
NO, THE CABBY, YOU KNOW, THE SAD TOSSER THAT COULDN'T PICK A WINNER IF HIS LIFE DEPENDED ON IT.
IT HAPPENS, EVEN TO THE WINDOW-LICKERS WE GET IN 'ERE.
NOT AT 500 TO BLOODY ONE IT DOESN'T...
WHAT?!
CHAS CHANDLER...AS I LIVE AND BREATHE.

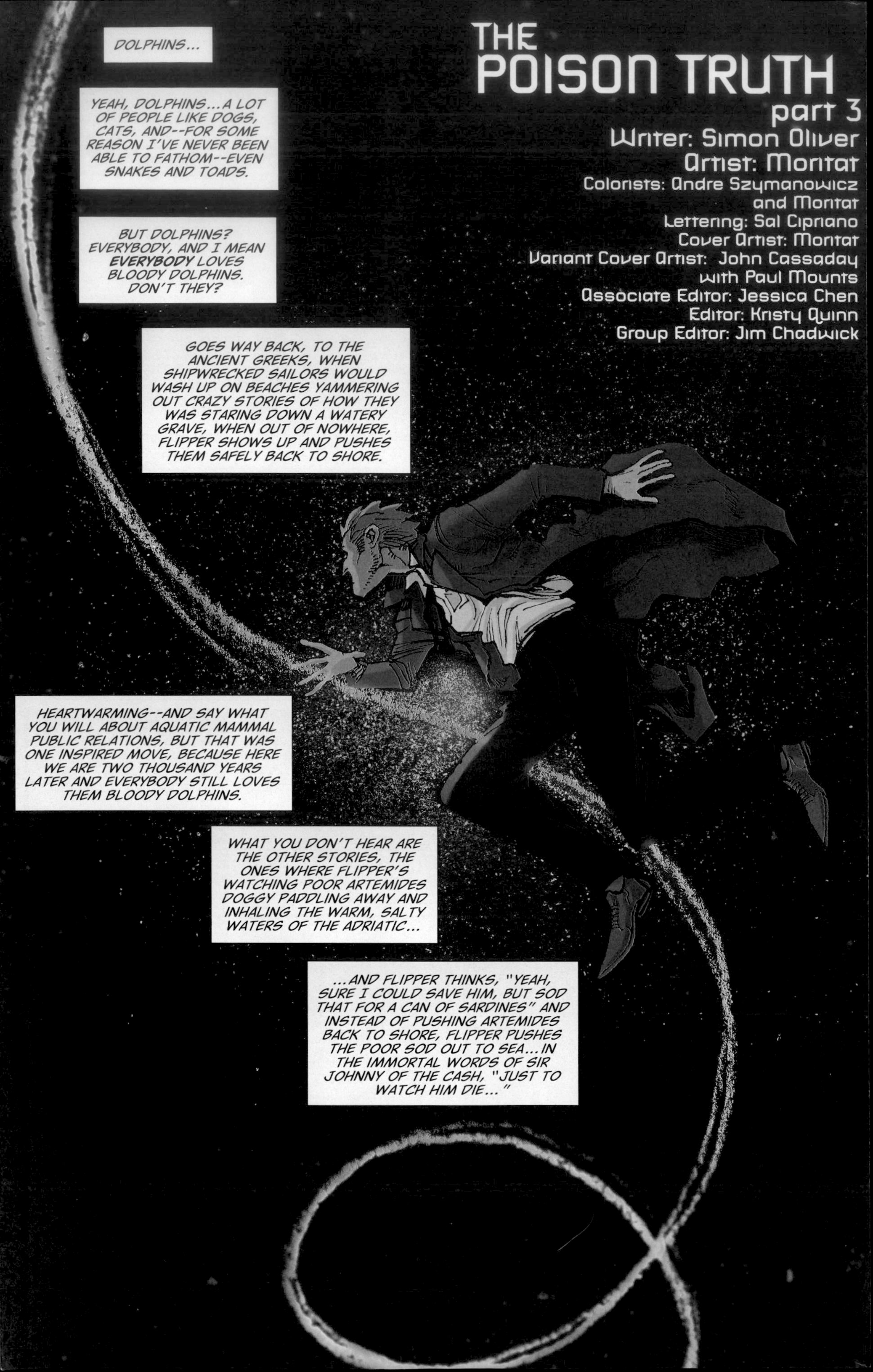
THE POISON TRUTH
part 3
Writer: Simon Oliver
Artist: Moritat
Colorists: Andre Szymanowicz and Moritat
Lettering: Sal Cipriano
Cover Artist: Moritat
Variant Cover Artist: John Cassaday with Paul Mounts
Associate Editor: Jessica Chen
Editor: Kristy Quinn
Group Editor: Jim Chadwick
DOLPHINS...
YEAH, DOLPHINS...A LOT OF PEOPLE LIKE DOGS, CATS, AND--FOR SOME REASON I'VE NEVER BEEN ABLE TO FATHOM--EVEN SNAKES AND TOADS.
BUT DOLPHINS? EVERYBODY, AND I MEAN EVERYBODY LOVES BLOODY DOLPHINS. DON'T THEY?
GOES WAY BACK, TO THE ANCIENT GREEKS, WHEN SHIPWRECKED SAILORS WOULD WASH UP ON BEACHES YAMMERING OUT CRAZY STORIES OF HOW THEY WAS STARING DOWN A WATERY GRAVE, WHEN OUT OF NOWHERE, FLIPPER SHOWS UP AND PUSHES THEM SAFELY BACK TO SHORE.
HEARTWARMING--AND SAY WHAT YOU WILL ABOUT AQUATIC MAMMAL PUBLIC RELATIONS, BUT THAT WAS ONE INSPIRED MOVE, BECAUSE HERE WE ARE TWO THOUSAND YEARS LATER AND EVERYBODY STILL LOVES THEM BLOODY DOLPHINS.
WHAT YOU DON'T HEAR ARE THE OTHER STORIES, THE ONES WHERE FLIPPER'S WATCHING POOR ARTEMIDES DOGGY PADDLING AWAY AND INHALING THE WARM, SALTY WATERS OF THE ADRIATIC...
...AND FLIPPER THINKS, "YEAH, SURE I COULD SAVE HIM, BUT SOD THAT FOR A CAN OF SARDINES" AND INSTEAD OF PUSHING ARTEMIDES BACK TO SHORE, FLIPPER PUSHES THE POOR SOD OUT TO SEA...IN THE IMMORTAL WORDS OF SIR JOHNNY OF THE CASH, "JUST TO WATCH HIM DIE..."

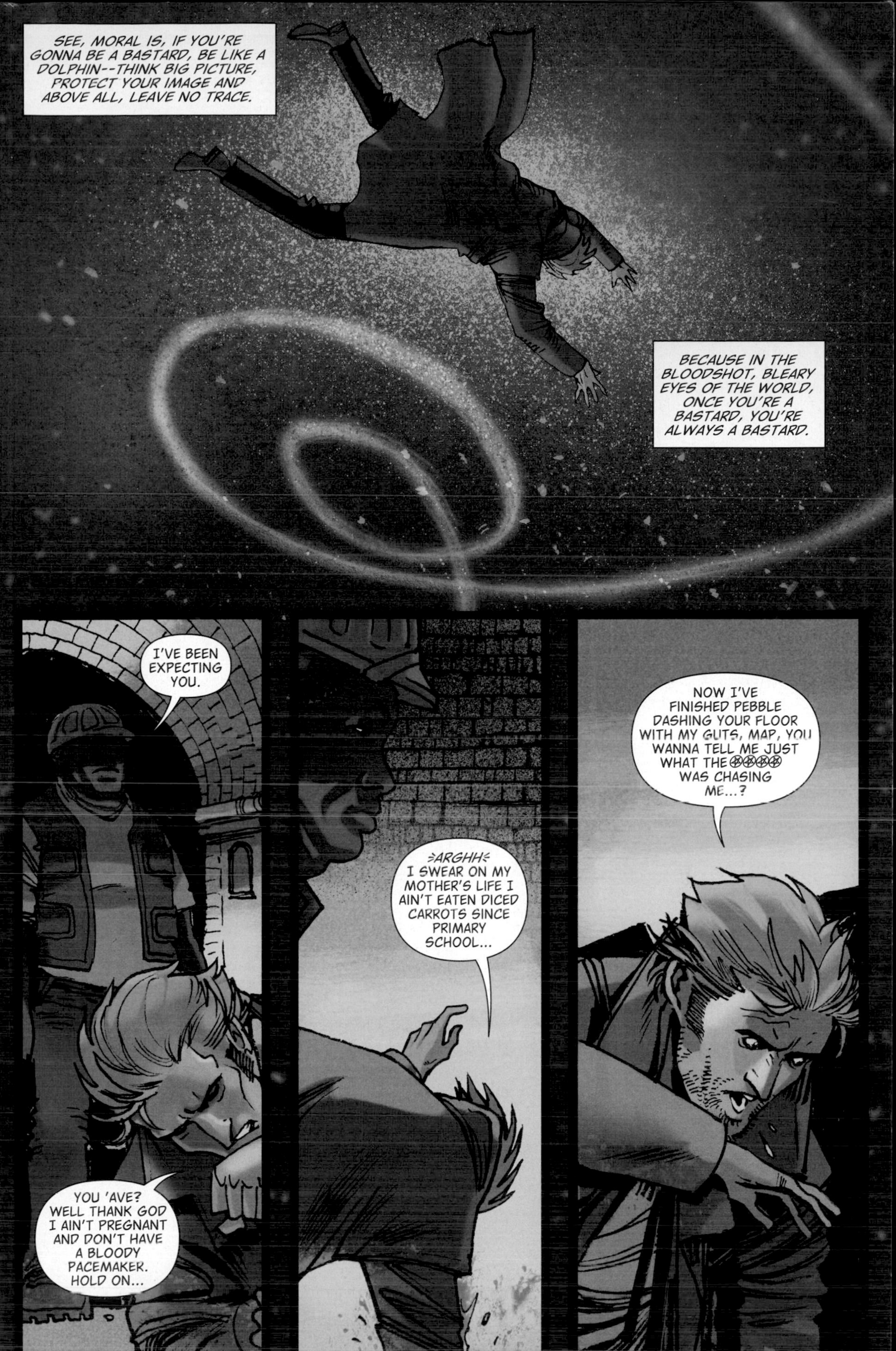
SEE, MORAL IS, IF YOU'RE GONNA BE A BASTARD, BE LIKE A DOLPHIN--THINK BIG PICTURE, PROTECT YOUR IMAGE AND ABOVE ALL, LEAVE NO TRACE.
BECAUSE IN THE BLOODSHOT, BLEARY EYES OF THE WORLD, ONCE YOU'RE A BASTARD, YOU'RE ALWAYS A BASTARD.
I'VE BEEN EXPECTING YOU.
YOU 'AVE? WELL THANK GOD I AIN'T PREGNANT AND DON'T HAVE A BLOODY PACEMAKER. HOLD ON...
ARGHH
I SWEAR ON MY MOTHER'S LIFE I AIN'T EATEN DICED CARROTS SINCE PRIMARY SCHOOL...
NOW I'VE FINISHED PEBBLE DASHING YOUR FLOOR WITH MY GUTS, MAP, YOU WANNA TELL ME JUST WHAT THE ⊛⊛⊛⊛ WAS CHASING ME...?

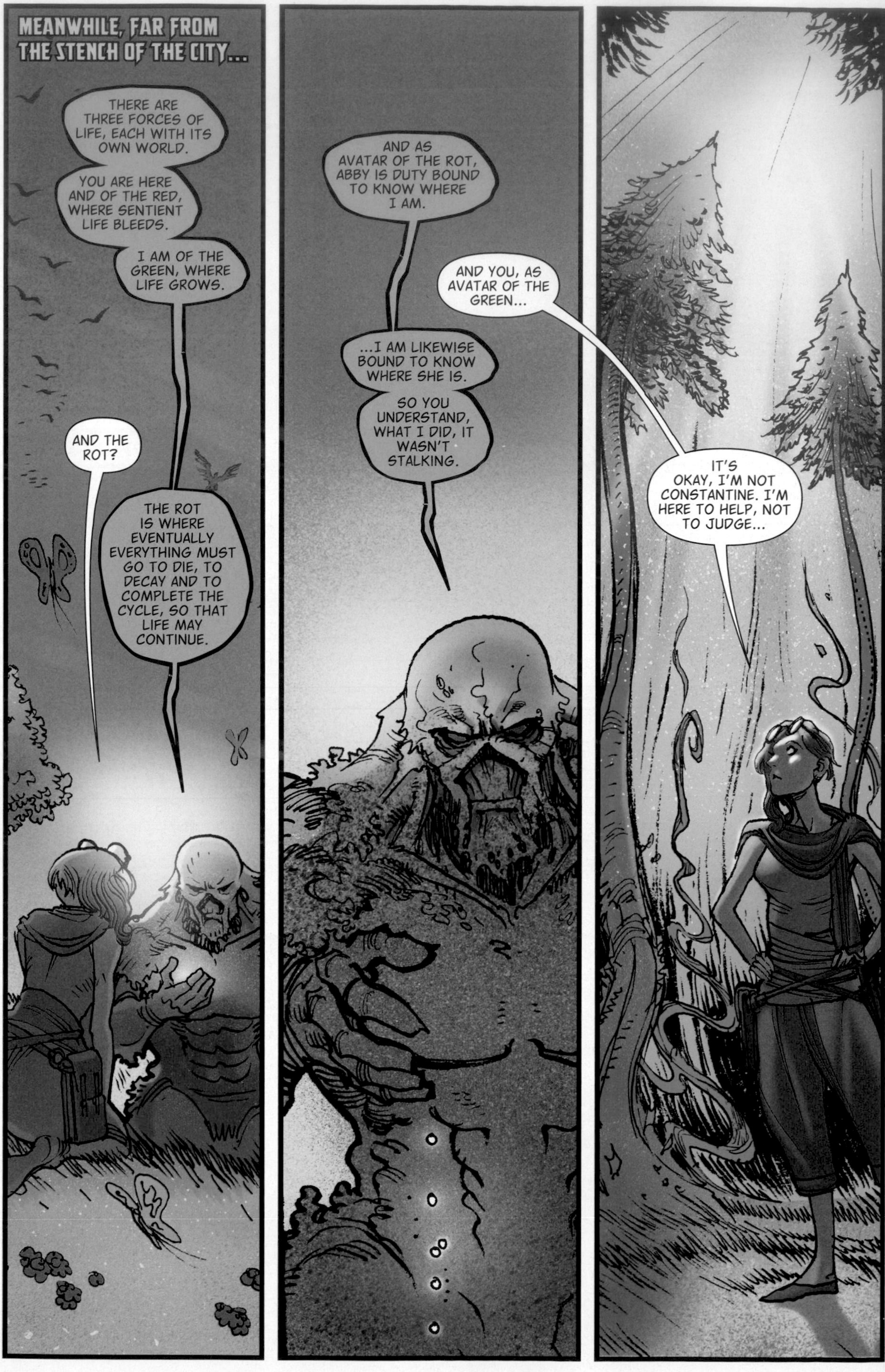

MEANWHILE, FAR FROM THE STENCH OF THE CITY...
THERE ARE THREE FORCES OF LIFE, EACH WITH ITS OWN WORLD.
YOU ARE HERE AND OF THE RED, WHERE SENTIENT LIFE BLEEDS.
I AM OF THE GREEN, WHERE LIFE GROWS.
AND THE ROT?
THE ROT IS WHERE EVENTUALLY EVERYTHING MUST GO TO DIE, TO DECAY AND TO COMPLETE THE CYCLE, SO THAT LIFE MAY CONTINUE.
AND AS AVATAR OF THE ROT, ABBY IS DUTY BOUND TO KNOW WHERE I AM.
...I AM LIKEWISE BOUND TO KNOW WHERE SHE IS.
SO YOU UNDERSTAND, WHAT I DID, IT WASN'T STALKING.
AND YOU, AS AVATAR OF THE GREEN...
IT'S OKAY, I'M NOT CONSTANTINE. I'M HERE TO HELP, NOT TO JUDGE...

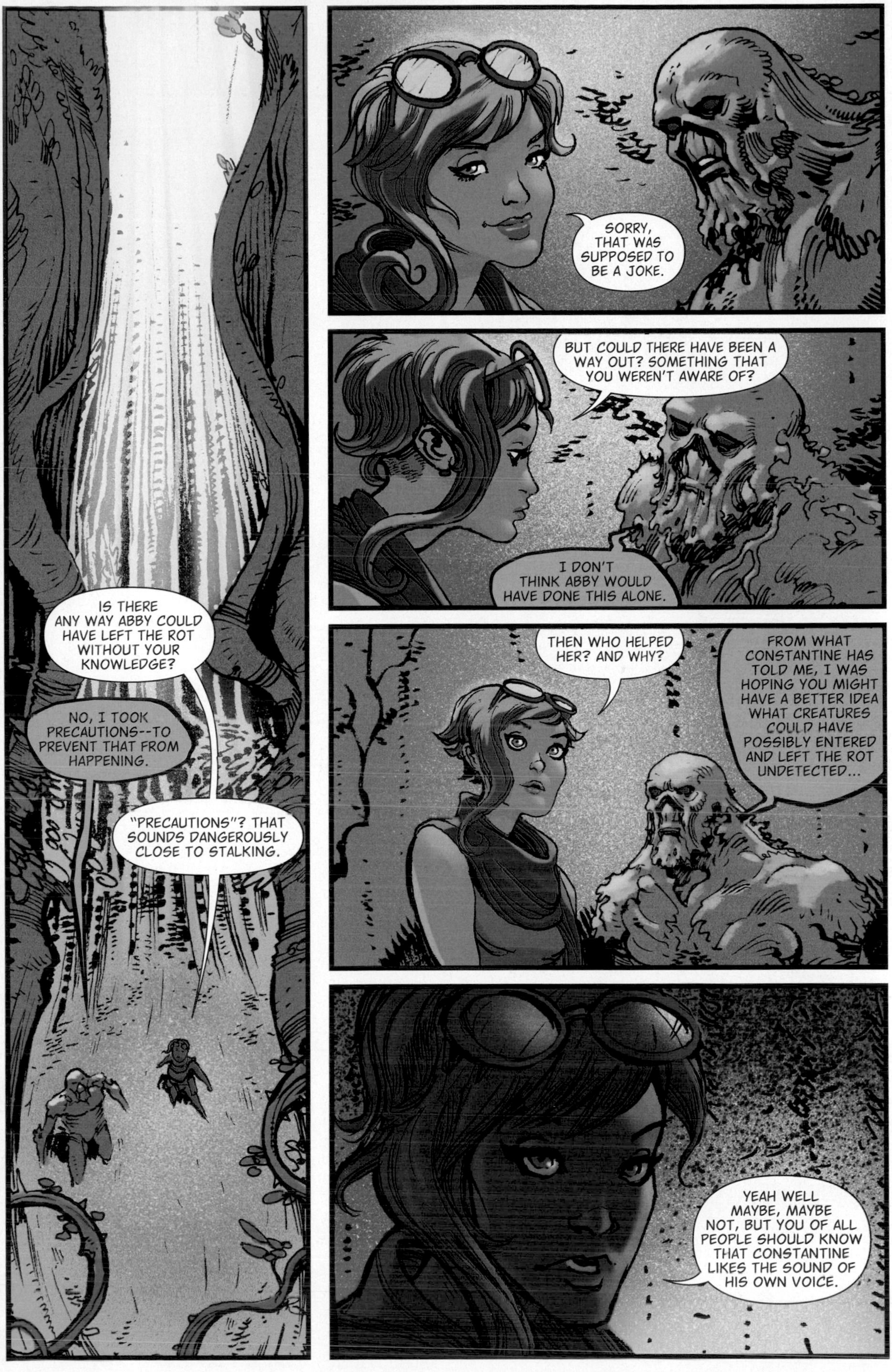
IS THERE ANY WAY ABBY COULD HAVE LEFT THE ROT WITHOUT YOUR KNOWLEDGE?
NO, I TOOK PRECAUTIONS--TO PREVENT THAT FROM HAPPENING.
"PRECAUTIONS"? THAT SOUNDS DANGEROUSLY CLOSE TO STALKING.
SORRY, THAT WAS SUPPOSED TO BE A JOKE.
BUT COULD THERE HAVE BEEN A WAY OUT? SOMETHING THAT YOU WEREN'T AWARE OF?
I DON'T THINK ABBY WOULD HAVE DONE THIS ALONE.
THEN WHO HELPED HER? AND WHY?
FROM WHAT CONSTANTINE HAS TOLD ME, I WAS HOPING YOU MIGHT HAVE A BETTER IDEA WHAT CREATURES COULD HAVE POSSIBLY ENTERED AND LEFT THE ROT UNDETECTED...
YEAH WELL MAYBE, MAYBE NOT, BUT YOU OF ALL PEOPLE SHOULD KNOW THAT CONSTANTINE LIKES THE SOUND OF HIS OWN VOICE.

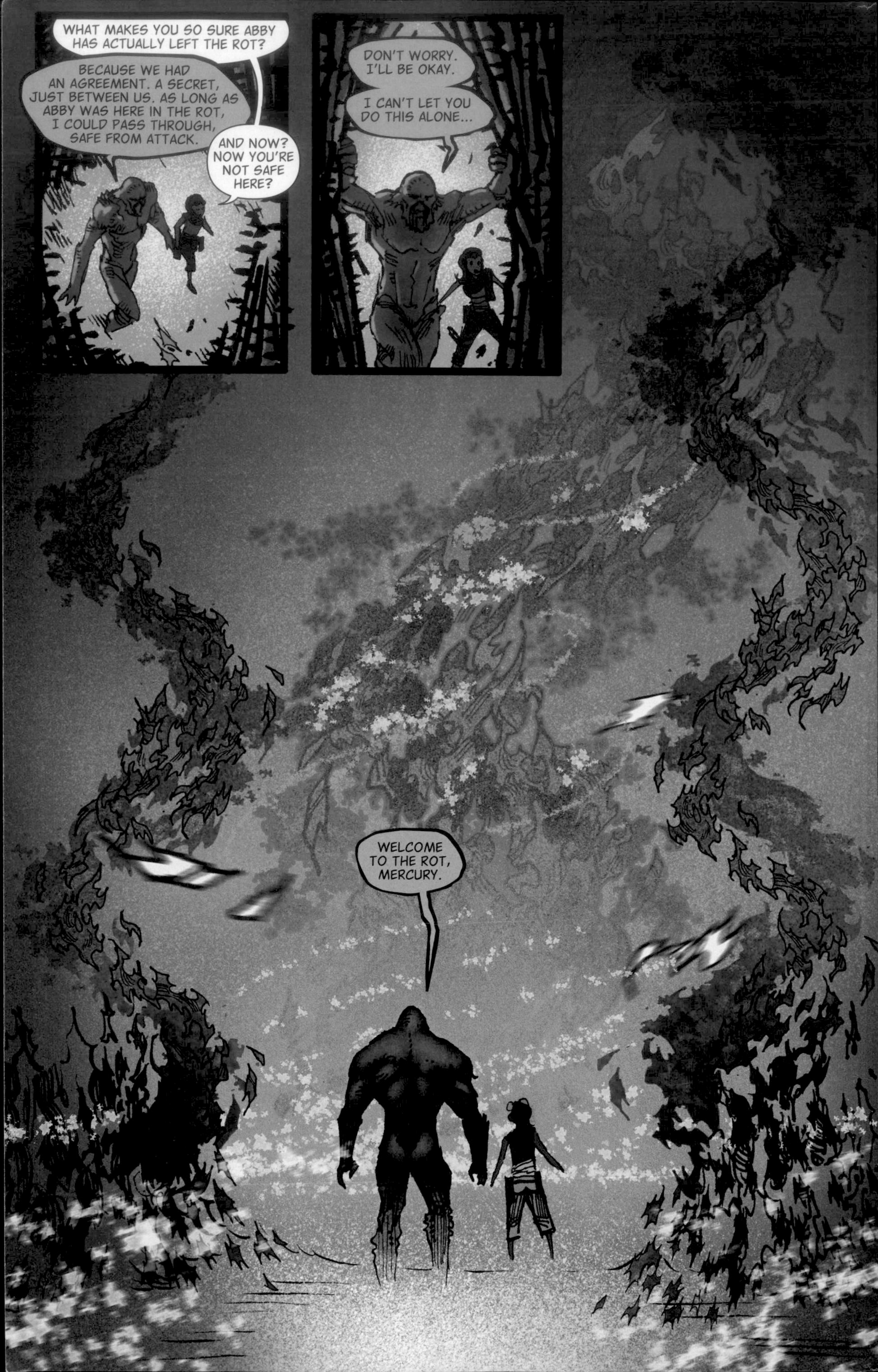
WHAT MAKES YOU SO SURE ABBY HAS ACTUALLY LEFT THE ROT?
BECAUSE WE HAD AN AGREEMENT. A SECRET, JUST BETWEEN US. AS LONG AS ABBY WAS HERE IN THE ROT, I COULD PASS THROUGH, SAFE FROM ATTACK.
AND NOW? NOW YOU'RE NOT SAFE HERE?
DON'T WORRY. I'LL BE OKAY.
I CAN'T LET YOU DO THIS ALONE...
WELCOME TO THE ROT, MERCURY.

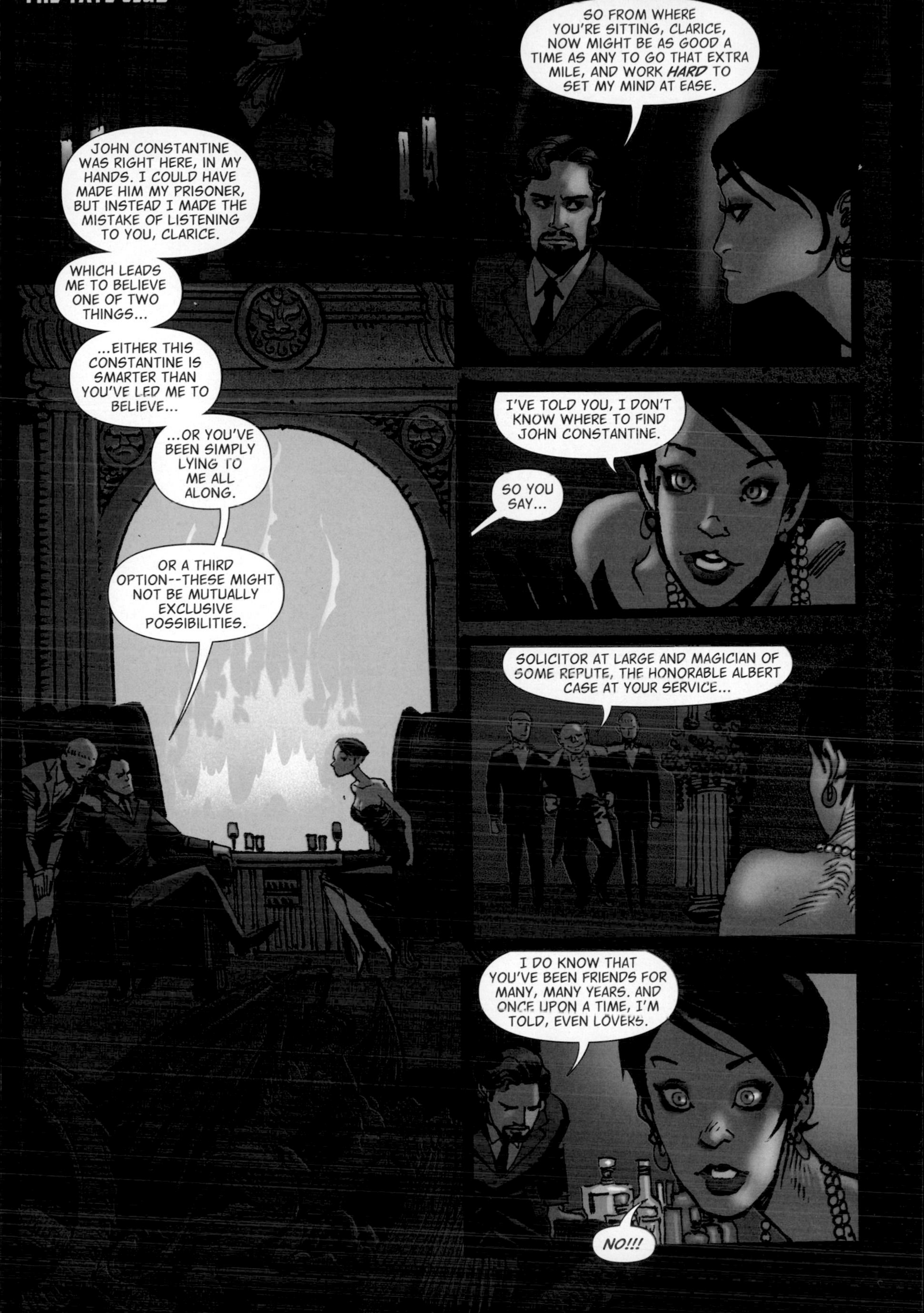
JOHN CONSTANTINE WAS RIGHT HERE, IN MY HANDS. I COULD HAVE MADE HIM MY PRISONER, BUT INSTEAD I MADE THE MISTAKE OF LISTENING TO YOU, CLARICE.
WHICH LEADS ME TO BELIEVE ONE OF TWO THINGS...
...EITHER THIS CONSTANTINE IS SMARTER THAN YOU'VE LED ME TO BELIEVE...
...OR YOU'VE BEEN SIMPLY LYING TO ME ALL ALONG.
OR A THIRD OPTION--THESE MIGHT NOT BE MUTUALLY EXCLUSIVE POSSIBILITIES.
SO FROM WHERE YOU'RE SITTING, CLARICE, NOW MIGHT BE AS GOOD A TIME AS ANY TO GO THAT EXTRA MILE, AND WORK *HARD* TO SET MY MIND AT EASE.
I'VE TOLD YOU, I DON'T KNOW WHERE TO FIND JOHN CONSTANTINE.
SO YOU SAY...
SOLICITOR AT LARGE AND MAGICIAN OF SOME REPUTE, THE HONORABLE ALBERT CASE AT YOUR SERVICE...
I DO KNOW THAT YOU'VE BEEN FRIENDS FOR MANY, MANY YEARS. AND ONCE UPON A TIME, I'M TOLD, EVEN LOVERS.
NO!!!

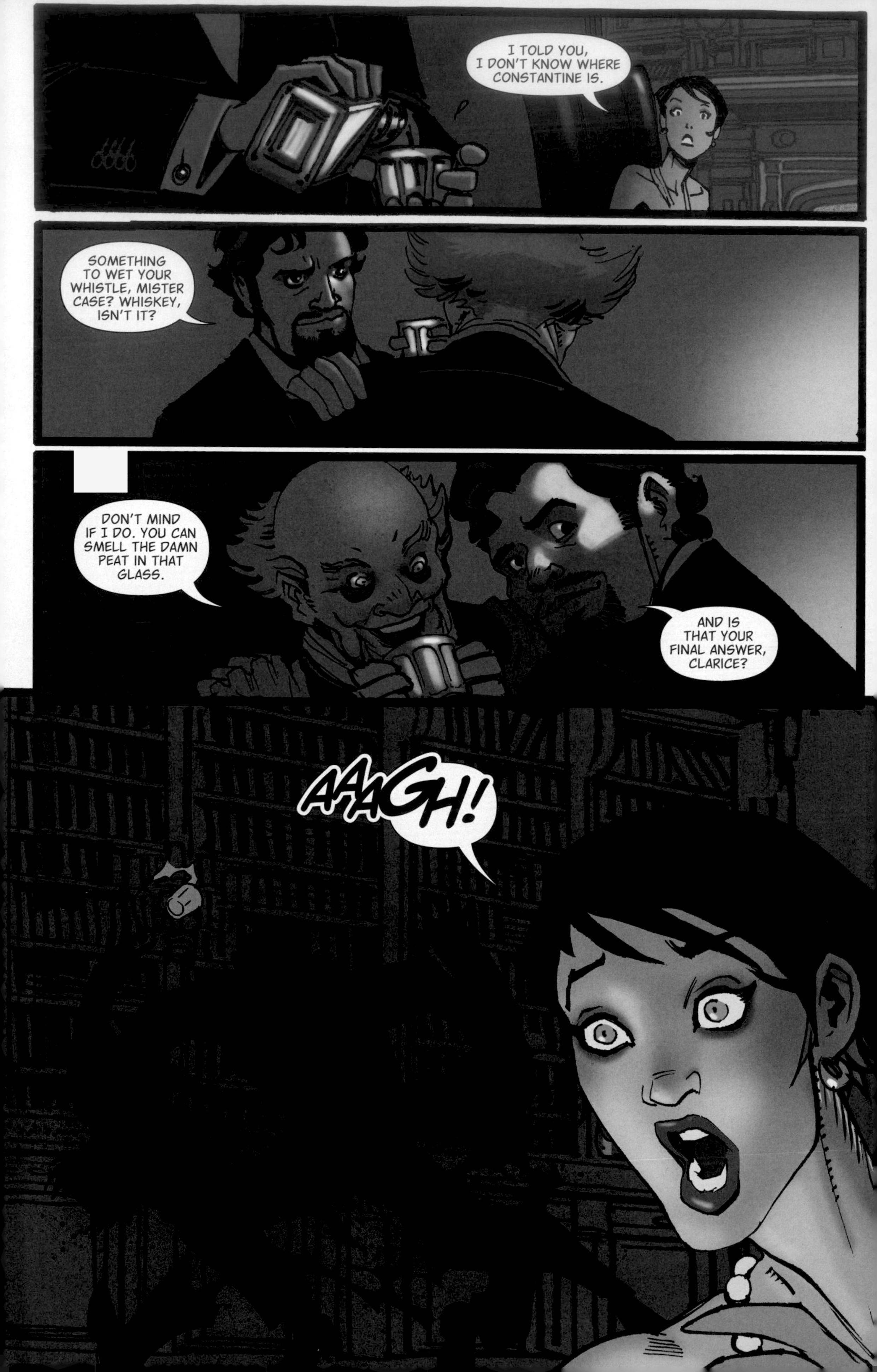
I TOLD YOU, I DON'T KNOW WHERE CONSTANTINE IS.
SOMETHING TO WET YOUR WHISTLE, MISTER CASE? WHISKEY, ISN'T IT?
DON'T MIND IF I DO. YOU CAN SMELL THE DAMN PEAT IN THAT GLASS.
AND IS THAT YOUR FINAL ANSWER, CLARICE?
AAAGH!

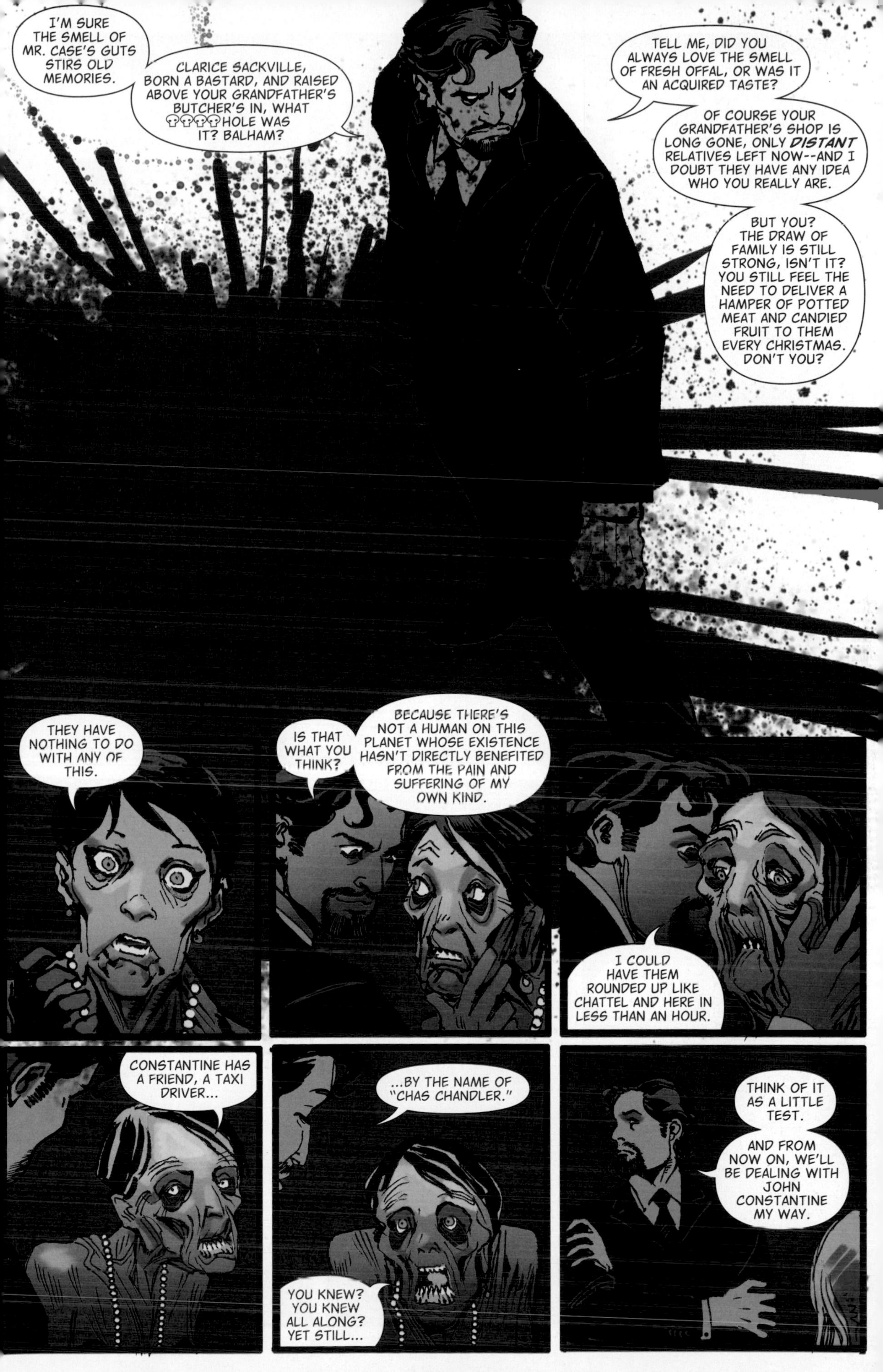
I'M SURE THE SMELL OF MR. CASE'S GUTS STIRS OLD MEMORIES.
CLARICE SACKVILLE, BORN A BASTARD, AND RAISED ABOVE YOUR GRANDFATHER'S BUTCHER'S IN, WHAT ☠☠☠☠HOLE WAS IT? BALHAM?
TELL ME, DID YOU ALWAYS LOVE THE SMELL OF FRESH OFFAL, OR WAS IT AN ACQUIRED TASTE?
OF COURSE YOUR GRANDFATHER'S SHOP IS LONG GONE, ONLY *DISTANT* RELATIVES LEFT NOW--AND I DOUBT THEY HAVE ANY IDEA WHO YOU REALLY ARE.
BUT YOU? THE DRAW OF FAMILY IS STILL STRONG, ISN'T IT? YOU STILL FEEL THE NEED TO DELIVER A HAMPER OF POTTED MEAT AND CANDIED FRUIT TO THEM EVERY CHRISTMAS. DON'T YOU?
THEY HAVE NOTHING TO DO WITH ANY OF THIS.
IS THAT WHAT YOU THINK?
BECAUSE THERE'S NOT A HUMAN ON THIS PLANET WHOSE EXISTENCE HASN'T DIRECTLY BENEFITED FROM THE PAIN AND SUFFERING OF MY OWN KIND.
I COULD HAVE THEM ROUNDED UP LIKE CHATTEL AND HERE IN LESS THAN AN HOUR.
CONSTANTINE HAS A FRIEND, A TAXI DRIVER...
...BY THE NAME OF "CHAS CHANDLER."
YOU KNEW? YOU KNEW ALL ALONG? YET STILL...
THINK OF IT AS A LITTLE TEST.
AND FROM NOW ON, WE'LL BE DEALING WITH JOHN CONSTANTINE MY WAY.

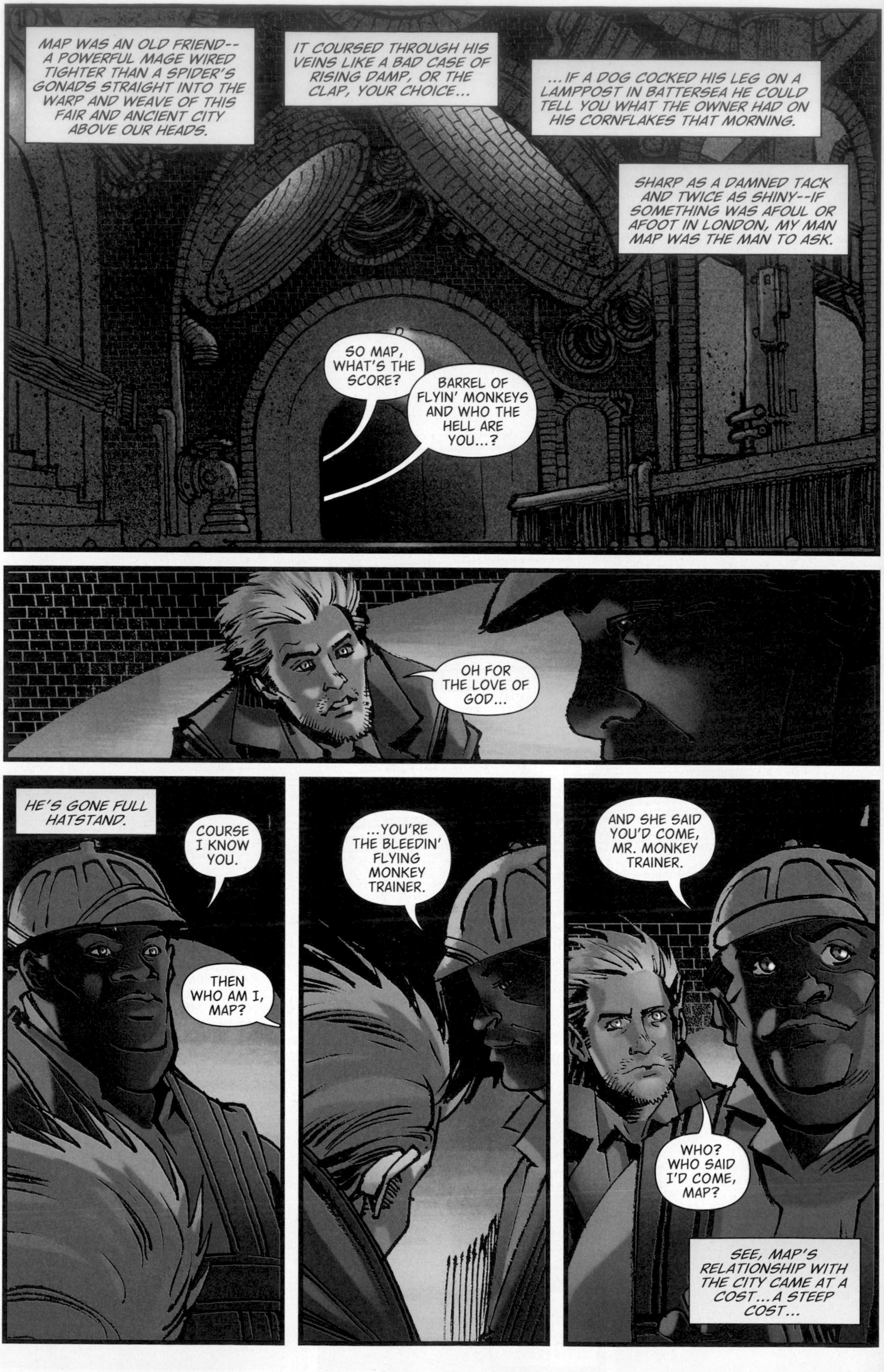
MAP WAS AN OLD FRIEND--A POWERFUL MAGE WIRED TIGHTER THAN A SPIDER'S GONADS STRAIGHT INTO THE WARP AND WEAVE OF THIS FAIR AND ANCIENT CITY ABOVE OUR HEADS.
IT COURSED THROUGH HIS VEINS LIKE A BAD CASE OF RISING DAMP, OR THE CLAP, YOUR CHOICE...
...IF A DOG COCKED HIS LEG ON A LAMPPOST IN BATTERSEA HE COULD TELL YOU WHAT THE OWNER HAD ON HIS CORNFLAKES THAT MORNING.
SHARP AS A DAMNED TACK AND TWICE AS SHINY--IF SOMETHING WAS AFOUL OR AFOOT IN LONDON, MY MAN MAP WAS THE MAN TO ASK.
SO MAP, WHAT'S THE SCORE?
BARREL OF FLYIN' MONKEYS AND WHO THE HELL ARE YOU...?
OH FOR THE LOVE OF GOD...
HE'S GONE FULL HATSTAND.
COURSE I KNOW YOU.
THEN WHO AM I, MAP?
...YOU'RE THE BLEEDIN' FLYING MONKEY TRAINER.
AND SHE SAID YOU'D COME, MR. MONKEY TRAINER.
WHO? WHO SAID I'D COME, MAP?
SEE, MAP'S RELATIONSHIP WITH THE CITY CAME AT A COST...A STEEP COST...

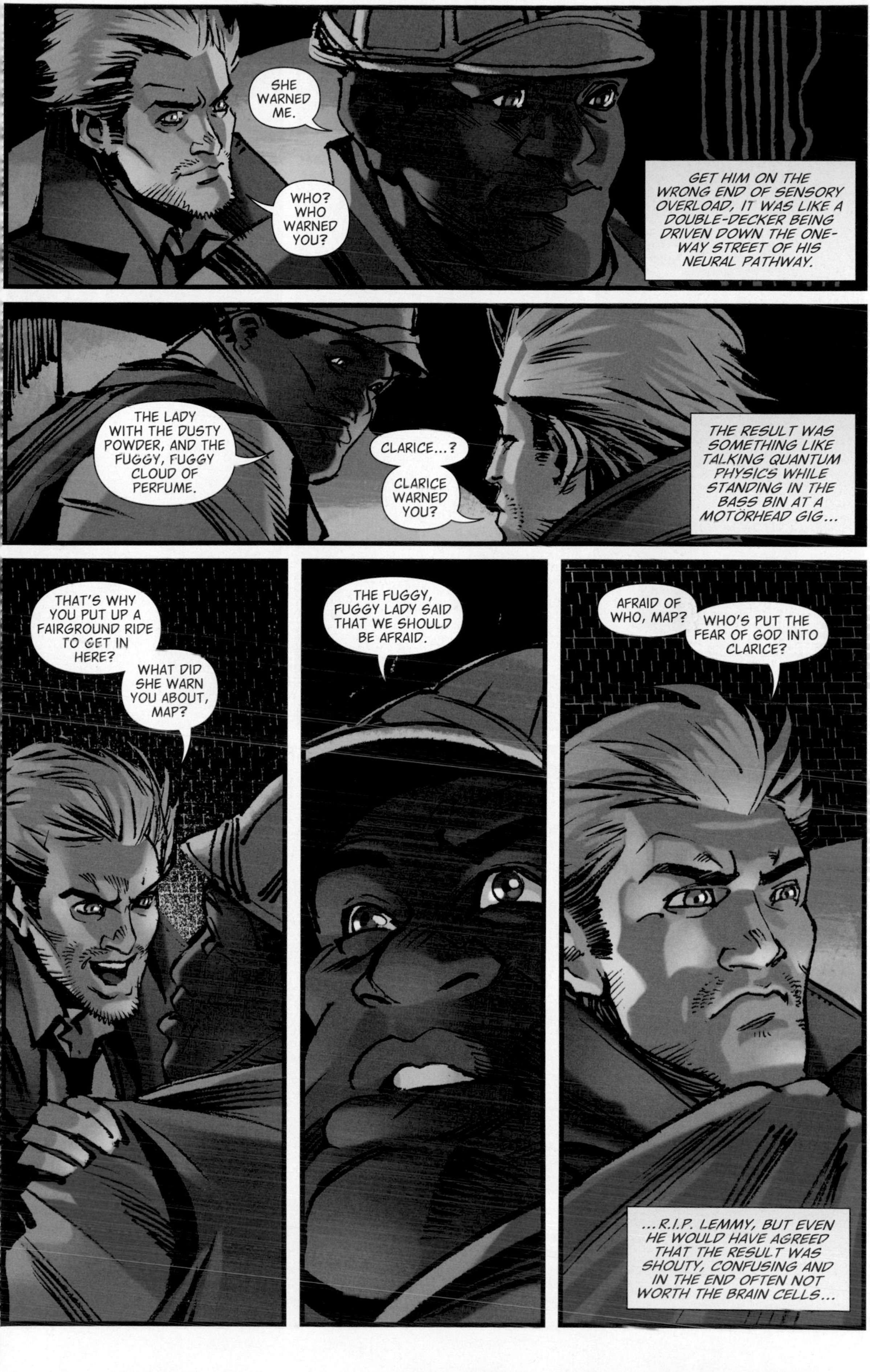
SHE WARNED ME.
WHO? WHO WARNED YOU?
GET HIM ON THE WRONG END OF SENSORY OVERLOAD, IT WAS LIKE A DOUBLE-DECKER BEING DRIVEN DOWN THE ONE-WAY STREET OF HIS NEURAL PATHWAY.
THE LADY WITH THE DUSTY POWDER, AND THE FUGGY, FUGGY CLOUD OF PERFUME.
CLARICE...?
CLARICE WARNED YOU?
THE RESULT WAS SOMETHING LIKE TALKING QUANTUM PHYSICS WHILE STANDING IN THE BASS BIN AT A MOTORHEAD GIG...
THAT'S WHY YOU PUT UP A FAIRGROUND RIDE TO GET IN HERE?
WHAT DID SHE WARN YOU ABOUT, MAP?
THE FUGGY, FUGGY LADY SAID THAT WE SHOULD BE AFRAID.
AFRAID OF WHO, MAP?
WHO'S PUT THE FEAR OF GOD INTO CLARICE?
...R.I.P. LEMMY, BUT EVEN HE WOULD HAVE AGREED THAT THE RESULT WAS SHOUTY, CONFUSING AND IN THE END OFTEN NOT WORTH THE BRAIN CELLS...

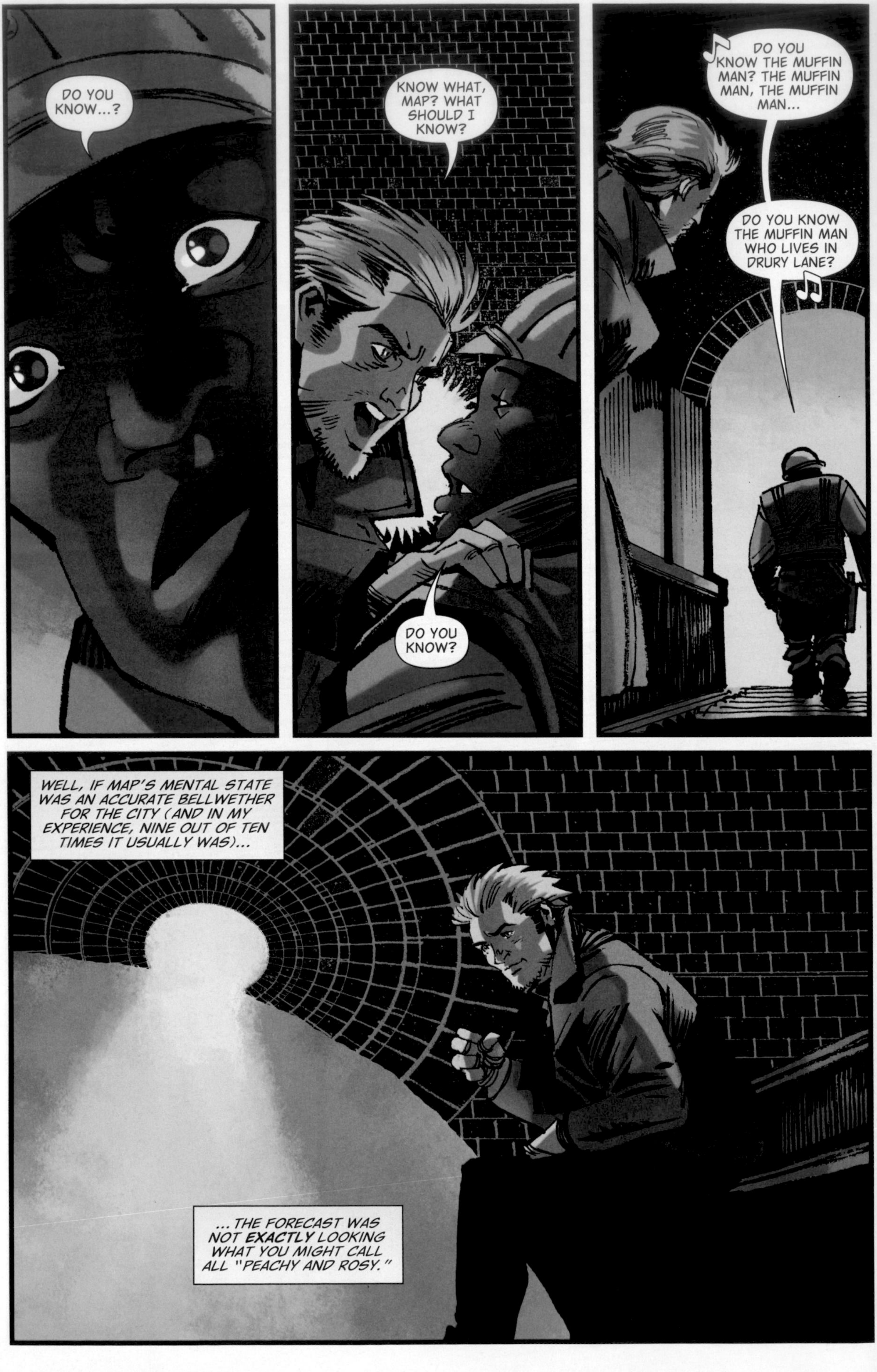
DO YOU KNOW...?
KNOW WHAT, MAP? WHAT SHOULD I KNOW?
DO YOU KNOW?
DO YOU KNOW THE MUFFIN MAN? THE MUFFIN MAN, THE MUFFIN MAN...
DO YOU KNOW THE MUFFIN MAN WHO LIVES IN DRURY LANE?
WELL, IF MAP'S MENTAL STATE WAS AN ACCURATE BELLWETHER FOR THE CITY (AND IN MY EXPERIENCE, NINE OUT OF TEN TIMES IT USUALLY WAS)...
...THE FORECAST WAS NOT EXACTLY LOOKING WHAT YOU MIGHT CALL ALL "PEACHY AND ROSY."

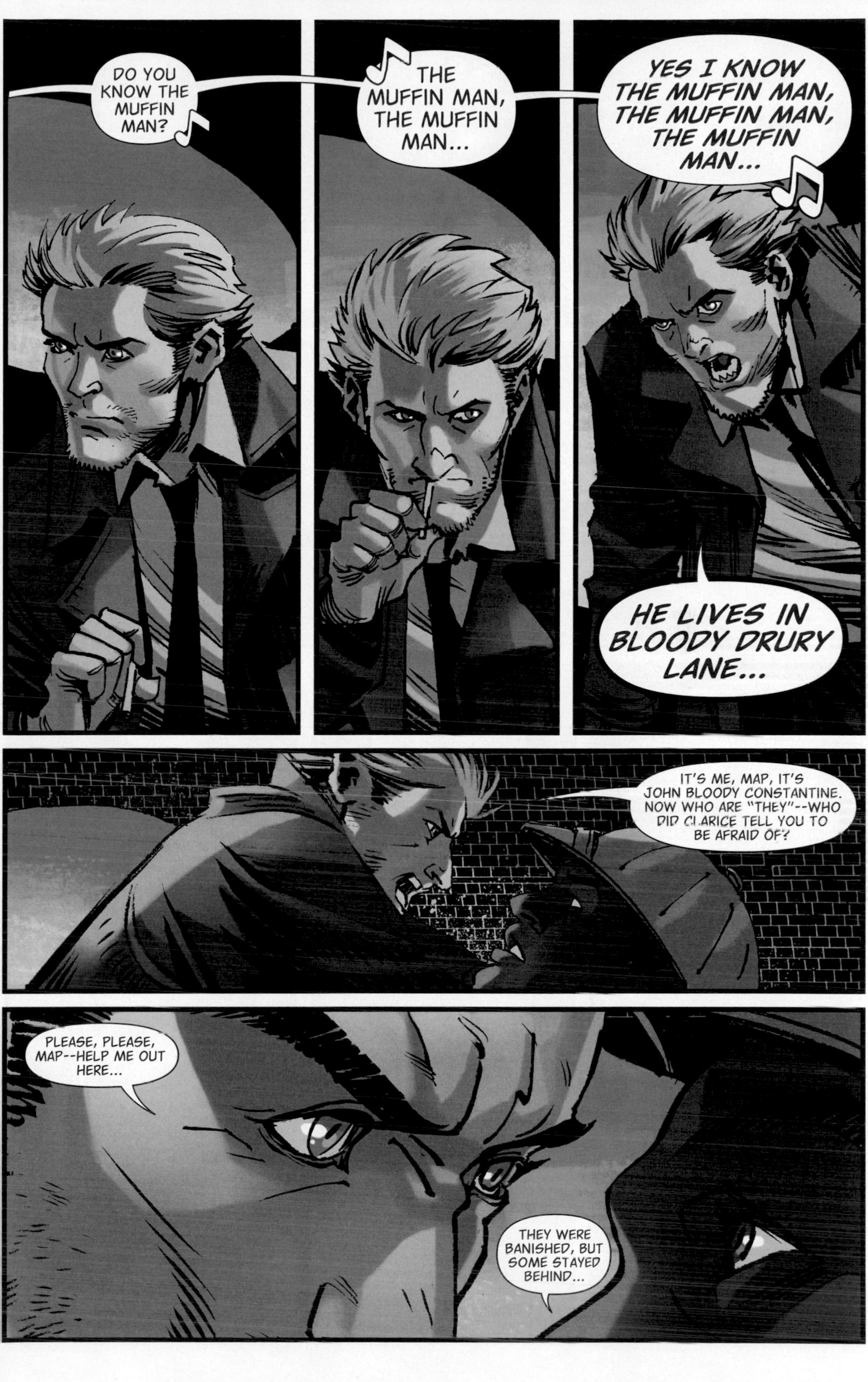
DO YOU KNOW THE MUFFIN MAN?
THE MUFFIN MAN, THE MUFFIN MAN...
YES I KNOW THE MUFFIN MAN, THE MUFFIN MAN, THE MUFFIN MAN...
HE LIVES IN BLOODY DRURY LANE...
IT'S ME, MAP, IT'S JOHN BLOODY CONSTANTINE. NOW WHO ARE "THEY"--WHO DID CLARICE TELL YOU TO BE AFRAID OF?
PLEASE, PLEASE, MAP--HELP ME OUT HERE...
THEY WERE BANISHED, BUT SOME STAYED BEHIND...

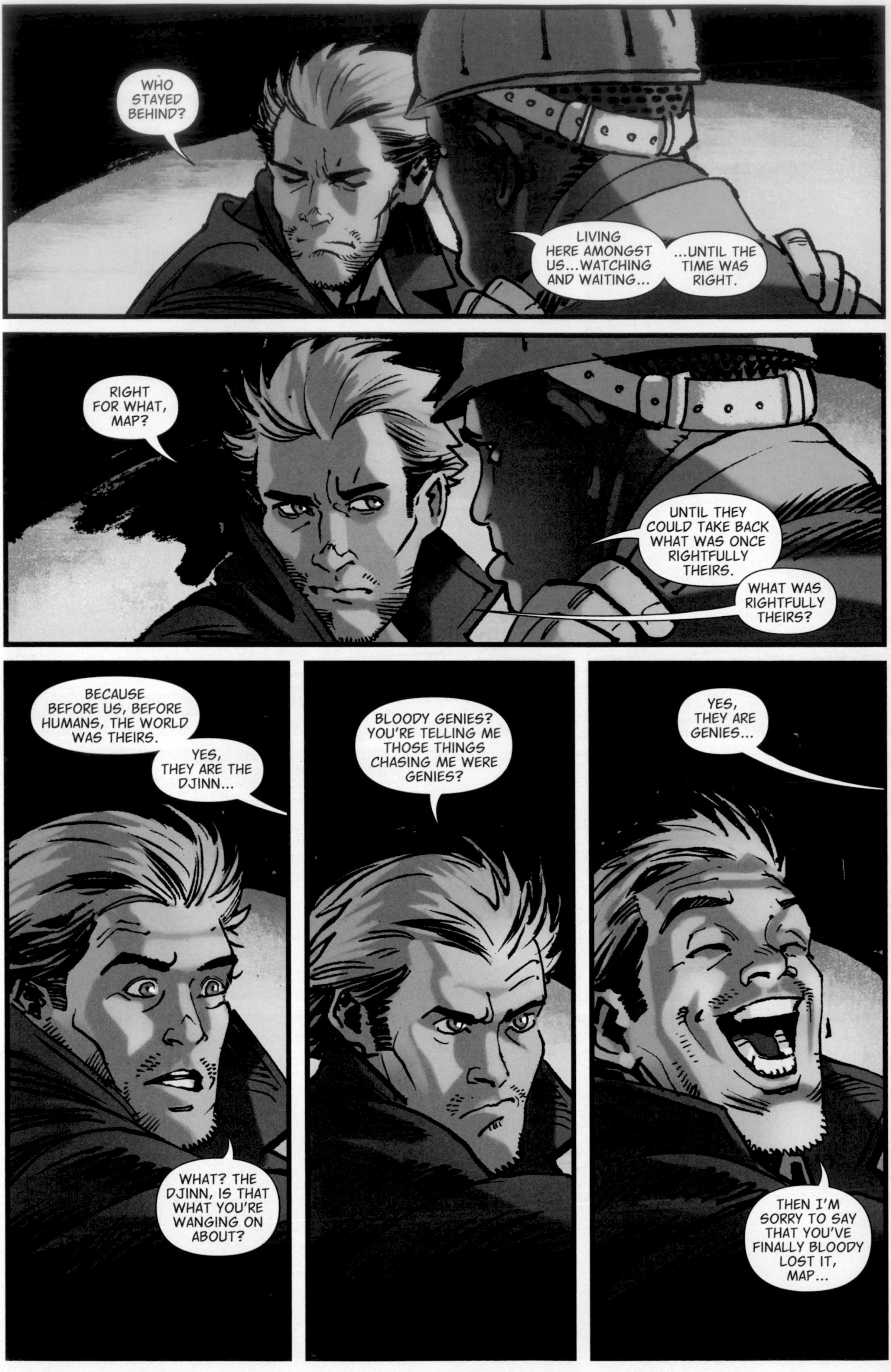
WHO STAYED BEHIND?
LIVING HERE AMONGST US...WATCHING AND WAITING...
...UNTIL THE TIME WAS RIGHT.
RIGHT FOR WHAT, MAP?
UNTIL THEY COULD TAKE BACK WHAT WAS ONCE RIGHTFULLY THEIRS.
WHAT WAS RIGHTFULLY THEIRS?
BECAUSE BEFORE US, BEFORE HUMANS, THE WORLD WAS THEIRS.
YES, THEY ARE THE DJINN...
WHAT? THE DJINN, IS THAT WHAT YOU'RE WANGING ON ABOUT?
BLOODY GENIES? YOU'RE TELLING ME THOSE THINGS CHASING ME WERE GENIES?
YES, THEY ARE GENIES...
THEN I'M SORRY TO SAY THAT YOU'VE FINALLY BLOODY LOST IT, MAP...

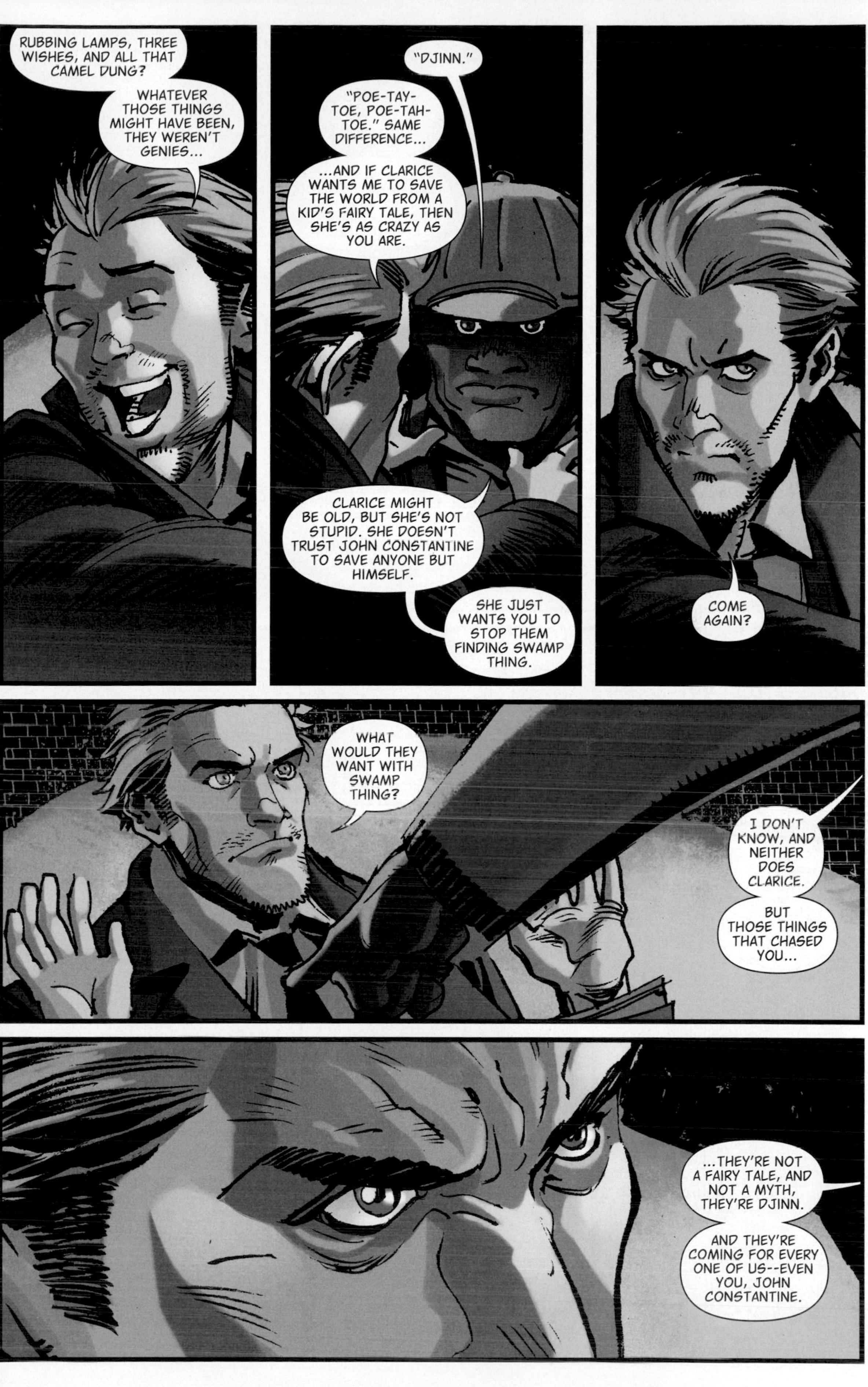
RUBBING LAMPS, THREE WISHES, AND ALL THAT CAMEL DUNG?
WHATEVER THOSE THINGS MIGHT HAVE BEEN, THEY WEREN'T GENIES...
"DJINN."
"POE-TAY-TOE, POE-TAH-TOE." SAME DIFFERENCE...
...AND IF CLARICE WANTS ME TO SAVE THE WORLD FROM A KID'S FAIRY TALE, THEN SHE'S AS CRAZY AS YOU ARE.
CLARICE MIGHT BE OLD, BUT SHE'S NOT STUPID. SHE DOESN'T TRUST JOHN CONSTANTINE TO SAVE ANYONE BUT HIMSELF.
SHE JUST WANTS YOU TO STOP THEM FINDING SWAMP THING.
COME AGAIN?
WHAT WOULD THEY WANT WITH SWAMP THING?
I DON'T KNOW, AND NEITHER DOES CLARICE.
BUT THOSE THINGS THAT CHASED YOU...
...THEY'RE NOT A FAIRY TALE, AND NOT A MYTH, THEY'RE DJINN.
AND THEY'RE COMING FOR EVERY ONE OF US--EVEN YOU, JOHN CONSTANTINE.

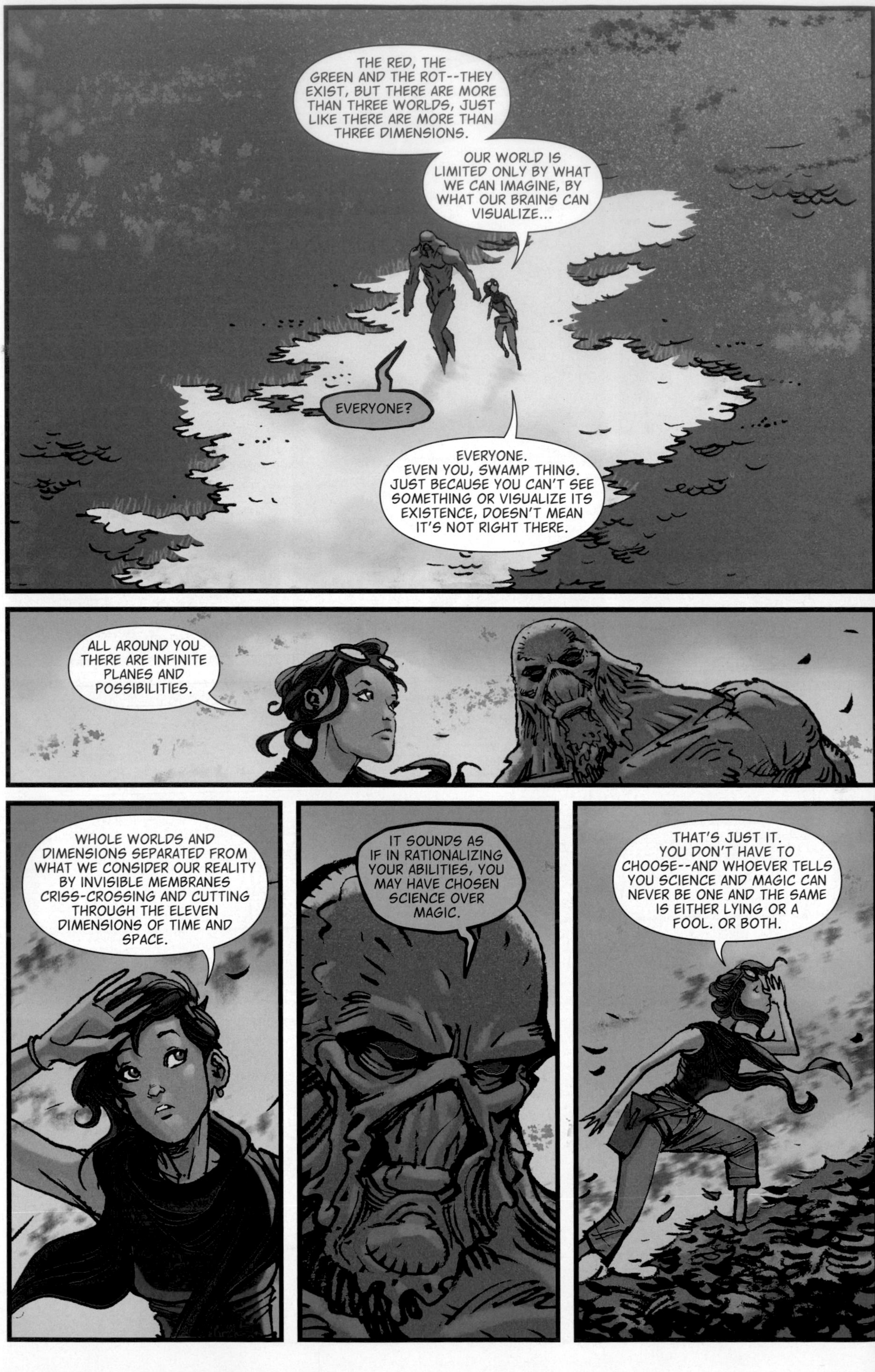
THE RED, THE GREEN AND THE ROT--THEY EXIST, BUT THERE ARE MORE THAN THREE WORLDS, JUST LIKE THERE ARE MORE THAN THREE DIMENSIONS.
OUR WORLD IS LIMITED ONLY BY WHAT WE CAN IMAGINE, BY WHAT OUR BRAINS CAN VISUALIZE...
EVERYONE?
EVERYONE. EVEN YOU, SWAMP THING. JUST BECAUSE YOU CAN'T SEE SOMETHING OR VISUALIZE ITS EXISTENCE, DOESN'T MEAN IT'S NOT RIGHT THERE.
ALL AROUND YOU THERE ARE INFINITE PLANES AND POSSIBILITIES.
WHOLE WORLDS AND DIMENSIONS SEPARATED FROM WHAT WE CONSIDER OUR REALITY BY INVISIBLE MEMBRANES CRISS-CROSSING AND CUTTING THROUGH THE ELEVEN DIMENSIONS OF TIME AND SPACE.
IT SOUNDS AS IF IN RATIONALIZING YOUR ABILITIES, YOU MAY HAVE CHOSEN SCIENCE OVER MAGIC.
THAT'S JUST IT. YOU DON'T HAVE TO CHOOSE--AND WHOEVER TELLS YOU SCIENCE AND MAGIC CAN NEVER BE ONE AND THE SAME IS EITHER LYING OR A FOOL. OR BOTH.

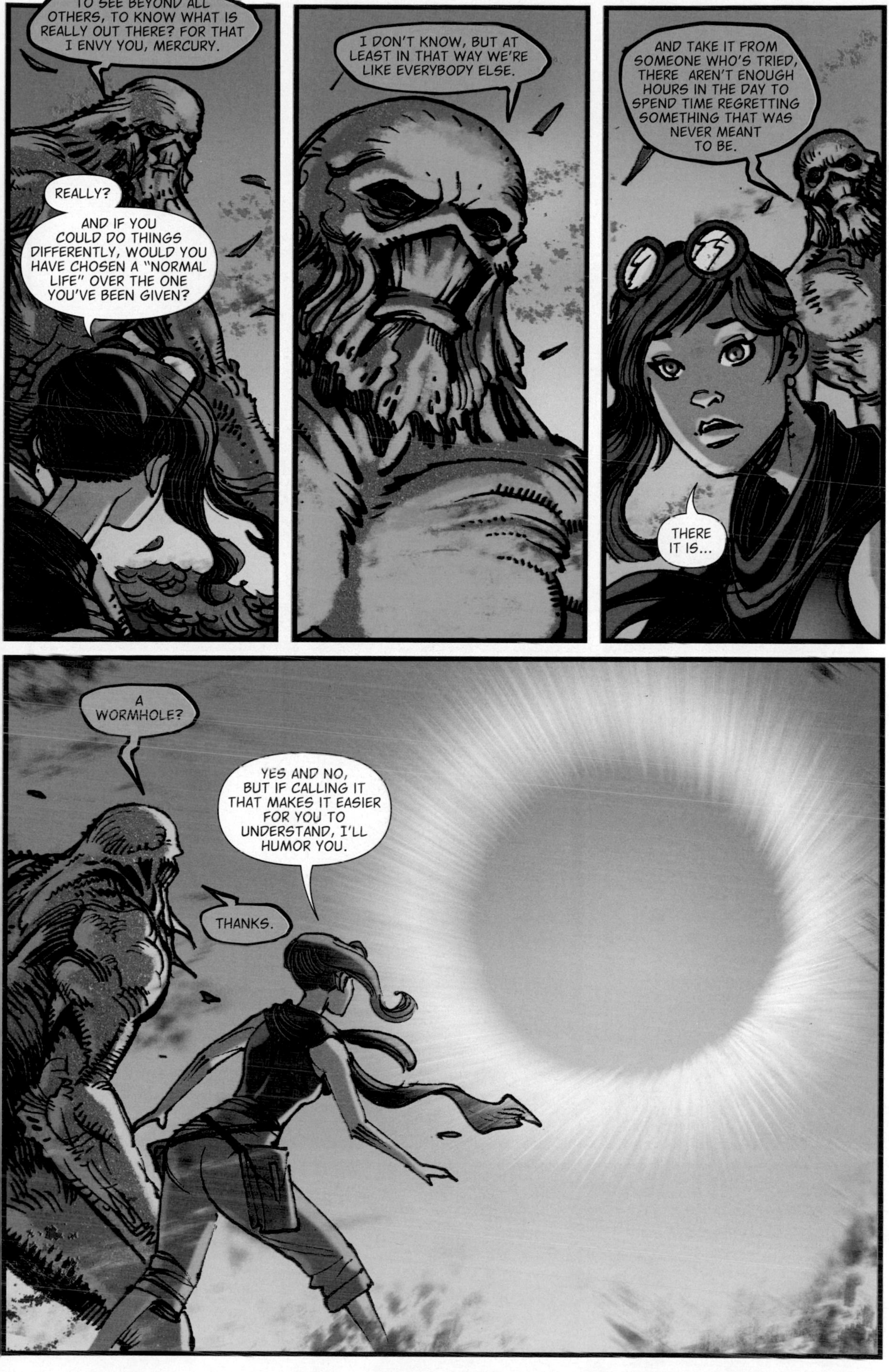
TO SEE BEYOND ALL OTHERS, TO KNOW WHAT IS REALLY OUT THERE? FOR THAT I ENVY YOU, MERCURY.
REALLY?
AND IF YOU COULD DO THINGS DIFFERENTLY, WOULD YOU HAVE CHOSEN A "NORMAL LIFE" OVER THE ONE YOU'VE BEEN GIVEN?
I DON'T KNOW, BUT AT LEAST IN THAT WAY WE'RE LIKE EVERYBODY ELSE.
AND TAKE IT FROM SOMEONE WHO'S TRIED, THERE AREN'T ENOUGH HOURS IN THE DAY TO SPEND TIME REGRETTING SOMETHING THAT WAS NEVER MEANT TO BE.
THERE IT IS...
A WORMHOLE?
YES AND NO, BUT IF CALLING IT THAT MAKES IT EASIER FOR YOU TO UNDERSTAND, I'LL HUMOR YOU.
THANKS.

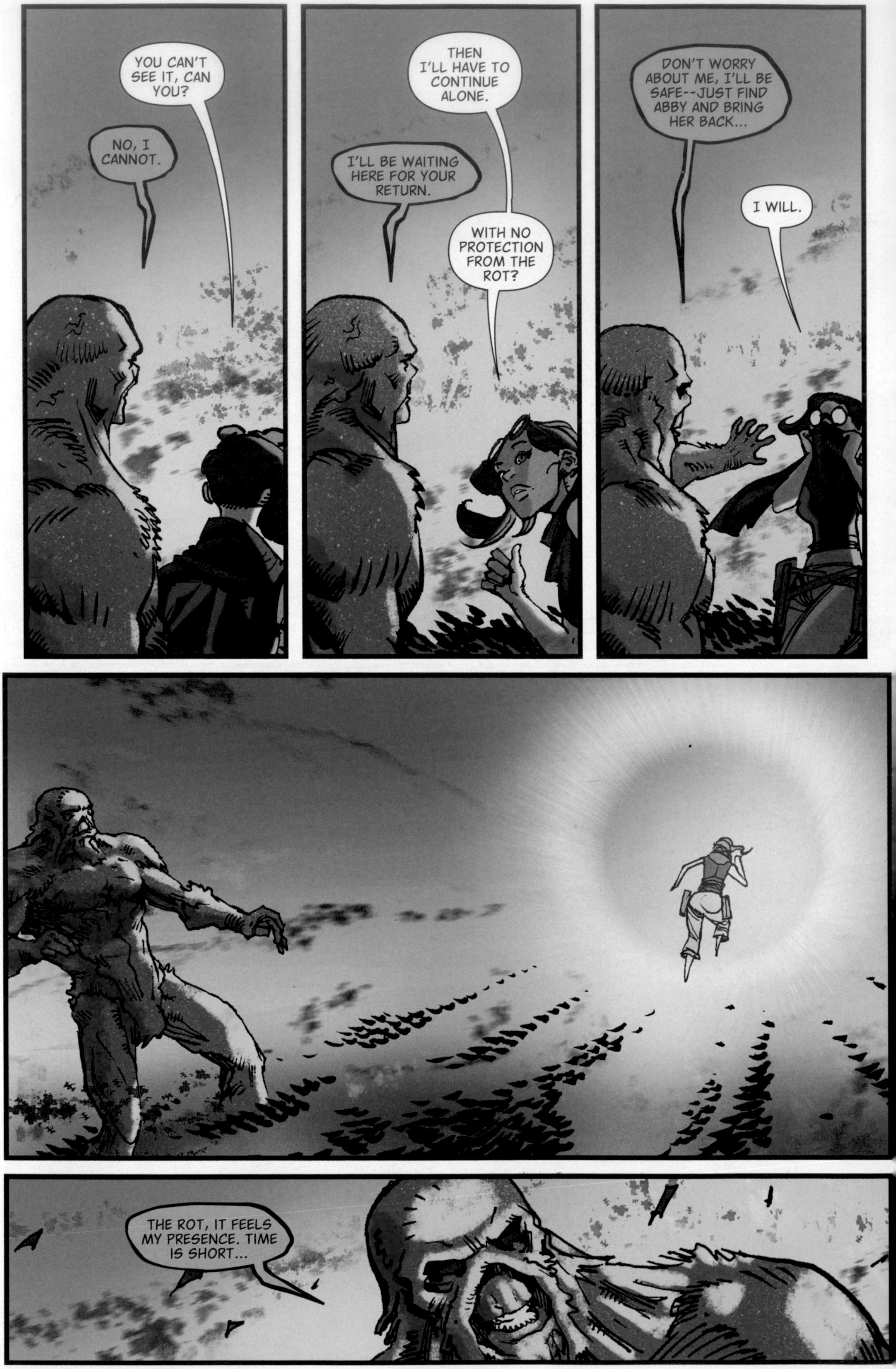

YOU CAN'T SEE IT, CAN YOU?
NO, I CANNOT.
THEN I'LL HAVE TO CONTINUE ALONE.
I'LL BE WAITING HERE FOR YOUR RETURN.
WITH NO PROTECTION FROM THE ROT?
DON'T WORRY ABOUT ME, I'LL BE SAFE--JUST FIND ABBY AND BRING HER BACK...
I WILL.
THE ROT, IT FEELS MY PRESENCE. TIME IS SHORT...

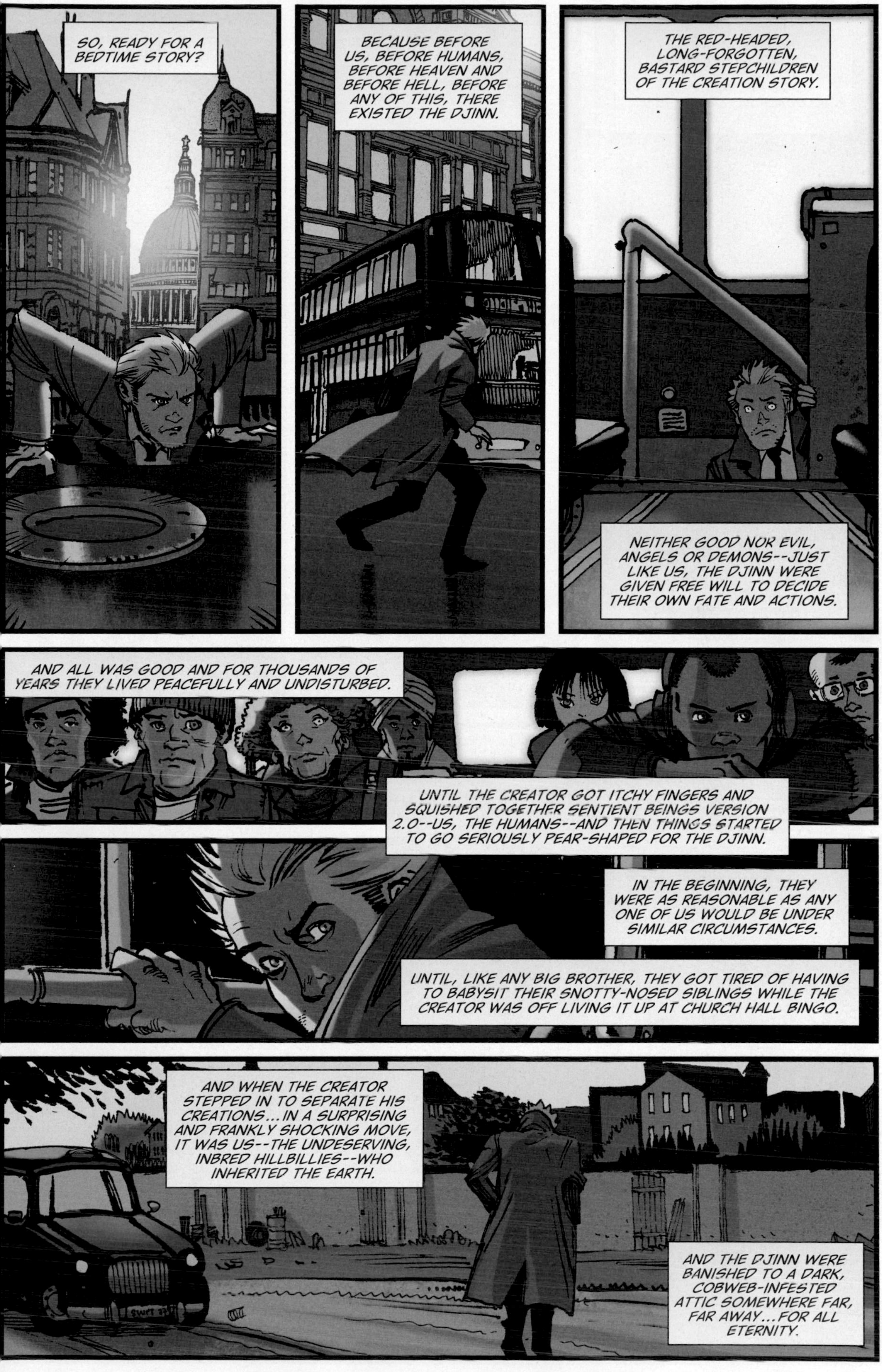
SO, READY FOR A BEDTIME STORY?
BECAUSE BEFORE US, BEFORE HUMANS, BEFORE HEAVEN AND BEFORE HELL, BEFORE ANY OF THIS, THERE EXISTED THE DJINN.
THE RED-HEADED, LONG-FORGOTTEN, BASTARD STEPCHILDREN OF THE CREATION STORY.
NEITHER GOOD NOR EVIL, ANGELS OR DEMONS--JUST LIKE US, THE DJINN WERE GIVEN FREE WILL TO DECIDE THEIR OWN FATE AND ACTIONS.
AND ALL WAS GOOD AND FOR THOUSANDS OF YEARS THEY LIVED PEACEFULLY AND UNDISTURBED.
UNTIL THE CREATOR GOT ITCHY FINGERS AND SQUISHED TOGETHER SENTIENT BEINGS VERSION 2.0--US, THE HUMANS--AND THEN THINGS STARTED TO GO SERIOUSLY PEAR-SHAPED FOR THE DJINN.
IN THE BEGINNING, THEY WERE AS REASONABLE AS ANY ONE OF US WOULD BE UNDER SIMILAR CIRCUMSTANCES.
UNTIL, LIKE ANY BIG BROTHER, THEY GOT TIRED OF HAVING TO BABYSIT THEIR SNOTTY-NOSED SIBLINGS WHILE THE CREATOR WAS OFF LIVING IT UP AT CHURCH HALL BINGO.
AND WHEN THE CREATOR STEPPED IN TO SEPARATE HIS CREATIONS... IN A SURPRISING AND FRANKLY SHOCKING MOVE, IT WAS US--THE UNDESERVING, INBRED HILLBILLIES--WHO INHERITED THE EARTH.
AND THE DJINN WERE BANISHED TO A DARK, COBWEB-INFESTED ATTIC SOMEWHERE FAR, FAR AWAY... FOR ALL ETERNITY.

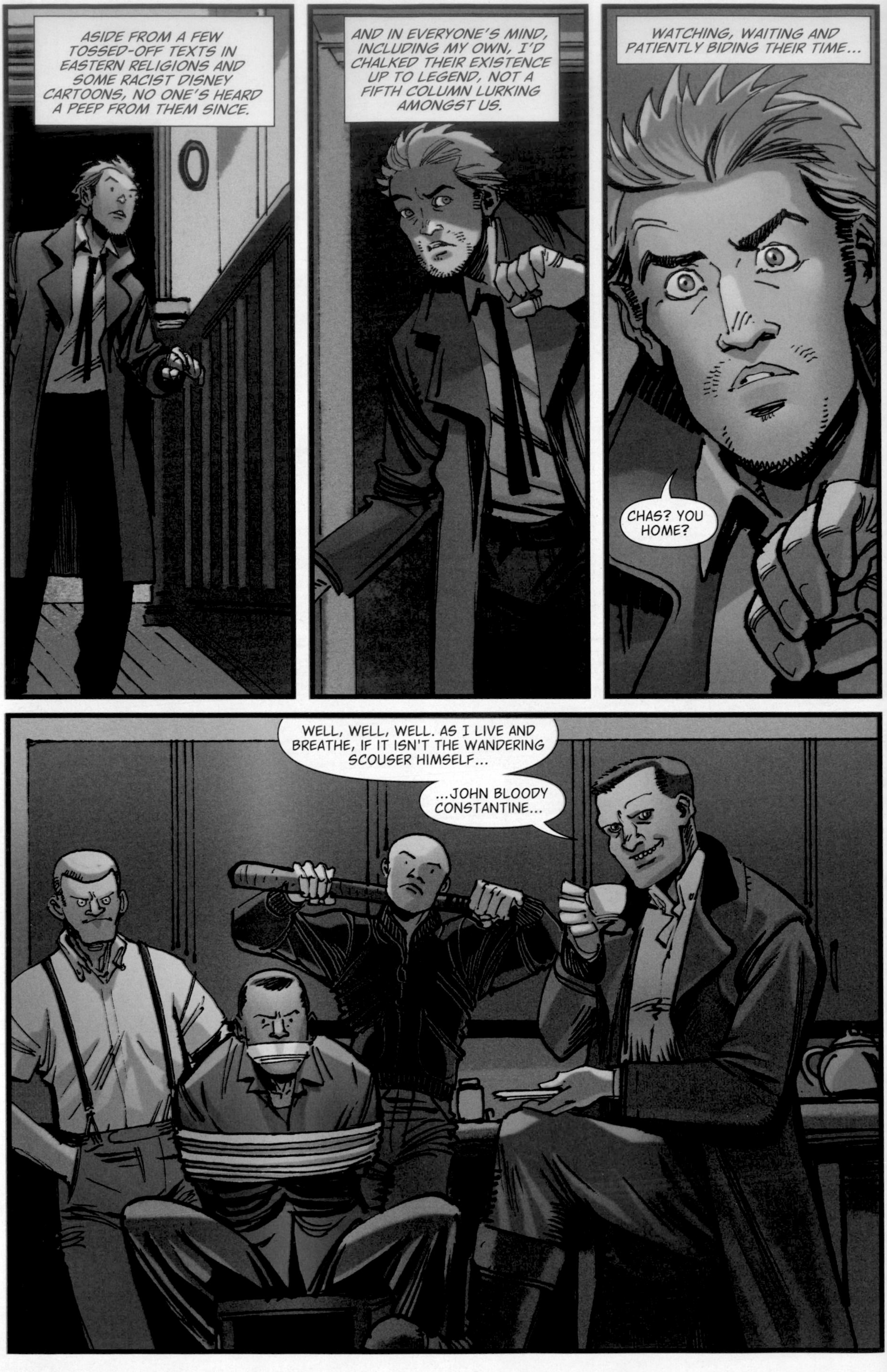
ASIDE FROM A FEW TOSSED-OFF TEXTS IN EASTERN RELIGIONS AND SOME RACIST DISNEY CARTOONS, NO ONE'S HEARD A PEEP FROM THEM SINCE.
AND IN EVERYONE'S MIND, INCLUDING MY OWN, I'D CHALKED THEIR EXISTENCE UP TO LEGEND, NOT A FIFTH COLUMN LURKING AMONGST US.
WATCHING, WAITING AND PATIENTLY BIDING THEIR TIME...
CHAS? YOU HOME?
WELL, WELL, WELL. AS I LIVE AND BREATHE, IF IT ISN'T THE WANDERING SCOUSER HIMSELF...
...JOHN BLOODY CONSTANTINE...

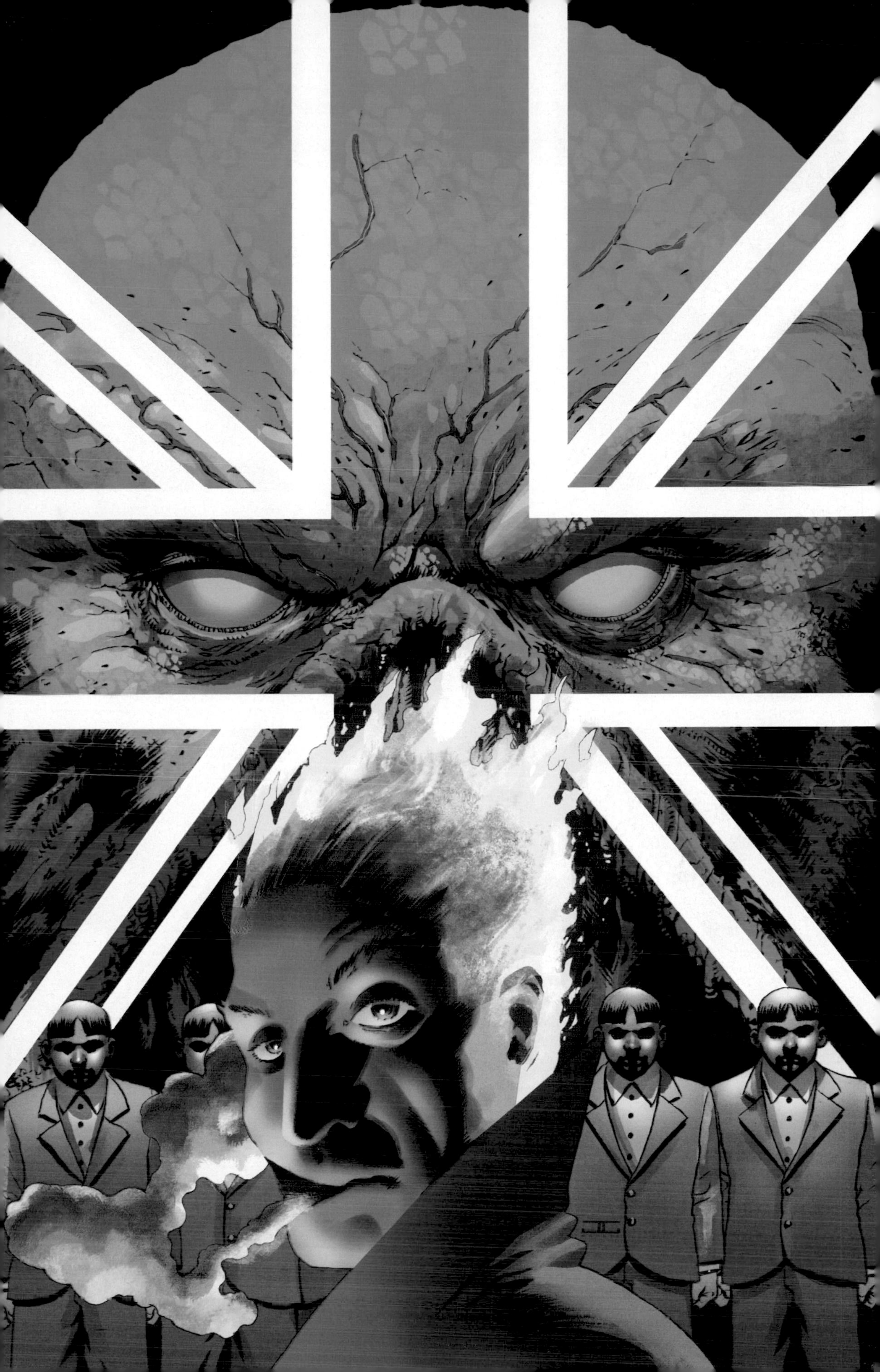

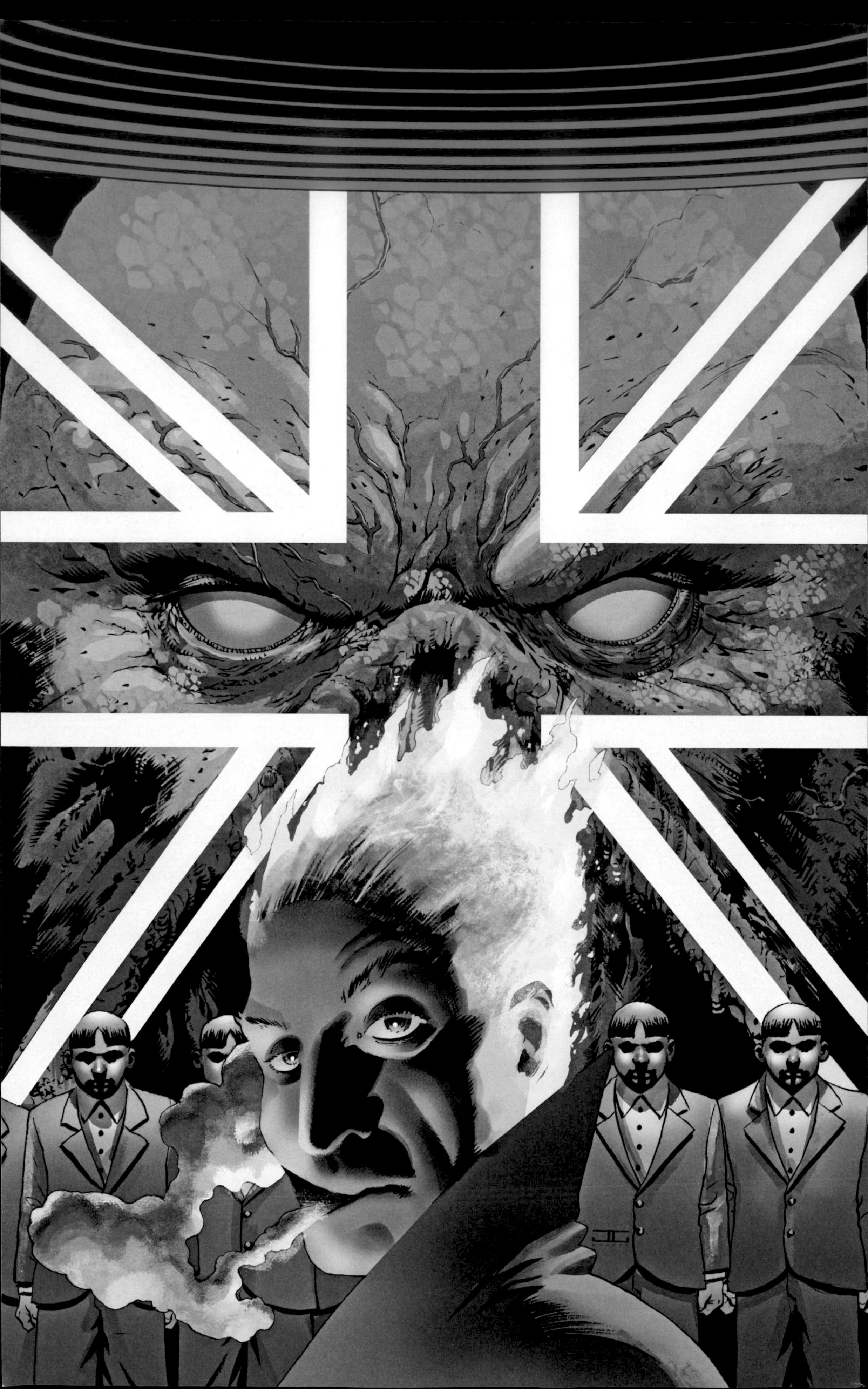

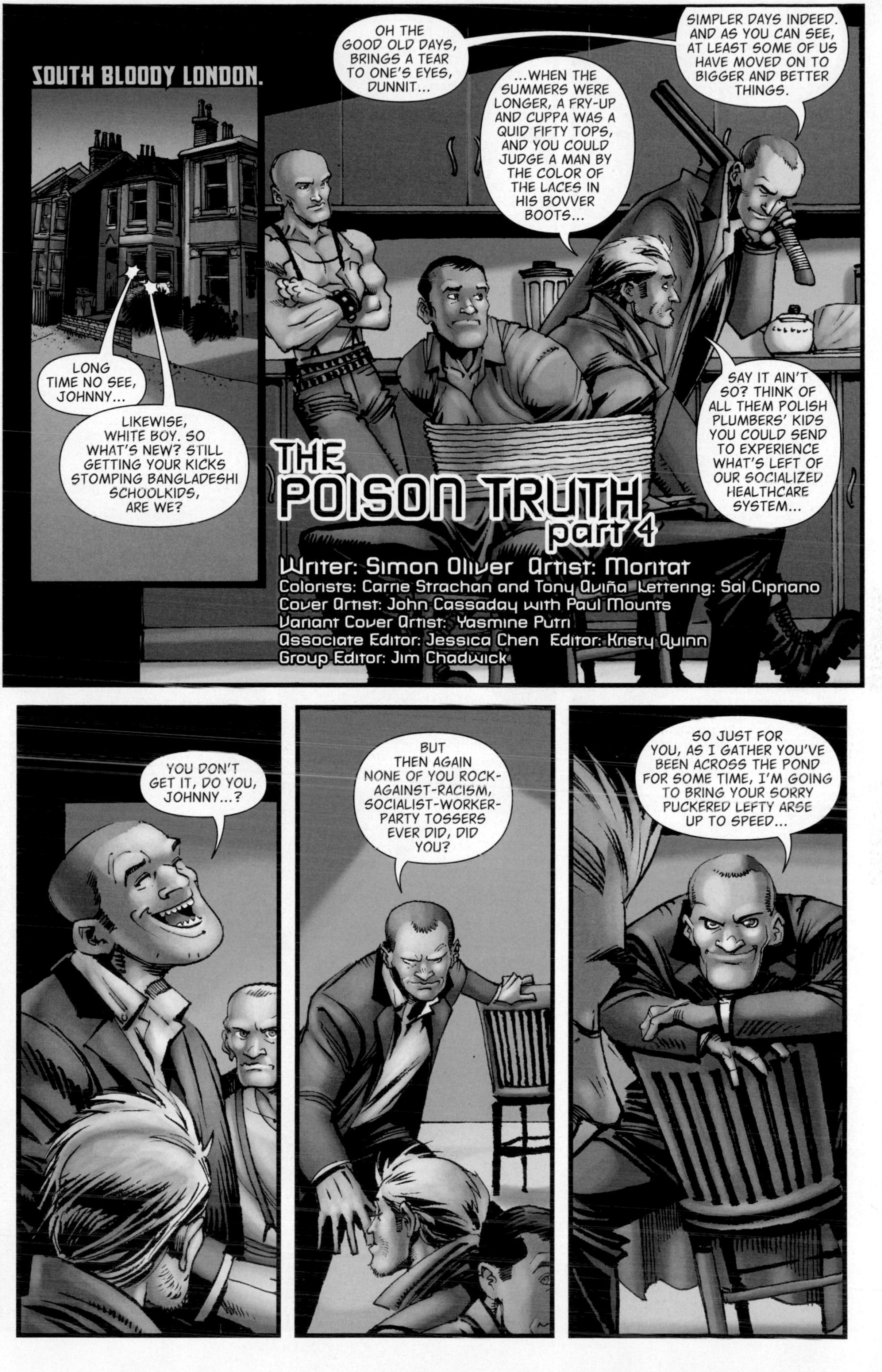
SOUTH BLOODY LONDON.
LONG TIME NO SEE, JOHNNY...
LIKEWISE, WHITE BOY. SO WHAT'S NEW? STILL GETTING YOUR KICKS STOMPING BANGLADESHI SCHOOLKIDS, ARE WE?
OH THE GOOD OLD DAYS, BRINGS A TEAR TO ONE'S EYES, DUNNIT...
...WHEN THE SUMMERS WERE LONGER, A FRY-UP AND CUPPA WAS A QUID FIFTY TOPS, AND YOU COULD JUDGE A MAN BY THE COLOR OF THE LACES IN HIS BOVVER BOOTS...
SIMPLER DAYS INDEED. AND AS YOU CAN SEE, AT LEAST SOME OF US HAVE MOVED ON TO BIGGER AND BETTER THINGS.
SAY IT AIN'T SO? THINK OF ALL THEM POLISH PLUMBERS' KIDS YOU COULD SEND TO EXPERIENCE WHAT'S LEFT OF OUR SOCIALIZED HEALTHCARE SYSTEM...
THE POISON TRUTH part 4
Writer: Simon Oliver Artist: Moritat
Colorists: Carrie Strachan and Tony Aviña Lettering: Sal Cipriano
Cover Artist: John Cassaday with Paul Mounts
Variant Cover Artist: Yasmine Putri
Associate Editor: Jessica Chen Editor: Kristy Quinn
Group Editor: Jim Chadwick
YOU DON'T GET IT, DO YOU, JOHNNY...?
BUT THEN AGAIN NONE OF YOU ROCK-AGAINST-RACISM, SOCIALIST-WORKER-PARTY TOSSERS EVER DID, DID YOU?
SO JUST FOR YOU, AS I GATHER YOU'VE BEEN ACROSS THE POND FOR SOME TIME, I'M GOING TO BRING YOUR SORRY PUCKERED LEFTY ARSE UP TO SPEED...

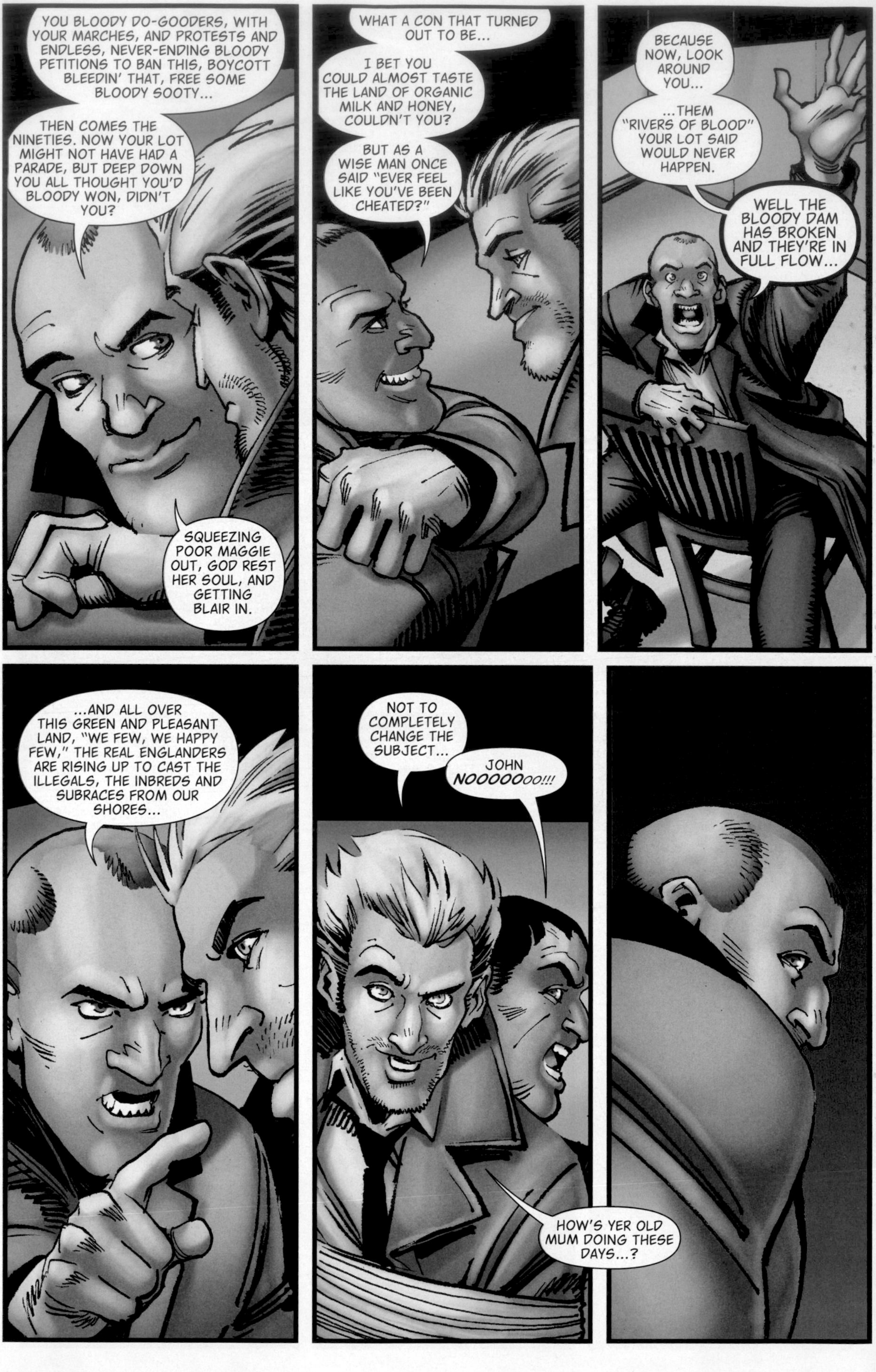
YOU BLOODY DO-GOODERS, WITH YOUR MARCHES, AND PROTESTS AND ENDLESS, NEVER-ENDING BLOODY PETITIONS TO BAN THIS, BOYCOTT BLEEDIN' THAT, FREE SOME BLOODY SOOTY...
THEN COMES THE NINETIES. NOW YOUR LOT MIGHT NOT HAVE HAD A PARADE, BUT DEEP DOWN YOU ALL THOUGHT YOU'D BLOODY WON, DIDN'T YOU?
SQUEEZING POOR MAGGIE OUT, GOD REST HER SOUL, AND GETTING BLAIR IN.
WHAT A CON THAT TURNED OUT TO BE...
I BET YOU COULD ALMOST TASTE THE LAND OF ORGANIC MILK AND HONEY, COULDN'T YOU?
BUT AS A WISE MAN ONCE SAID "EVER FEEL LIKE YOU'VE BEEN CHEATED?"
BECAUSE NOW, LOOK AROUND YOU...
...THEM "RIVERS OF BLOOD" YOUR LOT SAID WOULD NEVER HAPPEN.
WELL THE BLOODY DAM HAS BROKEN AND THEY'RE IN FULL FLOW...
...AND ALL OVER THIS GREEN AND PLEASANT LAND, "WE FEW, WE HAPPY FEW," THE REAL ENGLANDERS ARE RISING UP TO CAST THE ILLEGALS, THE INBREDS AND SUBRACES FROM OUR SHORES...
NOT TO COMPLETELY CHANGE THE SUBJECT...
JOHN NOOOOOoo!!!
HOW'S YER OLD MUM DOING THESE DAYS...?

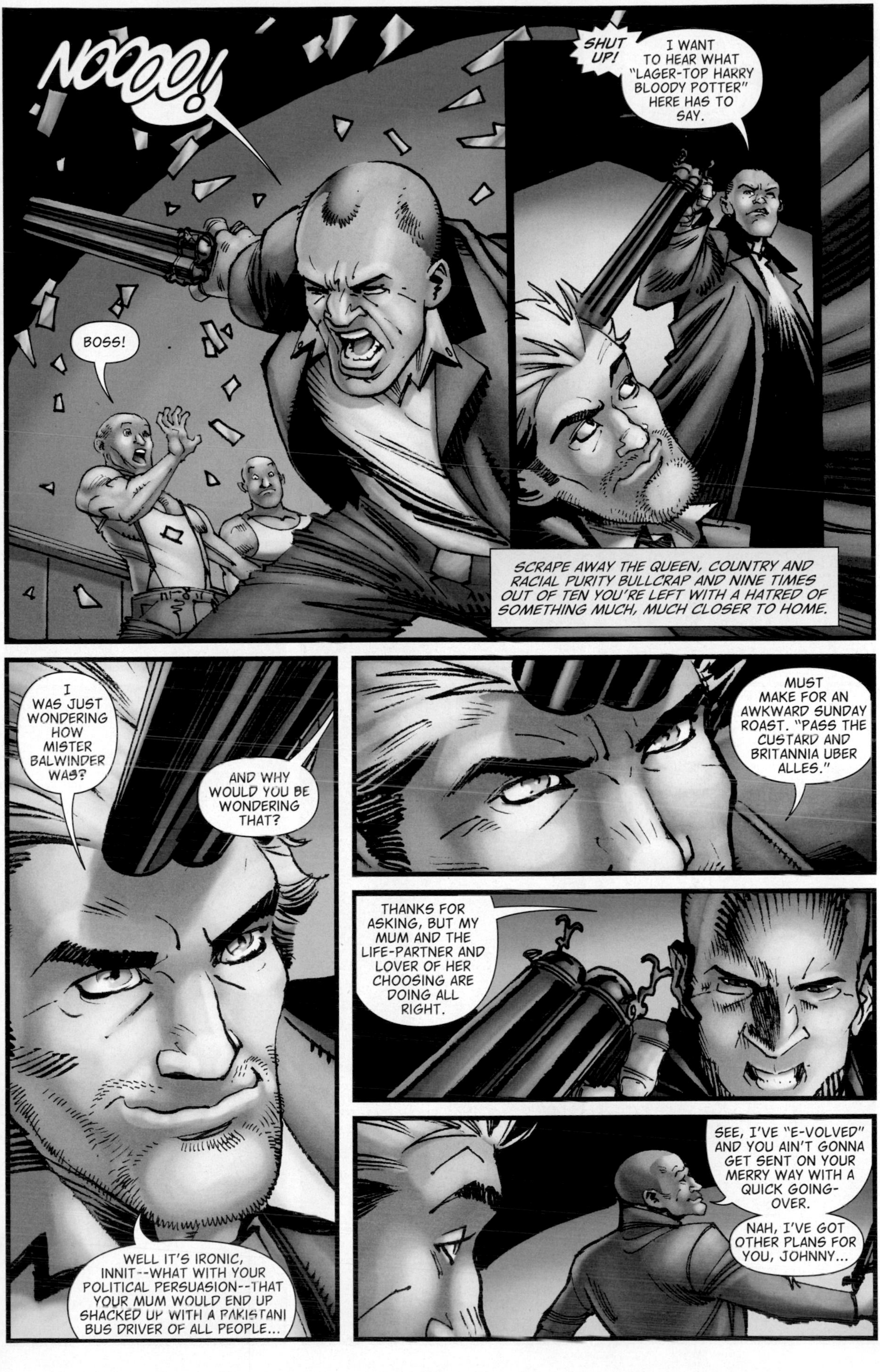
NOOOO!
SHUT UP!
I WANT TO HEAR WHAT "LAGER-TOP HARRY BLOODY POTTER" HERE HAS TO SAY.
BOSS!
SCRAPE AWAY THE QUEEN, COUNTRY AND RACIAL PURITY BULLCRAP AND NINE TIMES OUT OF TEN YOU'RE LEFT WITH A HATRED OF SOMETHING MUCH, MUCH CLOSER TO HOME.
I WAS JUST WONDERING HOW MISTER BALWINDER WAS?
AND WHY WOULD YOU BE WONDERING THAT?
WELL IT'S IRONIC, INNIT--WHAT WITH YOUR POLITICAL PERSUASION--THAT YOUR MUM WOULD END UP SHACKED UP WITH A PAKISTANI BUS DRIVER OF ALL PEOPLE...
MUST MAKE FOR AN AWKWARD SUNDAY ROAST. "PASS THE CUSTARD AND BRITANNIA UBER ALLES."
THANKS FOR ASKING, BUT MY MUM AND THE LIFE-PARTNER AND LOVER OF HER CHOOSING ARE DOING ALL RIGHT.
SEE, I'VE "E-VOLVED" AND YOU AIN'T GONNA GET SENT ON YOUR MERRY WAY WITH A QUICK GOING-OVER.
NAH, I'VE GOT OTHER PLANS FOR YOU, JOHNNY...

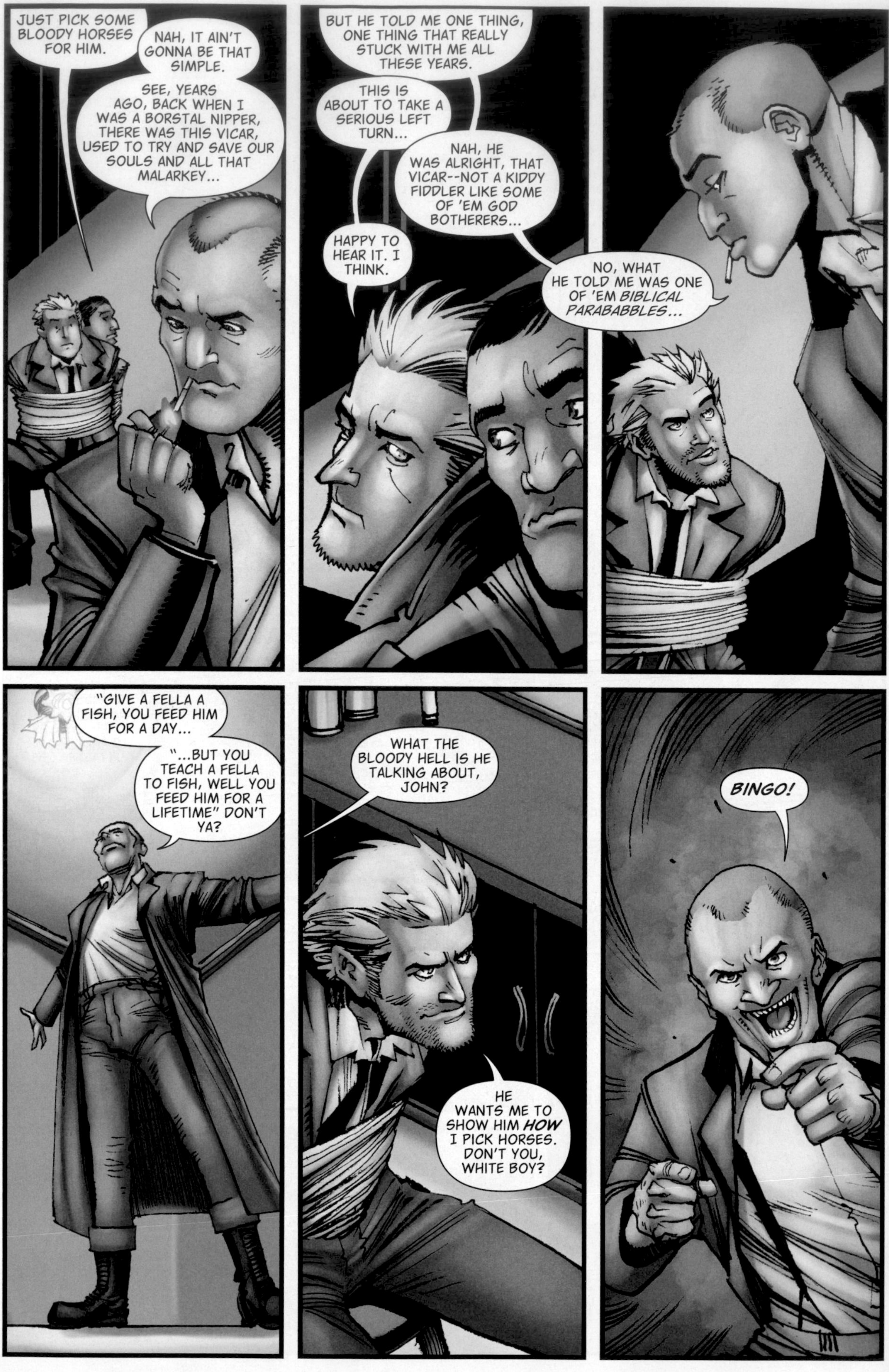
JUST PICK SOME BLOODY HORSES FOR HIM.
NAH, IT AIN'T GONNA BE THAT SIMPLE.
SEE, YEARS AGO, BACK WHEN I WAS A BORSTAL NIPPER, THERE WAS THIS VICAR, USED TO TRY AND SAVE OUR SOULS AND ALL THAT MALARKEY...
BUT HE TOLD ME ONE THING, ONE THING THAT REALLY STUCK WITH ME ALL THESE YEARS.
THIS IS ABOUT TO TAKE A SERIOUS LEFT TURN...
NAH, HE WAS ALRIGHT, THAT VICAR--NOT A KIDDY FIDDLER LIKE SOME OF 'EM GOD BOTHERERS...
HAPPY TO HEAR IT. I THINK.
NO, WHAT HE TOLD ME WAS ONE OF 'EM *BIBLICAL PARABABBLES*...
"GIVE A FELLA A FISH, YOU FEED HIM FOR A DAY...
"...BUT YOU TEACH A FELLA TO FISH, WELL YOU FEED HIM FOR A LIFETIME" DON'T YA?
WHAT THE BLOODY HELL IS HE TALKING ABOUT, JOHN?
HE WANTS ME TO SHOW HIM ***HOW*** I PICK HORSES. DON'T YOU, WHITE BOY?
BINGO!

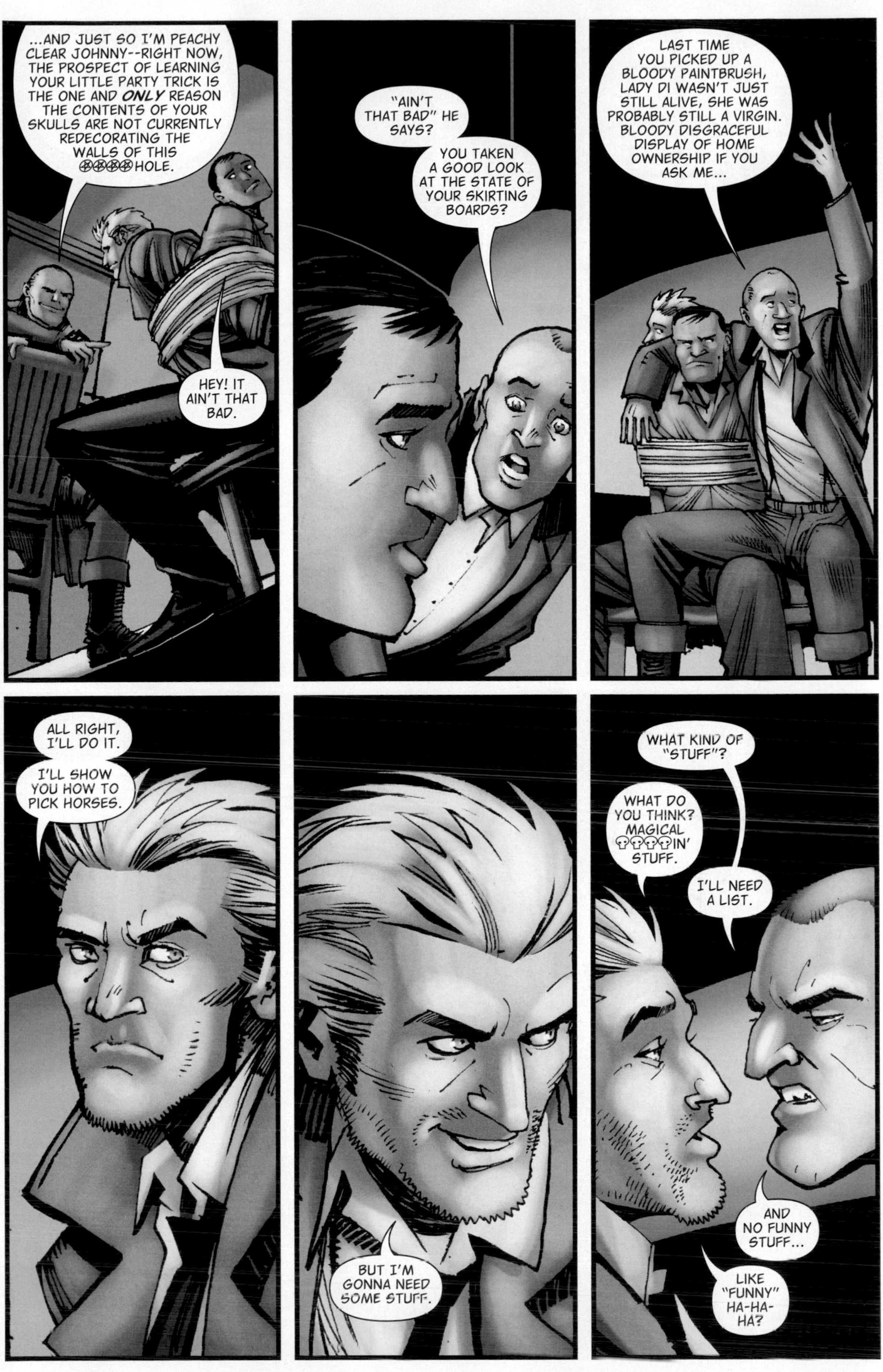
...AND JUST SO I'M PEACHY CLEAR JOHNNY--RIGHT NOW, THE PROSPECT OF LEARNING YOUR LITTLE PARTY TRICK IS THE ONE AND *ONLY* REASON THE CONTENTS OF YOUR SKULLS ARE NOT CURRENTLY REDECORATING THE WALLS OF THIS ⊗⊗⊗⊗ HOLE.
HEY! IT AIN'T THAT BAD.
"AIN'T THAT BAD" HE SAYS?
YOU TAKEN A GOOD LOOK AT THE STATE OF YOUR SKIRTING BOARDS?
LAST TIME YOU PICKED UP A BLOODY PAINTBRUSH, LADY DI WASN'T JUST STILL ALIVE, SHE WAS PROBABLY STILL A VIRGIN. BLOODY DISGRACEFUL DISPLAY OF HOME OWNERSHIP IF YOU ASK ME...
ALL RIGHT, I'LL DO IT.
I'LL SHOW YOU HOW TO PICK HORSES.
BUT I'M GONNA NEED SOME STUFF.
WHAT KIND OF "STUFF"?
WHAT DO YOU THINK? MAGICAL ☠☠☠☠IN' STUFF.
I'LL NEED A LIST.
AND NO FUNNY STUFF...
LIKE "FUNNY" HA-HA-HA?

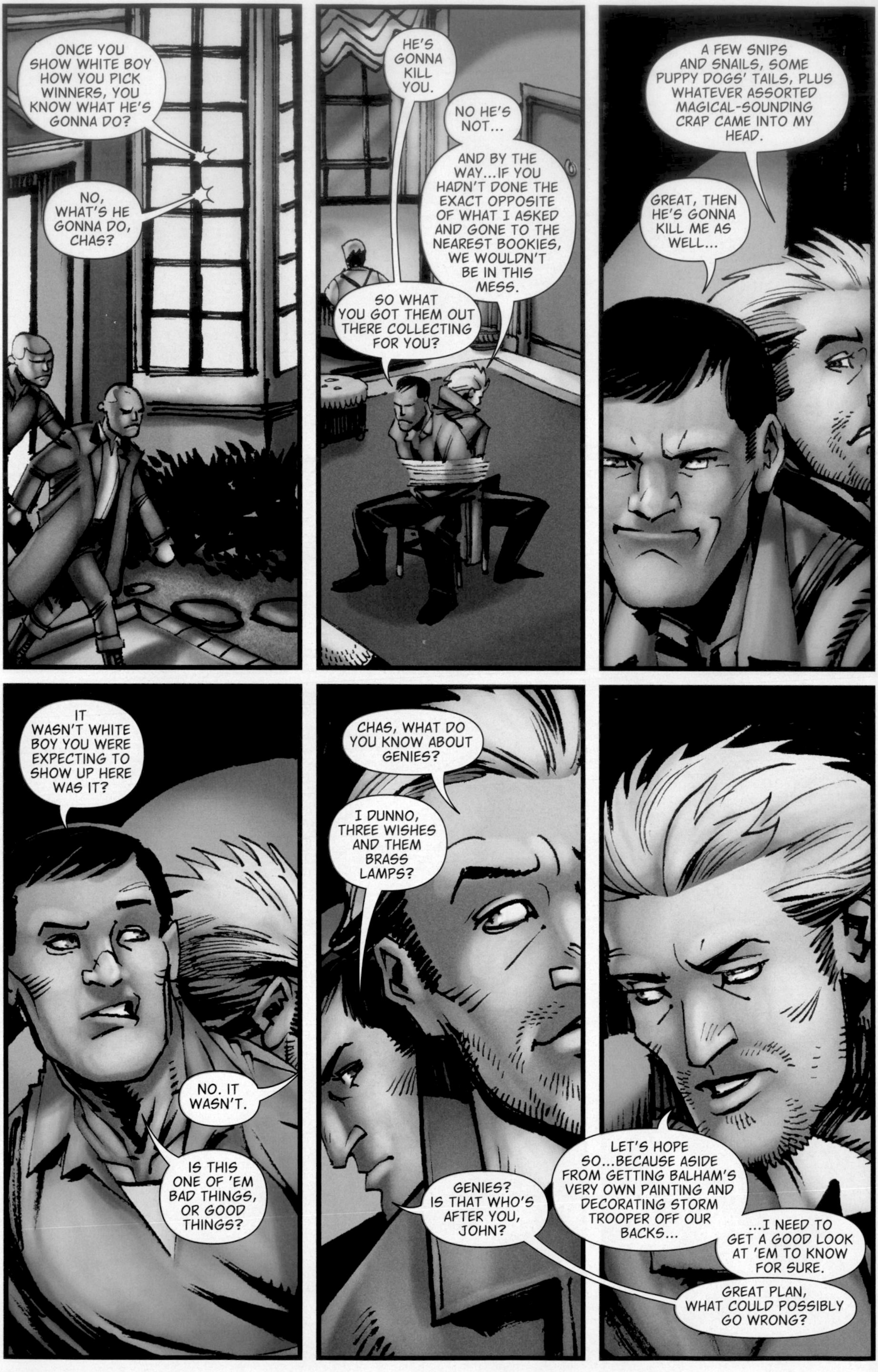
ONCE YOU SHOW WHITE BOY HOW YOU PICK WINNERS, YOU KNOW WHAT HE'S GONNA DO?
NO, WHAT'S HE GONNA DO, CHAS?
HE'S GONNA KILL YOU.
NO HE'S NOT...
AND BY THE WAY...IF YOU HADN'T DONE THE EXACT OPPOSITE OF WHAT I ASKED AND GONE TO THE NEAREST BOOKIES, WE WOULDN'T BE IN THIS MESS.
SO WHAT YOU GOT THEM OUT THERE COLLECTING FOR YOU?
A FEW SNIPS AND SNAILS, SOME PUPPY DOGS' TAILS, PLUS WHATEVER ASSORTED MAGICAL-SOUNDING CRAP CAME INTO MY HEAD.
GREAT, THEN HE'S GONNA KILL ME AS WELL...
IT WASN'T WHITE BOY YOU WERE EXPECTING TO SHOW UP HERE WAS IT?
NO. IT WASN'T.
IS THIS ONE OF 'EM BAD THINGS, OR GOOD THINGS?
CHAS, WHAT DO YOU KNOW ABOUT GENIES?
I DUNNO, THREE WISHES AND THEM BRASS LAMPS?
GENIES? IS THAT WHO'S AFTER YOU, JOHN?
LET'S HOPE SO...BECAUSE ASIDE FROM GETTING BALHAM'S VERY OWN PAINTING AND DECORATING STORM TROOPER OFF OUR BACKS...
...I NEED TO GET A GOOD LOOK AT 'EM TO KNOW FOR SURE.
GREAT PLAN, WHAT COULD POSSIBLY GO WRONG?

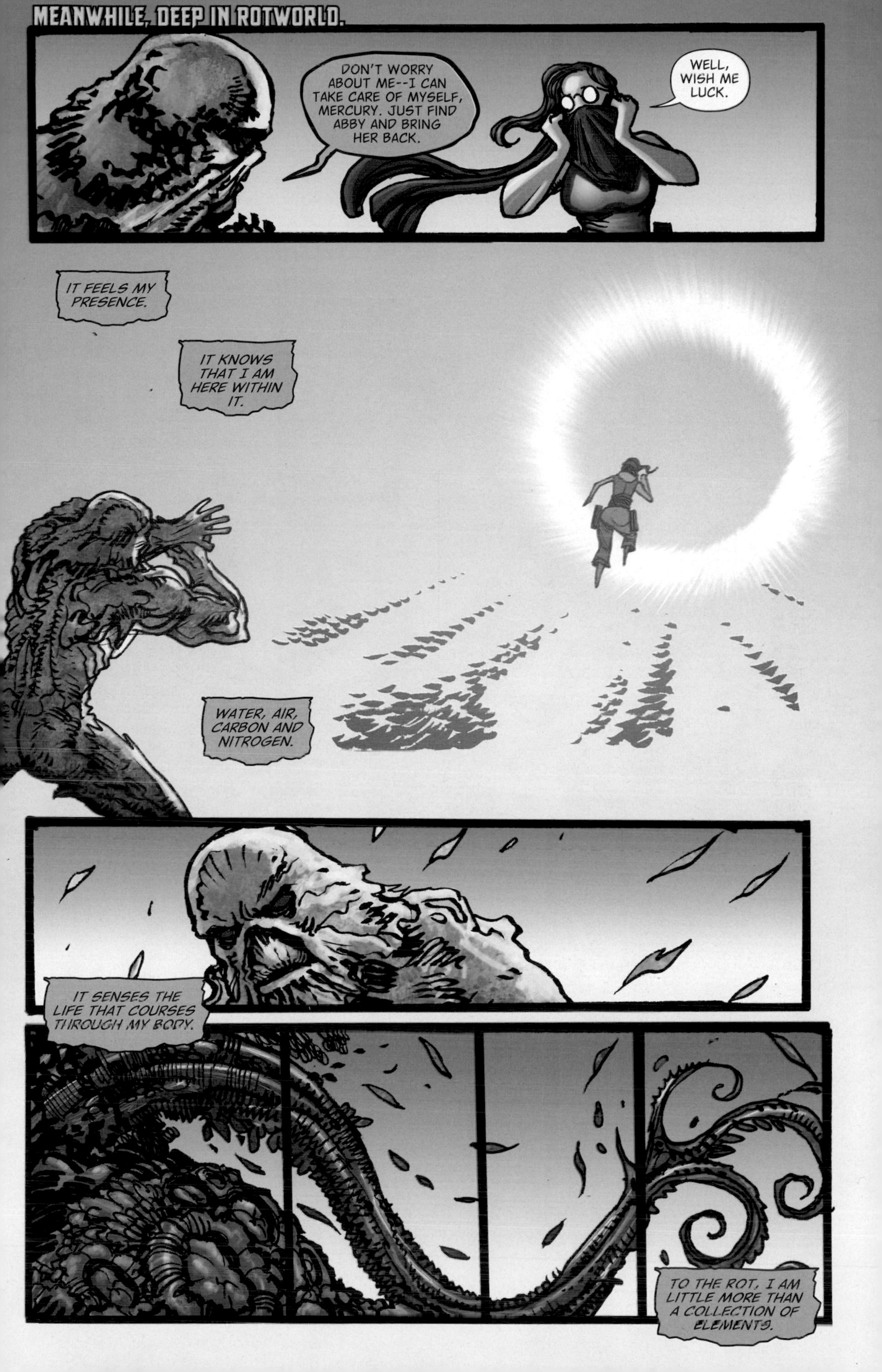
MEANWHILE, DEEP IN ROTWORLD.
DON'T WORRY ABOUT ME--I CAN TAKE CARE OF MYSELF, MERCURY. JUST FIND ABBY AND BRING HER BACK.
WELL, WISH ME LUCK.
IT FEELS MY PRESENCE.
IT KNOWS THAT I AM HERE WITHIN IT.
WATER, AIR, CARBON AND NITROGEN.
IT SENSES THE LIFE THAT COURSES THROUGH MY BODY.
TO THE ROT, I AM LITTLE MORE THAN A COLLECTION OF ELEMENTS.

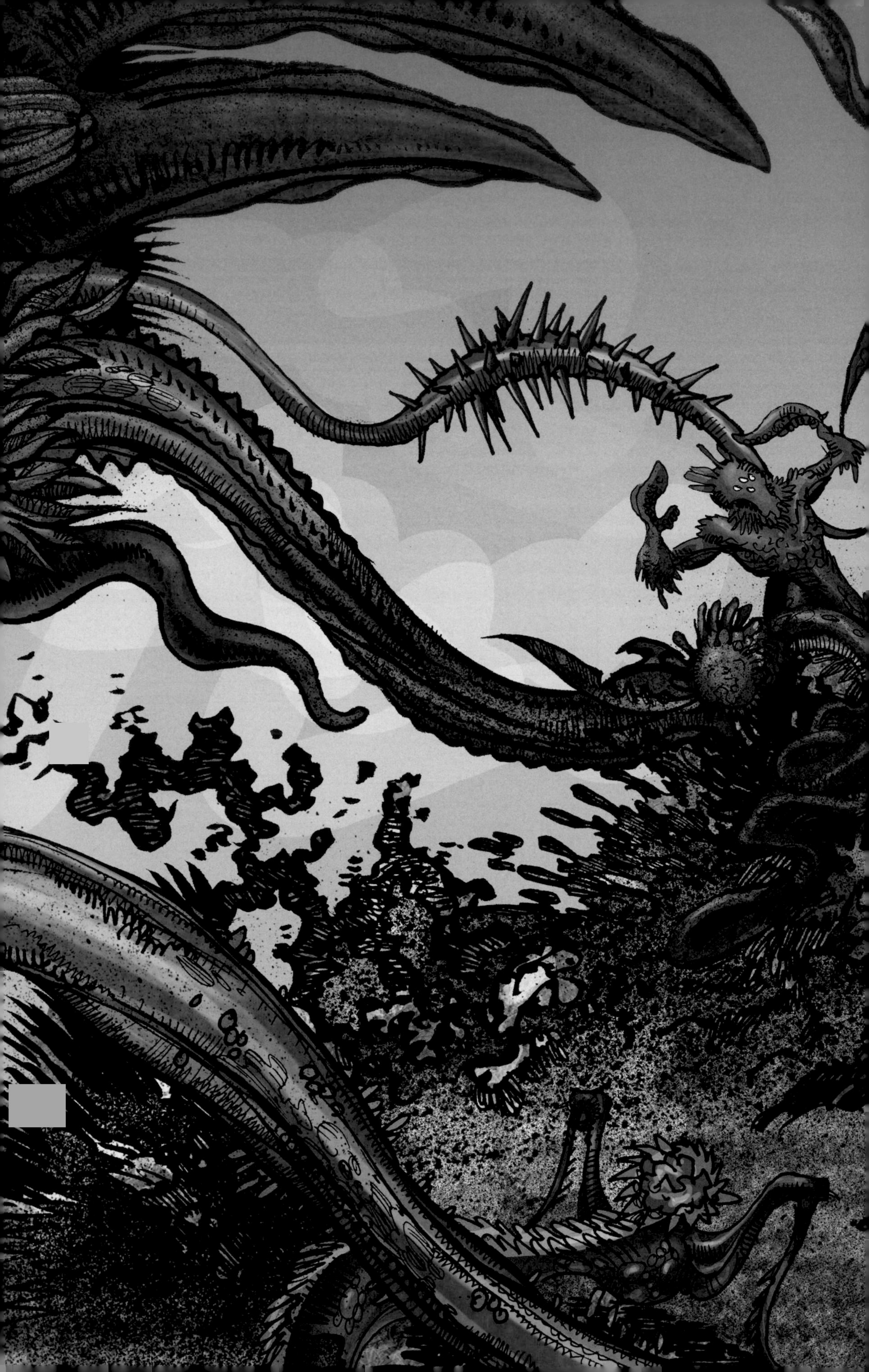

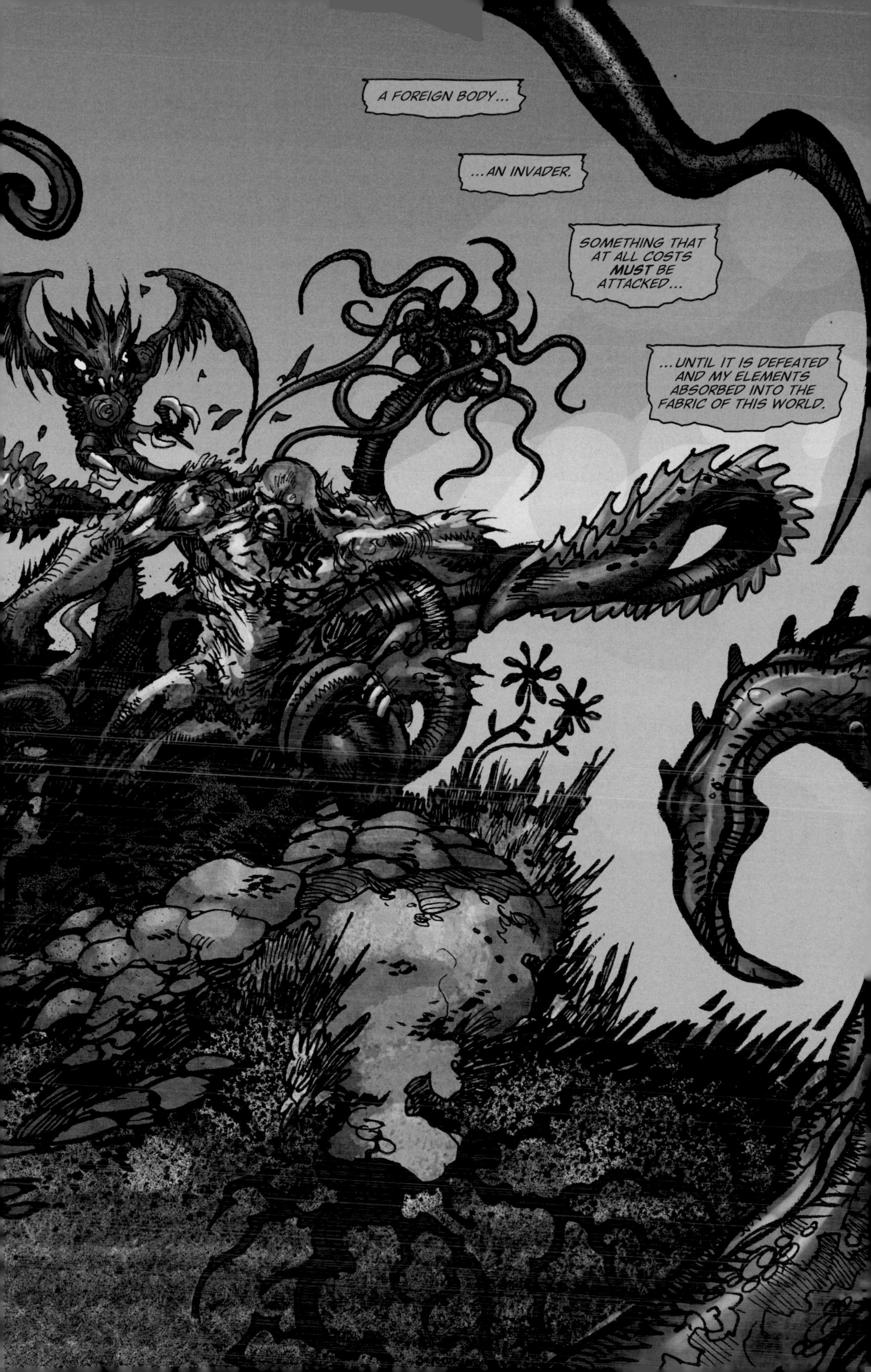
A FOREIGN BODY...
...AN INVADER.
SOMETHING THAT AT ALL COSTS MUST BE ATTACKED...
...UNTIL IT IS DEFEATED AND MY ELEMENTS ABSORBED INTO THE FABRIC OF THIS WORLD.

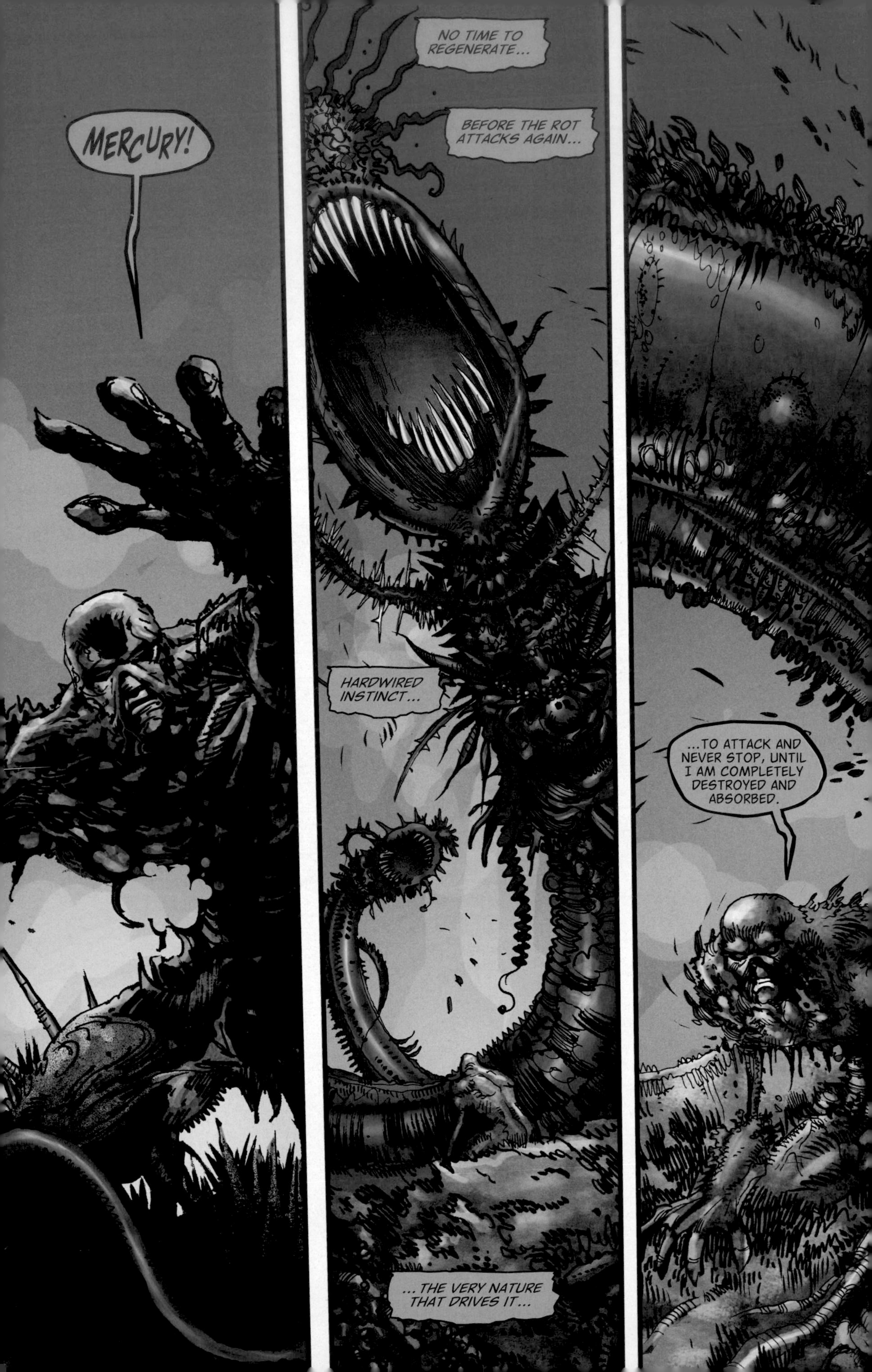
MERCURY!
NO TIME TO REGENERATE...
BEFORE THE ROT ATTACKS AGAIN...
HARDWIRED INSTINCT...
...THE VERY NATURE THAT DRIVES IT...
...TO ATTACK AND NEVER STOP, UNTIL I AM COMPLETELY DESTROYED AND ABSORBED.

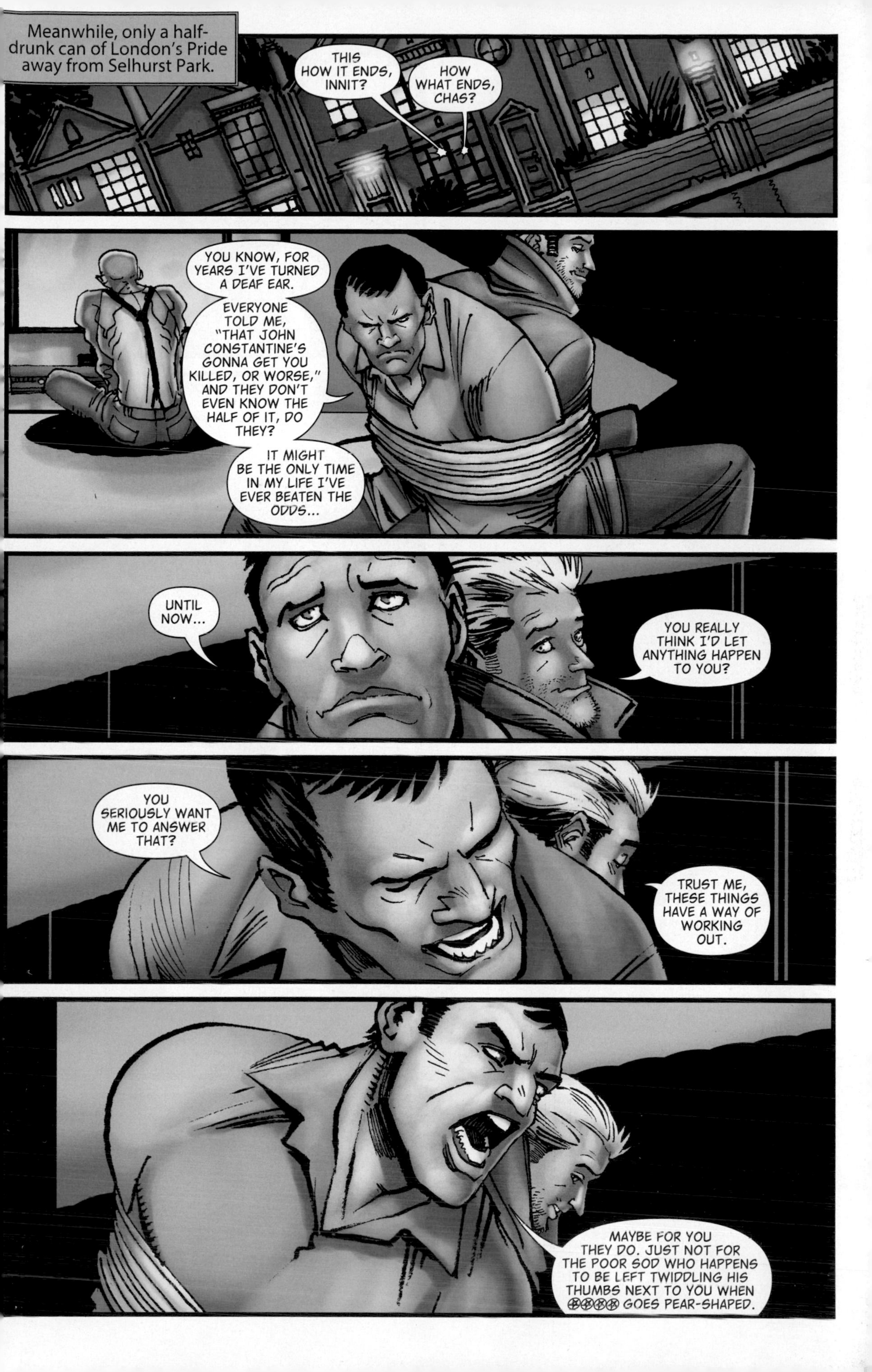
Meanwhile, only a half-drunk can of London's Pride away from Selhurst Park.
THIS HOW IT ENDS, INNIT?
HOW WHAT ENDS, CHAS?
YOU KNOW, FOR YEARS I'VE TURNED A DEAF EAR.
EVERYONE TOLD ME, "THAT JOHN CONSTANTINE'S GONNA GET YOU KILLED, OR WORSE," AND THEY DON'T EVEN KNOW THE HALF OF IT, DO THEY?
IT MIGHT BE THE ONLY TIME IN MY LIFE I'VE EVER BEATEN THE ODDS...
UNTIL NOW...
YOU REALLY THINK I'D LET ANYTHING HAPPEN TO YOU?
YOU SERIOUSLY WANT ME TO ANSWER THAT?
TRUST ME, THESE THINGS HAVE A WAY OF WORKING OUT.
MAYBE FOR YOU THEY DO. JUST NOT FOR THE POOR SOD WHO HAPPENS TO BE LEFT TWIDDLING HIS THUMBS NEXT TO YOU WHEN ⊗⊗⊗⊗ GOES PEAR-SHAPED.

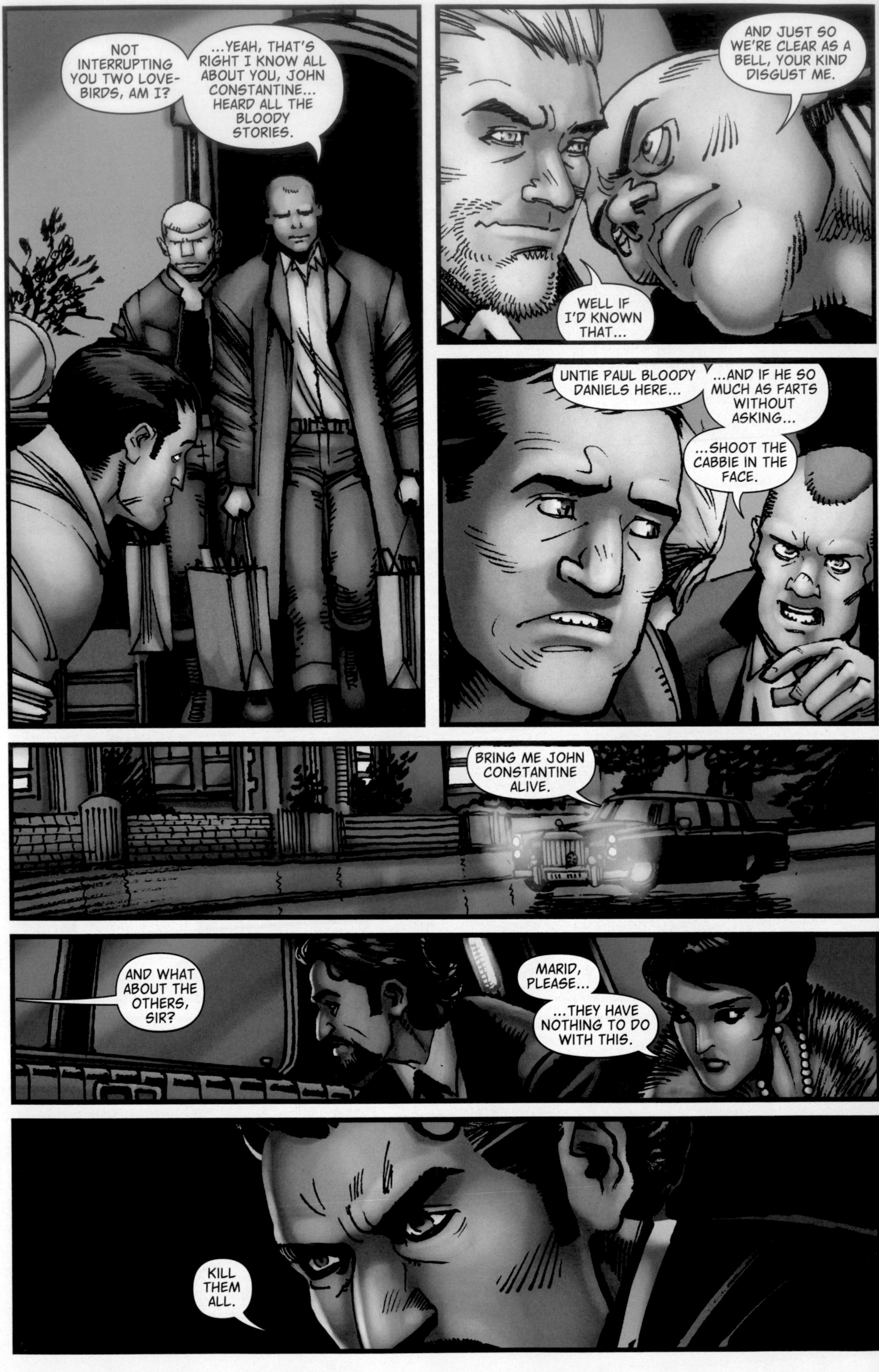
NOT INTERRUPTING YOU TWO LOVE-BIRDS, AM I?
...YEAH, THAT'S RIGHT I KNOW ALL ABOUT YOU, JOHN CONSTANTINE... HEARD ALL THE BLOODY STORIES.
AND JUST SO WE'RE CLEAR AS A BELL, YOUR KIND DISGUST ME.
WELL IF I'D KNOWN THAT...
UNTIE PAUL BLOODY DANIELS HERE...
...AND IF HE SO MUCH AS FARTS WITHOUT ASKING...
...SHOOT THE CABBIE IN THE FACE.
BRING ME JOHN CONSTANTINE ALIVE.
AND WHAT ABOUT THE OTHERS, SIR?
MARID, PLEASE...
...THEY HAVE NOTHING TO DO WITH THIS.
KILL THEM ALL.

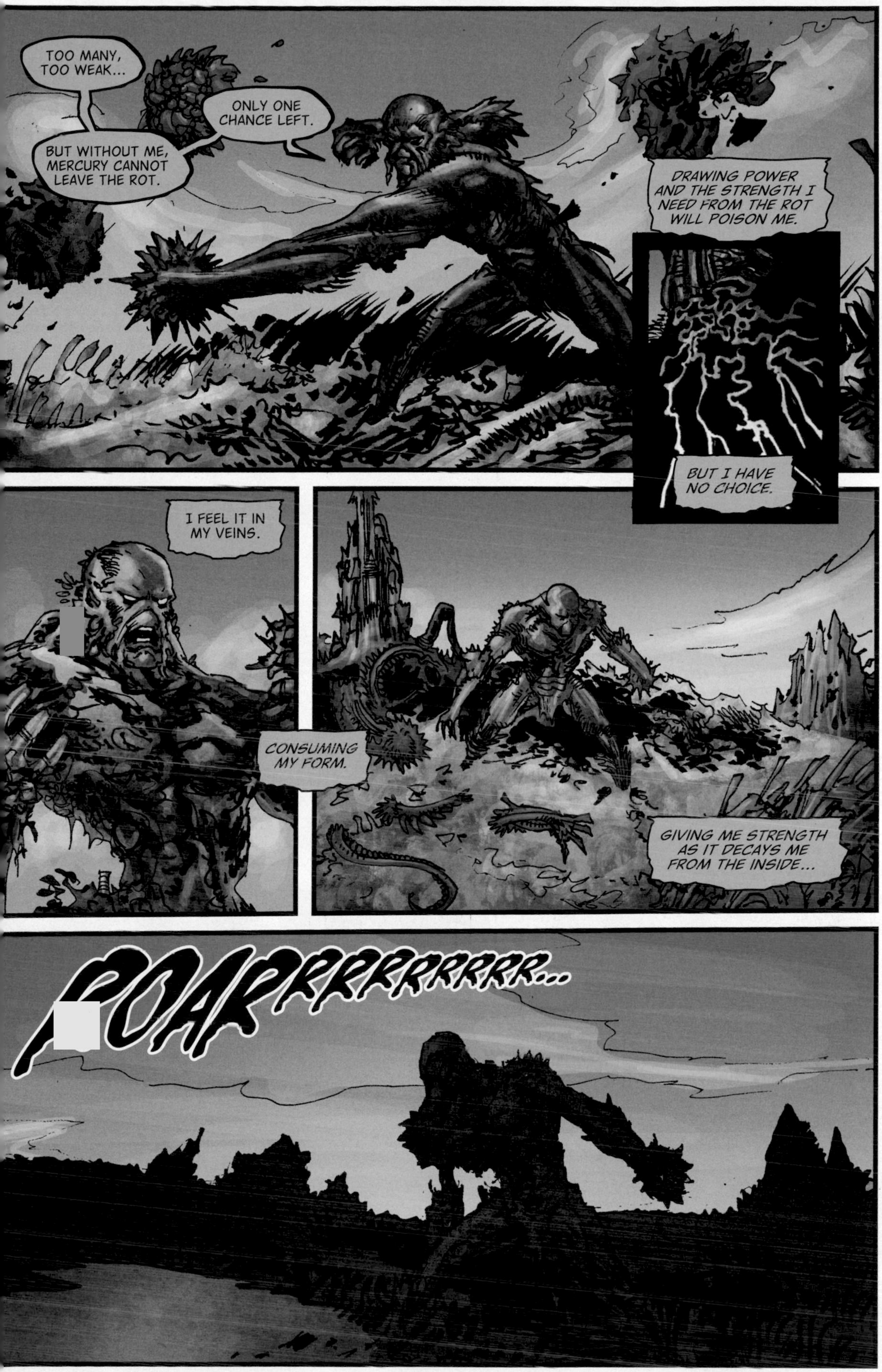
TOO MANY, TOO WEAK...
BUT WITHOUT ME, MERCURY CANNOT LEAVE THE ROT.
ONLY ONE CHANCE LEFT.
DRAWING POWER AND THE STRENGTH I NEED FROM THE ROT WILL POISON ME.
BUT I HAVE NO CHOICE.
I FEEL IT IN MY VEINS.
CONSUMING MY FORM.
GIVING ME STRENGTH AS IT DECAYS ME FROM THE INSIDE...
ROARRRRRRRRRR...

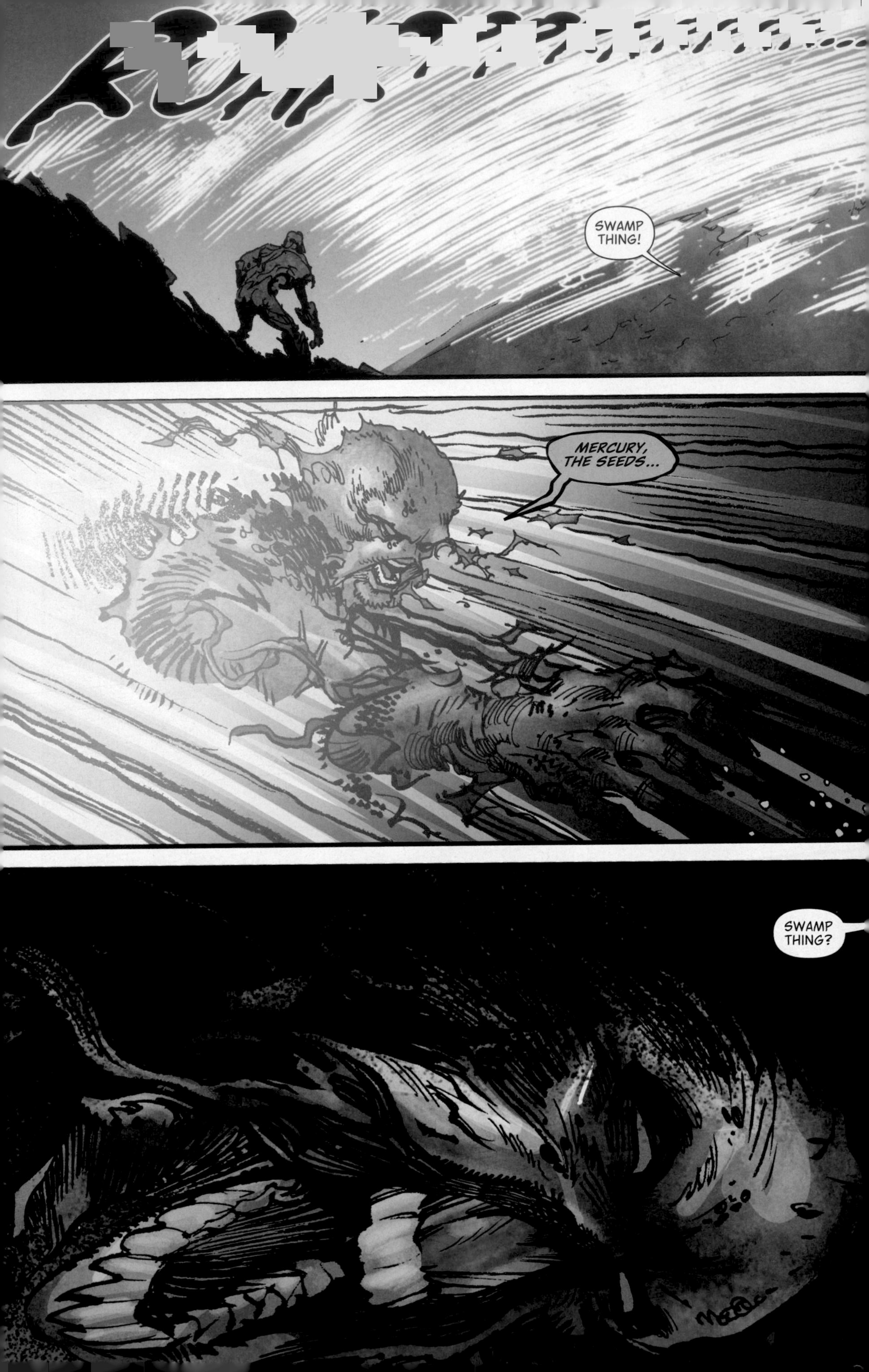
SWAMP THING!
MERCURY, THE SEEDS...
SWAMP THING?

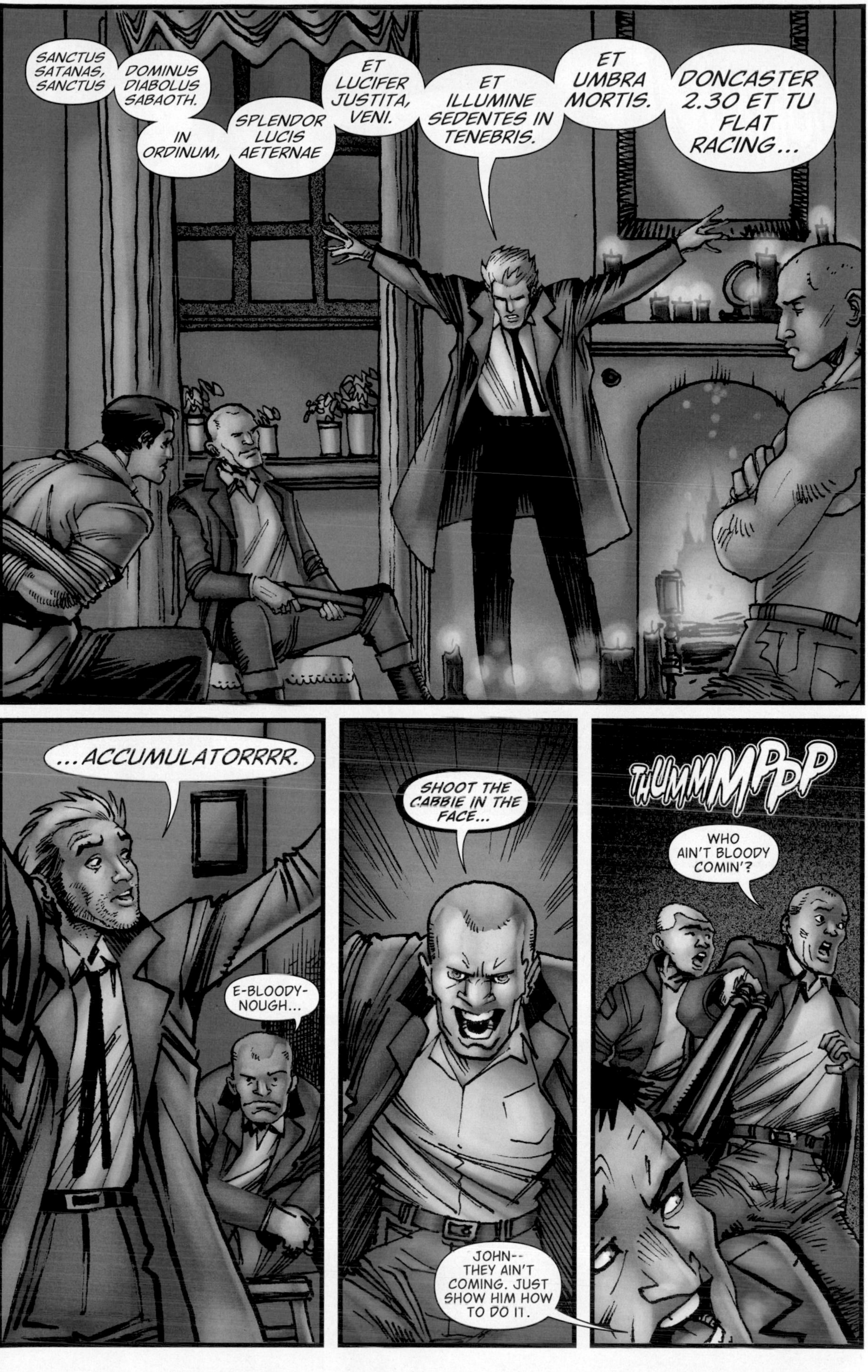
SANCTUS SATANAS, SANCTUS
DOMINUS DIABOLUS SABAOTH.
IN ORDINUM,
SPLENDOR LUCIS AETERNAE
ET LUCIFER JUSTITA, VENI.
ET ILLUMINE SEDENTES IN TENEBRIS.
ET UMBRA MORTIS.
DONCASTER 2.30 ET TU FLAT RACING...
...ACCUMULATORRRR.
E-BLOODY-NOUGH...
SHOOT THE CABBIE IN THE FACE...
JOHN-- THEY AIN'T COMING. JUST SHOW HIM HOW TO DO IT.
THUMMMPPP
WHO AIN'T BLOODY COMIN'?

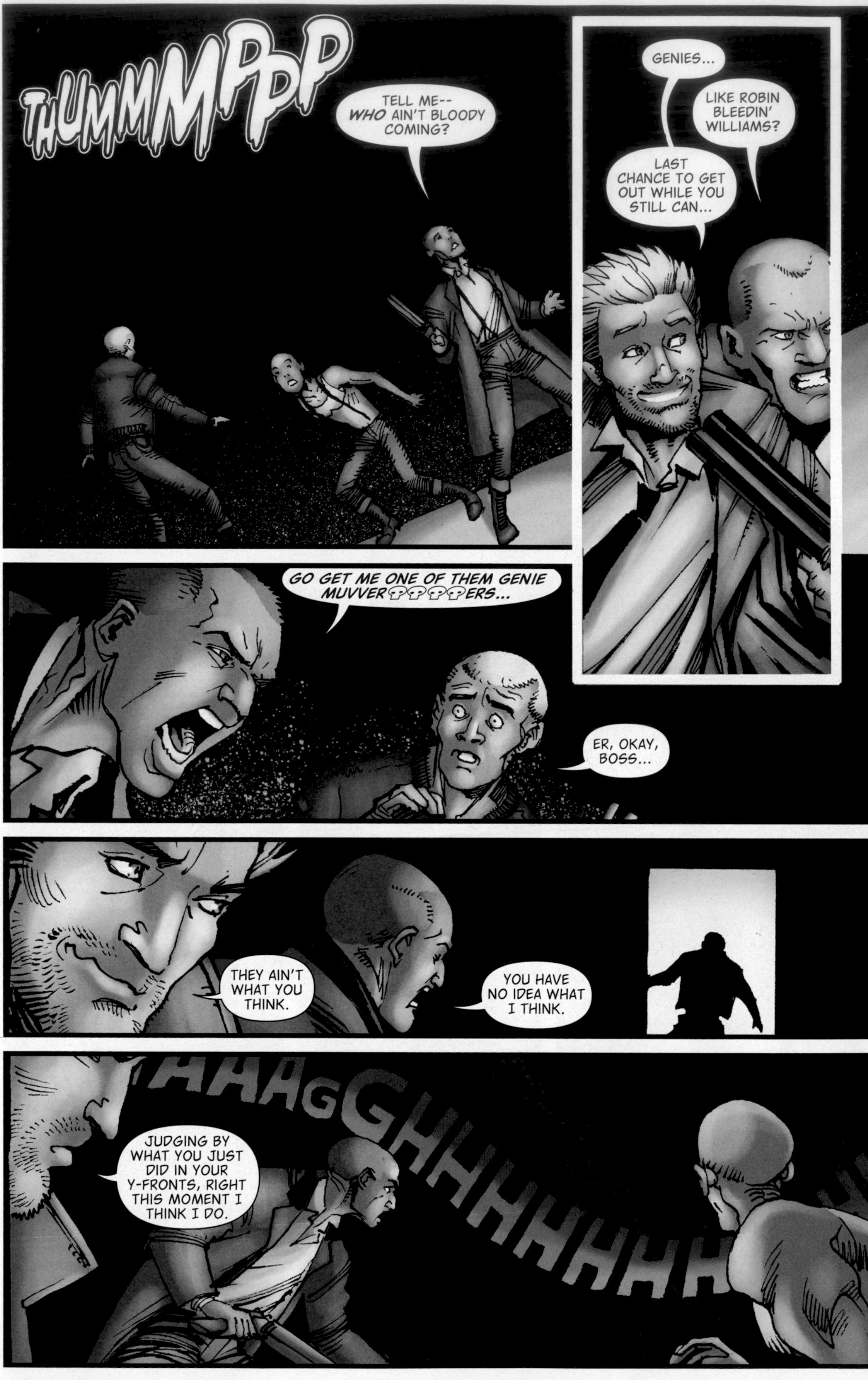
THUMMMPPP
TELL ME-- WHO AIN'T BLOODY COMING?
GENIES...
LIKE ROBIN BLEEDIN' WILLIAMS?
LAST CHANCE TO GET OUT WHILE YOU STILL CAN...
GO GET ME ONE OF THEM GENIE MUVVER☠☠☠☠ERS...
ER, OKAY, BOSS...
THEY AIN'T WHAT YOU THINK.
YOU HAVE NO IDEA WHAT I THINK.
AAAAGHHHHHHHHHH
JUDGING BY WHAT YOU JUST DID IN YOUR Y-FRONTS, RIGHT THIS MOMENT I THINK I DO.

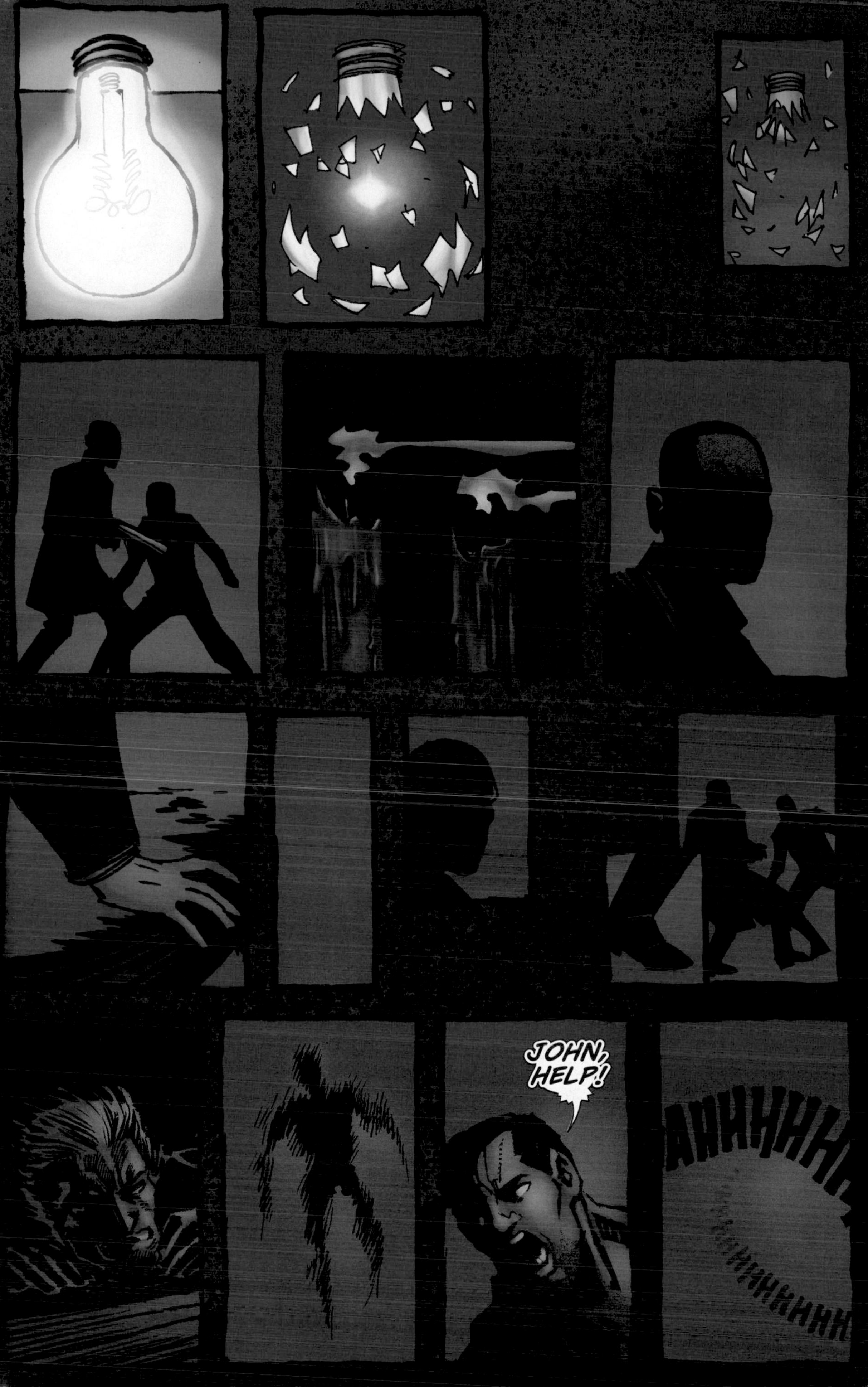
JOHN, HELP!
AHHHHHH
AHHHHHHHHHHH

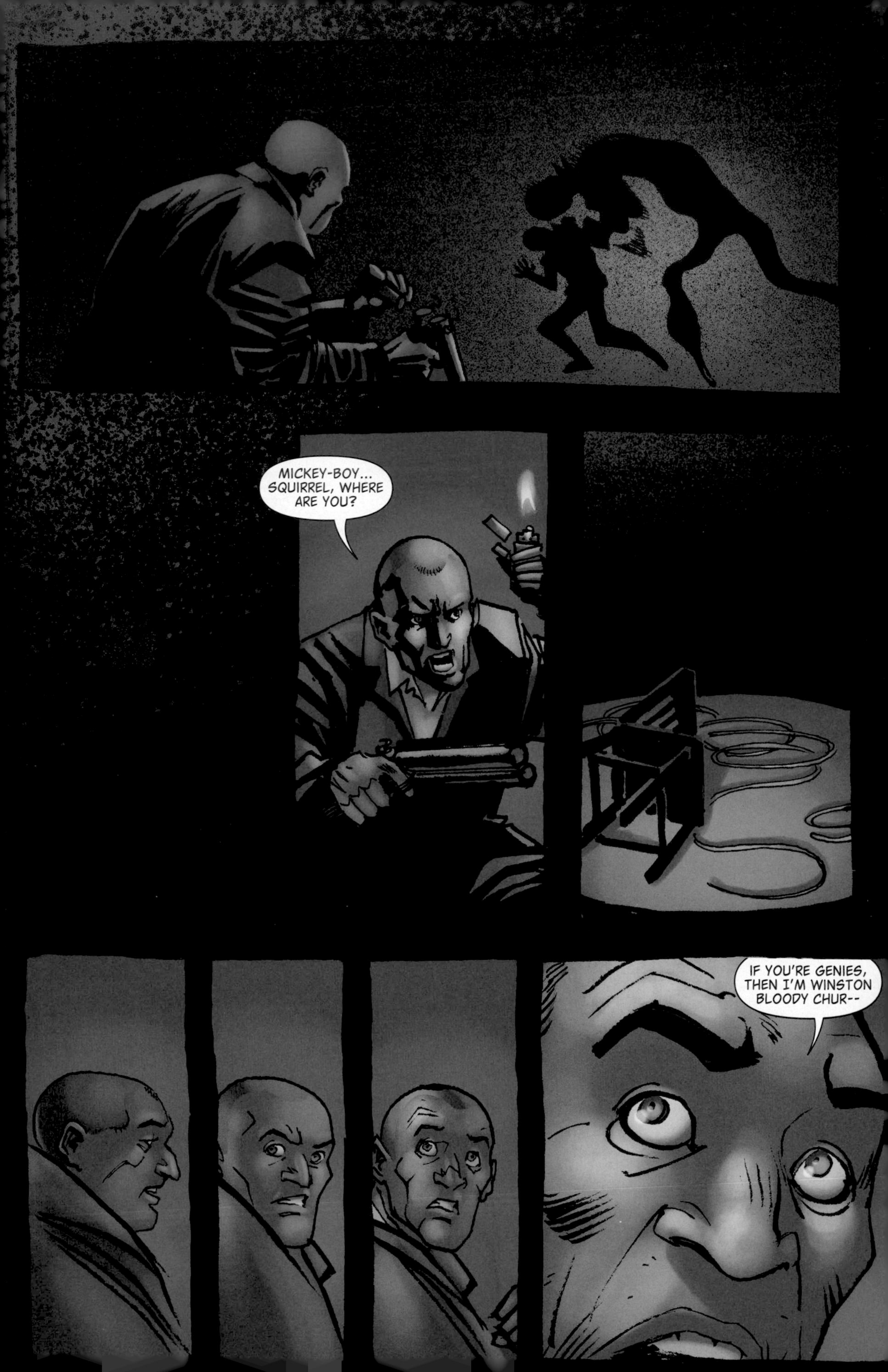
MICKEY-BOY... SQUIRREL, WHERE ARE YOU?
IF YOU'RE GENIES, THEN I'M WINSTON BLOODY CHUR--

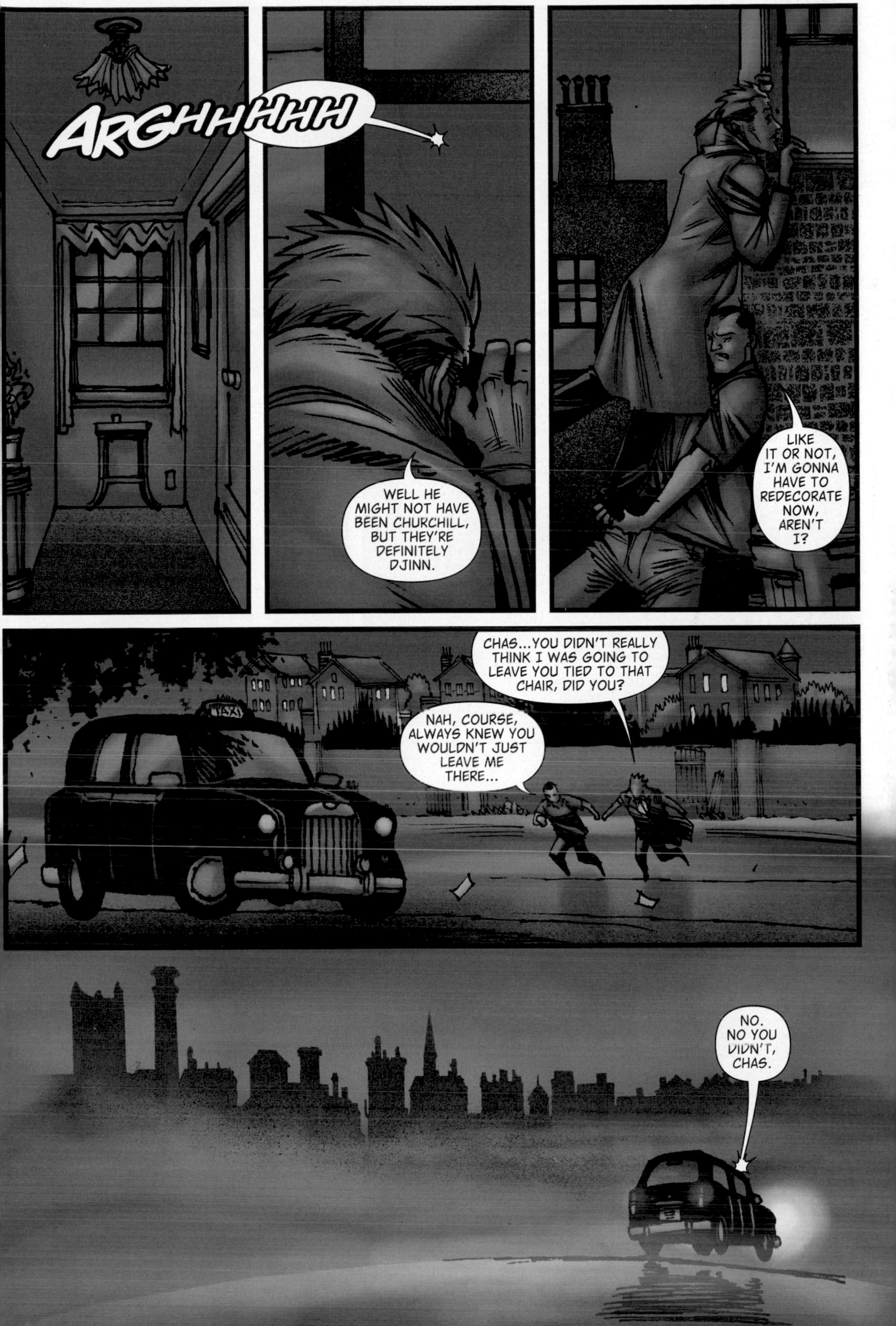
ARGHHHHHH
WELL HE MIGHT NOT HAVE BEEN CHURCHILL, BUT THEY'RE DEFINITELY DJINN.
LIKE IT OR NOT, I'M GONNA HAVE TO REDECORATE NOW, AREN'T I?
CHAS...YOU DIDN'T REALLY THINK I WAS GOING TO LEAVE YOU TIED TO THAT CHAIR, DID YOU?
NAH, COURSE, ALWAYS KNEW YOU WOULDN'T JUST LEAVE ME THERE...
NO. NO YOU DIDN'T, CHAS.

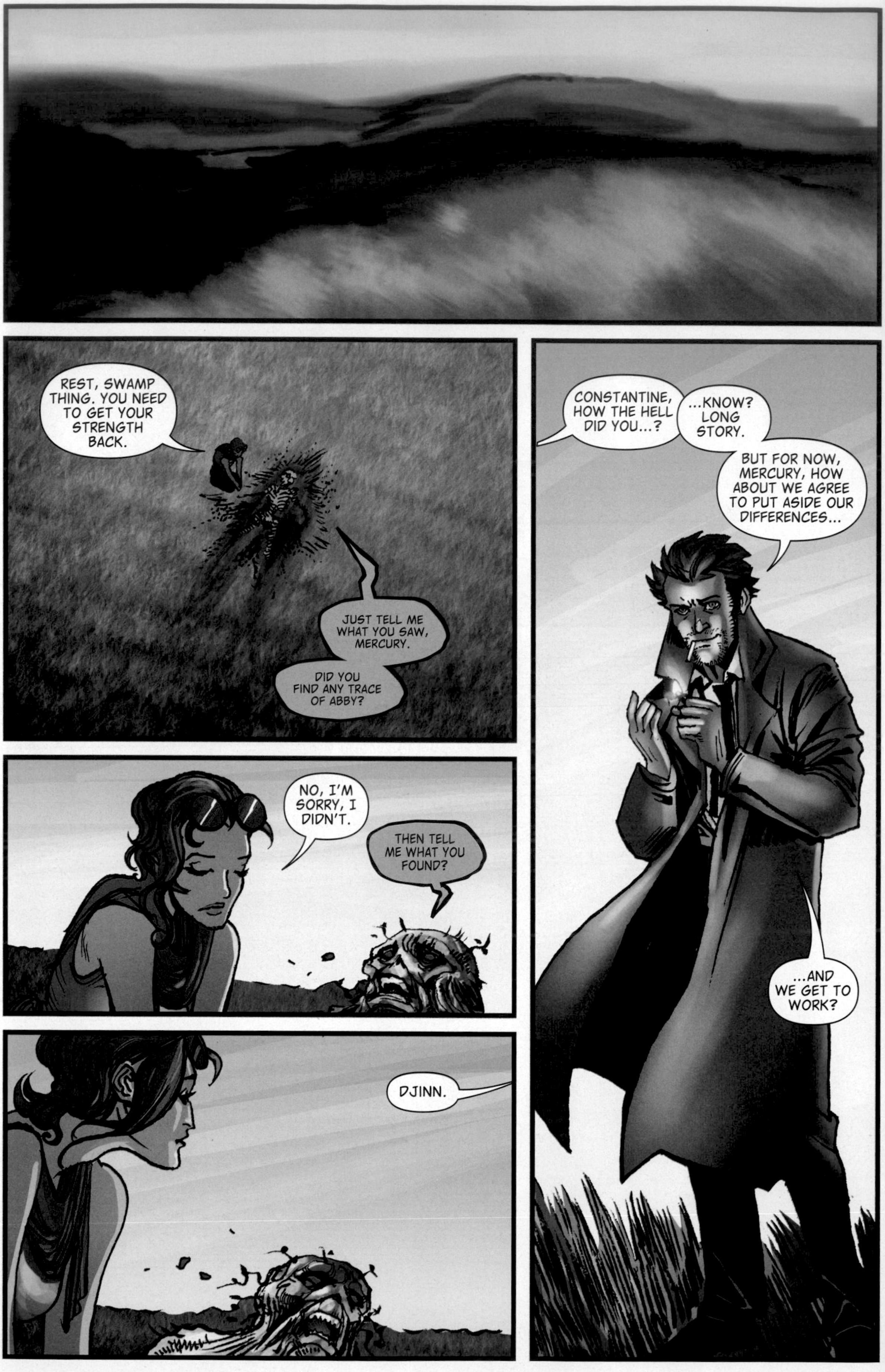
REST, SWAMP THING. YOU NEED TO GET YOUR STRENGTH BACK.
JUST TELL ME WHAT YOU SAW, MERCURY.
DID YOU FIND ANY TRACE OF ABBY?
CONSTANTINE, HOW THE HELL DID YOU...?
...KNOW? LONG STORY.
BUT FOR NOW, MERCURY, HOW ABOUT WE AGREE TO PUT ASIDE OUR DIFFERENCES...
...AND WE GET TO WORK?
NO, I'M SORRY, I DIDN'T.
THEN TELL ME WHAT YOU FOUND?
DJINN.

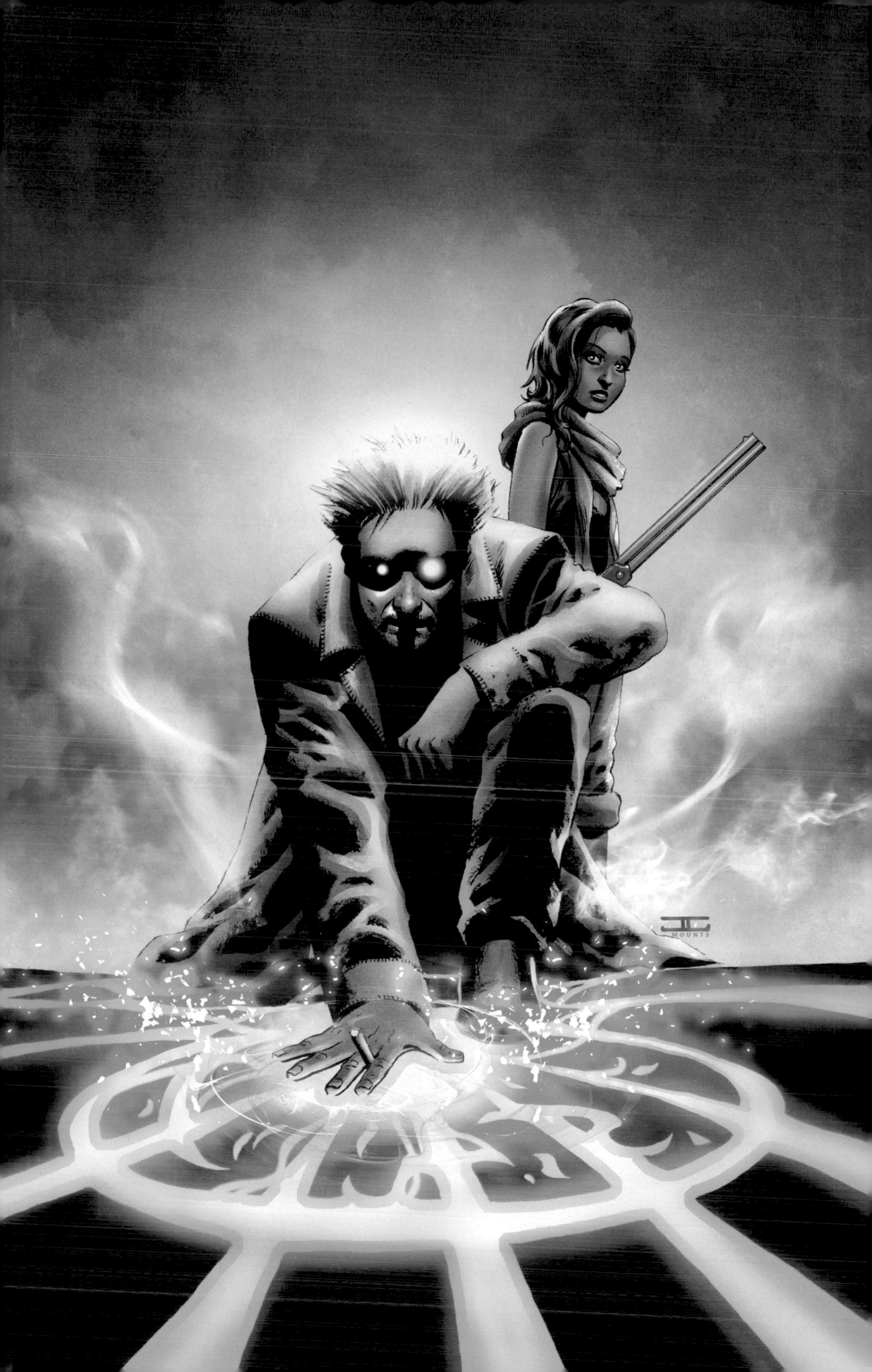

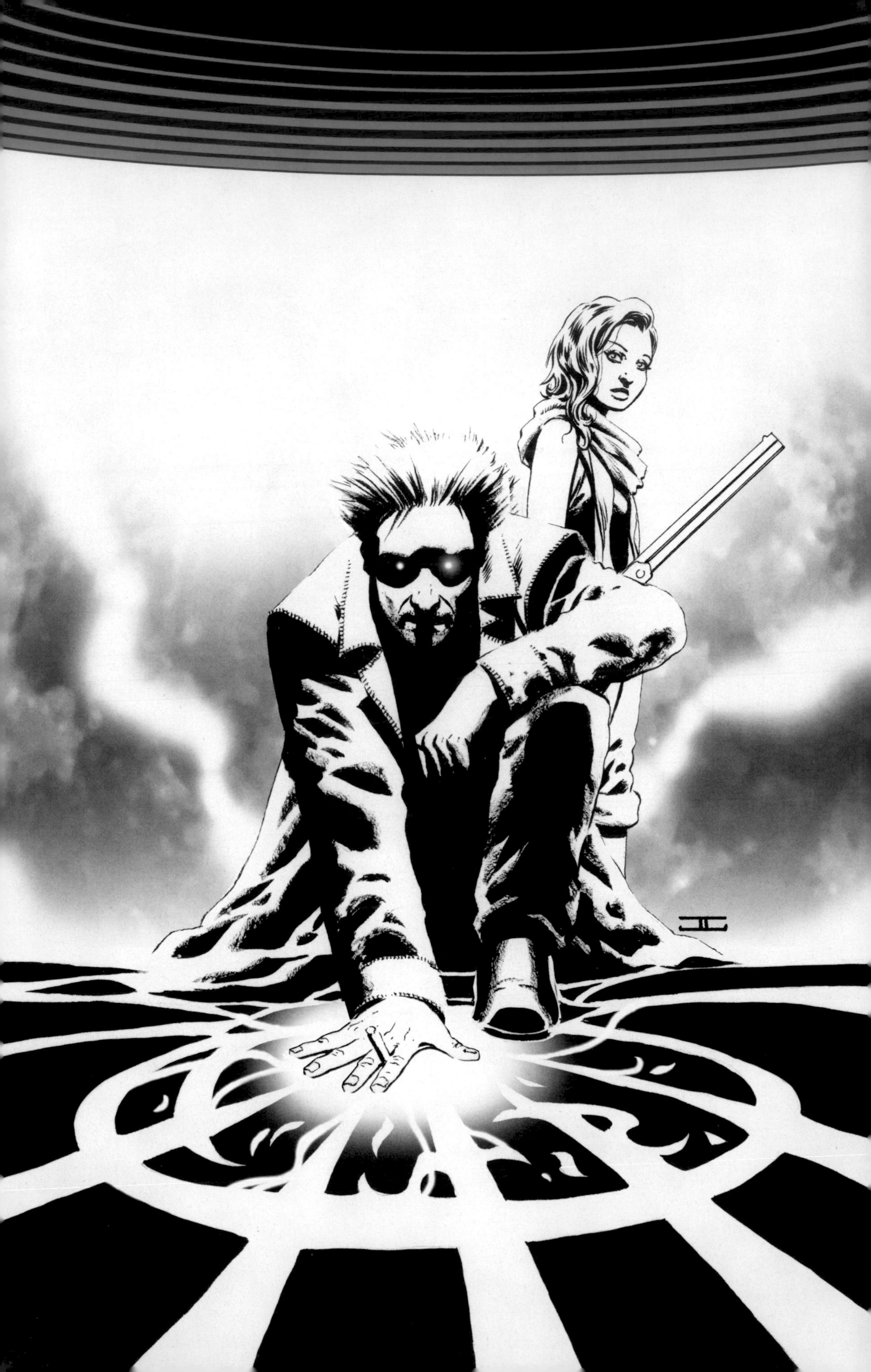

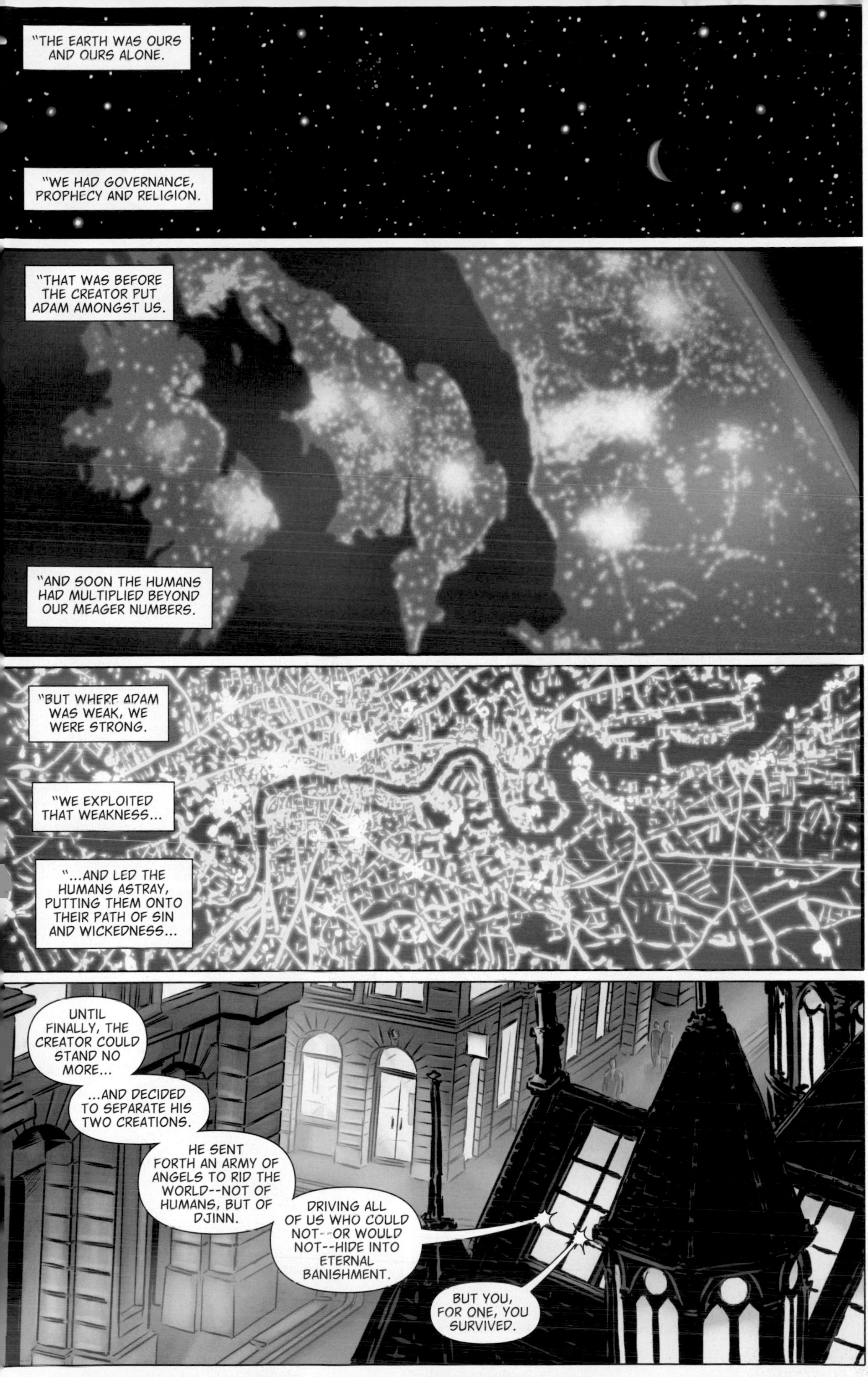
"THE EARTH WAS OURS AND OURS ALONE.
"WE HAD GOVERNANCE, PROPHECY AND RELIGION.
"THAT WAS BEFORE THE CREATOR PUT ADAM AMONGST US.
"AND SOON THE HUMANS HAD MULTIPLIED BEYOND OUR MEAGER NUMBERS.
"BUT WHERE ADAM WAS WEAK, WE WERE STRONG.
"WE EXPLOITED THAT WEAKNESS...
"...AND LED THE HUMANS ASTRAY, PUTTING THEM ONTO THEIR PATH OF SIN AND WICKEDNESS...
UNTIL FINALLY, THE CREATOR COULD STAND NO MORE...
...AND DECIDED TO SEPARATE HIS TWO CREATIONS.
HE SENT FORTH AN ARMY OF ANGELS TO RID THE WORLD--NOT OF HUMANS, BUT OF DJINN.
DRIVING ALL OF US WHO COULD NOT--OR WOULD NOT--HIDE INTO ETERNAL BANISHMENT.
BUT YOU, FOR ONE, YOU SURVIVED.

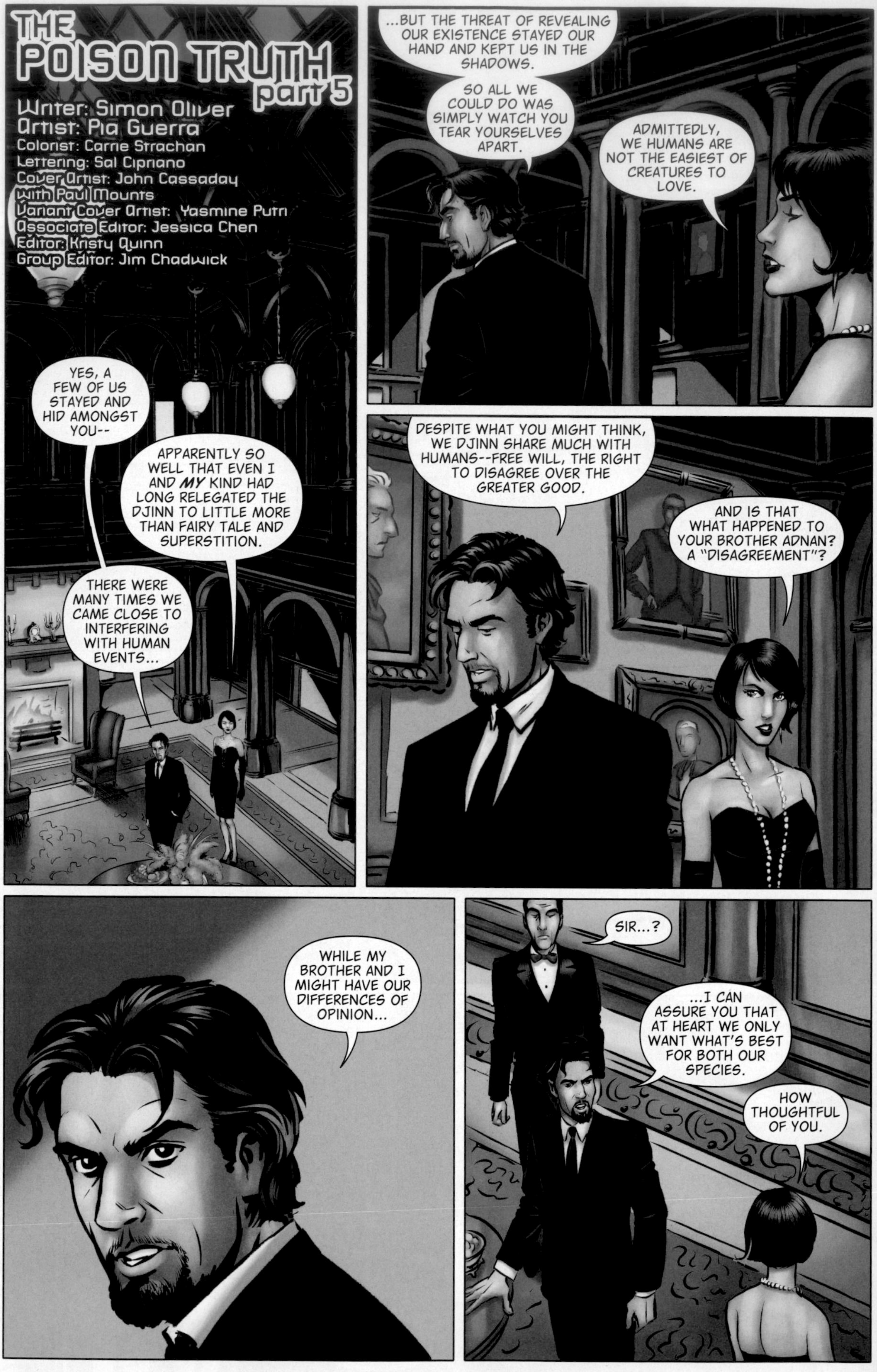
THE POISON TRUTH part 5
Writer: Simon Oliver
Artist: Pia Guerra
Colorist: Carrie Strachan
Lettering: Sal Cipriano
Cover Artist: John Cassaday with Paul Mounts
Variant Cover Artist: Yasmine Putri
Associate Editor: Jessica Chen
Editor: Kristy Quinn
Group Editor: Jim Chadwick
YES, A FEW OF US STAYED AND HID AMONGST YOU--
APPARENTLY SO WELL THAT EVEN I AND MY KIND HAD LONG RELEGATED THE DJINN TO LITTLE MORE THAN FAIRY TALE AND SUPERSTITION.
THERE WERE MANY TIMES WE CAME CLOSE TO INTERFERING WITH HUMAN EVENTS...
...BUT THE THREAT OF REVEALING OUR EXISTENCE STAYED OUR HAND AND KEPT US IN THE SHADOWS.
SO ALL WE COULD DO WAS SIMPLY WATCH YOU TEAR YOURSELVES APART.
ADMITTEDLY, WE HUMANS ARE NOT THE EASIEST OF CREATURES TO LOVE.
DESPITE WHAT YOU MIGHT THINK, WE DJINN SHARE MUCH WITH HUMANS--FREE WILL, THE RIGHT TO DISAGREE OVER THE GREATER GOOD.
AND IS THAT WHAT HAPPENED TO YOUR BROTHER ADNAN? A "DISAGREEMENT"?
WHILE MY BROTHER AND I MIGHT HAVE OUR DIFFERENCES OF OPINION...
SIR...?
...I CAN ASSURE YOU THAT AT HEART WE ONLY WANT WHAT'S BEST FOR BOTH OUR SPECIES.
HOW THOUGHTFUL OF YOU.

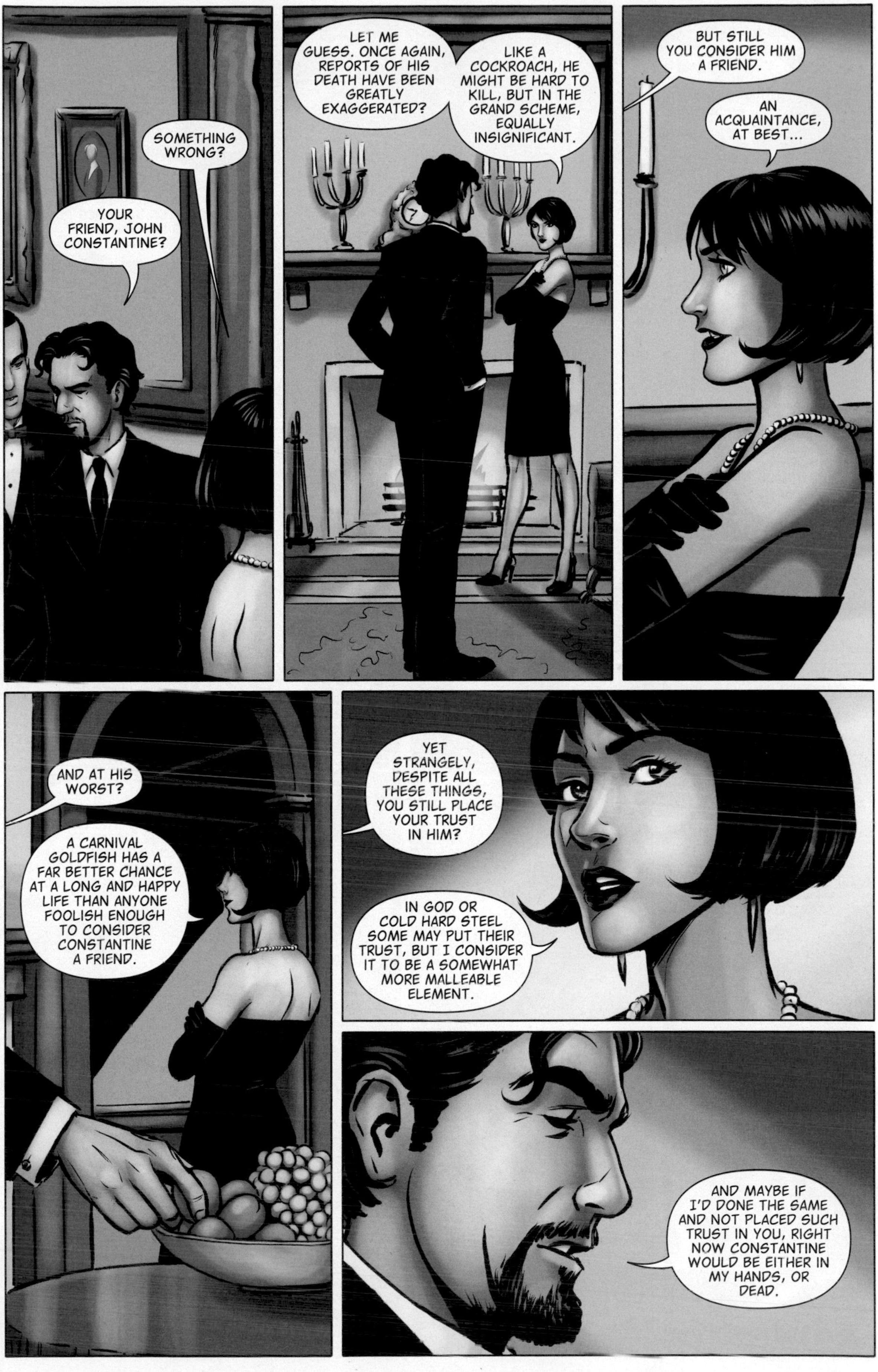
SOMETHING WRONG?
YOUR FRIEND, JOHN CONSTANTINE?
LET ME GUESS. ONCE AGAIN, REPORTS OF HIS DEATH HAVE BEEN GREATLY EXAGGERATED?
LIKE A COCKROACH, HE MIGHT BE HARD TO KILL, BUT IN THE GRAND SCHEME, EQUALLY INSIGNIFICANT.
BUT STILL YOU CONSIDER HIM A FRIEND.
AN ACQUAINTANCE, AT BEST...
AND AT HIS WORST?
A CARNIVAL GOLDFISH HAS A FAR BETTER CHANCE AT A LONG AND HAPPY LIFE THAN ANYONE FOOLISH ENOUGH TO CONSIDER CONSTANTINE A FRIEND.
YET STRANGELY, DESPITE ALL THESE THINGS, YOU STILL PLACE YOUR TRUST IN HIM?
IN GOD OR COLD HARD STEEL SOME MAY PUT THEIR TRUST, BUT I CONSIDER IT TO BE A SOMEWHAT MORE MALLEABLE ELEMENT.
AND MAYBE IF I'D DONE THE SAME AND NOT PLACED SUCH TRUST IN YOU, RIGHT NOW CONSTANTINE WOULD BE EITHER IN MY HANDS, OR DEAD.

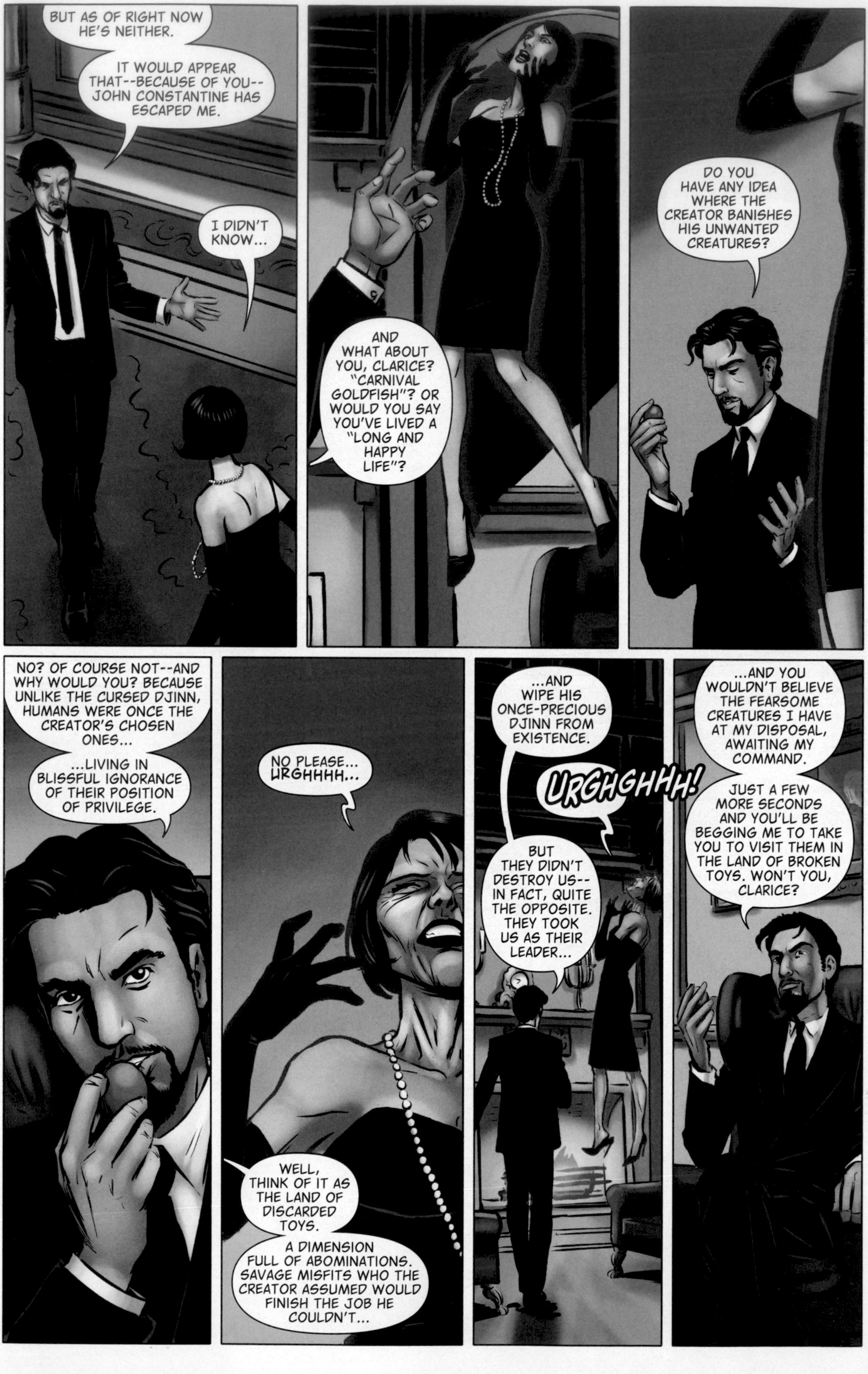
BUT AS OF RIGHT NOW HE'S NEITHER.
IT WOULD APPEAR THAT--BECAUSE OF YOU--JOHN CONSTANTINE HAS ESCAPED ME.
I DIDN'T KNOW...
AND WHAT ABOUT YOU, CLARICE? "CARNIVAL GOLDFISH"? OR WOULD YOU SAY YOU'VE LIVED A "LONG AND HAPPY LIFE"?
DO YOU HAVE ANY IDEA WHERE THE CREATOR BANISHES HIS UNWANTED CREATURES?
NO? OF COURSE NOT--AND WHY WOULD YOU? BECAUSE UNLIKE THE CURSED DJINN, HUMANS WERE ONCE THE CREATOR'S CHOSEN ONES...
...LIVING IN BLISSFUL IGNORANCE OF THEIR POSITION OF PRIVILEGE.
NO PLEASE... URGHHHH...
WELL, THINK OF IT AS THE LAND OF DISCARDED TOYS.
A DIMENSION FULL OF ABOMINATIONS. SAVAGE MISFITS WHO THE CREATOR ASSUMED WOULD FINISH THE JOB HE COULDN'T...
...AND WIPE HIS ONCE-PRECIOUS DJINN FROM EXISTENCE.
URGHGHHH!
BUT THEY DIDN'T DESTROY US--IN FACT, QUITE THE OPPOSITE. THEY TOOK US AS THEIR LEADER...
...AND YOU WOULDN'T BELIEVE THE FEARSOME CREATURES I HAVE AT MY DISPOSAL, AWAITING MY COMMAND.
JUST A FEW MORE SECONDS AND YOU'LL BE BEGGING ME TO TAKE YOU TO VISIT THEM IN THE LAND OF BROKEN TOYS. WON'T YOU, CLARICE?

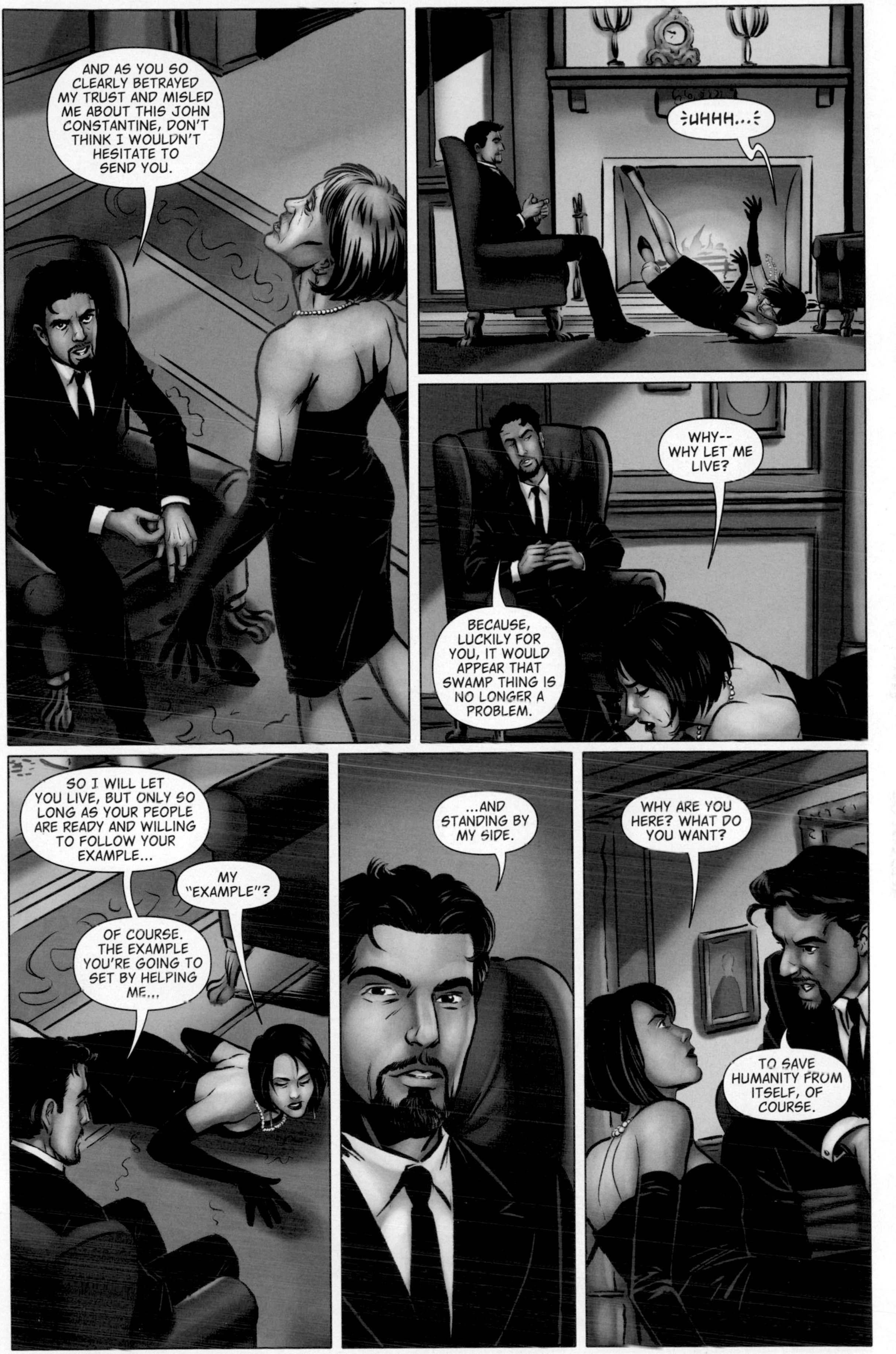
AND AS YOU SO CLEARLY BETRAYED MY TRUST AND MISLED ME ABOUT THIS JOHN CONSTANTINE, DON'T THINK I WOULDN'T HESITATE TO SEND YOU.
UHHH...
WHY-- WHY LET ME LIVE?
BECAUSE, LUCKILY FOR YOU, IT WOULD APPEAR THAT SWAMP THING IS NO LONGER A PROBLEM.
SO I WILL LET YOU LIVE, BUT ONLY SO LONG AS YOUR PEOPLE ARE READY AND WILLING TO FOLLOW YOUR EXAMPLE...
MY "EXAMPLE"?
OF COURSE. THE EXAMPLE YOU'RE GOING TO SET BY HELPING ME...
...AND STANDING BY MY SIDE.
WHY ARE YOU HERE? WHAT DO YOU WANT?
TO SAVE HUMANITY FROM ITSELF, OF COURSE.

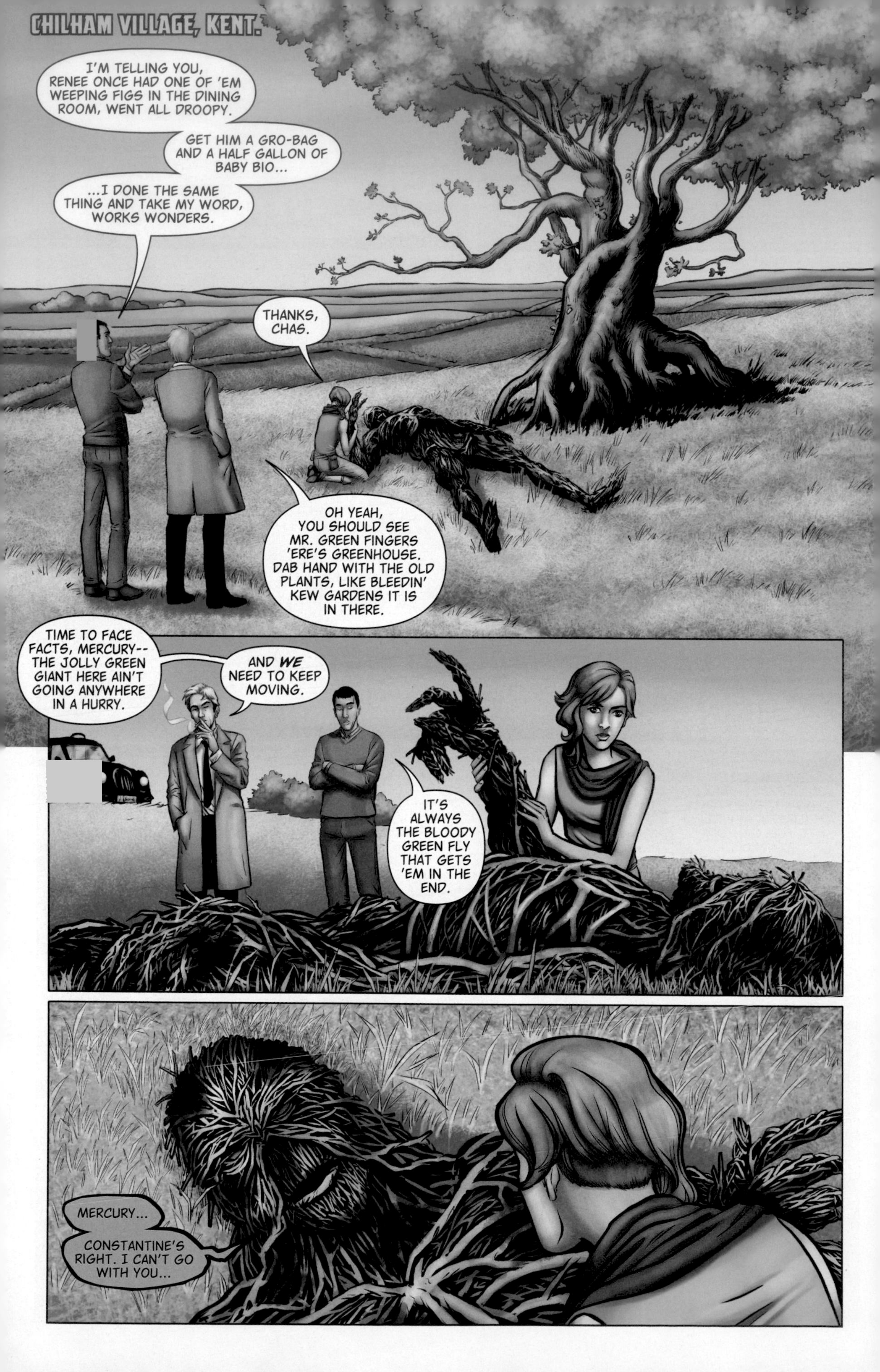
CHILHAM VILLAGE, KENT.
I'M TELLING YOU, RENEE ONCE HAD ONE OF 'EM WEEPING FIGS IN THE DINING ROOM, WENT ALL DROOPY.
GET HIM A GRO-BAG AND A HALF GALLON OF BABY BIO...
...I DONE THE SAME THING AND TAKE MY WORD, WORKS WONDERS.
THANKS, CHAS.
OH YEAH, YOU SHOULD SEE MR. GREEN FINGERS 'ERE'S GREENHOUSE. DAB HAND WITH THE OLD PLANTS, LIKE BLEEDIN' KEW GARDENS IT IS IN THERE.
TIME TO FACE FACTS, MERCURY-- THE JOLLY GREEN GIANT HERE AIN'T GOING ANYWHERE IN A HURRY.
AND *WE* NEED TO KEEP MOVING.
IT'S ALWAYS THE BLOODY GREEN FLY THAT GETS 'EM IN THE END.
MERCURY...
CONSTANTINE'S RIGHT. I CAN'T GO WITH YOU...

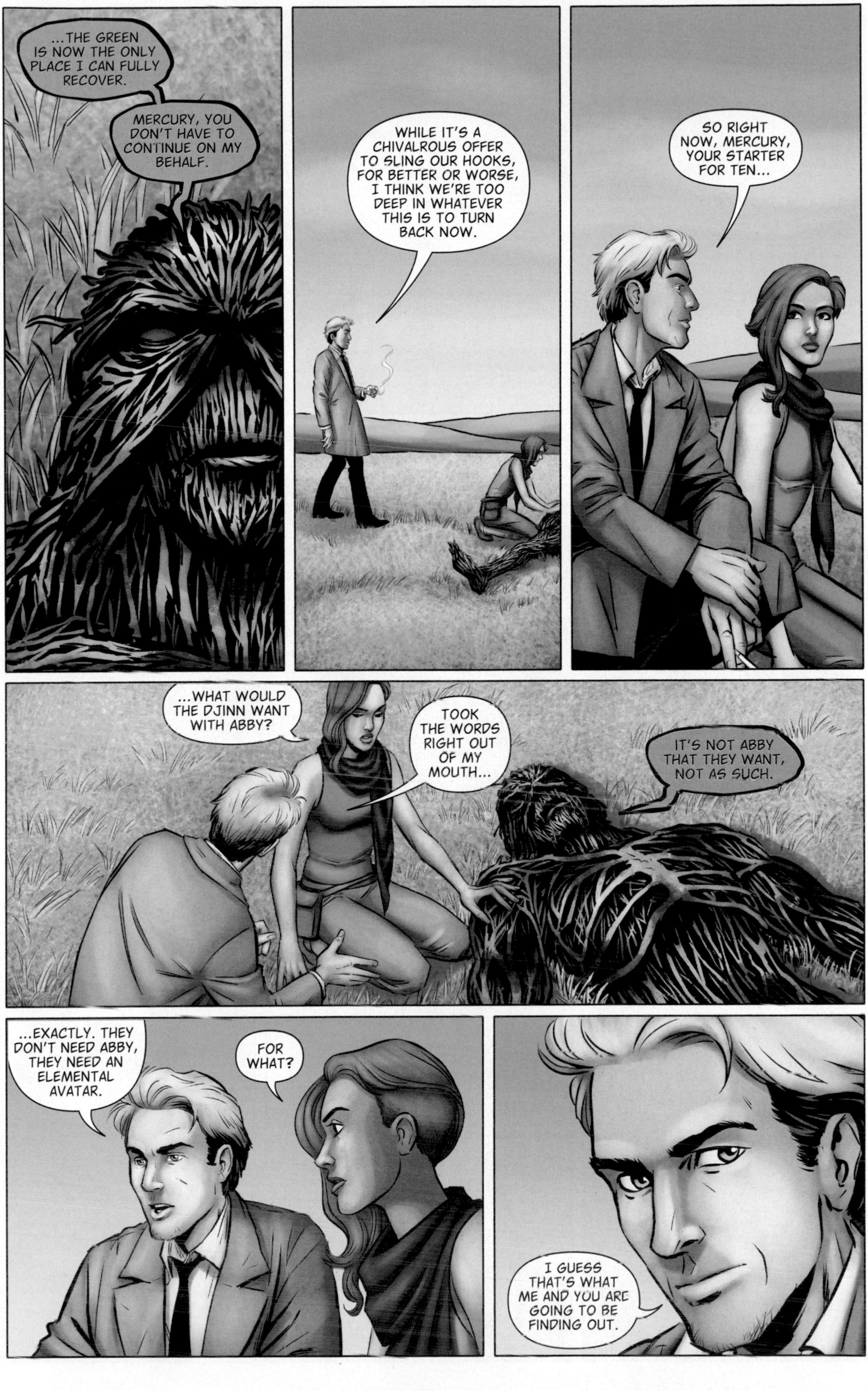
...THE GREEN IS NOW THE ONLY PLACE I CAN FULLY RECOVER.
MERCURY, YOU DON'T HAVE TO CONTINUE ON MY BEHALF.
WHILE IT'S A CHIVALROUS OFFER TO SLING OUR HOOKS, FOR BETTER OR WORSE, I THINK WE'RE TOO DEEP IN WHATEVER THIS IS TO TURN BACK NOW.
SO RIGHT NOW, MERCURY, YOUR STARTER FOR TEN...
...WHAT WOULD THE DJINN WANT WITH ABBY?
TOOK THE WORDS RIGHT OUT OF MY MOUTH...
IT'S NOT ABBY THAT THEY WANT, NOT AS SUCH.
...EXACTLY. THEY DON'T NEED ABBY, THEY NEED AN ELEMENTAL AVATAR.
FOR WHAT?
I GUESS THAT'S WHAT ME AND YOU ARE GOING TO BE FINDING OUT.

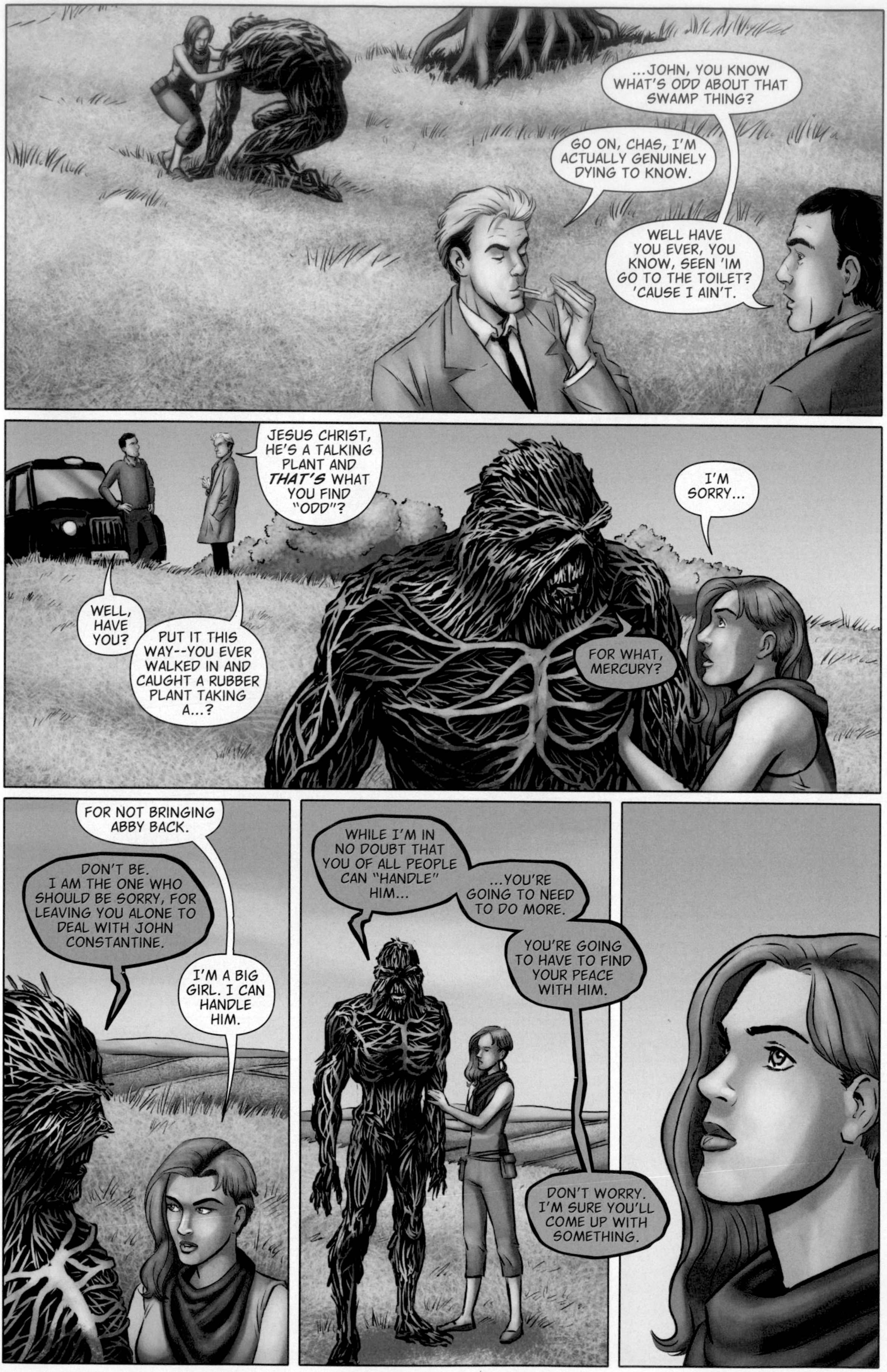
...JOHN, YOU KNOW WHAT'S ODD ABOUT THAT SWAMP THING?
GO ON, CHAS, I'M ACTUALLY GENUINELY DYING TO KNOW.
WELL HAVE YOU EVER, YOU KNOW, SEEN 'IM GO TO THE TOILET? 'CAUSE I AIN'T.
JESUS CHRIST, HE'S A TALKING PLANT AND *THAT'S* WHAT YOU FIND "ODD"?
WELL, HAVE YOU?
PUT IT THIS WAY--YOU EVER WALKED IN AND CAUGHT A RUBBER PLANT TAKING A...?
I'M SORRY...
FOR WHAT, MERCURY?
FOR NOT BRINGING ABBY BACK.
DON'T BE. I AM THE ONE WHO SHOULD BE SORRY, FOR LEAVING YOU ALONE TO DEAL WITH JOHN CONSTANTINE.
I'M A BIG GIRL. I CAN HANDLE HIM.
WHILE I'M IN NO DOUBT THAT YOU OF ALL PEOPLE CAN "HANDLE" HIM...
...YOU'RE GOING TO NEED TO DO MORE.
YOU'RE GOING TO HAVE TO FIND YOUR PEACE WITH HIM.
DON'T WORRY. I'M SURE YOU'LL COME UP WITH SOMETHING.

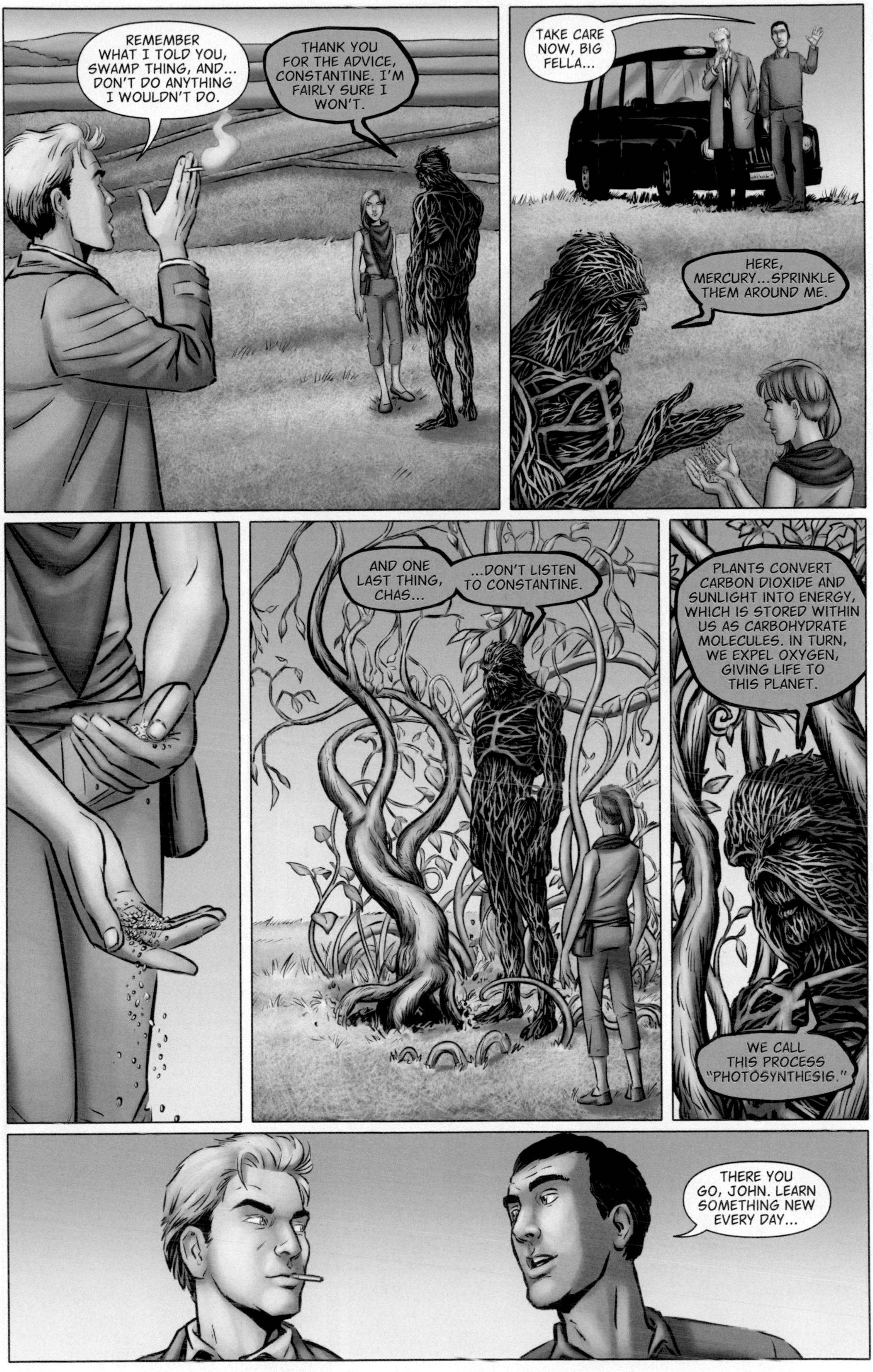
REMEMBER WHAT I TOLD YOU, SWAMP THING, AND... DON'T DO ANYTHING I WOULDN'T DO.
THANK YOU FOR THE ADVICE, CONSTANTINE. I'M FAIRLY SURE I WON'T.
TAKE CARE NOW, BIG FELLA...
HERE, MERCURY...SPRINKLE THEM AROUND ME.
AND ONE LAST THING, CHAS...
...DON'T LISTEN TO CONSTANTINE.
PLANTS CONVERT CARBON DIOXIDE AND SUNLIGHT INTO ENERGY, WHICH IS STORED WITHIN US AS CARBOHYDRATE MOLECULES. IN TURN, WE EXPEL OXYGEN, GIVING LIFE TO THIS PLANET.
WE CALL THIS PROCESS "PHOTOSYNTHESIS."
THERE YOU GO, JOHN. LEARN SOMETHING NEW EVERY DAY...

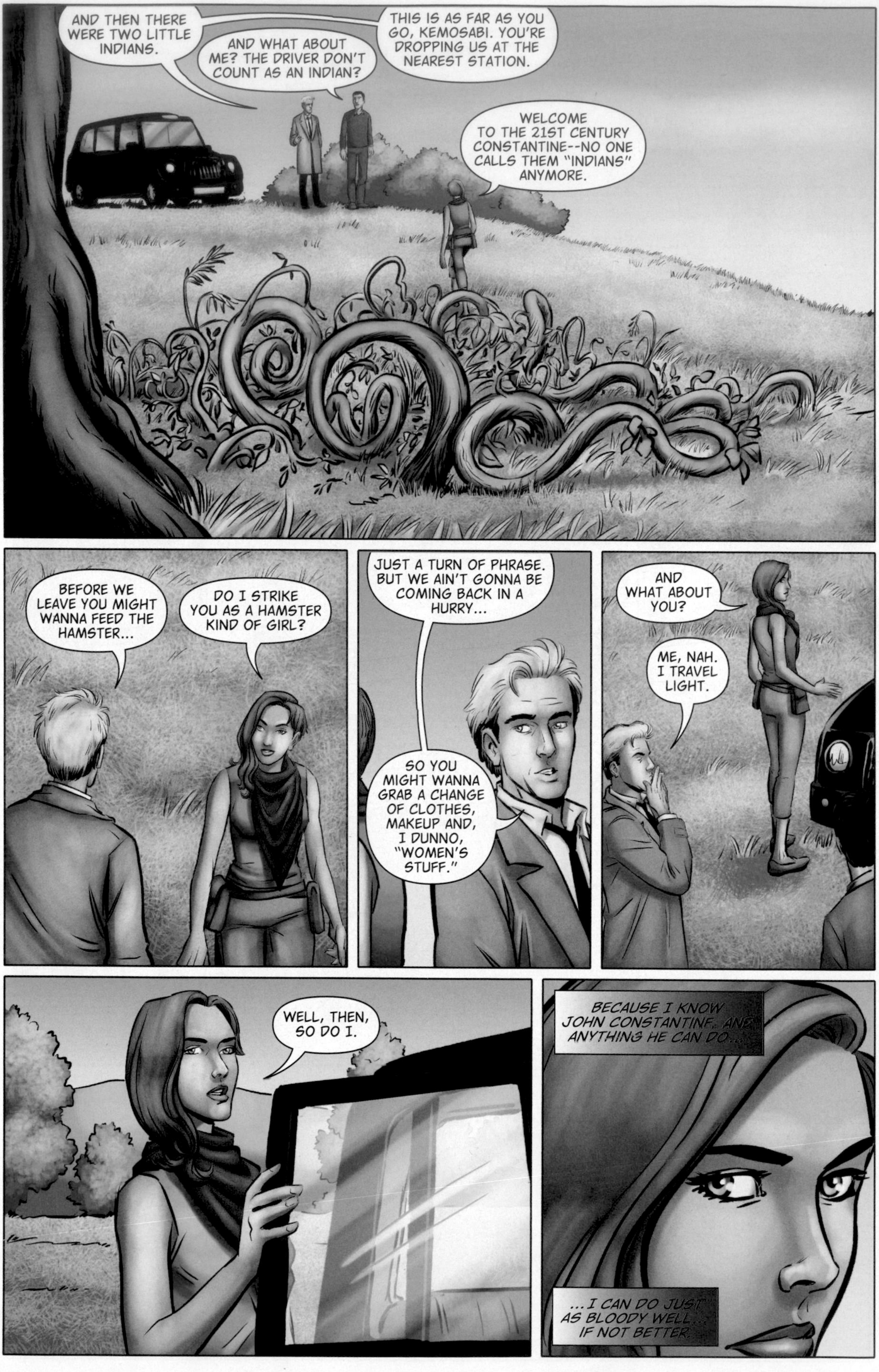
AND THEN THERE WERE TWO LITTLE INDIANS.
AND WHAT ABOUT ME? THE DRIVER DON'T COUNT AS AN INDIAN?
THIS IS AS FAR AS YOU GO, KEMOSABI. YOU'RE DROPPING US AT THE NEAREST STATION.
WELCOME TO THE 21ST CENTURY CONSTANTINE--NO ONE CALLS THEM "INDIANS" ANYMORE.
BEFORE WE LEAVE YOU MIGHT WANNA FEED THE HAMSTER...
DO I STRIKE YOU AS A HAMSTER KIND OF GIRL?
JUST A TURN OF PHRASE. BUT WE AIN'T GONNA BE COMING BACK IN A HURRY...
SO YOU MIGHT WANNA GRAB A CHANGE OF CLOTHES, MAKEUP AND, I DUNNO, "WOMEN'S STUFF."
AND WHAT ABOUT YOU?
ME, NAH. I TRAVEL LIGHT.
WELL, THEN, SO DO I.
BECAUSE I KNOW JOHN CONSTANTINE. AND ANYTHING HE CAN DO...
...I CAN DO JUST AS BLOODY WELL... IF NOT BETTER.

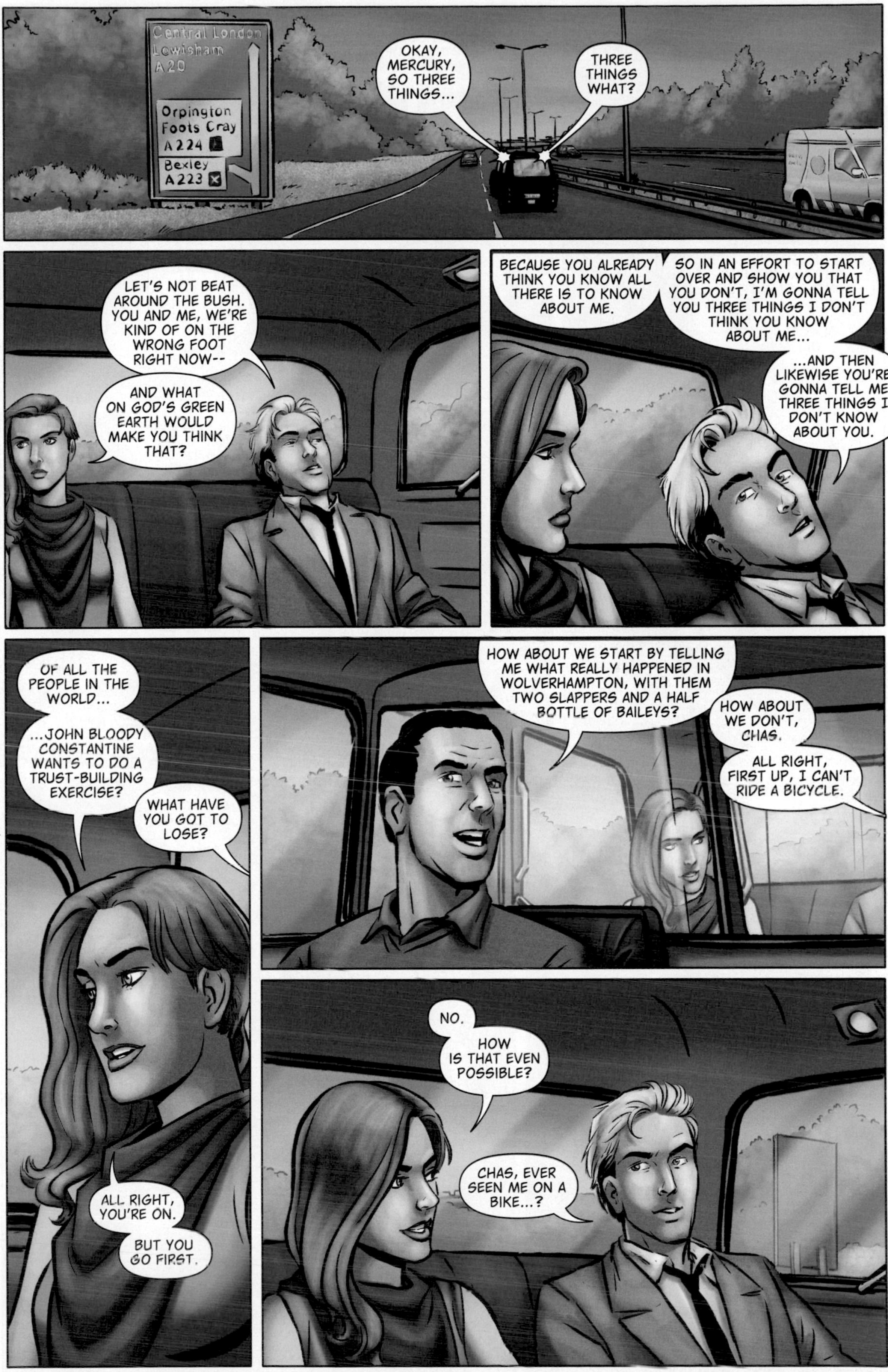
Central London
Lewisham
A20
Orpington
Foots Cray
A224
Bexley
A223
OKAY, MERCURY, SO THREE THINGS...
THREE THINGS WHAT?
LET'S NOT BEAT AROUND THE BUSH. YOU AND ME, WE'RE KIND OF ON THE WRONG FOOT RIGHT NOW--
AND WHAT ON GOD'S GREEN EARTH WOULD MAKE YOU THINK THAT?
BECAUSE YOU ALREADY THINK YOU KNOW ALL THERE IS TO KNOW ABOUT ME.
SO IN AN EFFORT TO START OVER AND SHOW YOU THAT YOU DON'T, I'M GONNA TELL YOU THREE THINGS I DON'T THINK YOU KNOW ABOUT ME...
...AND THEN LIKEWISE YOU'RE GONNA TELL ME THREE THINGS I DON'T KNOW ABOUT YOU.
OF ALL THE PEOPLE IN THE WORLD...
...JOHN BLOODY CONSTANTINE WANTS TO DO A TRUST-BUILDING EXERCISE?
WHAT HAVE YOU GOT TO LOSE?
ALL RIGHT, YOU'RE ON.
BUT YOU GO FIRST.
HOW ABOUT WE START BY TELLING ME WHAT REALLY HAPPENED IN WOLVERHAMPTON, WITH THEM TWO SLAPPERS AND A HALF BOTTLE OF BAILEYS?
HOW ABOUT WE DON'T, CHAS.
ALL RIGHT, FIRST UP, I CAN'T RIDE A BICYCLE.
NO.
HOW IS THAT EVEN POSSIBLE?
CHAS, EVER SEEN ME ON A BIKE...?

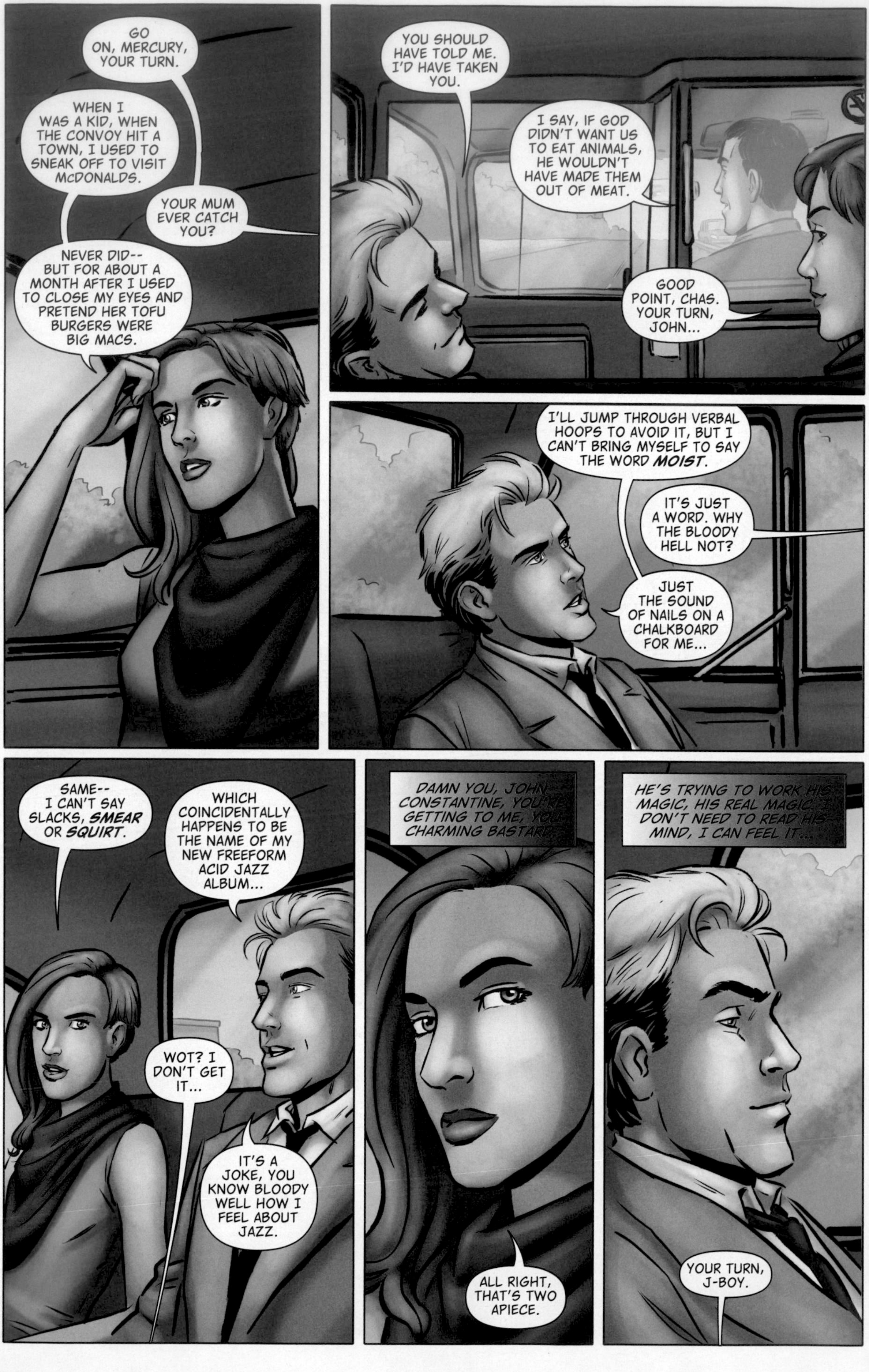
GO ON, MERCURY, YOUR TURN.
WHEN I WAS A KID, WHEN THE CONVOY HIT A TOWN, I USED TO SNEAK OFF TO VISIT McDONALDS.
YOUR MUM EVER CATCH YOU?
NEVER DID-- BUT FOR ABOUT A MONTH AFTER I USED TO CLOSE MY EYES AND PRETEND HER TOFU BURGERS WERE BIG MACS.
YOU SHOULD HAVE TOLD ME. I'D HAVE TAKEN YOU.
I SAY, IF GOD DIDN'T WANT US TO EAT ANIMALS, HE WOULDN'T HAVE MADE THEM OUT OF MEAT.
GOOD POINT, CHAS. YOUR TURN, JOHN...
I'LL JUMP THROUGH VERBAL HOOPS TO AVOID IT, BUT I CAN'T BRING MYSELF TO SAY THE WORD ***MOIST***.
IT'S JUST A WORD. WHY THE BLOODY HELL NOT?
JUST THE SOUND OF NAILS ON A CHALKBOARD FOR ME...
SAME-- I CAN'T SAY SLACKS, ***SMEAR*** OR ***SQUIRT***.
WHICH COINCIDENTALLY HAPPENS TO BE THE NAME OF MY NEW FREEFORM ACID JAZZ ALBUM...
WOT? I DON'T GET IT...
IT'S A JOKE, YOU KNOW BLOODY WELL HOW I FEEL ABOUT JAZZ.
DAMN YOU, JOHN CONSTANTINE, YOU'RE GETTING TO ME, YOU CHARMING BASTARD.
ALL RIGHT, THAT'S TWO APIECE.
HE'S TRYING TO WORK HIS MAGIC, HIS REAL MAGIC. I DON'T NEED TO READ HIS MIND, I CAN FEEL IT...
YOUR TURN, J-BOY.

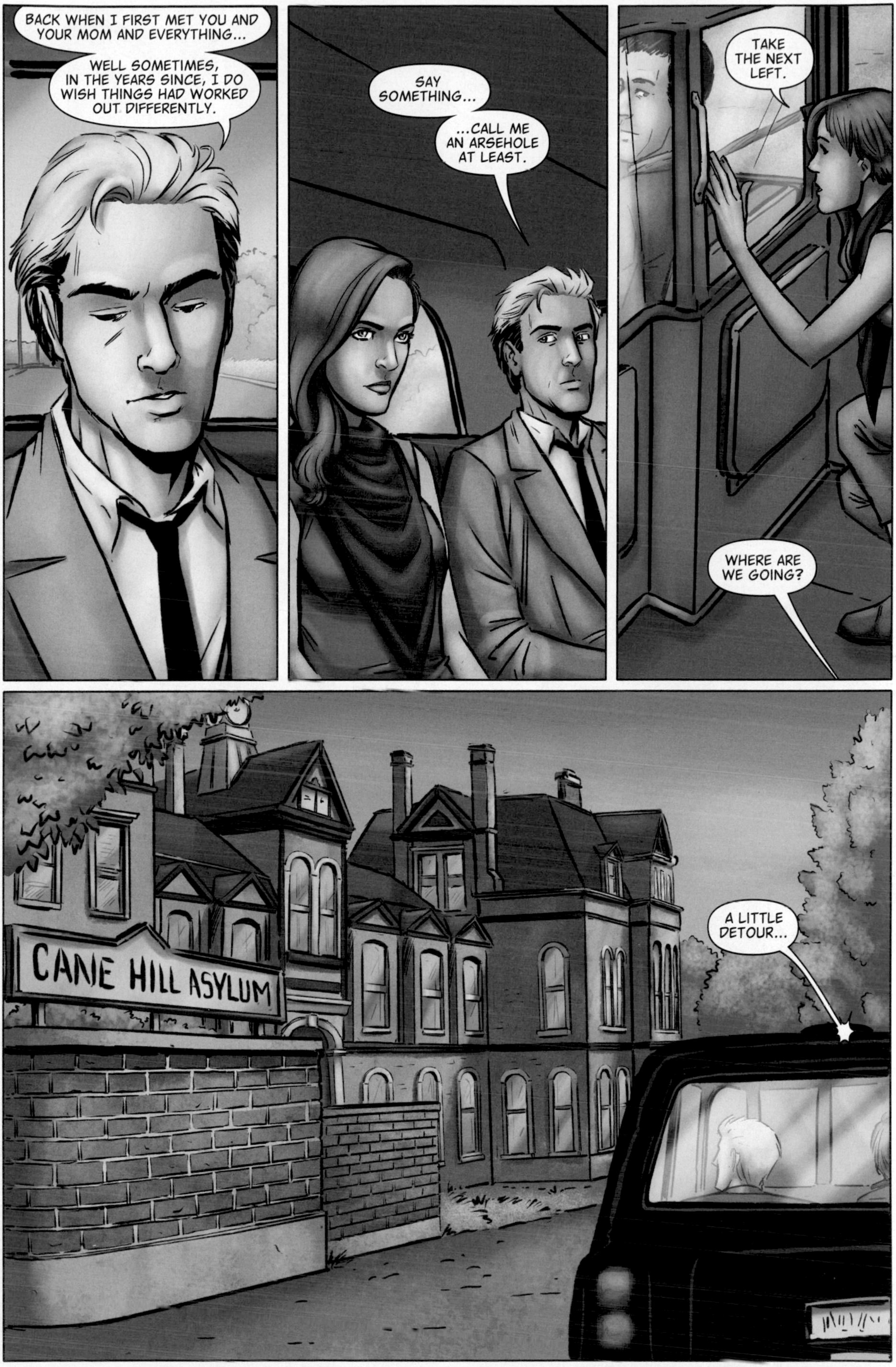
BACK WHEN I FIRST MET YOU AND YOUR MOM AND EVERYTHING...
WELL SOMETIMES, IN THE YEARS SINCE, I DO WISH THINGS HAD WORKED OUT DIFFERENTLY.
SAY SOMETHING...
...CALL ME AN ARSEHOLE AT LEAST.
TAKE THE NEXT LEFT.
WHERE ARE WE GOING?
CANE HILL ASYLUM
A LITTLE DETOUR...

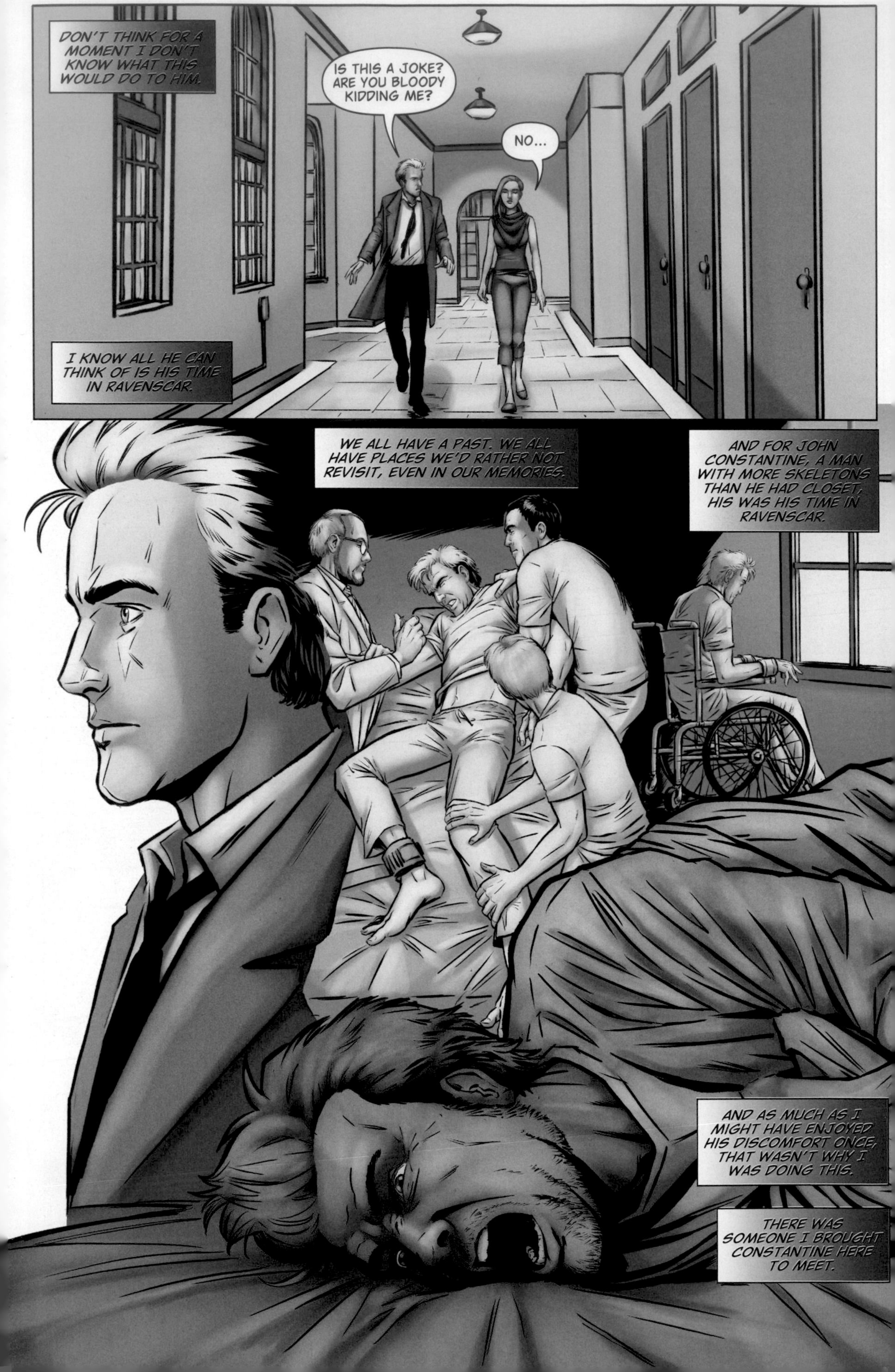
DON'T THINK FOR A MOMENT I DON'T KNOW WHAT THIS WOULD DO TO HIM.
IS THIS A JOKE? ARE YOU BLOODY KIDDING ME?
NO...
I KNOW ALL HE CAN THINK OF IS HIS TIME IN RAVENSCAR.
WE ALL HAVE A PAST. WE ALL HAVE PLACES WE'D RATHER NOT REVISIT, EVEN IN OUR MEMORIES.
AND FOR JOHN CONSTANTINE, A MAN WITH MORE SKELETONS THAN HE HAD CLOSET, HIS WAS HIS TIME IN RAVENSCAR.
AND AS MUCH AS I MIGHT HAVE ENJOYED HIS DISCOMFORT ONCE, THAT WASN'T WHY I WAS DOING THIS.
THERE WAS SOMEONE I BROUGHT CONSTANTINE HERE TO MEET.

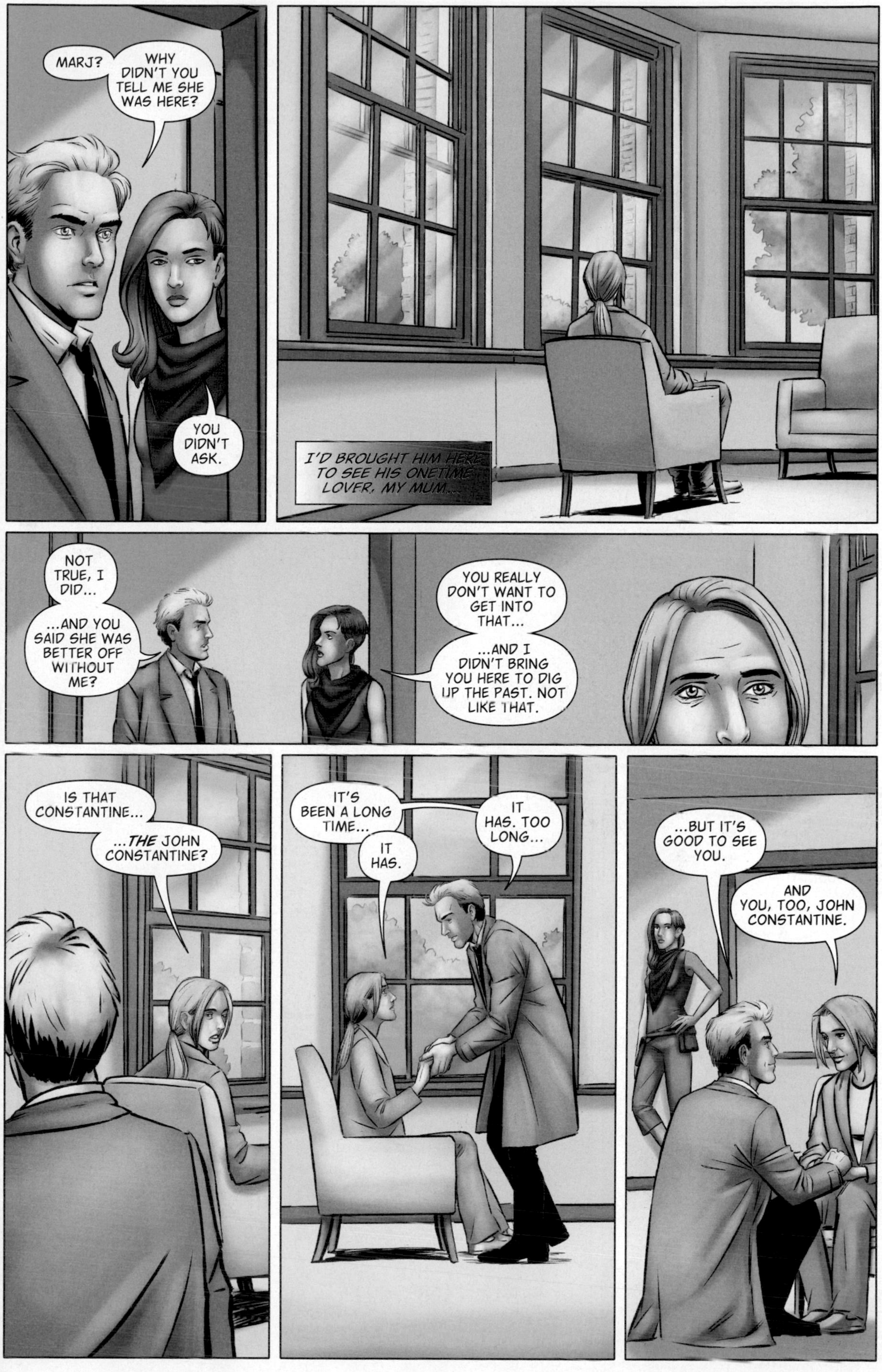
MARJ?
WHY DIDN'T YOU TELL ME SHE WAS HERE?
YOU DIDN'T ASK.
I'D BROUGHT HIM HERE TO SEE HIS ONETIME LOVER. MY MUM...
NOT TRUE, I DID...
...AND YOU SAID SHE WAS BETTER OFF WITHOUT ME?
YOU REALLY DON'T WANT TO GET INTO THAT...
...AND I DIDN'T BRING YOU HERE TO DIG UP THE PAST. NOT LIKE THAT.
IS THAT CONSTANTINE...
...*THE* JOHN CONSTANTINE?
IT'S BEEN A LONG TIME...
IT HAS.
IT HAS. TOO LONG...
...BUT IT'S GOOD TO SEE YOU.
AND YOU, TOO, JOHN CONSTANTINE.

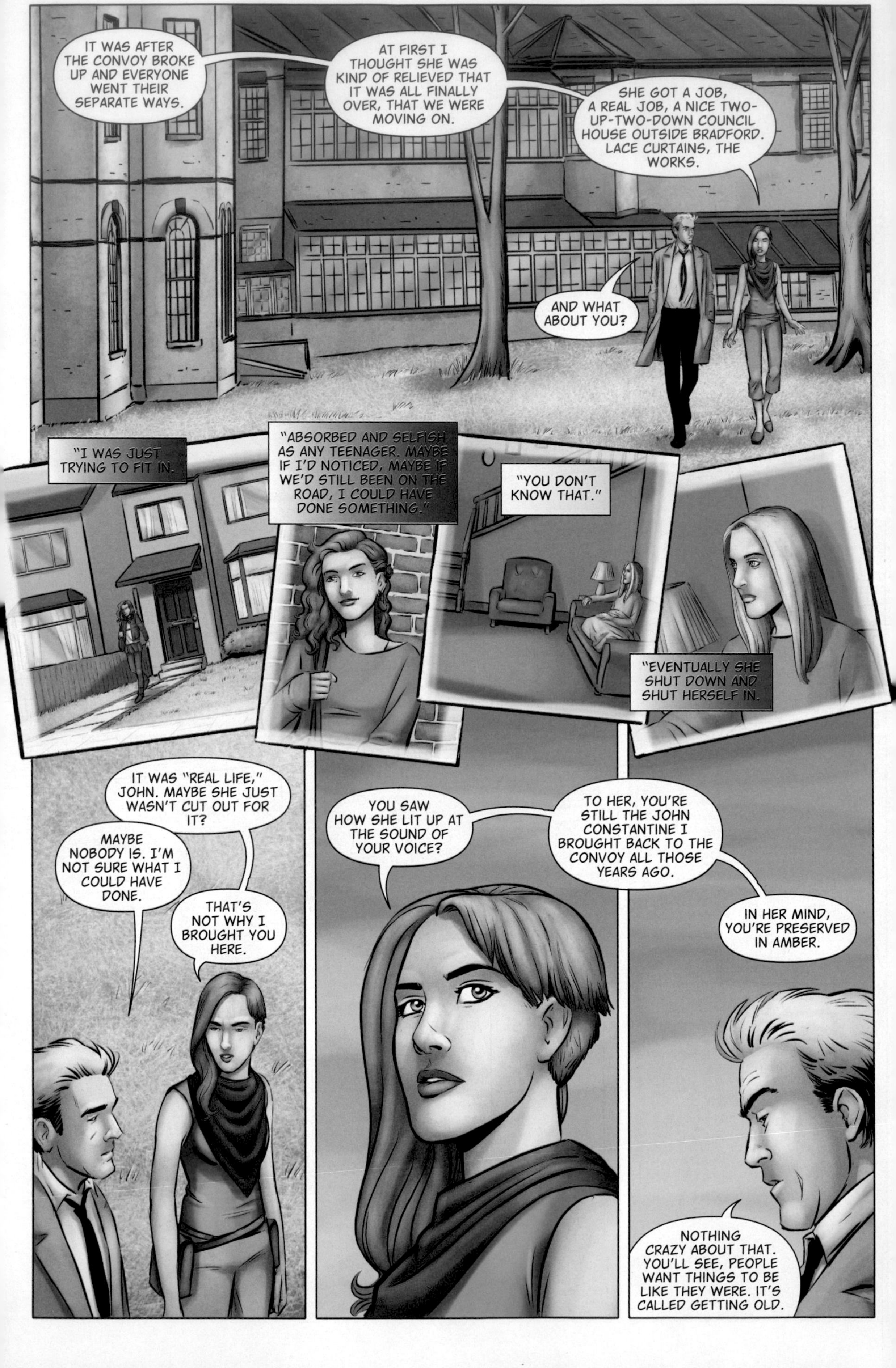
IT WAS AFTER THE CONVOY BROKE UP AND EVERYONE WENT THEIR SEPARATE WAYS.
AT FIRST I THOUGHT SHE WAS KIND OF RELIEVED THAT IT WAS ALL FINALLY OVER, THAT WE WERE MOVING ON.
SHE GOT A JOB, A REAL JOB, A NICE TWO-UP-TWO-DOWN COUNCIL HOUSE OUTSIDE BRADFORD. LACE CURTAINS, THE WORKS.
AND WHAT ABOUT YOU?
"I WAS JUST TRYING TO FIT IN.
"ABSORBED AND SELFISH AS ANY TEENAGER. MAYBE IF I'D NOTICED, MAYBE IF WE'D STILL BEEN ON THE ROAD, I COULD HAVE DONE SOMETHING."
"YOU DON'T KNOW THAT."
"EVENTUALLY SHE SHUT DOWN AND SHUT HERSELF IN.
IT WAS "REAL LIFE," JOHN. MAYBE SHE JUST WASN'T CUT OUT FOR IT?
MAYBE NOBODY IS. I'M NOT SURE WHAT I COULD HAVE DONE.
THAT'S NOT WHY I BROUGHT YOU HERE.
YOU SAW HOW SHE LIT UP AT THE SOUND OF YOUR VOICE?
TO HER, YOU'RE STILL THE JOHN CONSTANTINE I BROUGHT BACK TO THE CONVOY ALL THOSE YEARS AGO.
IN HER MIND, YOU'RE PRESERVED IN AMBER.
NOTHING CRAZY ABOUT THAT. YOU'LL SEE, PEOPLE WANT THINGS TO BE LIKE THEY WERE. IT'S CALLED GETTING OLD.

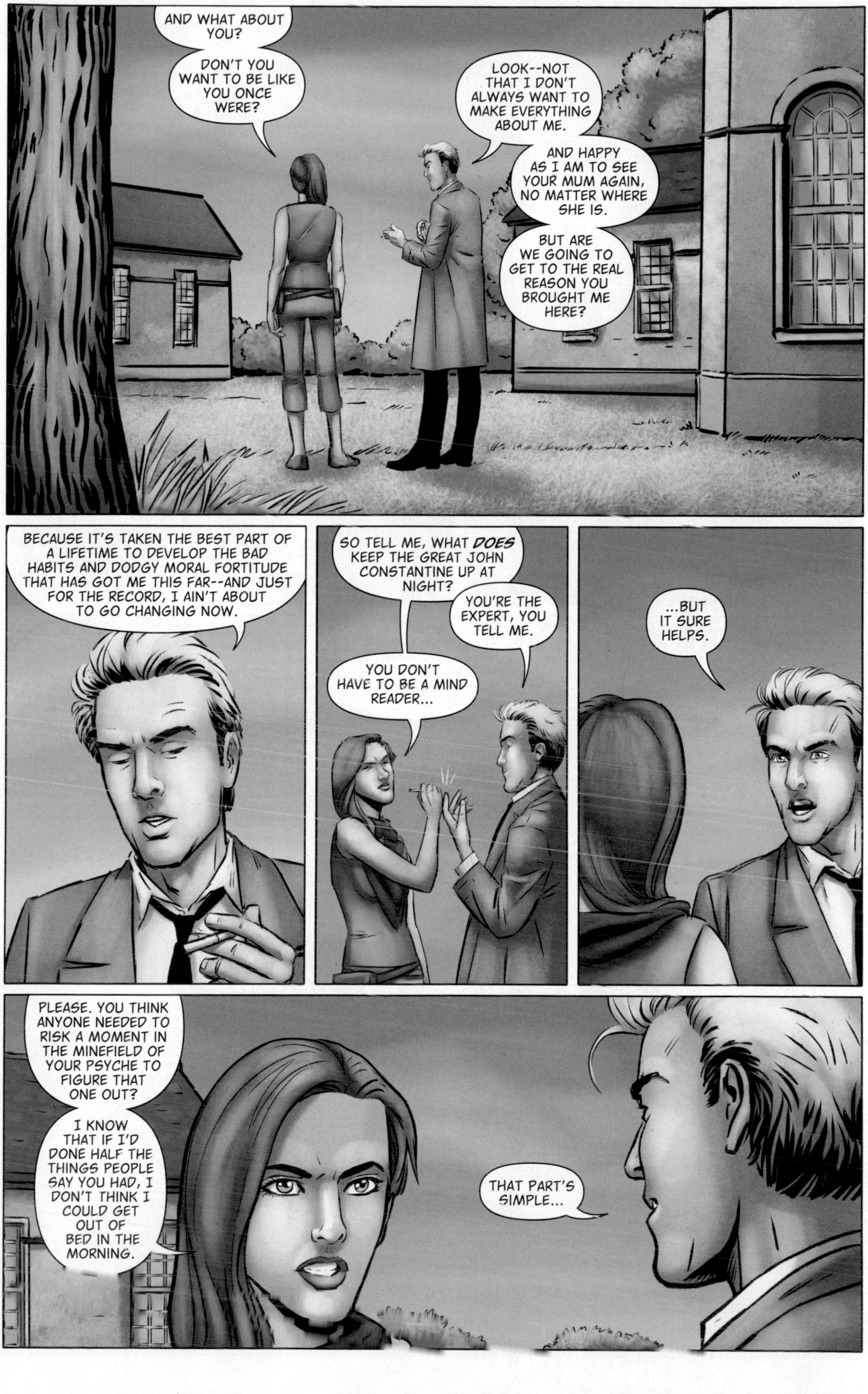
AND WHAT ABOUT YOU?
DON'T YOU WANT TO BE LIKE YOU ONCE WERE?
LOOK--NOT THAT I DON'T ALWAYS WANT TO MAKE EVERYTHING ABOUT ME.
AND HAPPY AS I AM TO SEE YOUR MUM AGAIN, NO MATTER WHERE SHE IS.
BUT ARE WE GOING TO GET TO THE REAL REASON YOU BROUGHT ME HERE?
BECAUSE IT'S TAKEN THE BEST PART OF A LIFETIME TO DEVELOP THE BAD HABITS AND DODGY MORAL FORTITUDE THAT HAS GOT ME THIS FAR--AND JUST FOR THE RECORD, I AIN'T ABOUT TO GO CHANGING NOW.
SO TELL ME, WHAT DOES KEEP THE GREAT JOHN CONSTANTINE UP AT NIGHT?
YOU'RE THE EXPERT, YOU TELL ME.
YOU DON'T HAVE TO BE A MIND READER...
...BUT IT SURE HELPS.
PLEASE. YOU THINK ANYONE NEEDED TO RISK A MOMENT IN THE MINEFIELD OF YOUR PSYCHE TO FIGURE THAT ONE OUT?
I KNOW THAT IF I'D DONE HALF THE THINGS PEOPLE SAY YOU HAD, I DON'T THINK I COULD GET OUT OF BED IN THE MORNING.
THAT PART'S SIMPLE...

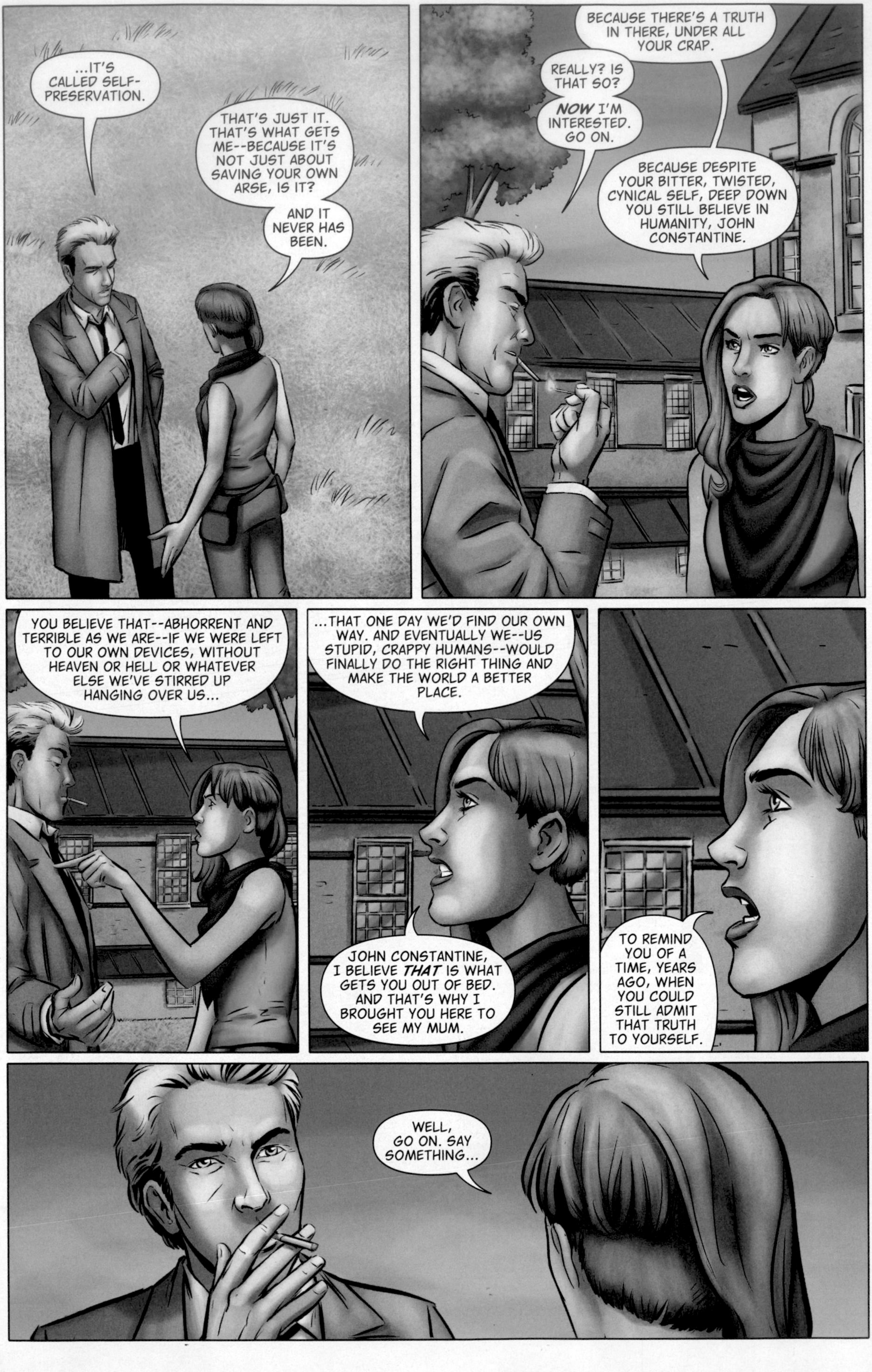
...IT'S CALLED SELF-PRESERVATION.
THAT'S JUST IT. THAT'S WHAT GETS ME--BECAUSE IT'S NOT JUST ABOUT SAVING YOUR OWN ARSE, IS IT?
AND IT NEVER HAS BEEN.
BECAUSE THERE'S A TRUTH IN THERE, UNDER ALL YOUR CRAP.
REALLY? IS THAT SO?
NOW I'M INTERESTED. GO ON.
BECAUSE DESPITE YOUR BITTER, TWISTED, CYNICAL SELF, DEEP DOWN YOU STILL BELIEVE IN HUMANITY, JOHN CONSTANTINE.
YOU BELIEVE THAT--ABHORRENT AND TERRIBLE AS WE ARE--IF WE WERE LEFT TO OUR OWN DEVICES, WITHOUT HEAVEN OR HELL OR WHATEVER ELSE WE'VE STIRRED UP HANGING OVER US...
...THAT ONE DAY WE'D FIND OUR OWN WAY. AND EVENTUALLY WE--US STUPID, CRAPPY HUMANS--WOULD FINALLY DO THE RIGHT THING AND MAKE THE WORLD A BETTER PLACE.
JOHN CONSTANTINE, I BELIEVE THAT IS WHAT GETS YOU OUT OF BED. AND THAT'S WHY I BROUGHT YOU HERE TO SEE MY MUM.
TO REMIND YOU OF A TIME, YEARS AGO, WHEN YOU COULD STILL ADMIT THAT TRUTH TO YOURSELF.
WELL, GO ON. SAY SOMETHING...

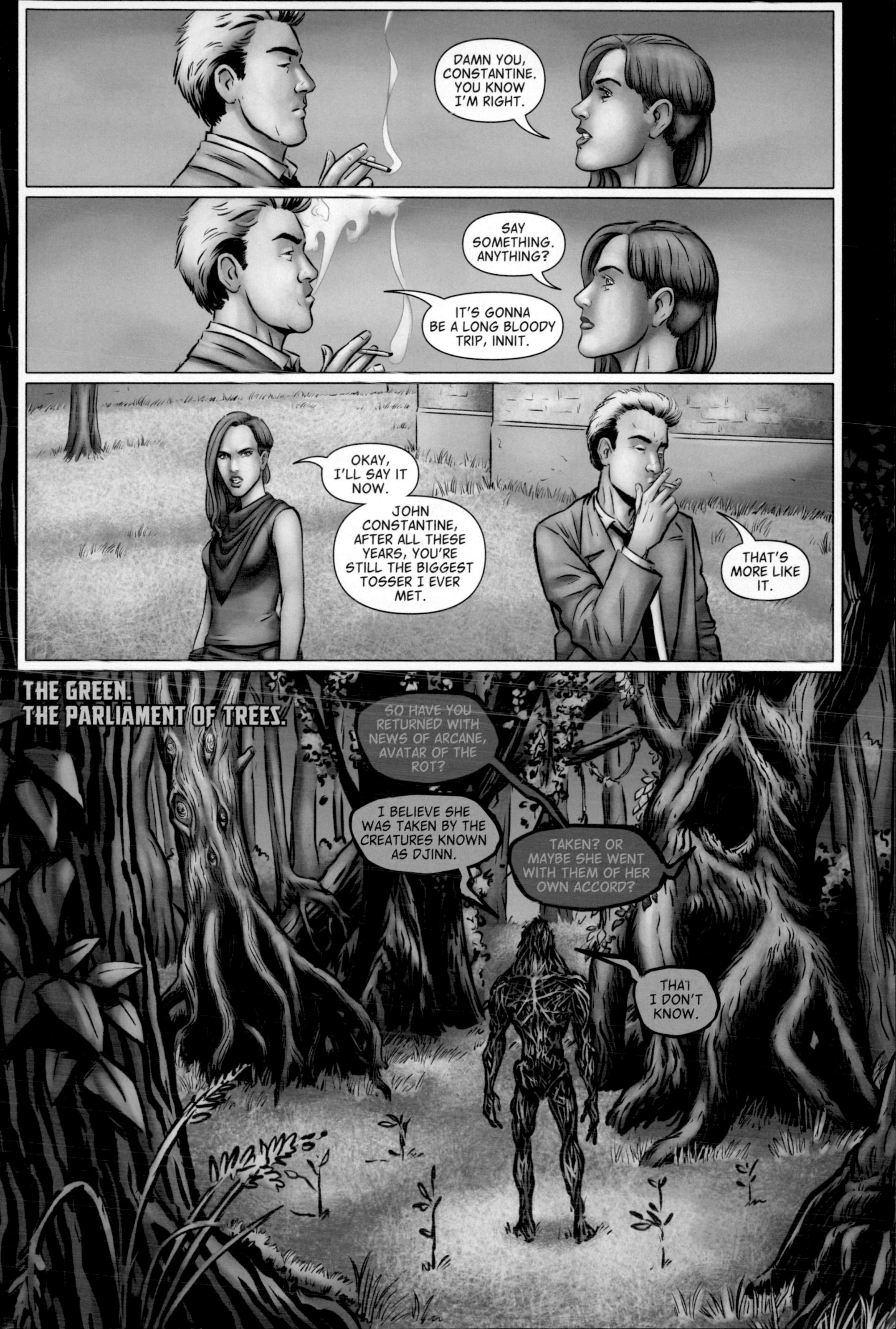
DAMN YOU, CONSTANTINE. YOU KNOW I'M RIGHT.
SAY SOMETHING. ANYTHING?
IT'S GONNA BE A LONG BLOODY TRIP, INNIT.
OKAY, I'LL SAY IT NOW.
JOHN CONSTANTINE, AFTER ALL THESE YEARS, YOU'RE STILL THE BIGGEST TOSSER I EVER MET.
THAT'S MORE LIKE IT.
THE GREEN. THE PARLIAMENT OF TREES.
SO HAVE YOU RETURNED WITH NEWS OF ARCANE, AVATAR OF THE ROT?
I BELIEVE SHE WAS TAKEN BY THE CREATURES KNOWN AS DJINN.
TAKEN? OR MAYBE SHE WENT WITH THEM OF HER OWN ACCORD?
THAT I DON'T KNOW.

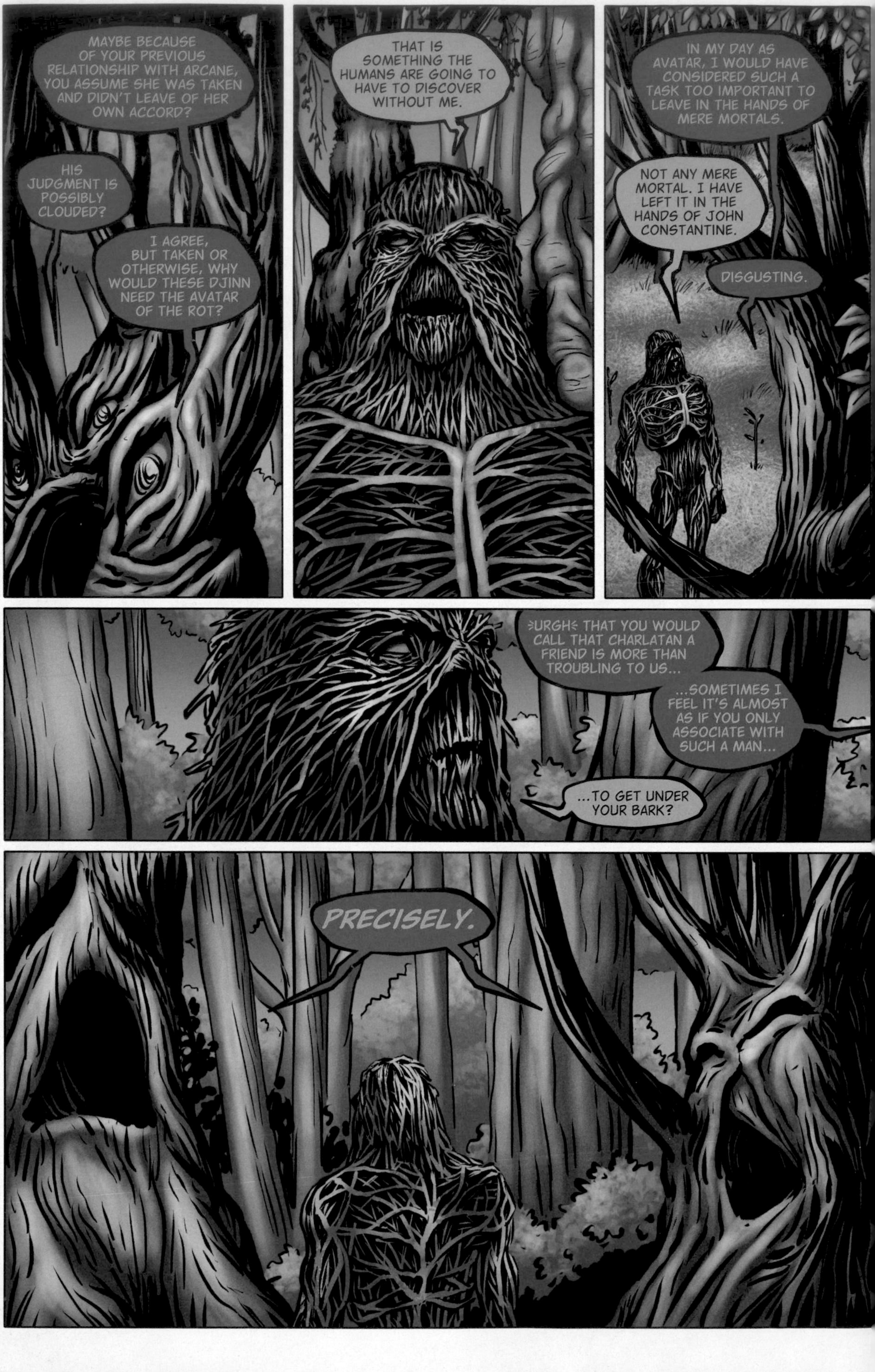
MAYBE BECAUSE OF YOUR PREVIOUS RELATIONSHIP WITH ARCANE, YOU ASSUME SHE WAS TAKEN AND DIDN'T LEAVE OF HER OWN ACCORD?
HIS JUDGMENT IS POSSIBLY CLOUDED?
I AGREE, BUT TAKEN OR OTHERWISE, WHY WOULD THESE DJINN NEED THE AVATAR OF THE ROT?
THAT IS SOMETHING THE HUMANS ARE GOING TO HAVE TO DISCOVER WITHOUT ME.
IN MY DAY AS AVATAR, I WOULD HAVE CONSIDERED SUCH A TASK TOO IMPORTANT TO LEAVE IN THE HANDS OF MERE MORTALS.
NOT ANY MERE MORTAL. I HAVE LEFT IT IN THE HANDS OF JOHN CONSTANTINE.
DISGUSTING.
URGH THAT YOU WOULD CALL THAT CHARLATAN A FRIEND IS MORE THAN TROUBLING TO US...
...SOMETIMES I FEEL IT'S ALMOST AS IF YOU ONLY ASSOCIATE WITH SUCH A MAN...
...TO GET UNDER YOUR BARK?
PRECISELY.

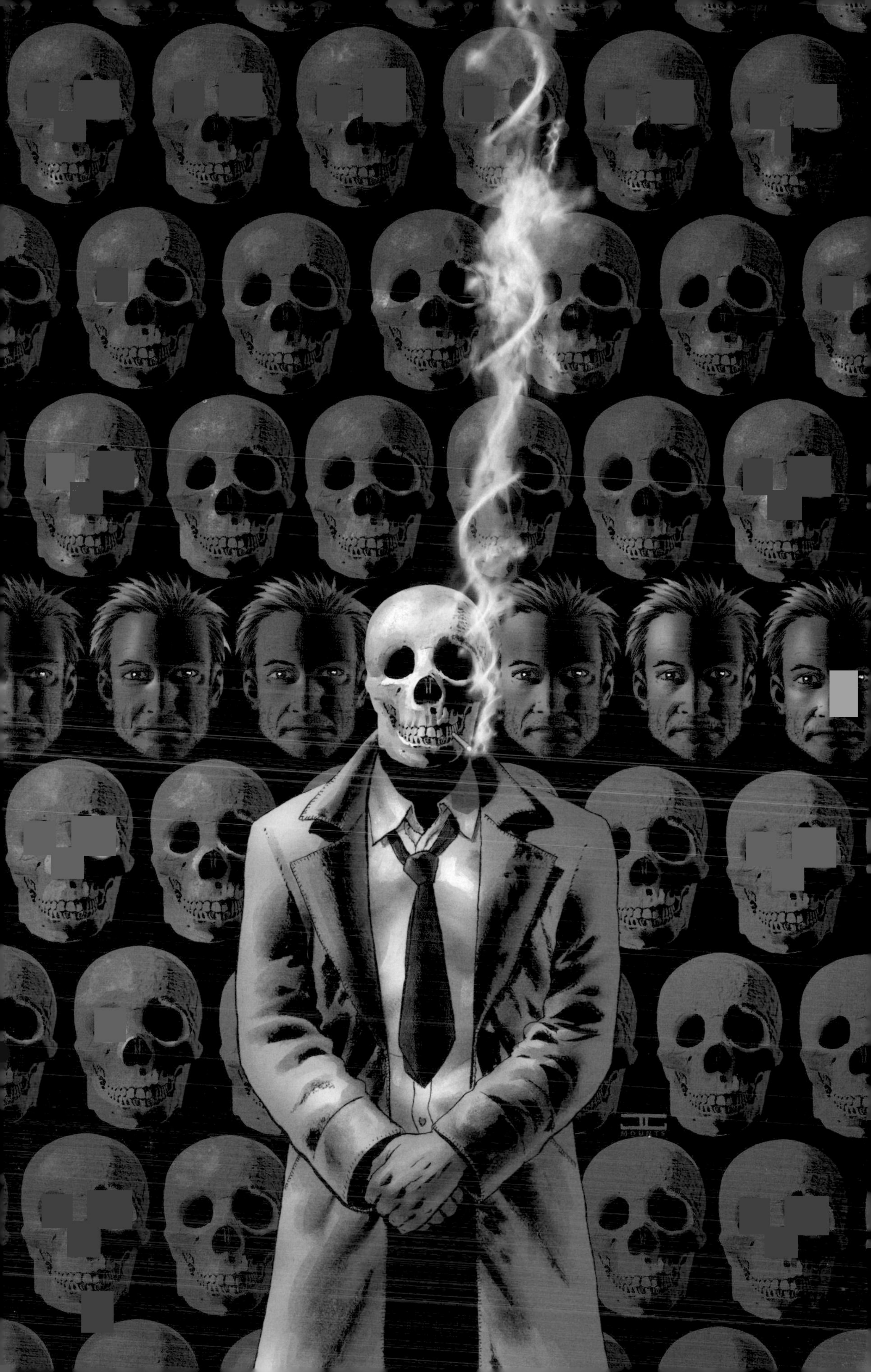

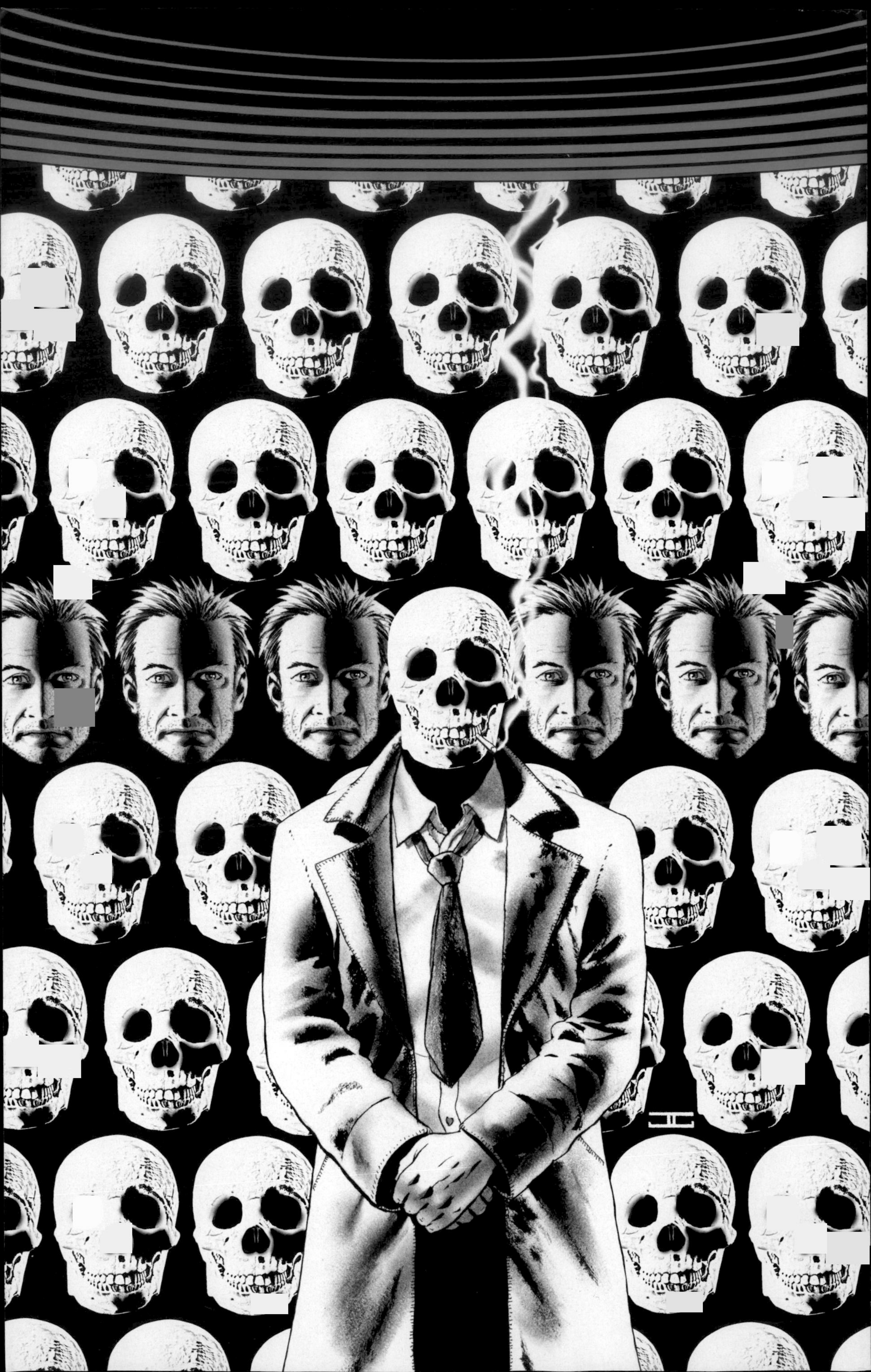

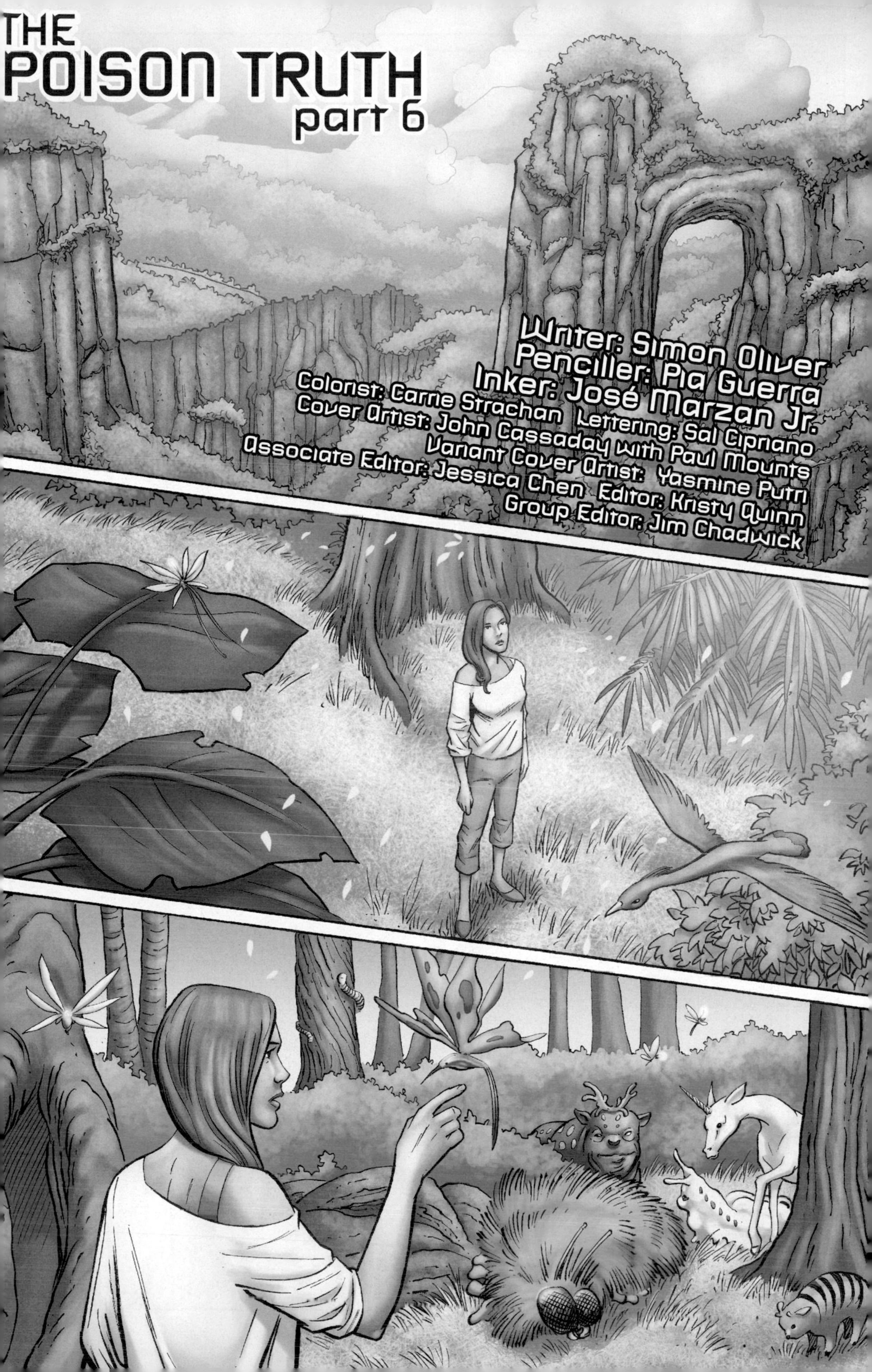
THE POISON TRUTH
part 6
Writer: Simon Oliver
Penciller: Pia Guerra
Inker: José Marzan Jr.
Colorist: Carrie Strachan Lettering: Sal Cipriano
Cover Artist: John Cassaday with Paul Mounts
Variant Cover Artist: Yasmine Putri
Associate Editor: Jessica Chen Editor: Kristy Quinn
Group Editor: Jim Chadwick

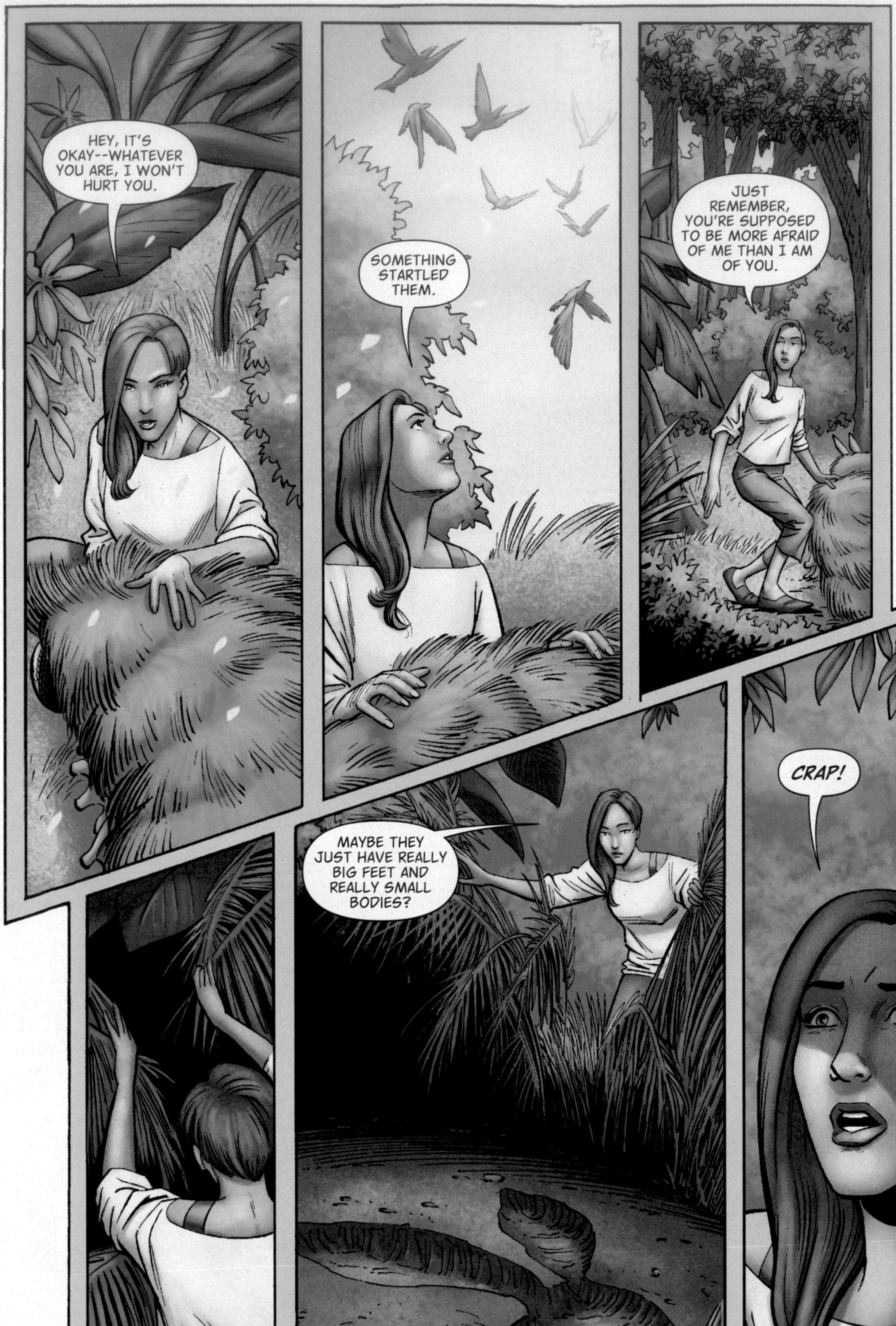
HEY, IT'S OKAY--WHATEVER YOU ARE, I WON'T HURT YOU.
SOMETHING STARTLED THEM.
JUST REMEMBER, YOU'RE SUPPOSED TO BE MORE AFRAID OF ME THAN I AM OF YOU.
MAYBE THEY JUST HAVE REALLY BIG FEET AND REALLY SMALL BODIES?
CRAP!

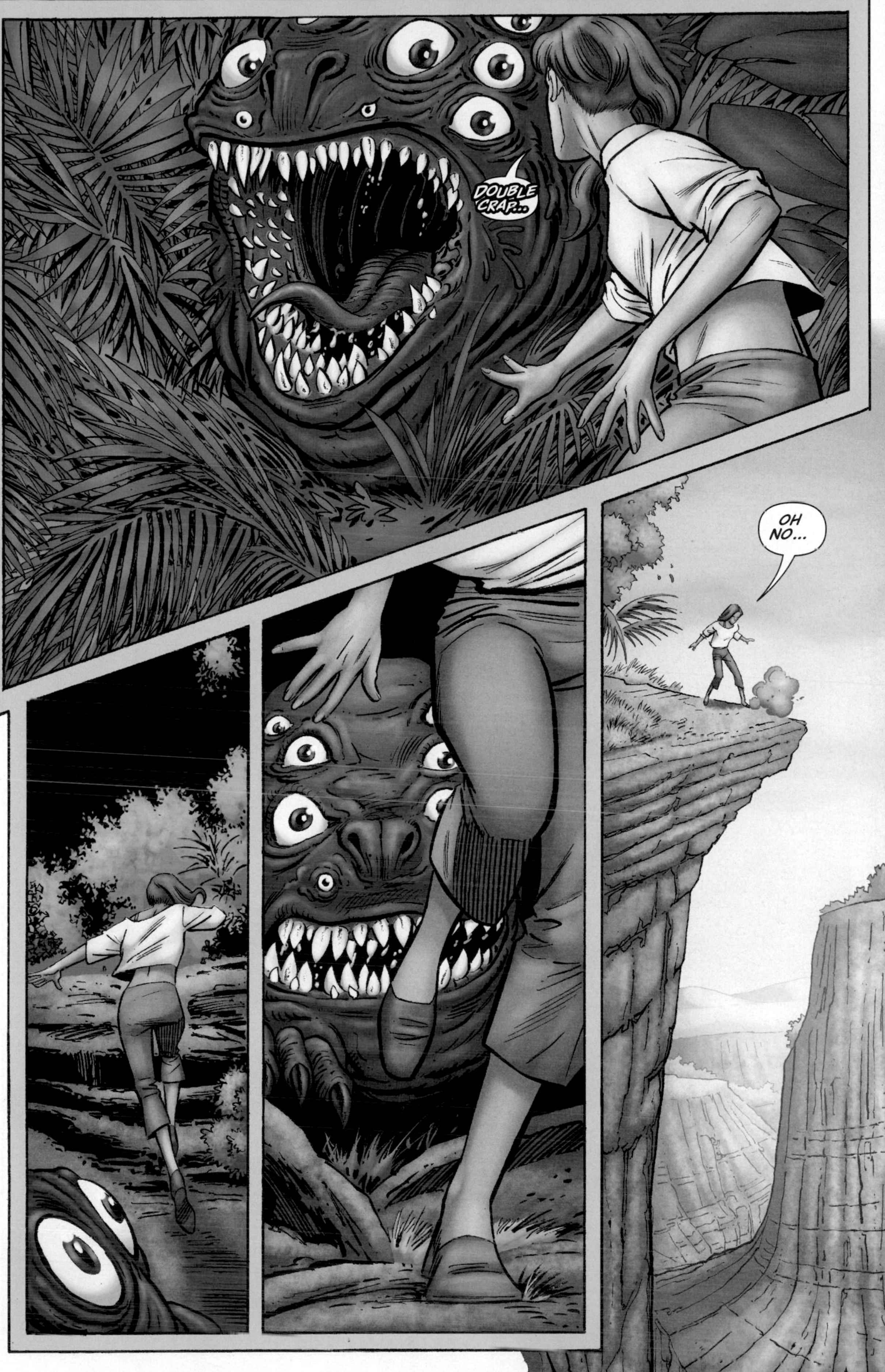
DOUBLE CRAP...
OH NO...

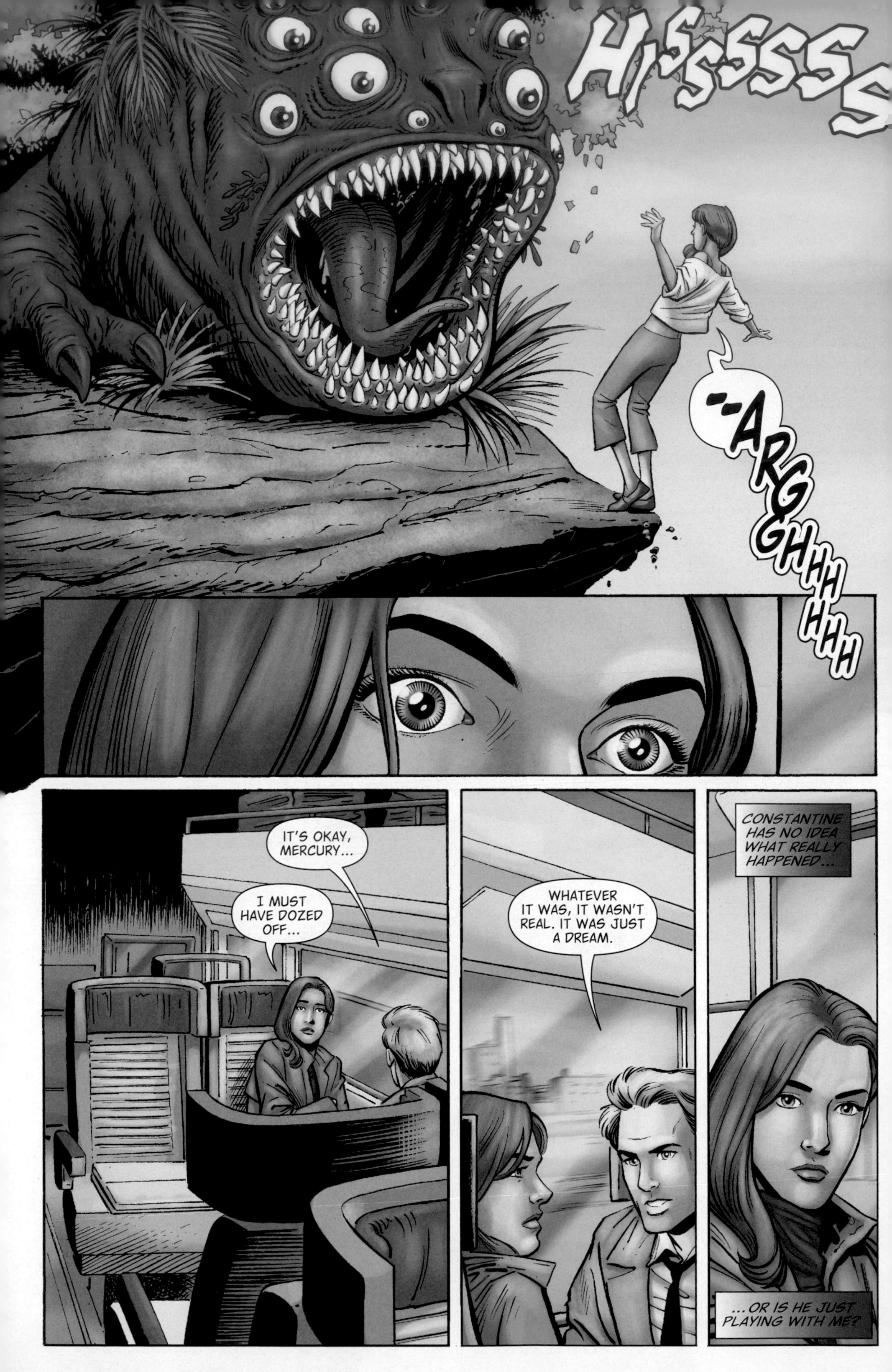
HISSSSSS
--ARGGHHHHHHH
IT'S OKAY, MERCURY...
I MUST HAVE DOZED OFF...
WHATEVER IT WAS, IT WASN'T REAL. IT WAS JUST A DREAM.
CONSTANTINE HAS NO IDEA WHAT REALLY HAPPENED...
...OR IS HE JUST PLAYING WITH ME?

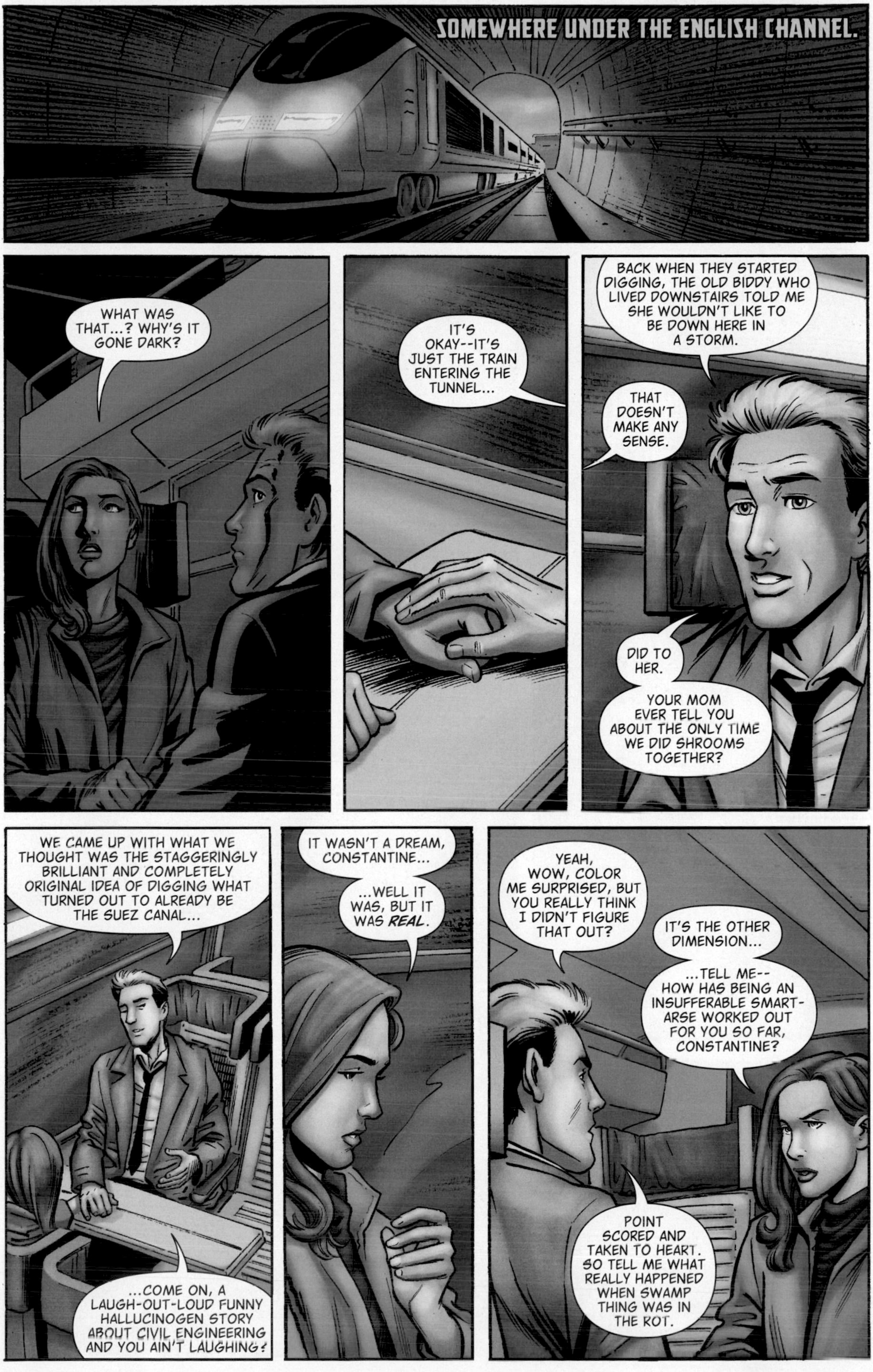

SOMEWHERE UNDER THE ENGLISH CHANNEL.
WHAT WAS THAT...? WHY'S IT GONE DARK?
IT'S OKAY--IT'S JUST THE TRAIN ENTERING THE TUNNEL...
BACK WHEN THEY STARTED DIGGING, THE OLD BIDDY WHO LIVED DOWNSTAIRS TOLD ME SHE WOULDN'T LIKE TO BE DOWN HERE IN A STORM.
THAT DOESN'T MAKE ANY SENSE.
DID TO HER.
YOUR MOM EVER TELL YOU ABOUT THE ONLY TIME WE DID SHROOMS TOGETHER?
WE CAME UP WITH WHAT WE THOUGHT WAS THE STAGGERINGLY BRILLIANT AND COMPLETELY ORIGINAL IDEA OF DIGGING WHAT TURNED OUT TO ALREADY BE THE SUEZ CANAL...
...COME ON, A LAUGH-OUT-LOUD FUNNY HALLUCINOGEN STORY ABOUT CIVIL ENGINEERING AND YOU AIN'T LAUGHING?
IT WASN'T A DREAM, CONSTANTINE...
...WELL IT WAS, BUT IT WAS *REAL*.
YEAH, WOW, COLOR ME SURPRISED, BUT YOU REALLY THINK I DIDN'T FIGURE THAT OUT?
IT'S THE OTHER DIMENSION...
...TELL ME--HOW HAS BEING AN INSUFFERABLE SMART-ARSE WORKED OUT FOR YOU SO FAR, CONSTANTINE?
POINT SCORED AND TAKEN TO HEART. SO TELL ME WHAT REALLY HAPPENED WHEN SWAMP THING WAS IN THE ROT.

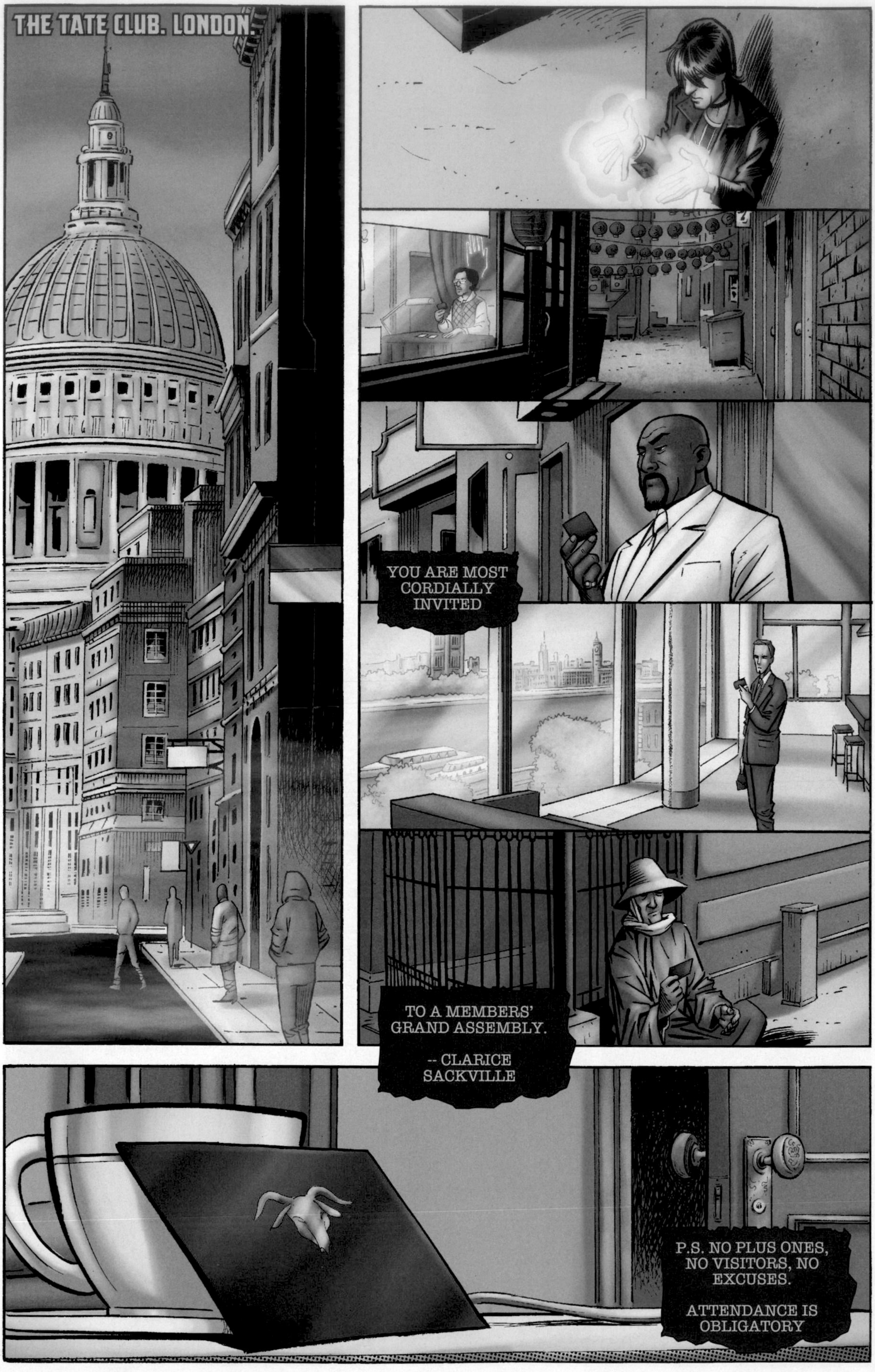
THE TATE CLUB. LONDON.
YOU ARE MOST CORDIALLY INVITED
TO A MEMBERS' GRAND ASSEMBLY.
-- CLARICE SACKVILLE
P.S. NO PLUS ONES, NO VISITORS, NO EXCUSES.
ATTENDANCE IS OBLIGATORY

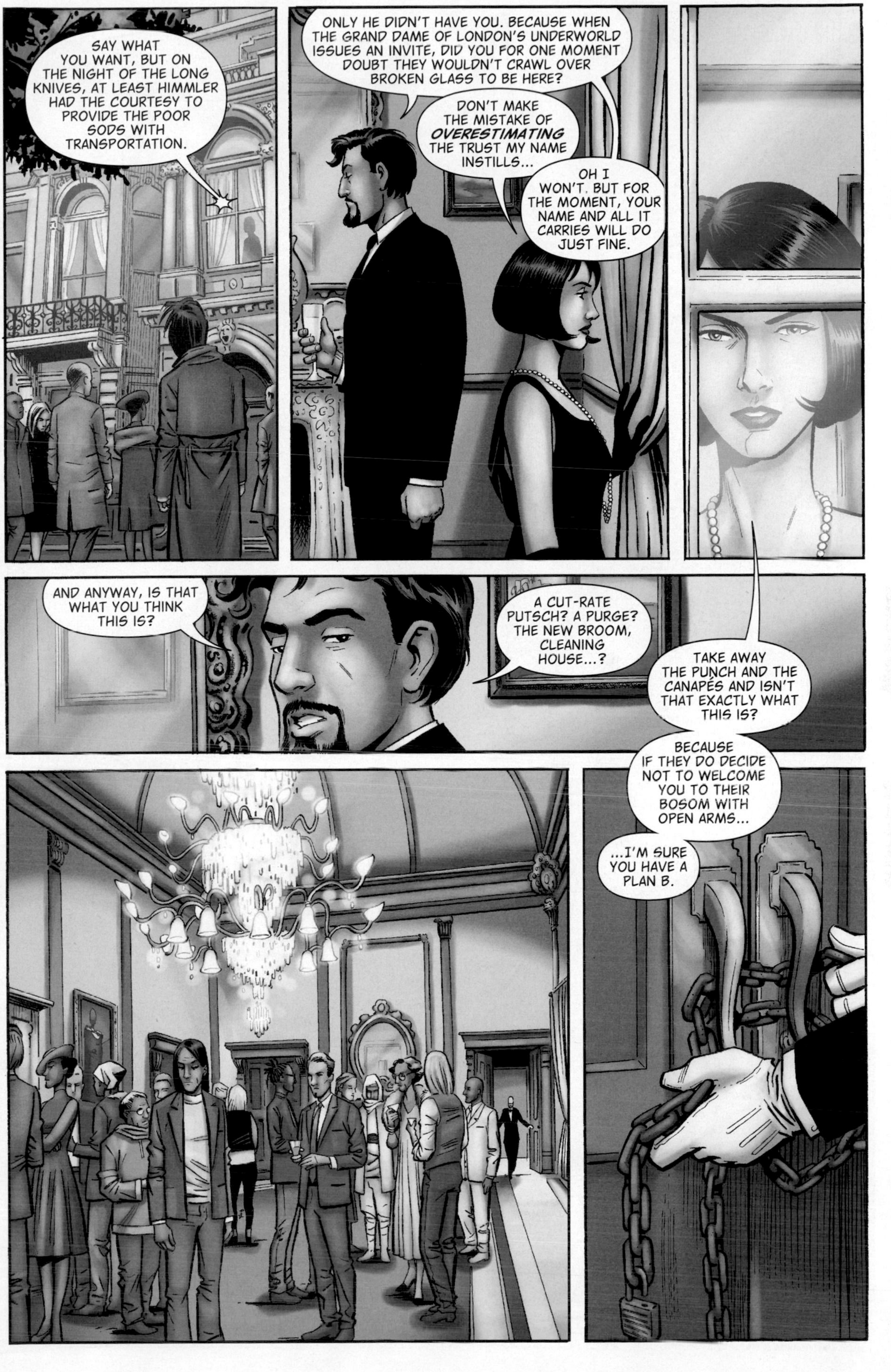
SAY WHAT YOU WANT, BUT ON THE NIGHT OF THE LONG KNIVES, AT LEAST HIMMLER HAD THE COURTESY TO PROVIDE THE POOR SODS WITH TRANSPORTATION.
ONLY HE DIDN'T HAVE YOU. BECAUSE WHEN THE GRAND DAME OF LONDON'S UNDERWORLD ISSUES AN INVITE, DID YOU FOR ONE MOMENT DOUBT THEY WOULDN'T CRAWL OVER BROKEN GLASS TO BE HERE?
DON'T MAKE THE MISTAKE OF *OVERESTIMATING* THE TRUST MY NAME INSTILLS...
OH I WON'T. BUT FOR THE MOMENT, YOUR NAME AND ALL IT CARRIES WILL DO JUST FINE.
AND ANYWAY, IS THAT WHAT YOU THINK THIS IS?
A CUT-RATE PUTSCH? A PURGE? THE NEW BROOM, CLEANING HOUSE...?
TAKE AWAY THE PUNCH AND THE CANAPÉS AND ISN'T THAT EXACTLY WHAT THIS IS?
BECAUSE IF THEY DO DECIDE NOT TO WELCOME YOU TO THEIR BOSOM WITH OPEN ARMS...
...I'M SURE YOU HAVE A PLAN B.

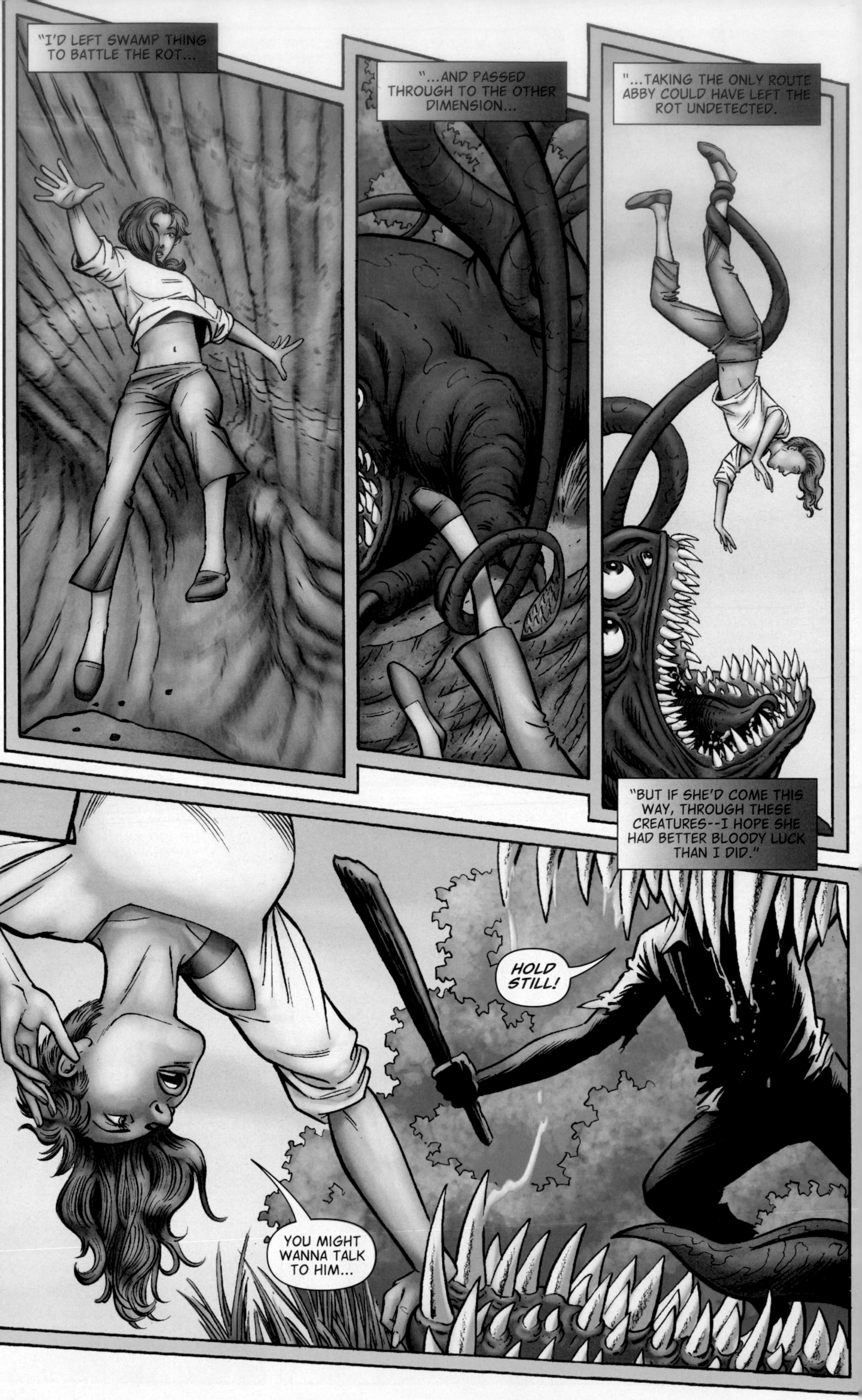
"I'D LEFT SWAMP THING TO BATTLE THE ROT...
"...AND PASSED THROUGH TO THE OTHER DIMENSION...
"...TAKING THE ONLY ROUTE ABBY COULD HAVE LEFT THE ROT UNDETECTED.
"BUT IF SHE'D COME THIS WAY, THROUGH THESE CREATURES--I HOPE SHE HAD BETTER BLOODY LUCK THAN I DID."
HOLD STILL!
YOU MIGHT WANNA TALK TO HIM...

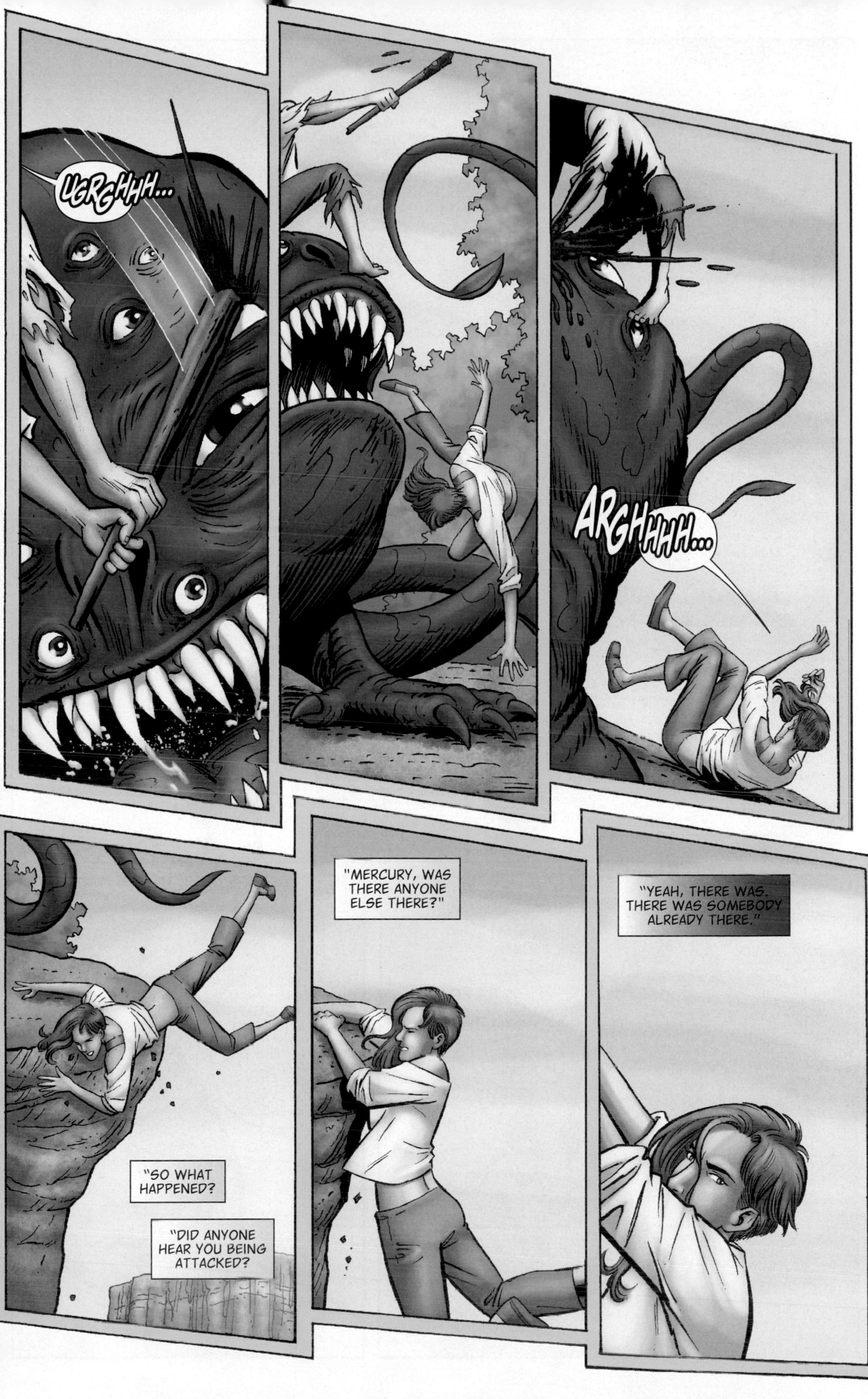
UGRGHHH...
ARGHHHH...
"MERCURY, WAS THERE ANYONE ELSE THERE?"
"SO WHAT HAPPENED?
"DID ANYONE HEAR YOU BEING ATTACKED?
"YEAH, THERE WAS. THERE WAS SOMEBODY ALREADY THERE."

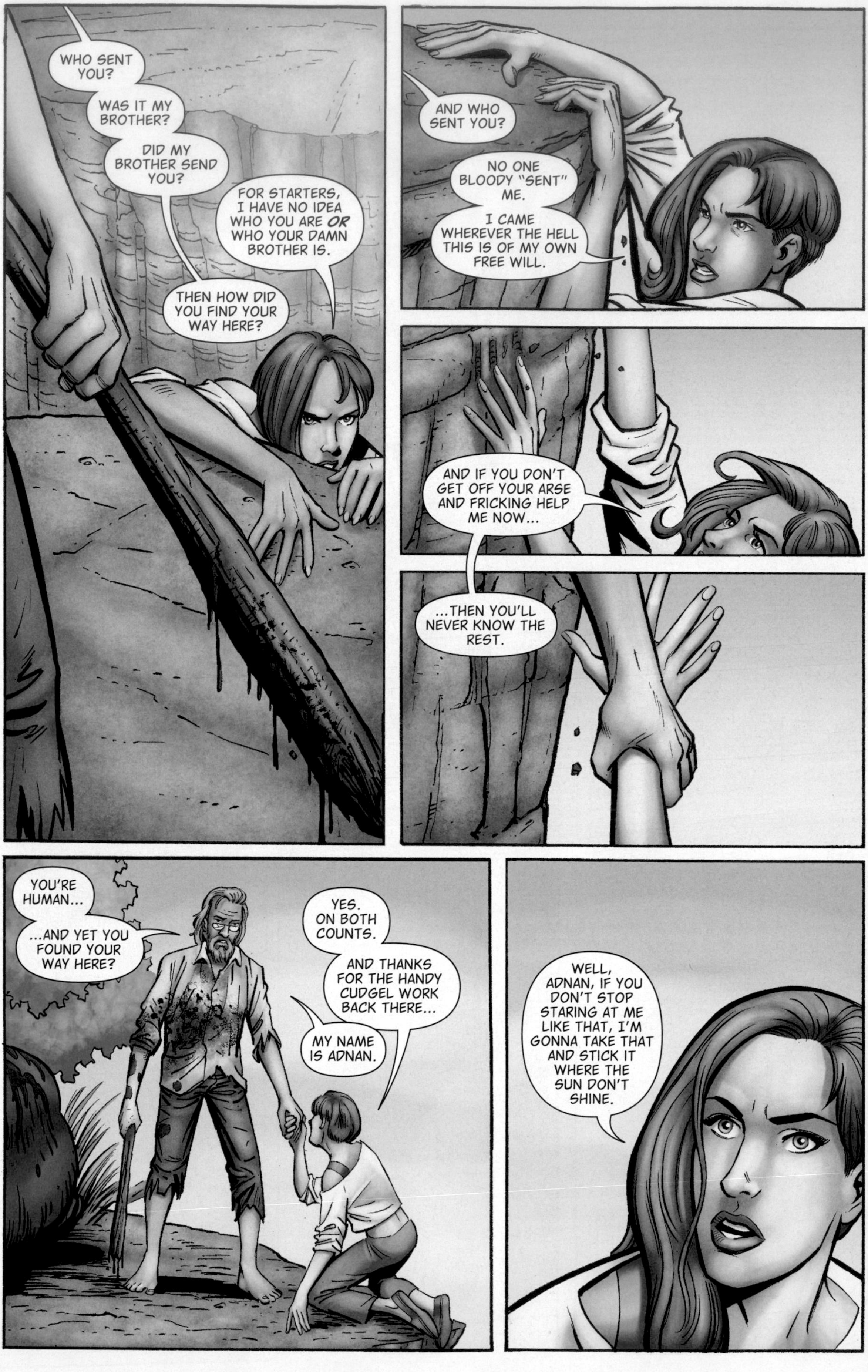
WHO SENT YOU?
WAS IT MY BROTHER?
DID MY BROTHER SEND YOU?
FOR STARTERS, I HAVE NO IDEA WHO YOU ARE *OR* WHO YOUR DAMN BROTHER IS.
THEN HOW DID YOU FIND YOUR WAY HERE?
AND WHO SENT YOU?
NO ONE BLOODY "SENT" ME.
I CAME WHEREVER THE HELL THIS IS OF MY OWN FREE WILL.
AND IF YOU DON'T GET OFF YOUR ARSE AND FRICKING HELP ME NOW...
...THEN YOU'LL NEVER KNOW THE REST.
YOU'RE HUMAN...
...AND YET YOU FOUND YOUR WAY HERE?
YES. ON BOTH COUNTS.
AND THANKS FOR THE HANDY CUDGEL WORK BACK THERE...
MY NAME IS ADNAN.
WELL, ADNAN, IF YOU DON'T STOP STARING AT ME LIKE THAT, I'M GONNA TAKE THAT AND STICK IT WHERE THE SUN DON'T SHINE.

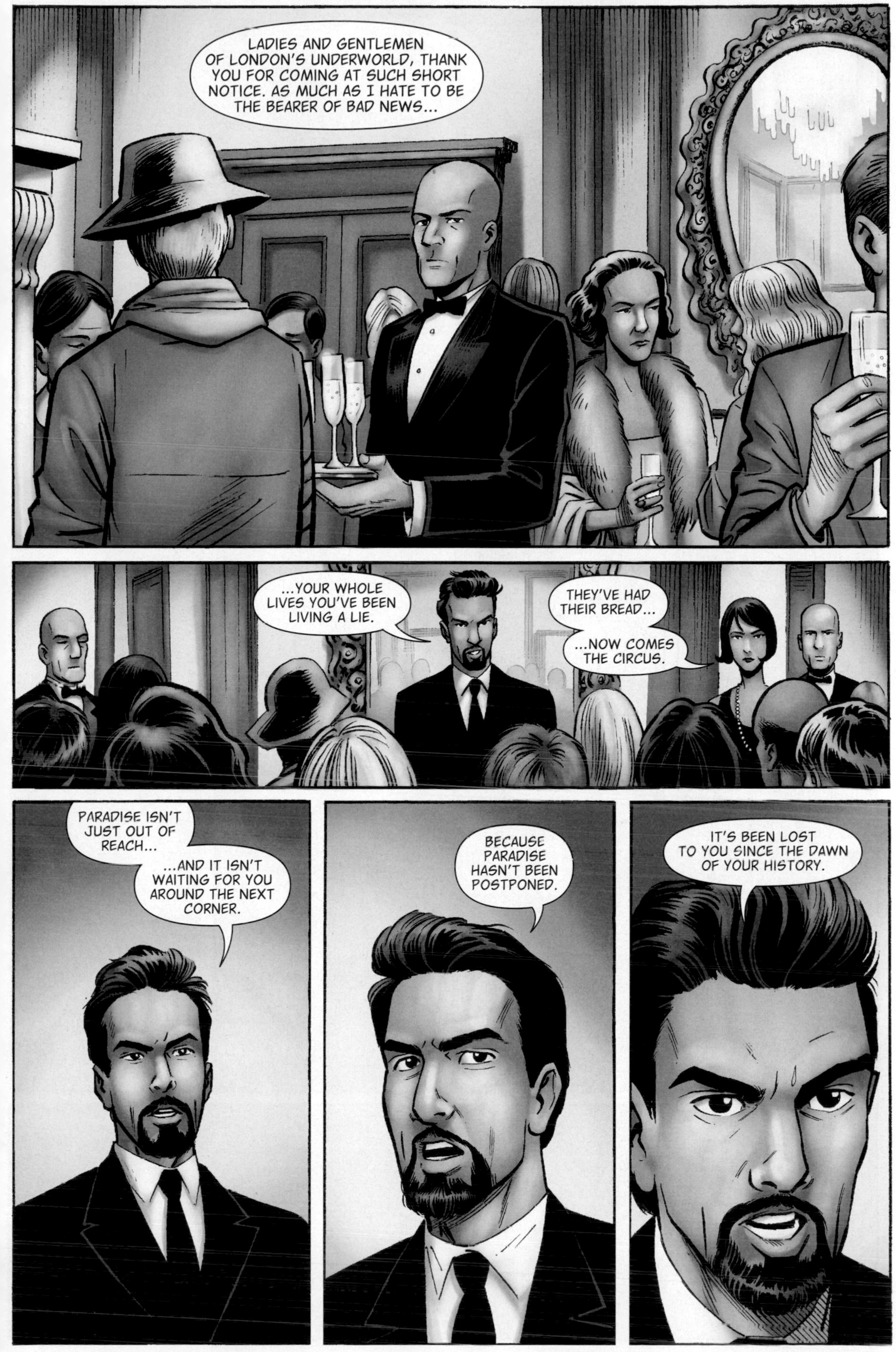
LADIES AND GENTLEMEN OF LONDON'S UNDERWORLD, THANK YOU FOR COMING AT SUCH SHORT NOTICE. AS MUCH AS I HATE TO BE THE BEARER OF BAD NEWS...
...YOUR WHOLE LIVES YOU'VE BEEN LIVING A LIE.
THEY'VE HAD THEIR BREAD...
...NOW COMES THE CIRCUS.
PARADISE ISN'T JUST OUT OF REACH...
...AND IT ISN'T WAITING FOR YOU AROUND THE NEXT CORNER.
BECAUSE PARADISE HASN'T BEEN POSTPONED.
IT'S BEEN LOST TO YOU SINCE THE DAWN OF YOUR HISTORY.

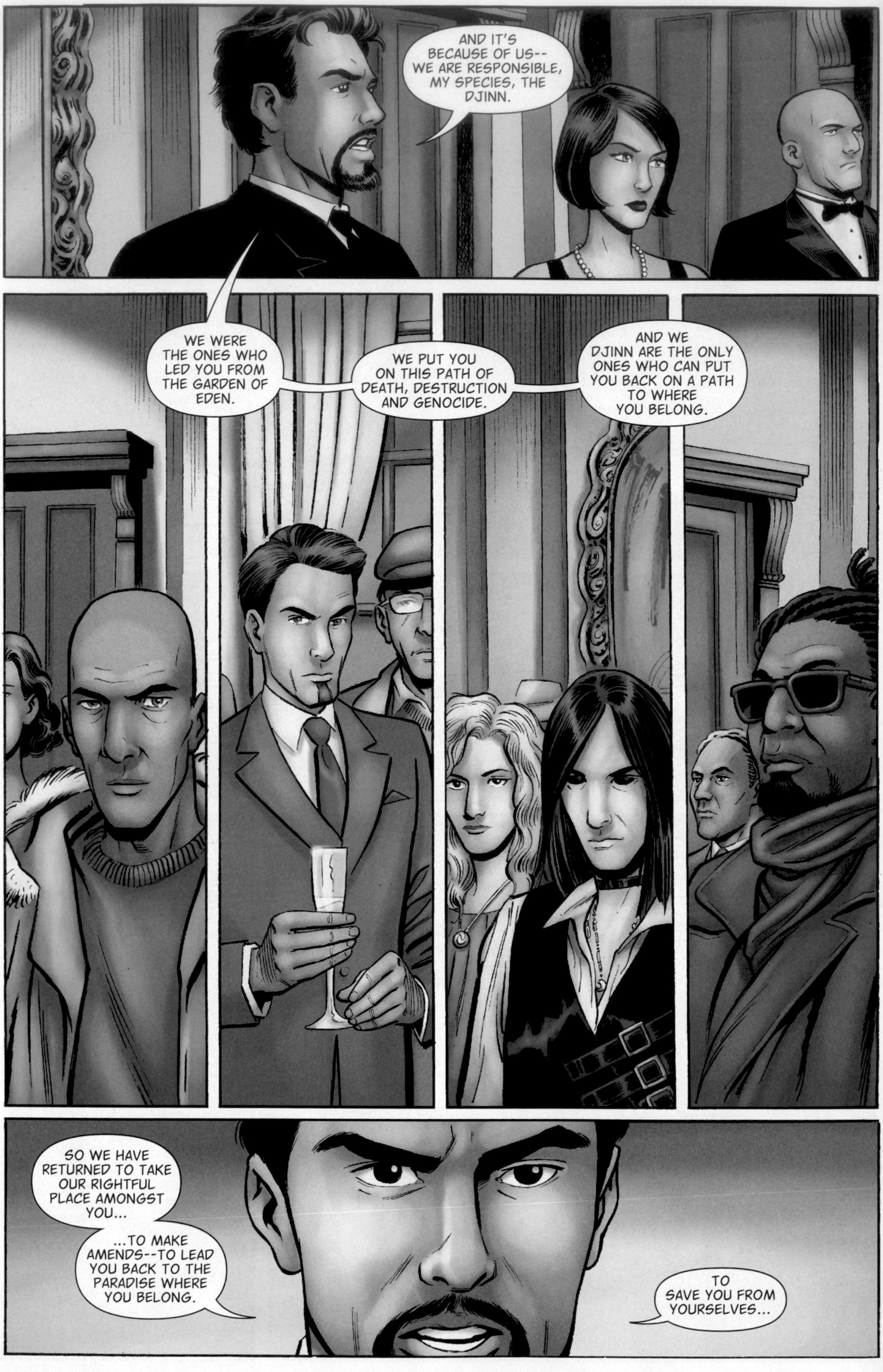
AND IT'S BECAUSE OF US-- WE ARE RESPONSIBLE, MY SPECIES, THE DJINN.
WE WERE THE ONES WHO LED YOU FROM THE GARDEN OF EDEN.
WE PUT YOU ON THIS PATH OF DEATH, DESTRUCTION AND GENOCIDE.
AND WE DJINN ARE THE ONLY ONES WHO CAN PUT YOU BACK ON A PATH TO WHERE YOU BELONG.
SO WE HAVE RETURNED TO TAKE OUR RIGHTFUL PLACE AMONGST YOU...
...TO MAKE AMENDS--TO LEAD YOU BACK TO THE PARADISE WHERE YOU BELONG.
TO SAVE YOU FROM YOURSELVES...

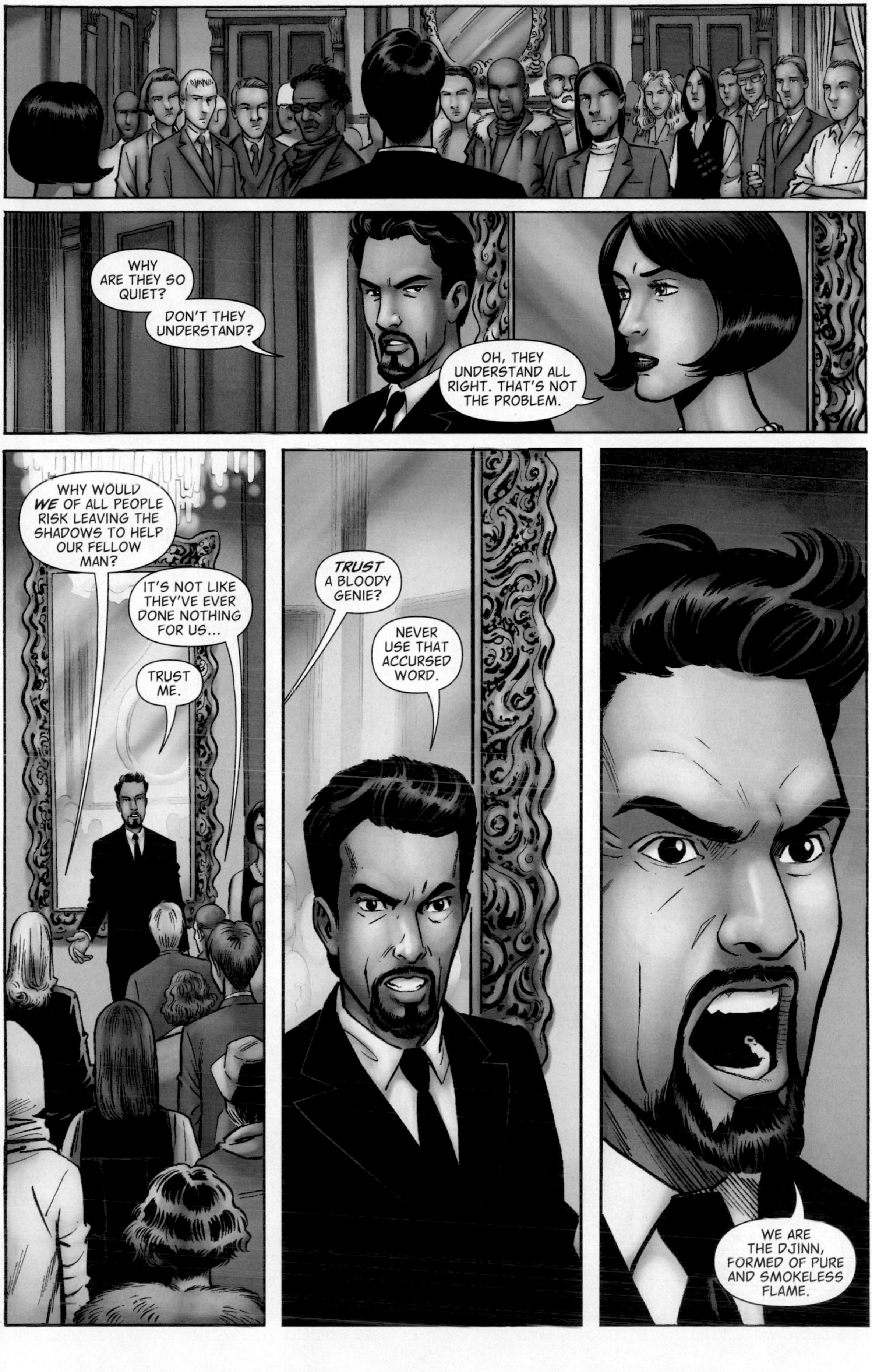
WHY ARE THEY SO QUIET?
DON'T THEY UNDERSTAND?
OH, THEY UNDERSTAND ALL RIGHT. THAT'S NOT THE PROBLEM.
WHY WOULD **WE** OF ALL PEOPLE RISK LEAVING THE SHADOWS TO HELP OUR FELLOW MAN?
IT'S NOT LIKE THEY'VE EVER DONE NOTHING FOR US...
TRUST ME.
TRUST A BLOODY GENIE?
NEVER USE THAT ACCURSED WORD.
WE ARE THE DJINN, FORMED OF PURE AND SMOKELESS FLAME.

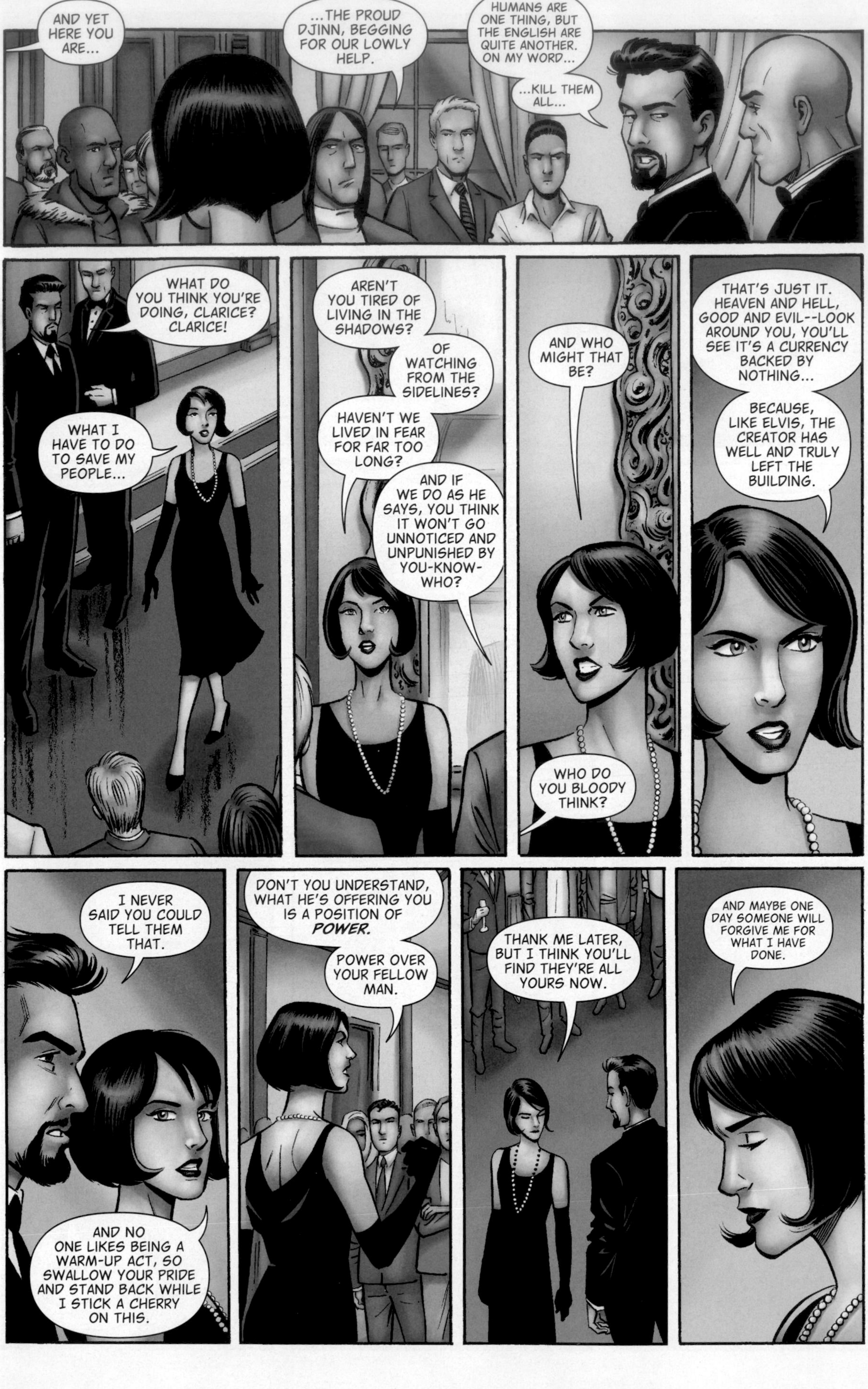
AND YET HERE YOU ARE...
...THE PROUD DJINN, BEGGING FOR OUR LOWLY HELP.
HUMANS ARE ONE THING, BUT THE ENGLISH ARE QUITE ANOTHER. ON MY WORD...
...KILL THEM ALL...
WHAT DO YOU THINK YOU'RE DOING, CLARICE? CLARICE!
WHAT I HAVE TO DO TO SAVE MY PEOPLE...
AREN'T YOU TIRED OF LIVING IN THE SHADOWS?
OF WATCHING FROM THE SIDELINES?
HAVEN'T WE LIVED IN FEAR FOR FAR TOO LONG?
AND IF WE DO AS HE SAYS, YOU THINK IT WON'T GO UNNOTICED AND UNPUNISHED BY YOU-KNOW-WHO?
AND WHO MIGHT THAT BE?
WHO DO YOU BLOODY THINK?
THAT'S JUST IT. HEAVEN AND HELL, GOOD AND EVIL--LOOK AROUND YOU, YOU'LL SEE IT'S A CURRENCY BACKED BY NOTHING...
BECAUSE, LIKE ELVIS, THE CREATOR HAS WELL AND TRULY LEFT THE BUILDING.
I NEVER SAID YOU COULD TELL THEM THAT.
AND NO ONE LIKES BEING A WARM-UP ACT, SO SWALLOW YOUR PRIDE AND STAND BACK WHILE I STICK A CHERRY ON THIS.
DON'T YOU UNDERSTAND, WHAT HE'S OFFERING YOU IS A POSITION OF POWER.
POWER OVER YOUR FELLOW MAN.
THANK ME LATER, BUT I THINK YOU'LL FIND THEY'RE ALL YOURS NOW.
AND MAYBE ONE DAY SOMEONE WILL FORGIVE ME FOR WHAT I HAVE DONE.

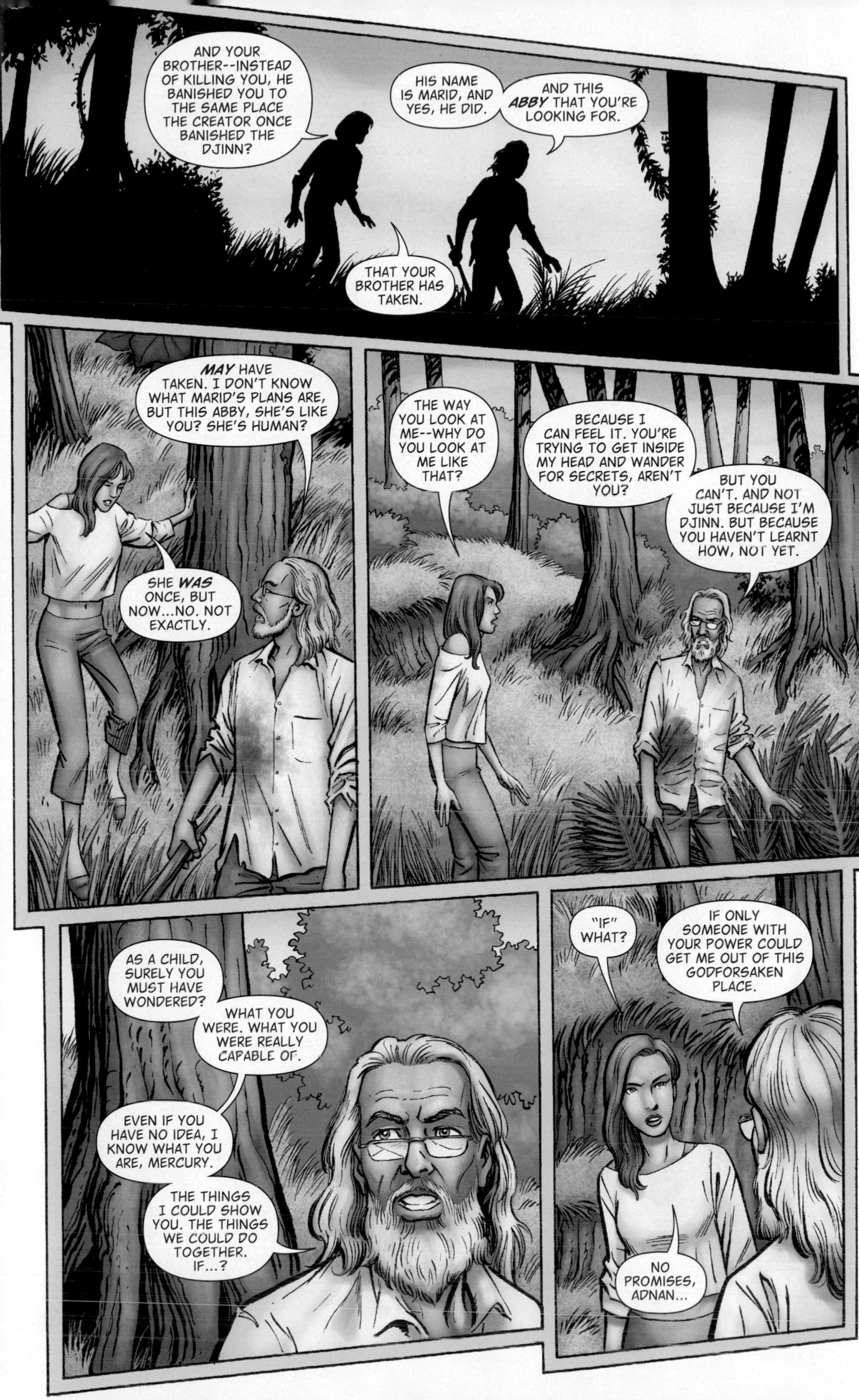
AND YOUR BROTHER--INSTEAD OF KILLING YOU, HE BANISHED YOU TO THE SAME PLACE THE CREATOR ONCE BANISHED THE DJINN?
HIS NAME IS MARID, AND YES, HE DID.
AND THIS ABBY THAT YOU'RE LOOKING FOR.
THAT YOUR BROTHER HAS TAKEN.
MAY HAVE TAKEN. I DON'T KNOW WHAT MARID'S PLANS ARE, BUT THIS ABBY, SHE'S LIKE YOU? SHE'S HUMAN?
SHE WAS ONCE, BUT NOW...NO. NOT EXACTLY.
THE WAY YOU LOOK AT ME--WHY DO YOU LOOK AT ME LIKE THAT?
BECAUSE I CAN FEEL IT. YOU'RE TRYING TO GET INSIDE MY HEAD AND WANDER FOR SECRETS, AREN'T YOU?
BUT YOU CAN'T. AND NOT JUST BECAUSE I'M DJINN. BUT BECAUSE YOU HAVEN'T LEARNT HOW, NOT YET.
AS A CHILD, SURELY YOU MUST HAVE WONDERED?
WHAT YOU WERE. WHAT YOU WERE REALLY CAPABLE OF.
EVEN IF YOU HAVE NO IDEA, I KNOW WHAT YOU ARE, MERCURY.
THE THINGS I COULD SHOW YOU. THE THINGS WE COULD DO TOGETHER. IF...?
"IF" WHAT?
IF ONLY SOMEONE WITH YOUR POWER COULD GET ME OUT OF THIS GODFORSAKEN PLACE.
NO PROMISES, ADNAN...

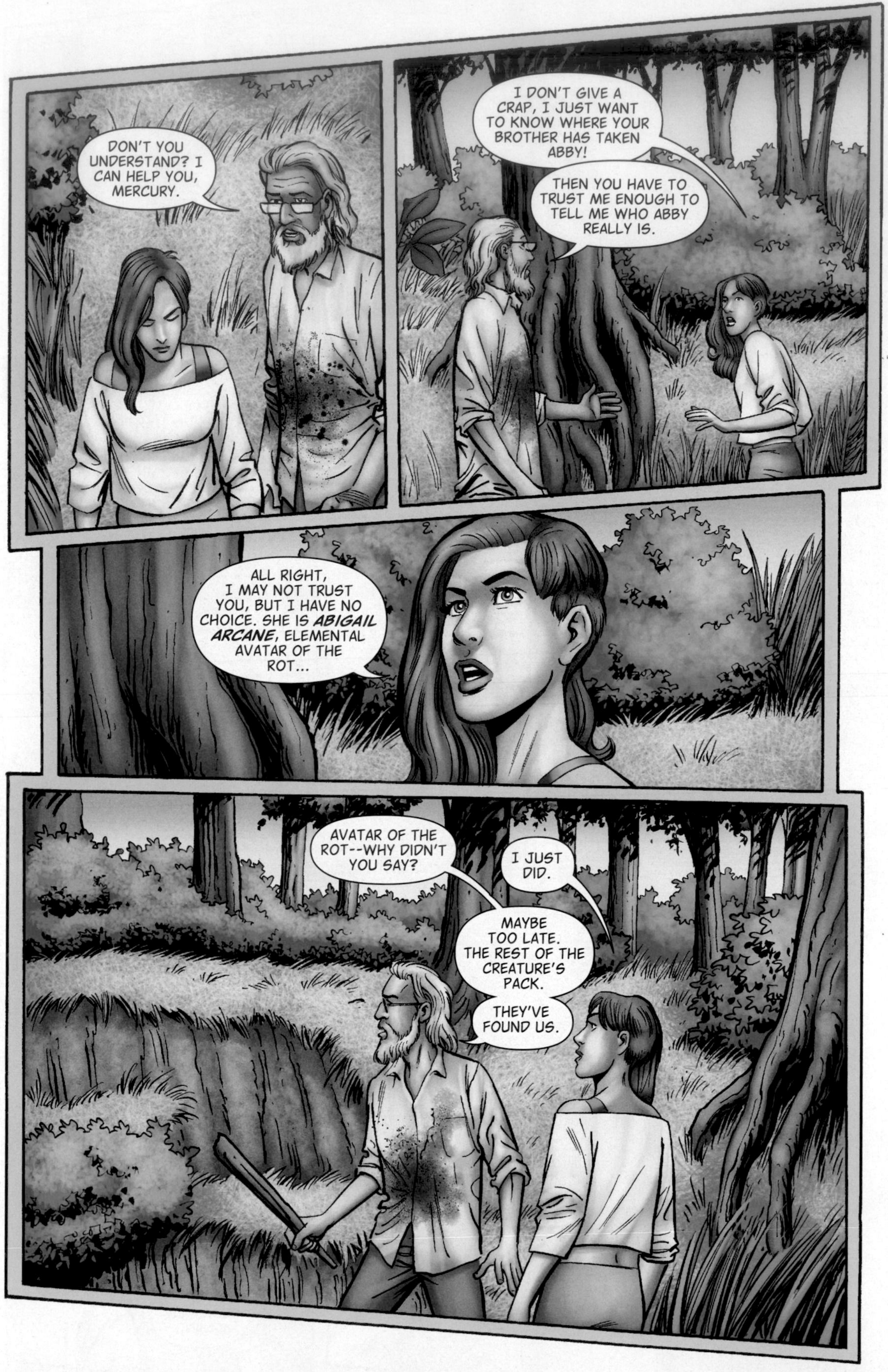

DON'T YOU UNDERSTAND? I CAN HELP YOU, MERCURY.
I DON'T GIVE A CRAP, I JUST WANT TO KNOW WHERE YOUR BROTHER HAS TAKEN ABBY!
THEN YOU HAVE TO TRUST ME ENOUGH TO TELL ME WHO ABBY REALLY IS.
ALL RIGHT, I MAY NOT TRUST YOU, BUT I HAVE NO CHOICE. SHE IS ***ABIGAIL ARCANE***, ELEMENTAL AVATAR OF THE ROT...
AVATAR OF THE ROT--WHY DIDN'T YOU SAY?
I JUST DID.
MAYBE TOO LATE. THE REST OF THE CREATURE'S PACK.
THEY'VE FOUND US.

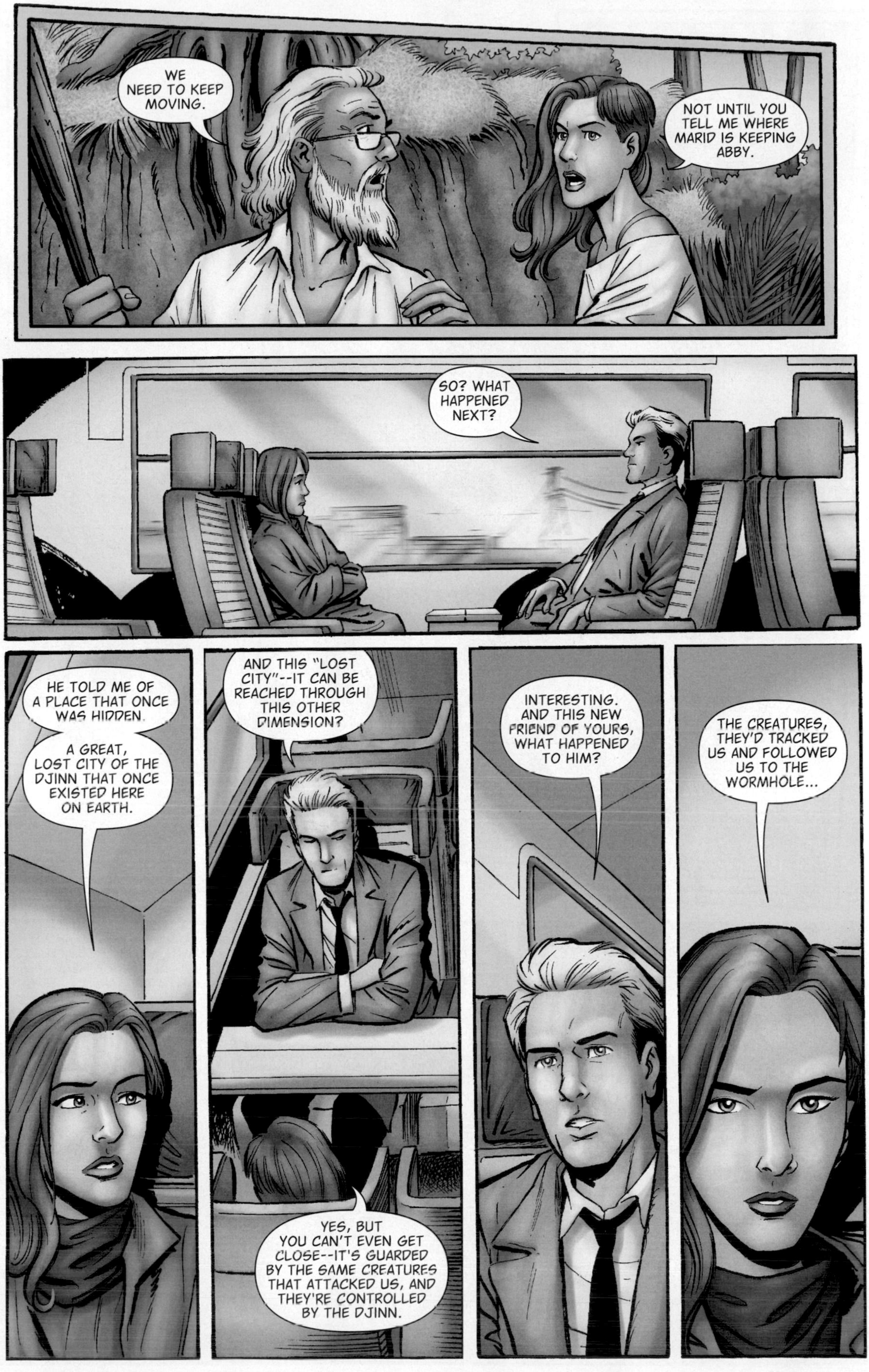
WE NEED TO KEEP MOVING.
NOT UNTIL YOU TELL ME WHERE MARID IS KEEPING ABBY.
SO? WHAT HAPPENED NEXT?
HE TOLD ME OF A PLACE THAT ONCE WAS HIDDEN.
A GREAT, LOST CITY OF THE DJINN THAT ONCE EXISTED HERE ON EARTH.
AND THIS "LOST CITY"--IT CAN BE REACHED THROUGH THIS OTHER DIMENSION?
YES, BUT YOU CAN'T EVEN GET CLOSE--IT'S GUARDED BY THE SAME CREATURES THAT ATTACKED US, AND THEY'RE CONTROLLED BY THE DJINN.
INTERESTING. AND THIS NEW FRIEND OF YOURS, WHAT HAPPENED TO HIM?
THE CREATURES, THEY'D TRACKED US AND FOLLOWED US TO THE WORMHOLE...

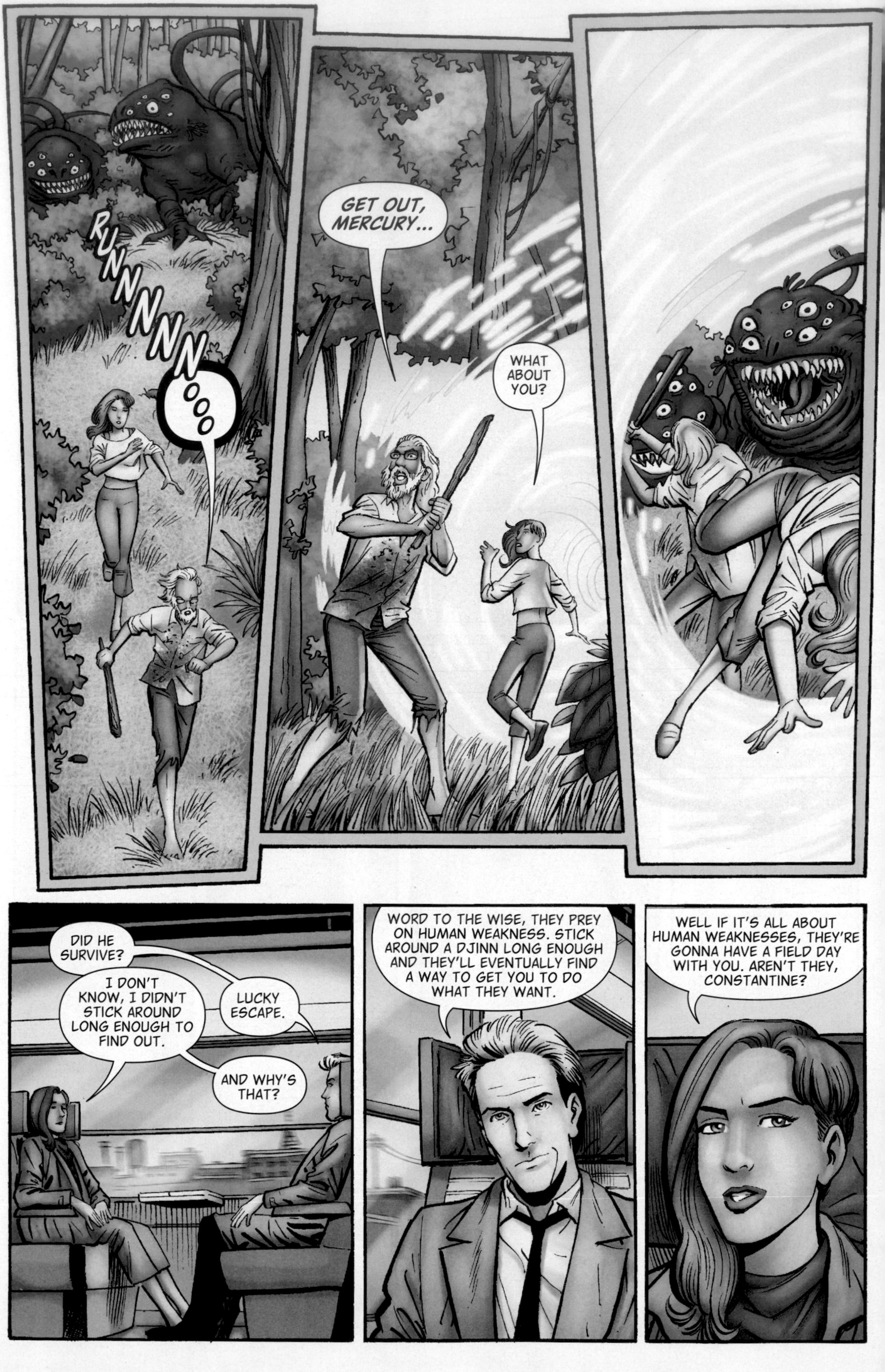
RUNNNNNNooo
GET OUT, MERCURY...
WHAT ABOUT YOU?
DID HE SURVIVE?
I DON'T KNOW, I DIDN'T STICK AROUND LONG ENOUGH TO FIND OUT.
LUCKY ESCAPE.
AND WHY'S THAT?
WORD TO THE WISE, THEY PREY ON HUMAN WEAKNESS. STICK AROUND A DJINN LONG ENOUGH AND THEY'LL EVENTUALLY FIND A WAY TO GET YOU TO DO WHAT THEY WANT.
WELL IF IT'S ALL ABOUT HUMAN WEAKNESSES, THEY'RE GONNA HAVE A FIELD DAY WITH YOU. AREN'T THEY, CONSTANTINE?

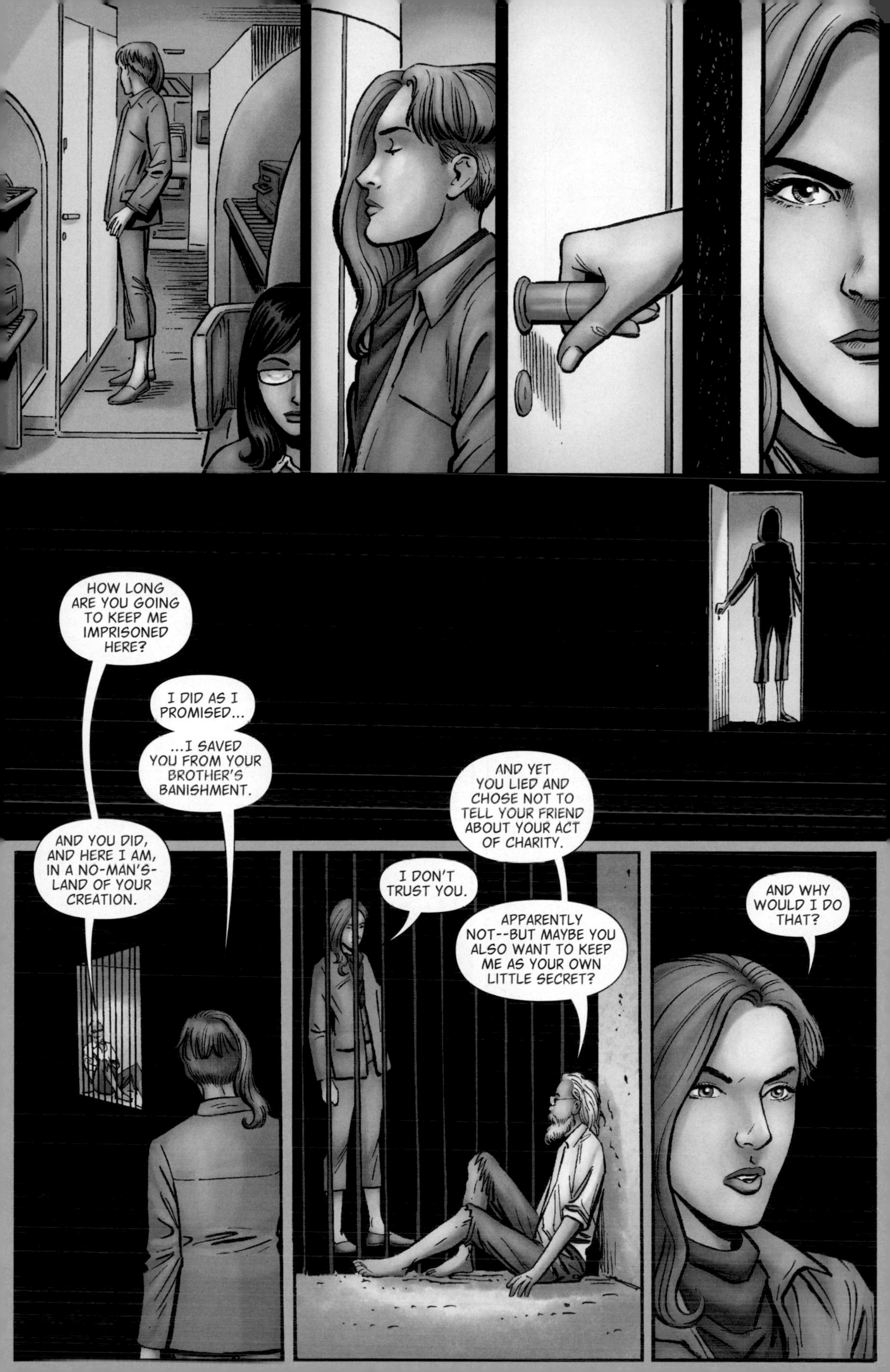
HOW LONG ARE YOU GOING TO KEEP ME IMPRISONED HERE?
I DID AS I PROMISED...
...I SAVED YOU FROM YOUR BROTHER'S BANISHMENT.
AND YOU DID, AND HERE I AM, IN A NO-MAN'S-LAND OF YOUR CREATION.
AND YET YOU LIED AND CHOSE NOT TO TELL YOUR FRIEND ABOUT YOUR ACT OF CHARITY.
I DON'T TRUST YOU.
APPARENTLY NOT--BUT MAYBE YOU ALSO WANT TO KEEP ME AS YOUR OWN LITTLE SECRET?
AND WHY WOULD I DO THAT?

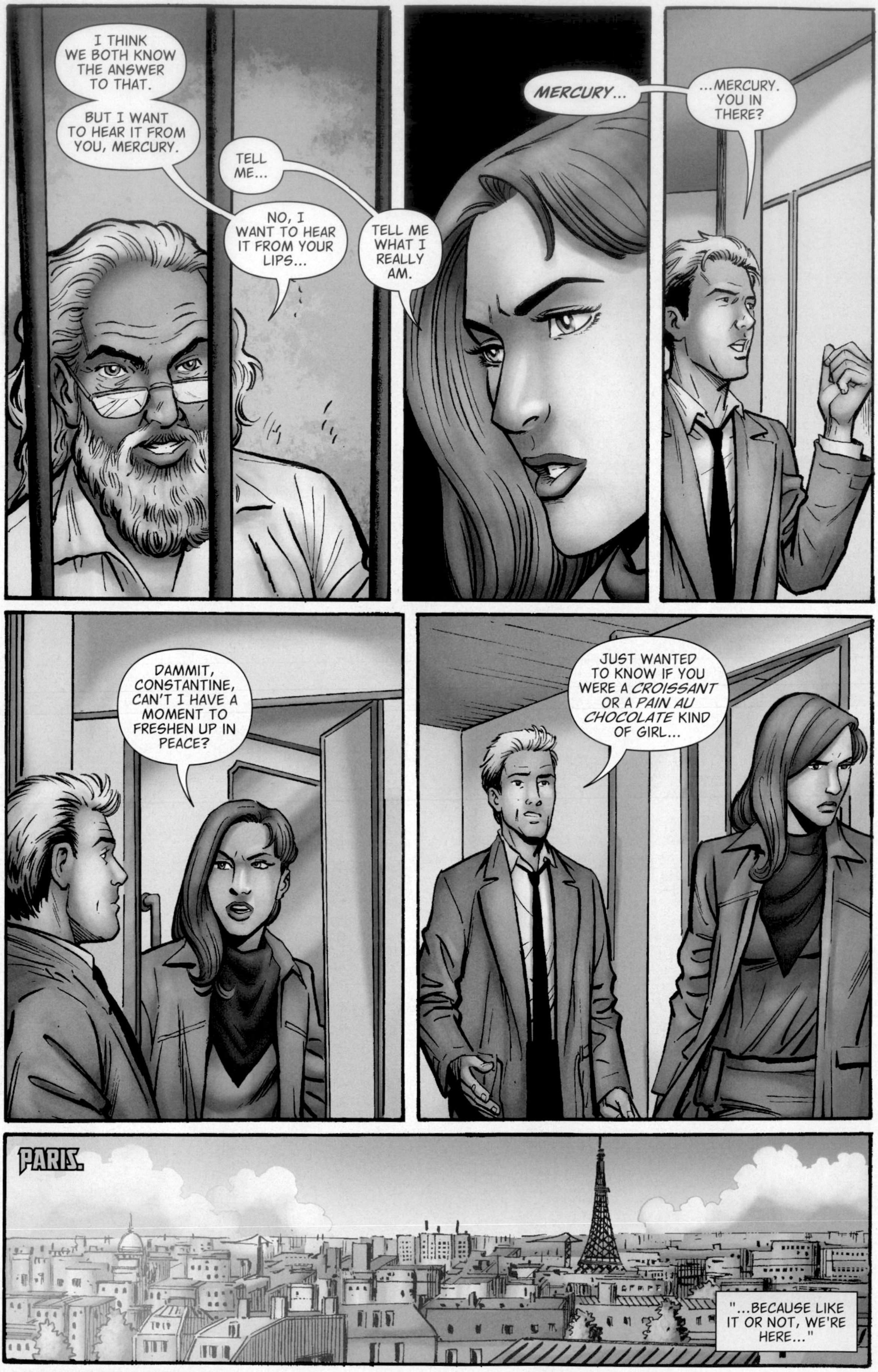
I THINK WE BOTH KNOW THE ANSWER TO THAT.
BUT I WANT TO HEAR IT FROM YOU, MERCURY.
NO, I WANT TO HEAR IT FROM YOUR LIPS...
TELL ME...
TELL ME WHAT I REALLY AM.
MERCURY...
...MERCURY. YOU IN THERE?
DAMMIT, CONSTANTINE, CAN'T I HAVE A MOMENT TO FRESHEN UP IN PEACE?
JUST WANTED TO KNOW IF YOU WERE A CROISSANT OR A PAIN AU CHOCOLATE KIND OF GIRL...
PARIS.
"...BECAUSE LIKE IT OR NOT, WE'RE HERE..."

THE HELLBLAZER

VARIANT COVER GALLERY

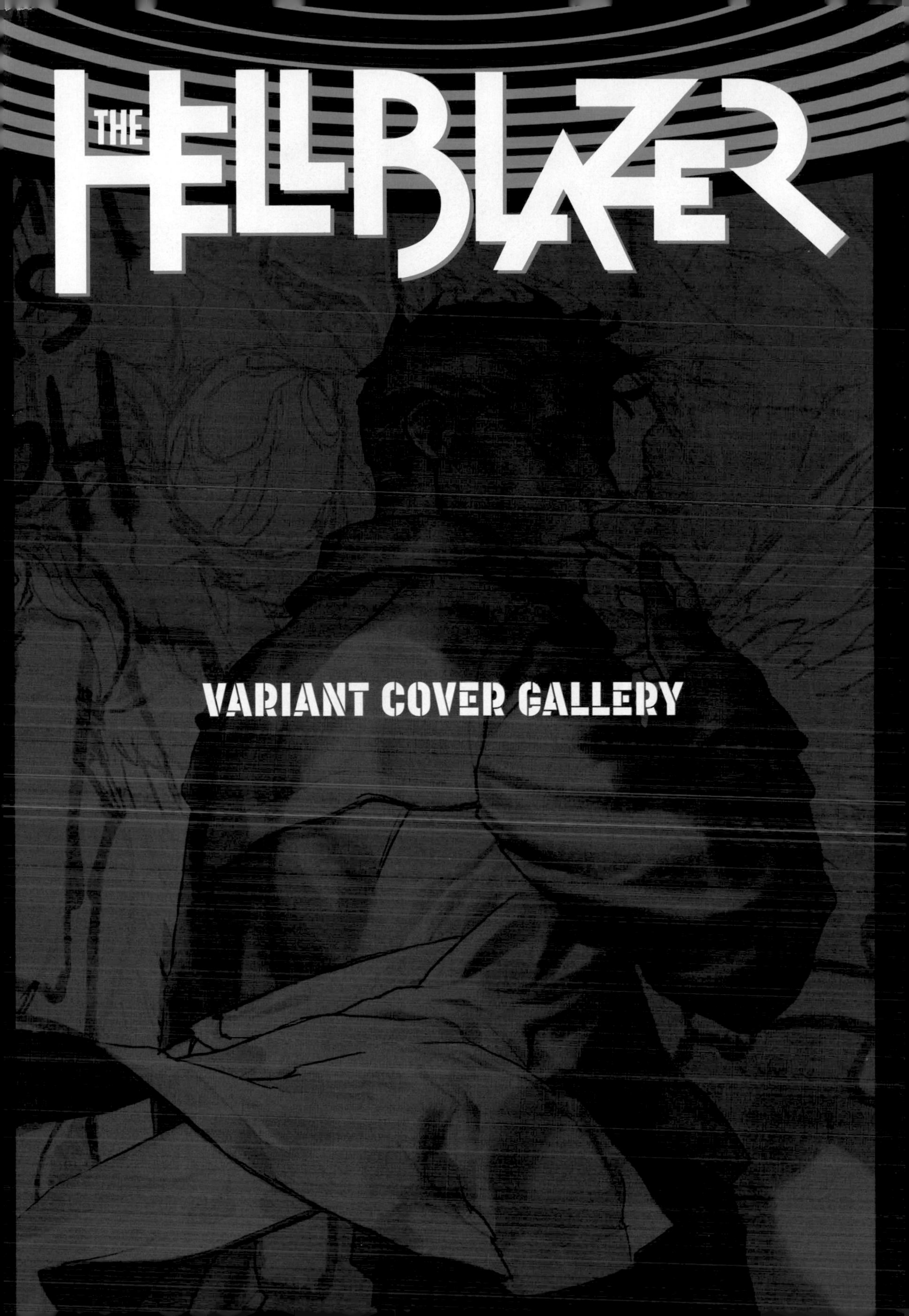

THE HELLBLAZER: REBIRTH #1 by DUNCAN FEGREDO

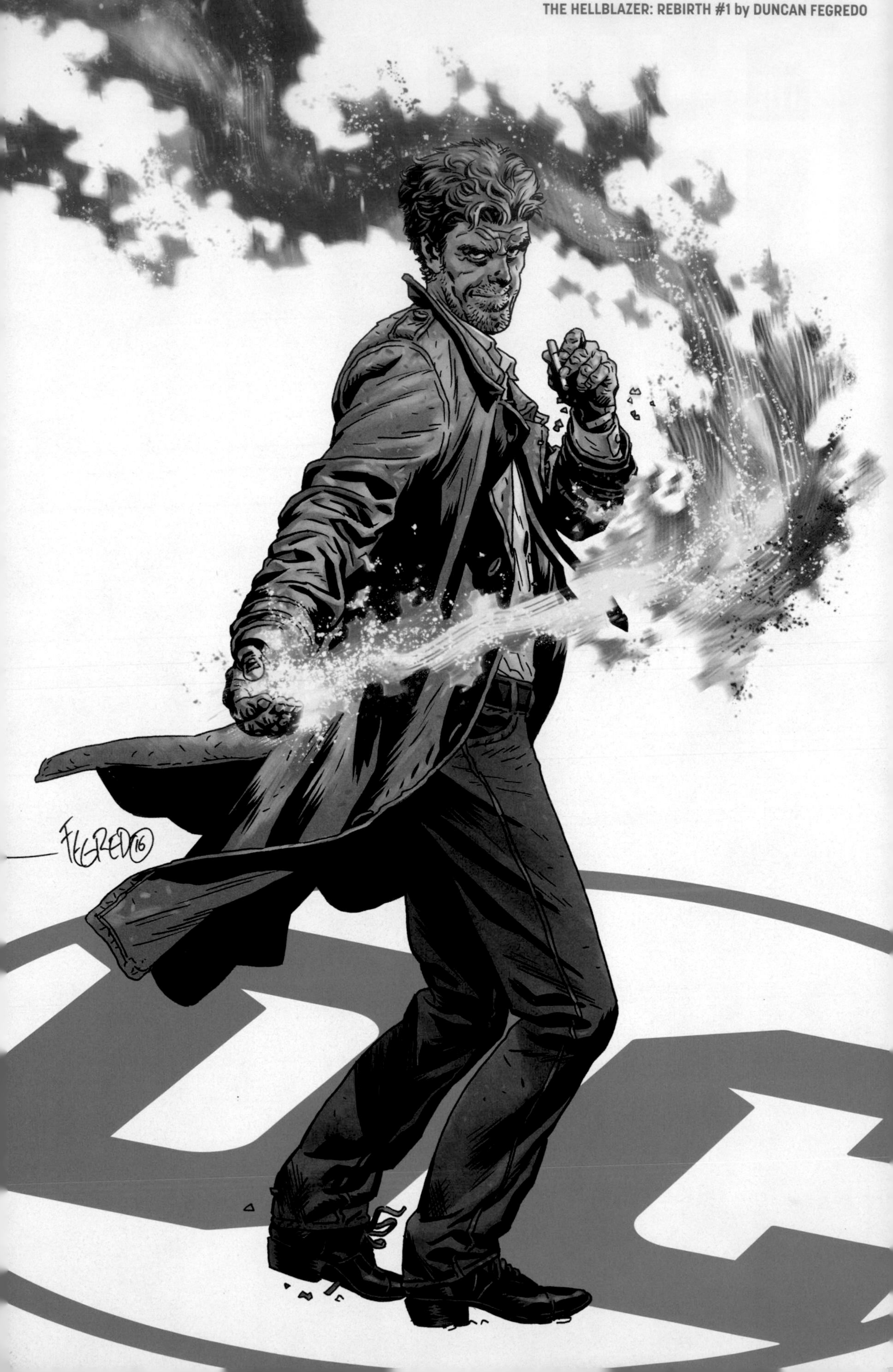
FEGREDO 16

THE HELLBLAZER #1 by JOHN CASSADAY with PAUL MOUNTS

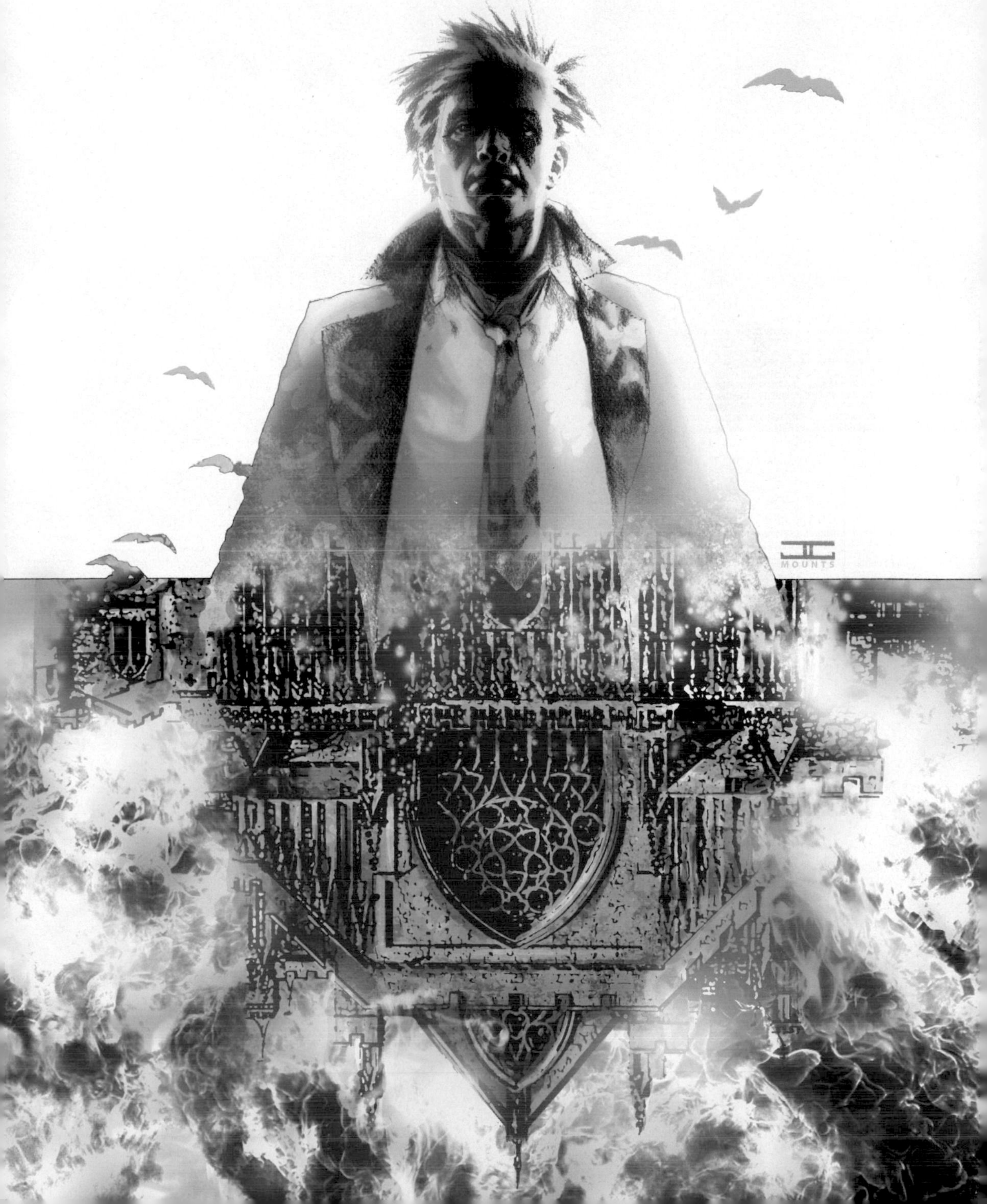

THE HELLBLAZER #2 by JOHN CASSADAY with PAUL MOUNTS

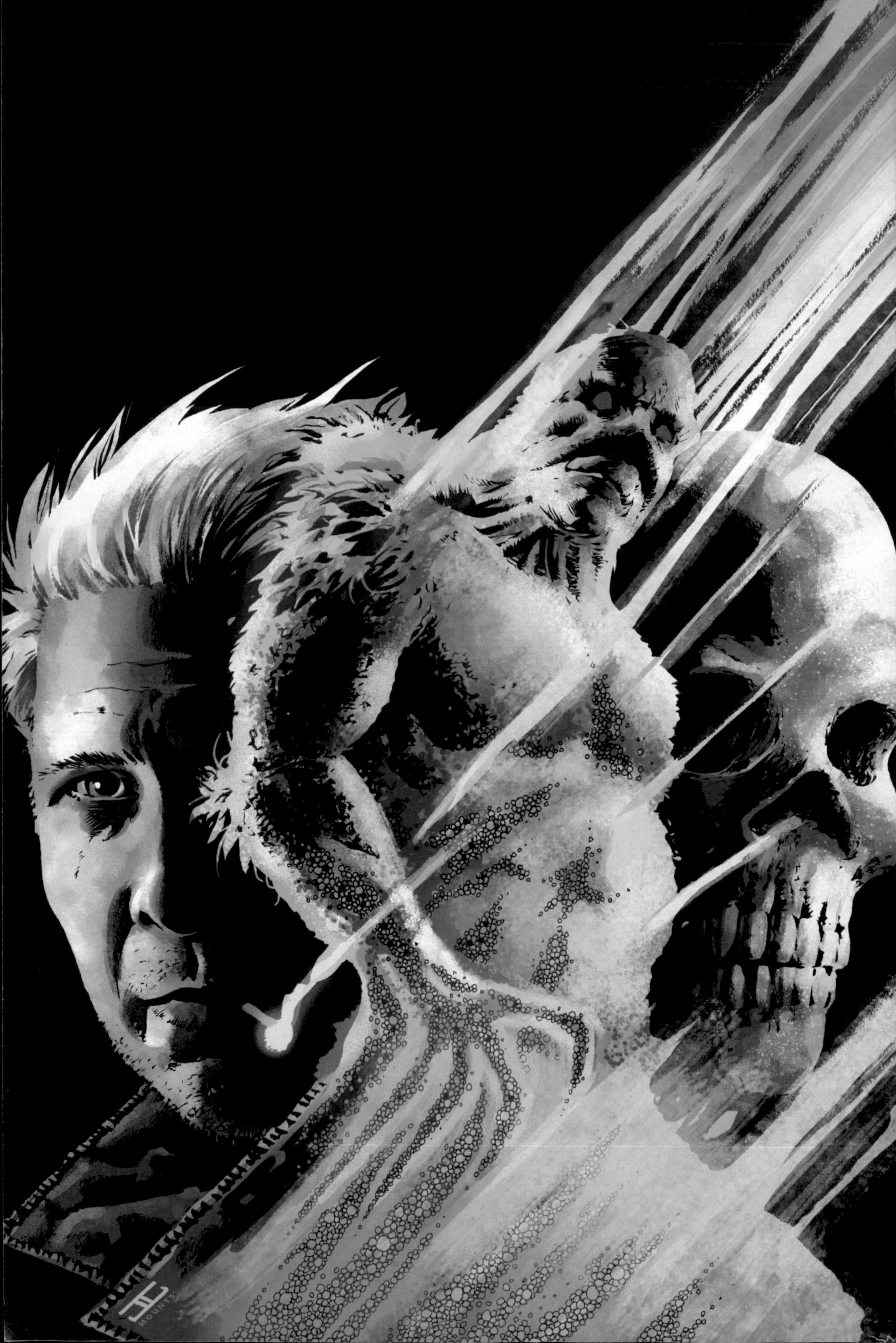

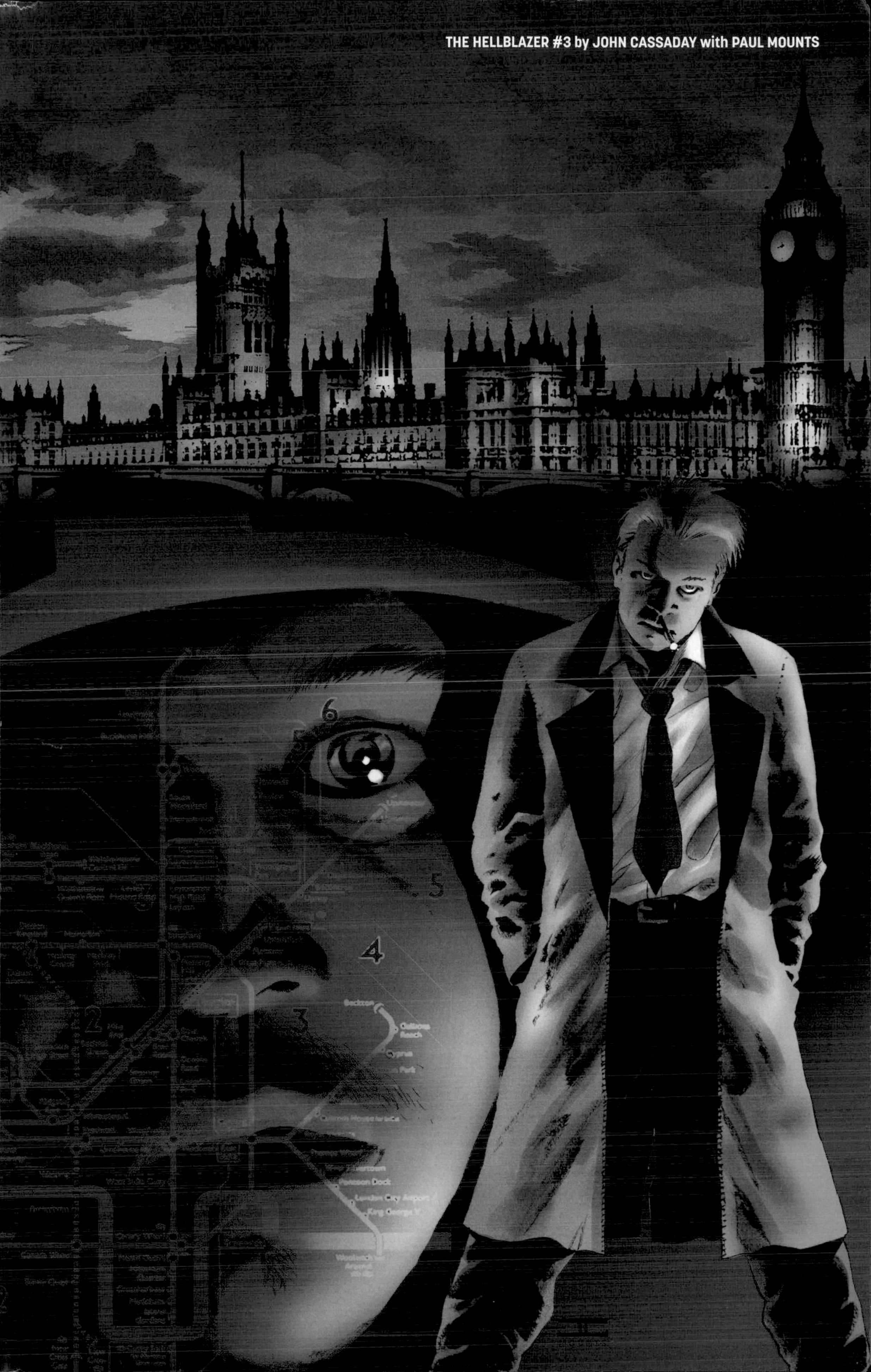

THE HELLBLAZER #3 by JOHN CASSADAY with PAUL MOUNTS

THE HELLBLAZER #4 by YASMINE PUTRI

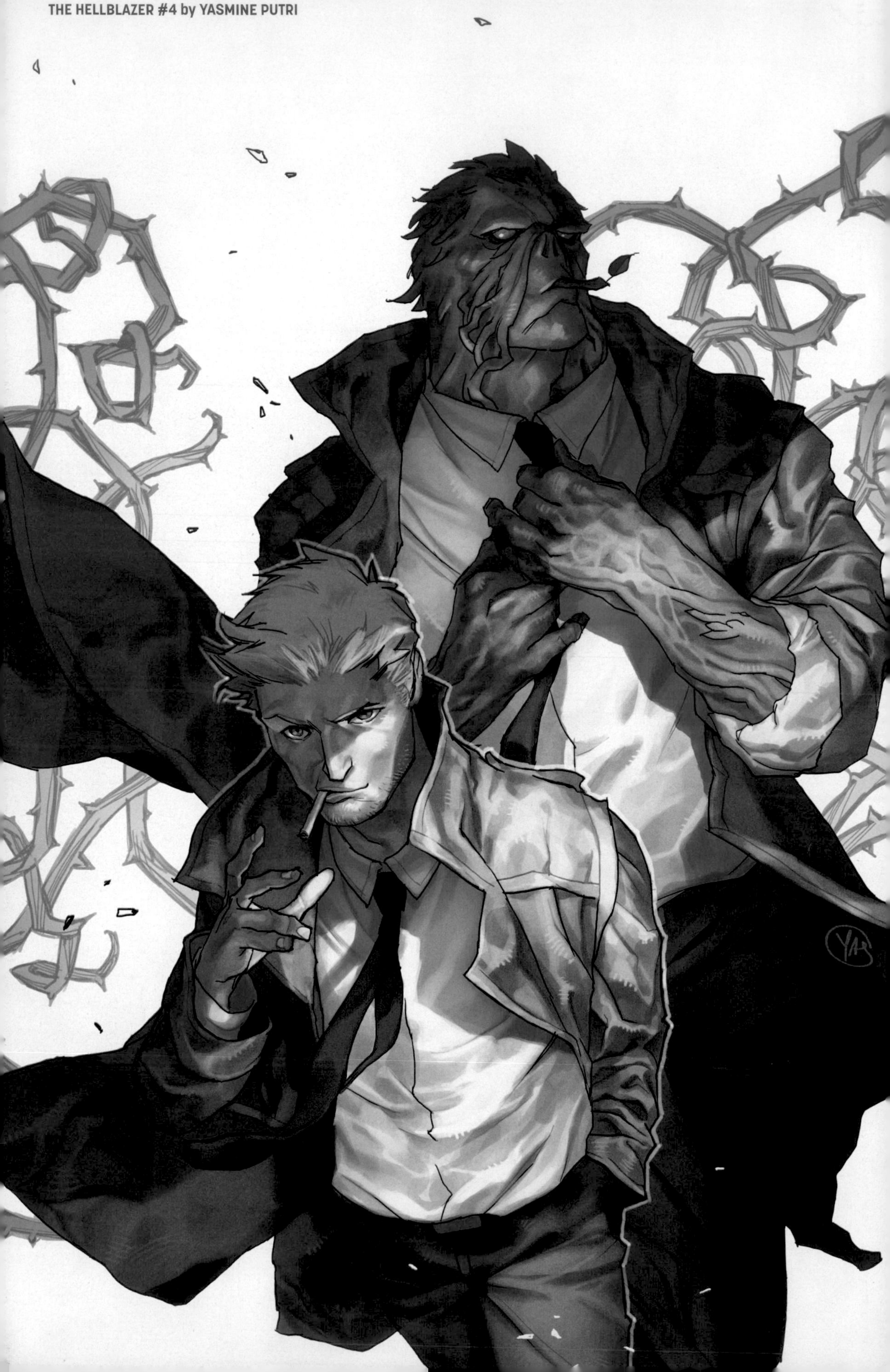

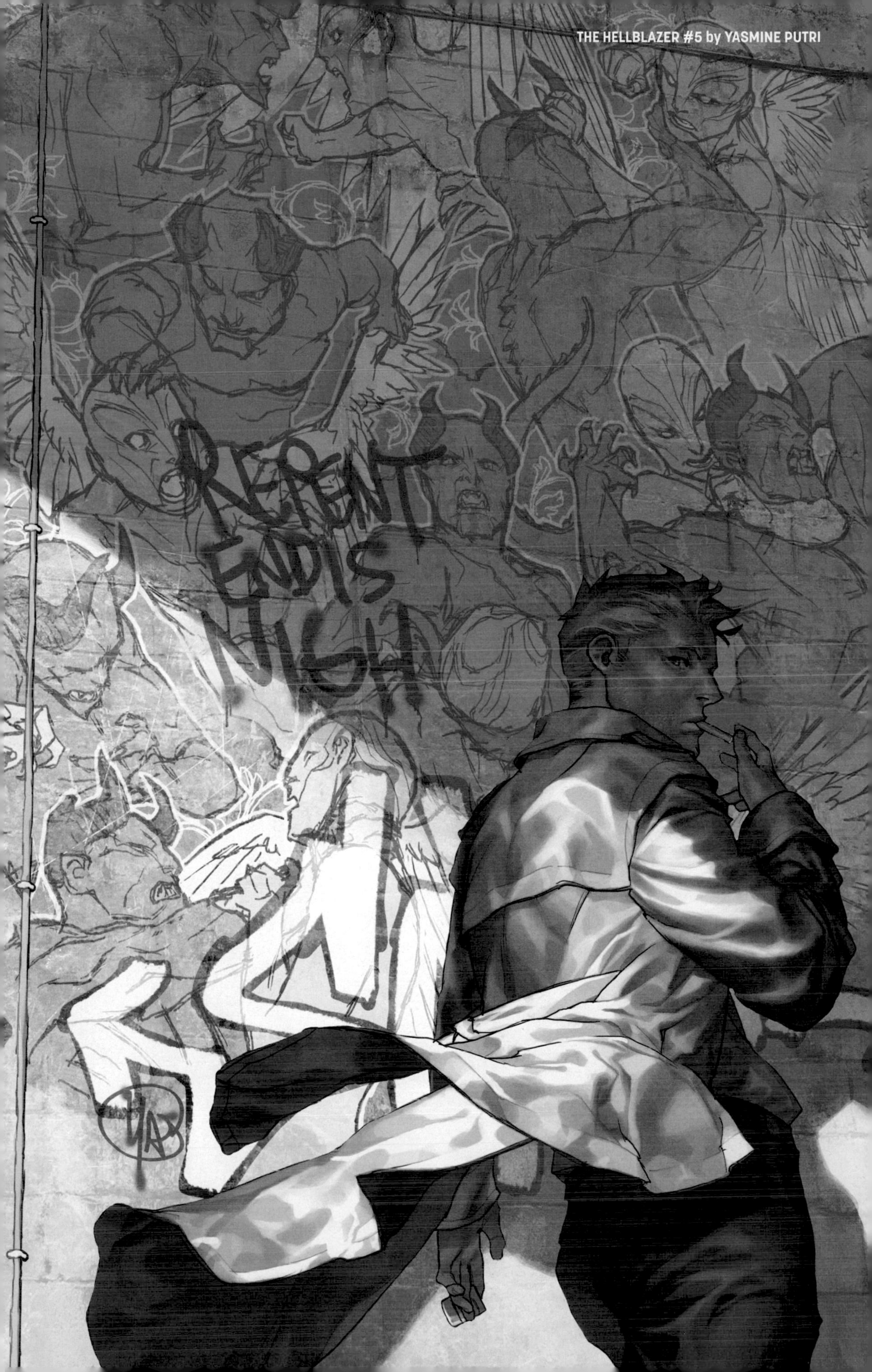
REPENT
END IS
NIGH

THE HELLBLAZER #6 by YASMINE PUTRI

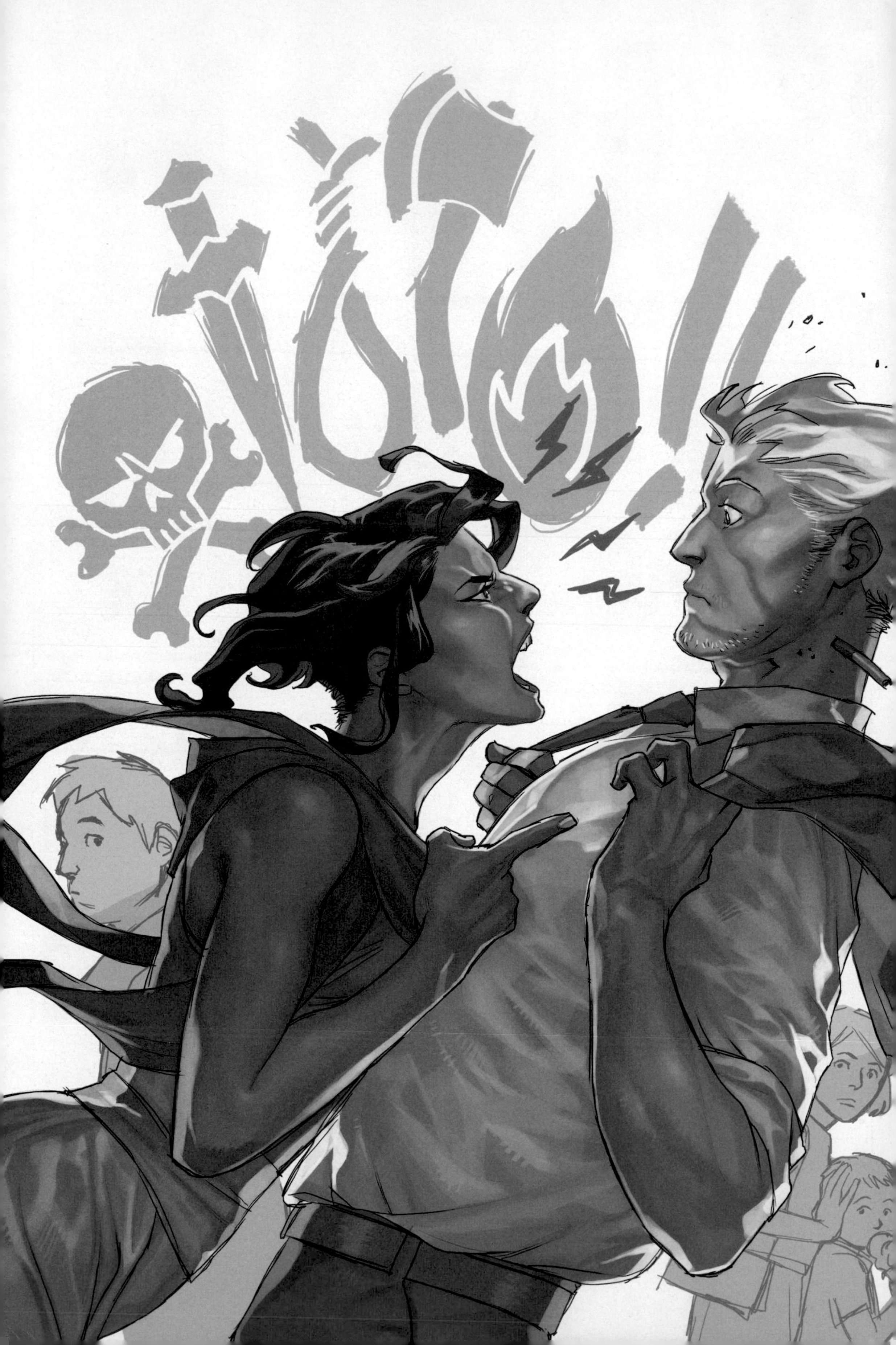

"It's nice to see one of the best comics of the late '80s return so strongly."
— **Comic Book Resources**

"It's high energy from page one through to the last page." — **BATMAN NEWS**

DC UNIVERSE REBIRTH

SUICIDE SQUAD

VOL. 1: THE BLACK VAULT

ROB WILLIAMS
with JIM LEE and others

VOL. 1 THE BLACK VAULT
ROB WILLIAMS • JIM LEE • PHILIP TAN • JASON FABOK • IVAN REIS • GARY FRANK

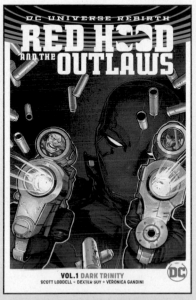

**THE HELLBLAZER VOL. 1:
THE POISON TRUTH**

**RED HOOD AND THE OUTLAWS VOL. 1:
DARK TRINITY**

**HARLEY QUINN VOL. 1:
DIE LAUGHING**

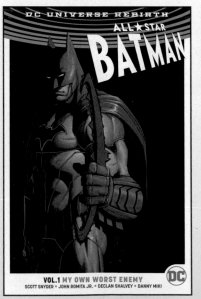